Talking with Children

Early childhood teachers know that the quality of child–teacher interactions has an impact on children's social and educational outcomes. Talking with children is central to early learning, but the significant details of high-quality conversations in early childhood settings are not always obvious. This handbook brings together experts from across the globe to share evidence of teachers talking with children in early learning environments. It applies the methodology of conversation analysis to questions about early childhood education, and shows why this method of studying discourse can be a valuable resource for professional development in early childhood. Each chapter of this handbook includes an up-to-date literature review; shows how interactional pedagogy can be achieved in everyday interactions; and demonstrates how to apply this learning in practice. It offers unique insights into real-life early childhood education practices, based on robust research findings, and provides practical advice for teaching and talking with children.

AMELIA CHURCH is a Senior Lecturer in the Melbourne Graduate School of Education at the University of Melbourne. Her research in early childhood education focuses on the quality of child-teacher interactions. Her books include *Preference Organization and Peer Disputes* (2009) and *Children's Knowledge-in-Interaction* (co-edited with Amanda Bateman, 2017).

AMANDA BATEMAN is Associate Professor in the School of Education at the University of Waikato. Amanda's research explores various aspects of early childhood education using a conversation analysis approach. Her books include *Conversation Analysis and Early Childhood Education* (2015), *Children's Knowledge-in-Interaction* (co-edited with Amelia Church, 2017), and *Children and Mental Health Talk* (co-edited, 2020).

Talking with Children

A Handbook on Interaction in Early Childhood Education

Edited by

AMELIA CHURCH
University of Melbourne

AMANDA BATEMAN
University of Waikato

CAMBRIDGE
UNIVERSITY PRESS

CAMBRIDGE
UNIVERSITY PRESS

University Printing House, Cambridge CB2 8BS, United Kingdom

One Liberty Plaza, 20th Floor, New York, NY 10006, USA

477 Williamstown Road, Port Melbourne, VIC 3207, Australia

314–321, 3rd Floor, Plot 3, Splendor Forum, Jasola District Centre, New Delhi – 110025, India

103 Penang Road, #05–06/07, Visioncrest Commercial, Singapore 238467

Cambridge University Press is part of the University of Cambridge.

It furthers the University's mission by disseminating knowledge in the pursuit of education, learning, and research at the highest international levels of excellence.

www.cambridge.org
Information on this title: www.cambridge.org/9781108845472
DOI: 10.1017/9781108979764

First published 2022

A catalogue record for this publication is available from the British Library

ISBN 978-1-108-84547-2 Hardback

For all the early childhood educators.

Contents

Figures

Tables

Contributors

Amanda Bateman is an Associate Professor in the Faculty of Education, University of Waikato. Her research involves using video data to analyse children's social interactions, and teacher-child pedagogical interactions. Dr Bateman has led research projects in Wales and New Zealand and is currently a co-investigator on a three-year New Zealand Marsden project investigating how early childhood centres support refugee children and families to belong in New Zealand. Findings from these projects have been disseminated through national and international conference presentations, academic journal articles, book chapters, and texts.

Jan Berenst is a retired Professor of Discourse & Learning at NHL Stenden University of Applied Sciences in Leeuwarden, the Netherlands. Previously, he worked as a senior lecturer and researcher at the Center for Language and Cognition of the University of Groningen, the Netherlands. He has published (amongst other things) on intercultural communication, teacher meetings, classroom interaction, (young) children's conversations, literacy development, and language pedagogy, including teaching materials on second language learning and reading comprehension. His recent research relates to the role of classroom interaction in the process of children's knowledge construction, and concerns especially the characteristics of peer interaction in inquiry learning in school.

Polly Björk-Willén is an Associate Professor Emerita in Educational Practice at Linköping University, Sweden. She has a background as a preschool teacher and has educated preschool teacher students for many years. Her research interest is in interactional studies in preschool, investigating (bilingual) children's language use, ethnicity and religion at preschool, language policy in families and preschool, as well as the moral and emotional socialization of children. Based on ethnomethodology and conversation analysis, her studies focus on multimodal interaction in mundane activities at preschool. She has published her research in international journals and contributed chapters in various Swedish as well as international anthologies.

Matthew Burdelski is Professor of Japanese Linguistics at Osaka University, Japan. His research uses multimodal conversation analysis to examine socialization practices within adult–child and peer interactions in family homes, neighbourhoods, classrooms, and preschools in Japan and the United States. He has published articles in various journals and edited volumes. He has recently co-edited a volume (with K. M. Howard) titled *Language Socialization in Classrooms: Culture, Interaction and Language Development* (2020, Cambridge University Press).

Asta Cekaite is a Professor in Child Studies at the Thematic Research Unit, Linköping University, Sweden. Her research involves an interdisciplinary approach to language, culture, and social interaction. Specific foci include social perspectives on bilingualism, embodiment, touch, emotion, and moral socialization. Empirical fields cover adult–child and children's peer group interactions in educational settings, and family in various cultural contexts (Sweden, United States, Japan). With M. Goodwin she has co-authored *Embodied Family Choreography: Practices of Control, Care and Mundane Creativity* (Routledge, 2018), and with L. Mondada she has co-edited *Touch in Social Interaction: Touch, Language and Body* (2021, Routledge).

Amelia Church is a Senior Lecturer in the Melbourne Graduate School of Education where she teaches research methods in early childhood education and applied conversation analysis (CA). Amelia's research focuses on child peer and child–teacher interactions, with an interest in how responsive engagement is collaboratively built in early learning environments. Her research has been published in a 2009 book on children's conflict, a 2017 collection of CA studies in early childhood education (co-edited with Amanda Bateman), and in international journals that focus on interaction research and learning in the early years.

Caroline Cohrssen is an Associate Professor in the Faculty of Education at The University of Hong Kong. Her research interests include children's learning in the years prior to school, with a focus on both the home learning environment and pre-school or centre-based settings. Much of her work is translated to practice in the form of curriculum support materials and teacher professional development.

Jakob Cromdal is Professor of Educational Practice in the Department of Behavioural Sciences and Learning, Linköping University, Sweden. He specializes in postcognitive approaches to social interaction – mainly ethnomethodology, conversation analysis, discursive psychology, and membership categorization analysis. He has published on a variety of topics analysing talk and embodied social conduct taking place in bilingual classrooms, playgrounds, driving-school cars, detention homes, emergency services, and youth helplines. His most recent projects focus on two settings for socialization in preschool: mealtimes and group outings passing through traffic environments.

Susan Danby is Professor in the Faculty of Education at Queensland University of Technology, Brisbane, Australia. She investigates children's lives across home and school contexts, and in clinical and helpline settings. Her 2019 Honorary Doctorate in Education at Uppsala University, Sweden, recognized her international leadership in child studies and young children's digital technologies, social interaction, and early childhood education. Australian Research Council projects, including a Future Fellowship, investigated young children's engagement with digital technologies. She is Director of the Australian Research Council Centre of Excellence for the Digital Child.

Marjolein Deunk is an Assistant Professor of Educational Sciences at the University of Groningen, the Netherlands. She has a background in developmental psychology and linguistics and received her Ph.D. from the Faculty of Arts at the University of Groningen. Her dissertation, titled *Discourse Practices in Preschool: Young Children's Participation in Everyday Classroom Activities*, appeared in 2009. Her areas of expertise include interactions in early childhood education, early literacy development, and diversity and inclusion in education. She teaches among others in the pre-service programme for primary teacher education, and in the international master programme in Educational Sciences, *Learning in Interaction*. She is a member of the Netherlands Comenius Network for teaching innovation in higher education.

Ann-Carita Evaldsson is Professor of Education at Uppsala University, Sweden. Her research draws on ethnographic and ethnomethodological, multimodal interactional approaches to children's everyday lives, their peer language practices, moral work, emotions, and identity work (gender, class, ethnicity, disability) in culturally diverse settings. She has published extensively in *Journal of Pragmatics*; *Research on Children and Social Interaction*; *Childhood*, *Text & Talk*; *Multilingua*; and *Emotional and Behavioral Difficulties*.

Anna Filipi is a Senior Lecturer in TESOL and Language Education at Monash University where she has taught since 2011. She has published extensively, and her research interests are in conversation analysis and young children's interactional competence, bilingualism and language switching in the foreign language classroom at school and at university, and L2 assessment. Her publications include *Toddler and Parent Interaction: The Organisation of Gaze, Pointing and Vocalization* (2009, John Benjamins) and *Conversation Analysis and Language Alternation: Capturing Transitions in the Classroom* (co-edited with N. Markee, 2018, John Benjamins).

Rod Gardner is an Honorary Associate Professor at the University of Queensland. He has been using conversation analysis for thirty years now, with an early interest in response tokens arising from his Ph.D. Recent research has focused on two areas: classroom interaction in the early years of schooling, with a co-authored book with Ilana Mushin on how instructions are delivered and how children implement those instructions in subsequent activities; and conversational interaction in a large team project, *Conversational Interaction in Aboriginal and Remote Australia*, which investigates both First Nations and Anglo communities.

Myrte Gosen is an Assistant Professor of Communication and Information Studies at the University of Groningen, the Netherlands. She received her Ph.D. from the same university in 2012. Her dissertation is titled '*Tracing Learning in Interaction. An Analysis of Shared Reading of Picture Books at Kindergarten*' and shows a research interest at the interface between education and communication. She has a particular interest in classroom interactions in relation to knowledge and she uses conversation analysis to identify the fundamental structures and practices in interaction that are related to knowledge construction. Besides her own teaching practices in the Communication and Information Studies programme, she is for instance also involved in the organization of an interdisciplinary summer school around analysing classroom interactions.

Frans Hiddink is a senior researcher in multilingualism and literacy at the NHL Stenden University of Applied Sciences in Leeuwarden, the Netherlands. Recently, he received his Ph.D. by conducting applied conversation analytic research on young children's reasoning and problem-solving during peer interaction in inquiry learning in either absence or presence of the teacher. Currently, Frans is investigating how classroom interactions in primary education in multilingual contexts can be enhanced. He has a particular interest in using conversation analysis in ways that help both (early childhood) educators and teacher training students to improve their own classroom practices. Among other things, he works as a teacher educator in the primary teacher training programme at the *Academy for Primary Education* of the same University, where he teaches courses that focus on classroom interaction and early childhood education.

Sandy Houen is a Senior Research Associate in the Faculty of Education at Queensland University of Technology, Brisbane, Australia. Her research interests include children's social interactions in home and classroom contexts, children's use of digital technology, and early childhood education. Sandy's Ph.D. work, which details how teachers can promote children's contributions to classroom discussions, offers fine-grained understandings of teacher–child interactions in preschool settings.

Magnus Karlsson is a Lecturer in Child & Youth studies at the University of Gothenburg. His research focuses on preschool children's everyday activities, moral work, peer relations and play, and teacher–child interaction. He is currently researching children's transformations of objects and their interactive achievement of space in play. His work draws on ethnomethodological conversation analysis and multimodal interactional approaches to participation in situated activities.

Friederike Kern is a Professor of German linguistics and didactics at Bielefeld University. After studying German literature, linguistics, and philosophy in Berlin and London, she was awarded a Ph.D. from the University of Hamburg. Her research interests include conversational analysis, language development, learning-in-interaction, classroom discourse, prosody, and gesture. Her publications include work on rhythm in Turkish German, on the development of storytelling in young schoolchildren, and on learning situations.

Mardi Kidwell is a Professor of Communication at the University of New Hampshire. She uses the method of conversation analysis to investigate fundamental interactional processes in the areas of very young children's interaction and also police–citizen interaction. She is particularly interested in children's early engagement techniques and their emerging orientations to social norms, in addition to issues of conflict and social control that apply to both children's and policing contexts. She began her career studying children's interaction as a Ph.D. student, working on the Very Young Children Project at UC Santa Barbara. Her research has appeared in a number of international journals and anthologies.

Christine Lee is a Post-Doctoral scholar at UCLA's School of Education and Information Studies. She received her Ph.D. from the Urban Schooling division at UCLA's Graduate School of Education. She collaborates with teachers in design-based research to examine how learning occurs through dramatic play. Her research focuses on designing and implementing play-based learning, how play can support instructional interactions, the importance of affect and identity, and service-learning.

Jessica Nina Lester is an Associate Professor of Inquiry Methodology in the School of Education at Indiana University, Bloomington. Her scholarship focuses on discourse and conversation analysis, disability studies, and more general concerns related to qualitative research. Most recently, she co-authored the book *Doing Qualitative Research in a Digital World* with Sage publications (2022). She has most recently published in journals such as *Qualitative Inquiry* and *Discourse Studies*. At Indiana University, she teaches graduate level courses focused on discourse and conversation analysis.

Ekaterina Moore is Associate Professor of Clinical Education at Rossier School of Education, University of Southern California. Her research interests are in classroom language socialization and discourse. Her work includes examination of Russian preschool and Heritage language classrooms.

Ilana Mushin is a Reader in Linguistics at the University of Queensland. Her research interests include the pragmatics of evidentiality and epistemics and she is the author of the monograph *Evidentiality and Epistemological Stance* (2002, John Benjamins). She and Rod Gardner have collaborated on a number of projects investigating engagement with learning in Early Years Schooling, including in Australian First Nations schools. Their forthcoming book, to be published by Routledge in 2021, focuses on procedural instructions and task accomplishment as evidence of children's' development as school learners in the first year of formal schooling.

Kadek Ratih Dwi Oktarini (Ratih Oktarini) completed her Ph.D. in the School of Humanities, Nanyang Technological University, in 2017. Her thesis is titled '*Flirtatious Sequence in Indonesian: A Conversation Analytic* *and Membership Categorization Analytic Approach*'. Much of the analysis in her Ph.D. project relied on detailed observation of participants' non-verbal behaviour, such as bodily posture, gaze direction, and hand movement. In turn, it forced her to learn a new skill: making line drawings fit for multimodal analysis illustration. After completing her Ph.D., she continues producing and improving her skill in making line drawings amidst her activity as a researcher on Conversational Indonesian and Institutional Talk. Her line drawing portfolio can be accessed from her ResearchGate Page 'Ratih Oktarini', Project 'Conversation Analysis Line Drawing'.

Michelle O'Reilly is an Associate Professor of Communication in Mental Health at the University of Leicester, working in both the School of Media, Communication and Sociology and the Department of Neuroscience, Psychology and Behaviour. Michelle is also a Research Consultant and Quality Improvement Advisor for Leicestershire Partnership NHS Trust. Michelle is a Senior Fellow of the Higher Education Academy and is also a Chartered Psychologist in Health. Michelle has specific interests in child and adolescent mental health. Michelle undertakes research in self-harm and suicidal behaviour, neurodevelopmental conditions, and child mental health services, such as mental health assessments and family therapy.

Annukka Pursi is a Lecturer at the Faculty of Educational Sciences, University of Helsinki, Finland. She has published several papers on the organization of two-year-old children's play. Her research focuses on how shared understanding is created and maintained in adult-child interaction in the context of early childhood education.

Laura Sterponi is Professor of Language, Literacy, and Culture at UC Berkeley. She combines methods from interactional linguistics, conversation analysis, and linguistic anthropology to investigate naturally occurring uses of language, oral and written, in a range of institutional contexts and with different populations. Leveraging micro-analysis of interactional practices, her scholarship engages more macro issues such as linguistic competence in autism, language and literacy ideologies in educational settings, and communication in healthcare encounters.

Kirsten Stoewer is a Lecturer in the Department of Behavioural Sciences and Learning at Linköping University, where she received her Ph.D. Her doctoral thesis uses conversation analysis to examine teacher-student interaction during English mother tongue instruction in Sweden, in particular various verbal and multimodal aspects of language work as it arises and is developed. Kirsten teaches pre-service preschool and primary school teachers at Linköping University.

Akira Takada is currently a Professor in the Graduate School of Asian and African Area Studies at Kyoto University, Japan. He has led various research projects where he uses conversation analysis and language socialization approaches to delve into caregiver-child interactions and ethnic identity, and is currently working on a project exploring the cultural formation of responsibility in early childhood. He has conducted intensive field researches in Botswana, Namibia, and Japan. He is the author of books including *The Ecology of Playful Childhood: The Diversity and Resilience of Caregiver-Child Interactions among the San of Southern Africa* (2020, Palgrave Macmillan). His research has also been published in various academic journals including *Cognitive Science*, *Frontiers in Psychology*, *Journal of Pragmatics*, *Language & Communication*, *PLoS ONE*, *Research on Children and Social Interaction*, and in edited volumes including the *Handbook of Language Socialization* (2012, Blackwell).

Maryanne Theobald is Associate Professor in the School of Early Childhood and Inclusive Education at Queensland University of Technology. Maryanne has over thirty years' experience in early childhood education and care (ECEC) and she currently coordinates foundational units in QUT's initial teaching education programmes and postgraduate programmes. Maryanne's interactional research has practical application for real world ECEC educational and social matters, including children's rights, friendships, communication in culturally and linguistically diverse settings and playgrounds, as well as children's experiences with digital technologies. Maryanne is co-editor of *Research on Children and Social Interaction* (RCSI). She has gained international recognition as an exceptional teacher and mentor, having been appointed as a Senior Fellow in the Higher Education Academy (United Kingdom).

Betty Yu is Professor in the Speech, Language, and Hearing Sciences Department at San Francisco State University. Her research focuses on heritage language maintenance and bilingualism in autistic children from minoritized language communities. She is interested in understanding communication between children and their parents, teachers, and peers as an interactional achievement not only defined by the management of two or more linguistic codes, but also by the coordination of sociocultural meaning within everyday routines. Her research also examines how parent–child interactions are shaped by the broader discourses, practices, and ideologies related to disability and race.

Acknowledgements

Our special thanks and acknowledgement to the authors for contributing during the ongoing crisis of the global coronavirus pandemic. We are honored to be your friends and colleagues. We have missed seeing you in person to talk through these ideas, and we dedicate this book to you. We are grateful to *all* the authors in this Handbook; we wanted to make research in ethnomethodology and conversation analysis (EMCA) accessible and useful to early childhood practitioners, and the contributing authors have generously given their time and expertise to achieve this project.

EMCA scholars are lovely people, and we have benefitted from their advice and constructive encouragement throughout our careers. Every conference and data session reveals new insights, and conversation analysts display a pervasive enthusiasm for understanding how talk works and what this means for how we navigate our social lives. A particular mention to Liz Stokoe and Rein Sikveland for sharing their experience of using conversation analysis (CA) for professional development and developing the Conversation Analytic Role-play Method (CARM).

We thank our colleagues in early childhood education for reviewing chapters: Sara Archard, Sonja Ardnt, Wendy Carss, Alison Clark, Jeanette Clarkin-Phillips, Caroline Cohrssen, Bronya Dean, Tricia Eadie, Catriona Elek, Susie Garvis, Jeanne Iorio, Friederike Kern, Penny Levickis, Angie Mashford-Scott, Hoanna McMillan, Sue Mentha, Linda Mitchell, Edith Nicolas, Louise Paatsch, Maryanne Theobald, Jane Waters, and Sarah Young. Thanks to Andrew Winnard, Izzie Collins, and the team at Cambridge University Press, and the reviewers who provided such helpful feedback on the proposal for this Handbook.

Amelia would like to thank her teachers Marion and Barry Church, Candy Goodwin, and the late Collette Tayler; the Melbourne Graduate School of Education for a six-month sabbatical; and colleagues at MGSE for being such great role models. Amanda thanks those who have guided her throughout her EMCA early childhood journey, Chuck and Candy Goodwin and their UCLA co-op lab, Asta Cekaite and her Swedish early childhood interaction lab, the wonderful members of the University of Waikato Early Years Research Centre, and all of her past and present early childhood students in Wales and New Zealand from whom she has learnt so much.

Finally – and most importantly – we are grateful to the children, families, and teachers involved in the studies detailed throughout this Handbook. They allowed researchers into their lives and learning spaces to videorecord everyday interactions. We learn so much from these early childhood communities and thank them for opening their doors to research.

Notes on Transcription Conventions

The transcription conventions used throughout this book were first published in Sacks, Schegloff, and Jefferson (1974), and developed by Gail Jefferson (2004). There are theoretical, methodological, and practical concerns in how transcripts aim to capture spoken and embodied interaction (see Gardner, 2001; Hepburn and Bolden, 2012; Mondada, 2018; Ochs, 1979), but here we simply provide the conventions as a reference for the chapters that follow. In this Handbook, we have used the core conventions used in conversation analysis listed below; any additional conventions used by authors will be explained in their chapter.

These conventions were first developed when researchers used typewriters rather than computers, so were limited to the keys available. Symbols used do not mark punctuation, but instead are employed to capture some detail of how the talk is done.

.	falling intonation
,	slightly rising or continuing intonation
?	rising intonation
¿	intonation that rises more than a comma but less than a question mark
::	lengthened syllable
↓	sharp fall in pitch
↑	sharp rise in pitch
[ ]	overlapping talk
( )	unintelligible stretch
(0.5)	length of silence in tenths of a second
> <	increase in tempo, rushed stretch of talk
< >	slower tempo
hh	audible outbreath
.hh	audible inbreath
° °	talk that is quieter than the surrounding talk
(( ))	description of accompanying behaviour
→	points to a phenomena of particular interest, to be discussed by the author

Gardner, R. (2001). *When Listeners Talk: Response Tokens and Listener Stance*. Amsterdam: John Benjamins.

Hepburn, A., and Bolden, G. B. (2012). The conversation analytic approach to data collection. In J. Sidnell & T. Stivers (eds.), *The Handbook of Conversation Analysis* (pp. 57–76). Hoboken, NJ: Wiley.

Jefferson, G. (2004). Glossary of transcript symbols with an introduction. In G. H. Lerner (ed.), *Conversation Analysis: Studies from the First Generation* (pp. 43–59). Philadelphia, PA: John Benjamins.

Mondada, L. (2018). Multiple temporalities of language and body in interaction: challenges for transcribing multimodality, *Research on Language and Social Interaction*, 51(1), 85–106.

Ochs, E. (1979). Transcription as theory. In E. Ochs and B. Schieffelin (eds.), *Developmental Pragmatics*. New York, NY: Academic Press.

Sacks, H., Schegloff, E.A., and Jefferson, G. (1974). A simplest systematics for the organization of turn-taking for conversation. *Language*, 50(4), 696–735.

Introduction

AMELIA CHURCH AND AMANDA BATEMAN

Talking with Children

In early childhood education and care (ECEC), the importance of extended conversations with children is emphasized through professional practice principles (i.e. what teachers should do) and in learning outcomes for children (i.e. what children should be able to do). Early childhood curricula, frameworks, or statements of learning goals for young children necessarily respond to the historical, educational, and political priorities of their communities. There is, however, a universal understanding of the primacy of talk-in-interaction as both the medium of learning *and* a skill for children to develop. All early childhood curricula reference the fundamental importance of talking with children.

Early childhood curricula do not, however, specify *how* talking with children might be done. The deliberate lack of explicit directions on how to talk with children allows teachers to develop pedagogical strategies that incorporate each child's experiences, abilities, and interests, forming a continuum of learning from their home and community environments. The flexibility and responsivity of curriculum frameworks for early childhood education – frameworks developed and evaluated through national education and care policy – enables teachers to create individualized learning for the children and families they work with. The fact that early childhood curricula are not prescriptive aligns with a sociocultural approach to education where programmes can adapt and respond to the needs of local communities. It does mean, however, that the practices to implement national curricula and enable learning outcomes are less visible to teachers; this illusiveness can be problematic, as learning outcomes for children *are* specified in ECEC curricula. Teachers know where they are going (i.e. learning goals) and why (i.e. professional knowledge, beliefs, and theory), but they are not always sure how to initiate, navigate, and extend conversations with children throughout this journey.

Research reveals the extraordinary range of skills required for engaging in learning interactions with infants, toddlers, and young children in everyday moments. Studies in pedagogy demonstrate the demands on early childhood teachers to continually notice, recognize, and respond to each child's interests to extend their learning in meaningful and relevant ways. Teaching requires complex skills of observation to notice when a child is engaged in an activity that presents itself as an opportunity for learning-in-interaction, an acute sense of the appropriate time and approach to use to initiate purposeful interactions, and skilful understanding of how to engage in talk in ways that extend each child's learning. Teaching as a responsive and intentional practice can be demanding and requires a renewable source of professional knowledge.

The aim of this Handbook is to support the professional learning needs of early childhood teachers. We aim to make empirical evidence accessible to teachers, using data that illuminates the how of high-quality learning interactions in early childhood settings. The intention is not to provide a checklist of practices, but instead to illustrate how key concepts and principles in early childhood education are realized through everyday talk-in-interaction. Extracts of video recordings provided in each chapter reveal child-teacher interaction in specific settings, and the authors distil implications for pedagogy by identifying the sequences of actions that provide opportunities for learning. In this Handbook, we are able to show how existing research in ethnomethodology and conversation analysis (EMCA) provides (1) empirical evidence of children's competencies, (2) illustration of teaching practices from original data rather than analytic summaries, and (3) accessible and practical resources to inform teacher reflection and practice.

This introductory chapter has three goals. First, we explain why evidence from conversation analytic research is useful and accessible as a professional learning resource in early childhood education. We then briefly identify the scope of conversation analytic research in early childhood education to show readers the sorts – and source – of knowledge available. Finally, we introduce the scope of topics in this Handbook to describe how each chapter contributes to a professional body of knowledge for early childhood educators.

Research in Conversation Analysis for Professional Learning

Conversation analysis (CA) originates in sociology and explores how people use language to achieve social actions. By paying very close attention to how people talk with one another – through careful transcribing of spoken and embodied features of talk-in-interaction – video recordings of everyday interactions reveal the systematic and sequentially organized nature of talk (see Lester & O'Reilly, 2019, and Sidnell, 2010 for practical introductions; and

Heritage, 1984, Schegloff, 2007, and Sidnell & Stivers, 2013, for a more detailed review). The origins, approach, and methods of conversation analysis are outlined in the next chapter. In this introduction, we will limit the discussion to the sorts of questions about early childhood education CA can ask and answer, and why this method of studying discourse can be a valuable resource for professional development in early childhood.

The method of CA relies upon collecting (video-recorded) examples of everyday interactions, then analysing sequences of interaction repeatedly through the process of transcription. Using video recordings rather than subsequent analysis as the data means that social practices remain available for scrutiny and review by other audiences. As Harvey Sacks noted, not only do recordings of interaction allow the researcher to re-visit the data for analysis but 'others could look at what I had studied, and make of it what they could, if they wanted to be able to disagree with me' (Sacks, 1995, p. 622). This transparency of method means the original data is accessible for teachers, making visible the practices that enable children to engage in creative thinking, problem solving, and conceptual understanding. Data from CA research is available – but underemployed – for professional learning and reflection.

Elsewhere, the method of CA has proven useful as a means of professional development and training. Elizabeth Stokoe developed the Conversation Analytic Role-play Method (CARM; Stokoe, 2014) as a means of sharing findings – turn by turn – with project participants. Professor Stokoe, Rein Sikveland, and their colleagues have shown that the analytic features of CA provide a means of presenting *practical* professional insights for police in interviewing suspects (Stokoe & Edwards, 2008), for crisis negotiations (Sikveland, Kevoe-Feldman, & Stokoe, 2021), for mediators encouraging complainants to engage with mediation services (Stokoe 2013a), and for GP clinic administrators to better meet the needs of patients (Stokoe, Sikveland, & Symonds, 2016). Rather than simply sharing findings or reporting back outcomes of a study, CARM allows professionals to identify the constituent parts of effective communication practices in sequences of interaction typical in their own professional lives, by approaching the data as a conversation analyst would, interrogating why certain actions are responded to in particular ways (see Pomerantz & Fehr, 1997; Stokoe, 2011). Importantly, training relies on examples of *real* rather than role-play interactions (Stokoe, 2013b).

CARM proves valuable as a method of professional learning for early childhood teachers (Church & Bateman, 2019a), because sharing video-recorded data with teachers provides unique insights and prompts for reflection (Cherrington, 2018; Nolan, Paatsch, & Scull, 2018). Early childhood teachers typically work in small teams, and opportunities for informal or formal peer discussions and professional reflection can be limited (Molla & Nolan, 2019). Deconstructing a sequence of talk-in-interaction between children and teachers by identifying the trajectory set up by each subsequent turn at talk allows early childhood teachers to identify the practices which enable children's participation (Church & Bateman, 2019b); essentially encouraging teachers to discover the research findings related to their own practice themselves. Such analysis of one's own interactions with children offers a valuable resource for reflective practice.

There are other productive methodologies for investigating interactions in early learning environments, but CA, with its insistence on repeatedly returning to original recordings of interactions, allows us to see what actually happens, rather than what we assume or recall to have been central to interactions with children. We see how children contribute to learning sequences and find evidence of their competencies that may not be immediately visible in the busy life of an early learning centre. Data from CA research provide a sort of detailed eavesdropping otherwise unavailable to teachers given the demands of their daily professional responsibilities.

Research in Conversation Analysis and Early Childhood Education

Given the volume of CA research in early childhood in the past forty years, an adequate summary cannot be provided in this chapter. Instead, the Handbook as a whole aims to bring together this body of research – from sociology, linguistic anthropology, applied linguistics, psychology, education, and childhood studies – as a resource for early childhood educators. We should point out that there is a wealth of CA research on interactions within family contexts, detailing interactions with very young children and their parents (e.g. Filipi, 2009, 2019; Keel, 2016; Morita, 2019) and between siblings and other family members (e.g. Galatolo & Caronia, 2018; Goodwin, 2017; Takada & Kawashima, 2017). This research reveals children's socially constructed knowledge of the world and relationships, and provides a developmental account of learning insofar as children's competencies are revealed in talk-in-interaction (Gardner & Forrester, 2010; Wootton, 2006). Obviously young children learn across settings, primarily at home with parents, siblings, and other family members. Indeed, CA research in family interactions (e.g. Burdelski, 2019a; Butler & Edwards, 2018; Goodwin & Cekaite, 2018; Searles, 2019) has much to offer early childhood teachers in understanding children's knowledge-in-interaction.

The focus of this Handbook, however, is evidence gathered in early learning environments and the first year of primary school; the extracts and discussion speak directly to the practices and professional experience of early childhood teachers. Conversation analytic research in early childhood settings broadly responds to two main themes: the structure of question-and-answer sequences between groups of children and their teacher(s), and the social organization of peer relationships. An interest in how pedagogy and peer socialization are managed in and through multilingualism, where speakers shift between languages, is also an enduring focus for CA research. Regardless of the aims of individual projects, however, the process of teaching and learning – or the praxis of education – is invariably documented in CA research, because the data records sequences of interaction in children's early learning environments.

Question-and-answer sequences, unsurprisingly, are a focus for many researchers as the locus for learning-in-interaction. CA research has shown how question design influences the likelihood of children contributing their ideas, positioning the child as expert and qualified to make suggestions (e.g. Baraldi, 2015; Bateman, 2015; Ekberg, Danby, Houen, Davidson, & Thorpe, 2017; Houen, Danby, Farrell, & Thorpe, 2016), and that extended pauses make it possible for children to formulate and contribute their ideas (e.g. Cohrssen, Church, & Tayler, 2014). More recently, learning interactions supported by and engaging with digital technologies have been studied, as research funding has been directed towards the role of information and communication technologies (ICT) in young children's learning (e.g. Danby, Davidson, Theobald, Houen, & Thorpe, 2017; Danby, Fleer, Davidson, & Hatzigianni, 2018). Studies of interaction also consider children's agency when talking with teachers, exploring what rights and resources they have to influence topics and trajectories of learning activities (e.g. Church & Bateman, 2019b; Theobald & Kultti, 2012). Notably, intentional teaching is not limited to task-based activities, as skilful teachers extend opportunities for learning by supporting exploration of concepts during play (e.g. Dalgren, 2017; Pursi, 2019).

Conversation analysts are interested in how people construct social actions – including how group membership is organized and talked into being – so peer relationships in early childhood have received a great deal of attention. This includes how friendships are maintained during play activities, documenting the linguistic, environmental, and knowledge resources children draw on to maintain alliances (e.g. Bateman, 2012; Butler, 2008; Cromdal, 2001; Theobald, 2017). Studies of peer relationships also document how inclusion or exclusion from the group is negotiated in interaction (e.g. Evaldsson & Tellgren, 2009; Kultti & Odenbring, 2015). This includes observations of peer conflict, because conversation analysts have sought to identify how social status is collaboratively achieved and continually negotiated through peer interactions (e.g. Burdelski, 2020; Cekaite, 2020; Church, 2009; Danby & Baker, 1998; Goodwin, 1990, 2006; Moore & Burdelski, 2020). Disputes and imaginative play also provide opportunities for children to establish a locally regulated moral order (Björk-Willén, 2018; Danby & Theobald, 2012).

The common thread in these studies is that each turn at talk provides us with evidence of what the speaker has made of the previous turns at talk (Schegloff & Sacks, 1973). This understanding is on display for teachers, for children, and for the researchers observing and recording the interaction. Importantly, each turn at talk can be used as a resource for another person to build a subsequent turn, because talk is cumulative (Goodwin, 2018). CA research pays attention to particular features of the talk made salient by the speakers themselves. Furthermore, talking with children draws upon and *displays* conceptual and cultural knowledge, linguistic resources, working theories, emotional regulation, socialization rules, and so on (Bateman, 2013; Cekaite, 2013).

Research in this Handbook

One of the challenges of dividing a text and nominating topics as chapters is that the structure of this book does not reflect the fact that practices are distributed across early childhood programmes. For example, 'wellbeing' or 'multilingualism' are not distinct elements of early learning, but rather permeate and are woven into children's experiences. Similarly, we are not able to reflect the diversity of early childhood education settings, nor diversity within communities. Children bring to early childhood education a myriad of languages, cultural funds of knowledge, and lived experience. Teachers have different opportunities for securing qualifications and engaging in professional learning, and centres and families have different resources to draw on to support children to thrive. Therefore, it is important to acknowledge that we are not able to detail all elements of early learning curricula or approaches and philosophy of education. Instead, what we have collected here is the existing expertise on interactions in international early learning environments from experienced CA researchers. The topics are defined by the available empirical evidence in CA research.

We should emphasize the heterogeneity of early childhood settings, as children and families have diverse cultural, linguistic, ethnic, educational, and socioeconomic backgrounds, with a range of experiences, abilities, and expectations. There is always a risk when holding up examples of practice of inadvertently claiming a notion of 'best' or common practice. Yet the 'ideal' is teaching and learning approaches that respond to the individual needs of each child, embedded within knowledge drawn from family and community. We know that there is no one size that suits all, but at the same time we do not want the rich diversity of children's experiences to prohibit efforts to detail the learning interactions we *have* observed, to illustrate for teachers the often opaque process of collaboratively building extended sequences of talk.

Finally, the Handbook cannot capture all elements of early childhood curricula; instead, we share topics in which each author has expertise and empirical research evidence. The first section details the practices of talk-in-interaction, introducing teachers to concepts from CA and the machinery of learning interactions. The interactional practices explained and illustrated in the first section of the book support the reader to engage with the content of the next sections, which provide details of interaction in common strands of early childhood education programmes. This second section of the Handbook then details practices in key learning areas and outcomes in early childhood curricula, highlighting how their implementation is achieved as a collaborative effort between children and their teachers. The third section of the Handbook details practices that apply across topics of learning and provides teachers with practical insights into key principles of early childhood education.

Part I: Talk as Social Action

Chapter 1: Conversation Analysis for Early Childhood Education

In the first chapter, we (with Susan Danby) provide an introduction to the methodology and methods of CA, explaining the features of interaction that allow us to make sense of each other in conversation. The aim is to introduce the reader to the procedures used in CA research studies, so that the subsequent chapters are accessible. The first chapter is also designed to establish why CA is ideally suited to documenting children's participation in learning-in-interaction, and making the moment-by-moment practices of pedagogy transparent for professional reflection.

Chapter 2: Sequences

Children learn about interaction *in* interaction. In this chapter Mardi Kidwell shows us how toddlers use sequences of action to establish joint attention with caregivers. We see that the relative positioning of turns – one after the other – allows for intersubjectivity or 'how two individuals come to share their minds' (Kern, Chapter 4, this volume) and how children use actions to express intention in systematic ways. This chapter shows us the where and how of responsive engagement with children from a very young age.

Chapter 3: Participation

Through close analysis of child-teacher interactions in outdoor learning environments, Amanda Bateman shows how the theories of the zone of proximal development (Vygotsky), scaffolding (Bruner), and guided participation (Rogoff) can be understood using CA's detailing of participation frameworks. Participation in this light reveals how embodied practices (how teachers position their bodies) and the design of sequences of turns (eliciting expanded responses from children) structure the organization and possibilities of pedagogy.

Chapter 4: Embodiment

Talking with children draws on a range of interactional resources to achieve collaborative and cooperative social action. Where other disciplines may refer to 'nonverbal' behaviour, conversation analysts are able to show how the physical body and objects in the environment are used simultaneously with talk to accomplish intersubjectivity. Friederike Kern provides a thorough review of this research in early childhood, illustrating how gesture, gaze, touch, and orientation to objects are coordinated for specific purposes by children and adults.

Chapter 5: Emotion

Language and embodied resources are used to convey and respond to emotional states. In this chapter, Asta Cekaite illustrates how children's emotions (sadness, laughter, empathy, compassion, among others) are displayed and interpreted in social interaction, and how teachers respond to these displays as opportunities for learning early socialization practices.

Chapter 6: Socialization

Language socialization is a field of study in its own right, and in this chapter, Matt Burdelski illustrates how CA studies contribute to understanding language-in-interaction as the vehicle for how children learn to go about being in the world, in ways that reference and constitute social norms and locally ratified practices (i.e. doing the 'right' thing, at the 'right' time, in the 'right' way).

Chapter 7: Epistemics

The relative knowledge of teachers and children is central to teaching and learning. Mushin and Gardner's overview of epistemics in interactional research (i.e. who knows what and how this knowledge is displayed and oriented to) illustrates the locus of visible learning as an interactional achievement.

Part II: Pedagogy in Interaction

Chapter 8: Literacy

Marjolein Deunk, Myrte Gosen, Frans Hiddink, and Jan Berenst show us how children's emergent literacy knowledge is constructed in everyday activities, through shared book reading and collaborative writing activities. Notably, the teacher is not the only authority in learning about literacy, as the data illustrates how peer scaffolding supports understanding both the form (e.g. which letter to use) and function (e.g. writing an invitation) of environmental print.

Chapter 9: Storytelling

Early childhood teachers understand that storytelling is fundamental to children's learning, their knowledge of the world around them, and is foundational to emerging literacy. In this chapter, Anna Filipi shows us how adults co-tell stories with young children, using sequences of questions to elicit children's accounts of characters and events, with data that shows children's increasing capacity to contribute novel content to a story.

Chapter 10: Digital Technology

Computers, tablets, and smartphones are ubiquitous in children's lives. In this chapter, Susan Danby and Sandra Houen illustrate how digital technology (e.g. web browsing) can provide opportunities for educators to co-create interaction that supports inquiry-based learning, problem solving, and conceptual engagement.

Chapter 11: Mathematics

The data in this chapter shows how talking about mathematics and spatial thinking can be co-constructed in play-based pedagogy. Caroline Cohrssen's analysis reveals how teachers can introduce mathematical concepts into a building and map-making activity, and can simultaneously achieve assessment-in-interaction (i.e. establishing whether the children have mastered relational prepositions such as 'under', 'on top of', or 'in between') while taking on a participant role in highly creative and boisterous play.

Chapter 12: Creativity

This chapter provides readers with an extended example of children's creative role-playing in the context of designing, demonstrating, and enacting their own script about marine ecosystems. Christine Lee explains that creating space (by providing resources *and* the time and freedom for children's spontaneous creative play), valuing children's agency, and extending creativity across the curriculum all support creativity in science learning.

Chapter 13: Multilingualism

Education programmes are often built on assumptions of monolingualism, despite the fact of – and the cognitive and social benefits of – childhood multilingualism. Jacob Cromdal and Kirsten Stoewer encourage us to recalibrate our understanding of childhood multilingualism, by moving away from a monolingual bias in our understanding of language development, to accommodate the interactional competence displayed and deployed by children when drawing on more than one language. The chapter demonstrates how language alternation (shifting between languages) for specific purposes is a common social practice and can be harnessed for learning interactions with children.

Chapter 14: Belonging

Belonging is an essential element of early childhood programmes, where children's sense of being part of the group is foundational to teaching and learning. In this chapter, Polly Björk-Willén details belonging as a visible social practice constructed in everyday interactions in early learning environments, specifically in greeting children using relevant linguistic and embodied resources (i.e. using the child's first language, hugging, and encouraging children to greet each other on arrival at preschool).

Part III: Interaction and Inclusion

Chapter 15: Play

Annukka Pursi illustrates how a teacher uses playful encounters with toddlers as a means for the children to manage the distress of being separated from parents in the morning. This chapter encourages educators to see how they can adopt playful stances for intentional purposes (i.e. supporting children to self-regulate emotions) throughout everyday interactions with children.

Chapter 16: Mental Health and Wellbeing

Wellbeing is a concept familiar to early childhood educators, but professional knowledge of the mental health needs of children is less commonly understood. Michelle O'Reilly and Jessica Nina Lester provide data of clinical interviews with primary-school-aged children illustrating how particular question design – and sequences of questions – can elicit children's experience of their own emotional state and needs. An understanding of clinical practice in children's mental health, and provision of a 'communication toolkit', can be a resource for early childhood educators to engage in sensitive conversations with children and/or families.

Chapter 17: Neurodiversity

Laura Sterponi and Betty Yu show us how important it is to consider the immediately local context of conversations when assessing children's competencies. They show that six-year-old children with autism use a range of strategies in interaction, and that these strategies are used in interactionally relevant ways. The chapter argues for a shift in our understanding of children's communicative competences, and illustrates, through careful analysis, the skills that are missed if talk-in-interaction is only viewed from neurotypical stances.

Chapter 18: Friendships

Social friendships indelibly influence children's experience of early learning environments, and in the preschool years, friendships with other children increasingly influence their social life. Maryanne Theobald explains the complexity in how children negotiate peer relationships in joining play, claiming ownership of objects and games, how they collaborate (or not) in joint projects and pretend play, and how they navigate cultural and linguistic diversity in establishing and cultivating friendships.

Chapter 19: Conflict

Conflict is ever-present in early learning environments, but *how* children's arguments are managed is highly dependent on teacher approaches to conflict resolution. Amelia Church and Ekaterina Moore detail how children can be supported to find solutions to peer disagreements and how a teacher can scaffold the implementation of a consensus – developed and decided upon by the children themselves – to resume collaborative play.

Chapter 20: Morality

Ann-Carita Evaldson and Magnus Karlsson show us how morality is talked into being – and how children can resist the moral framework imposed by teachers in a discussion about excluding peers. This chapter details how accounts are treated by children and teachers, to resist, reprimand and re-negotiate behaviour that is sanctioned or encouraged in peer play.

Chapter 21: Family

In the final chapter, Akira Takada shares observations of family interactions with very young children, illustrating in very fine detail how the coordination of actions between speakers is an apparatus for socializing children into the valences of the family and the broader community. The data was recorded in the homes of families in Japan, and the analysis carefully unfolds how learning is a socially constructed activity, with interactional practices that can be observed across a range of contexts.

Summary

Throughout, this Handbook provides extracts of familiar, everyday interactions in early childhood settings, and illuminates these interactions to show us evidence of children's competencies, the achievement of intersubjectivity, and the skillful work of *responsive* engagement in early childhood education. Contributing authors have shared their empirical data and insights to detail the 'how' of early learning interactions. Essentially, the aim of this Handbook is to make the evidence from research in conversation analysis accessible for professional learning and practice in early childhood education. We invite readers to engage with this evidence in light of their own practice and expertise, and to consider how they can extend or expand everyday interactions when talking with children.

References

Baraldi, C. (2015). Promotion of migrant children's epistemic status and authority in early school life. *International Journal of Early Childhood*, 47(1), 5–25.

Bateman, A. (2012). Forging friendships: the use of collective pro-terms by preschool children. *Discourse Studies*, 14(2), 165–180.

Bateman, A. (2013). Responding to children's answers: questions embedded in the social context of early childhood education, *Early Years: An International Research Journal*, 33(2), 275–289.

Bateman, A. (2015). *Conversation Analysis and Early Childhood Education: The Co-Production of Knowledge and Relationships*. Farnham, Surrey: Ashgate.

Björk-Willén, P. (2018). Learning to apologize: moral socialization as an interactional practice in preschool. *Research on Children and Social Interaction*, 2(2), 177–194.

Burdelski, M. (2019a), Young children's multimodal participation in storytelling: analysing talk and gesture in Japanese family interaction. *Research on Children and Social Interaction*, 3(1–2), 6–35.

Burdelski, M. (2020) 'Say can I borrow it': teachers and children managing peer conflict in a Japanese preschool. *Linguistics and Education*, 59, 100758.

Butler, C. W. (2008). *Talk and Social Interaction in the Playground*. Aldershot, Surrey: Ashgate.

Butler, C. W., and Edwards, D. (2018). Children's whining in family interaction. *Research on Language and Social Interaction*, 51(1), 52–66.

Cekaite, A. (2013). Socializing emotionally and morally appropriate peer group conduct through classroom discourse. *Linguistics and Education*, 24(4), 511–522.

Cekaite, A. (2020). Triadic conflict mediation as socialisation into perspective taking in Swedish preschools. *Linguistics and Education*, 59, 100753.

Cherrington, S. (2018) Early childhood teachers' thinking and reflection: a model of current practice in New Zealand. *Early Years*, 38(3), 316–332,

Church, A. (2009). *Preference Organization Peer Disputes: How Young Children Resolve Conflict*. Aldershot, Surrey: Ashgate.

Church, A., and Bateman, A. (2019a). Methodology and professional development: Conversation Analytic Role-play Method (CARM) for early childhood education. *Journal of Pragmatics*, 143(1), 242–254.

Church, A., and Bateman, A. (2019b). Children's right to participate: how can teachers extend child-initiated learning sequences? *International Journal of Early Childhood*, 51(3). https://doi.org/10.1007/s13158-019-00250-7

Cohrssen, C., Church, A., and Taylor, C. (2014). Purposeful pauses: teacher talk during early childhood mathematics activities. *International Journal of Early Years Education*, 22(2), 169–183.

Cromdal, J. (2001). 'Can I be with?': negotiating play entry in a bilingual school. *Journal of Pragmatics*, 33(4), 453–515.

Dalgren, S. (2017). Questions and answers, a seesaw and embodied action: how children respond in informing sequences. In A. Bateman and A. Church (eds.), *Children's Knowledge-in-Interaction: Studies in Conversation Analysis* (pp. 37–56). Singapore: Springer.

Danby, S., and Baker, C. (1998). How to be masculine in the block area. *Childhood*, 5 (2), 151–175.

Danby, S., and Theobald, M. (eds.) (2012). *Disputes in Everyday Life: Social and Moral Orders of Children and Young People (Sociological Studies of Children and Youth, Vol. 15)*. Bingley: Emerald Publishing.

Danby, S., Davidson, C., Given, L. M., and Thorpe, K. (2016). Composing an email: social interaction in a preschool classroom. In S. Garvis and N. Lemon (eds.), *Understanding Digital Technologies and Young Children: An International Perspective* (pp. 5–17). London: Routledge.

Danby, S., Davidson, C., Theobald, M., Houen, S., and Thorpe, K. (2017). Pretend play and technology: young children making sense of their everyday social worlds. In D. Pike, S. Lynch, and C. A. Beckett (eds.), *Multidisciplinary Perspectives on Play from Birth and Beyond* (pp. 231–245). Berlin: Springer.

Danby, S. J., Fleer, M., Davidson, C., and Hatzigianni, M. (2018). *Digital Childhoods: Technologies and Children's Everyday Lives*. Singapore: Springer.

Department of Education. (2009). *Belonging, Being and Becoming: The Early Years Learning Framework for Australia (EYLF)*. Canberra, Australia: Department of Education.

Ekberg, S., Danby, S. Houen, S., Davidson, C., and Thorpe, K. (2017). Soliciting and pursuing suggestions: practices for contemporaneously managing student-centred and curriculum-focused activities. *Linguistics and Education*, 42, 65–73.

Evaldsson, A-C., and Tellgren, B. (2009). 'Don't enter – it's dangerous': negotiations for power and exclusion in pre-school girls' play interactions. *Educational and Child Psychology*, 26(2), 9–18.

Filipi, A. (2009). *Toddler and Parent Interaction: The Organization of Gaze, Pointing and Vocalization*. Amsterdam: John Benjamins.

Filipi, A. (2019). Snapshots of tellings in interactions between adults and children aged two, three and three and a half in an Australian context. *Research on Children and Social Interaction*, 3(1–2), 119–143.

Galatolo, R., and Caronia, L. (2018). Morality at dinnertime: the sense of the other as a practical accomplishment in family interaction. *Discourse & Society*, 29(1), 43–62.

Gardner, H., and Forrester, M. (eds.). (2010). *Analysing Interactions in Childhood: Insights from Conversation Analysis*. Oxford: Wiley-Blackwell.

Gardner, R. (2019). Classroom interaction research: the state of the art. *Research on Language and Social Interaction*, 52(3), 212–226.

Goodwin, C. (2018). *Cooperative Action*. Cambridge: Cambridge University Press.

Goodwin, M. H. (1990). *He-Said-She-Said: Talk as Social Organisation among Black Children*. Bloomington, IN: Indiana University Press.

Goodwin, M. H. (2006). *The Hidden Life of Girls: Games of Stance, Status, and Exclusion*. Oxford: Blackwell.

Goodwin, M. H. (2017). Sibling sociality: participation and apprenticeship across contexts. *Research on Children and Social Interaction*, 1(1), 4–29.

Goodwin, M. H., and Cekaite, A. (2018). *Embodied Family Choreography: Practices of Control, Care, and Mundane Creativity*. London: Routledge.

Heritage, J. (1984). *Garfinkel and Ethnomethodology*. Cambridge: Polity Press.

Houen, S., Danby, S., Farrell, A., and Thorpe, K. (2016). 'I wonder what you know …' teachers designing requests for factual information. *Teaching and Teacher Education*, 59, 68–78.

Keel, S. (2016). *Socialization: Parent-Child Interaction in Everyday Life*. London: Routledge.

Kultti, A., and Odenbring, Y. (2015). Collective and individual dimensions in peer positioning in early childhood education. *Early Child Development and Care*, 185(6), 868–882.

Lester, J. N., and O'Reilly, M. (2019). *Applied Conversation Analysis*. Thousand Oaks, CA: Sage.

Ministry of Education (1996; 2017). *Te whāriki: He whāriki mātauranga mō ngā mokopuna o Aotearoa: Early childhood curriculum*. Wellington, New Zealand.

Molla, T., and Nolan, A. (2019). Identifying professional functionings of early childhood educators. *Professional Development in Education*, 45(4), 551–566.

Mondada, L. (2019). Transcribing silent actions: a multimodal approach of sequence organization. *Social Interaction. Video-Based Studies of Human Sociality*, 2(1). https://doi.org/10.7146/si.v2i1.113150

Moore, E., and Burdelski, M. (2020). Peer conflict and language socialization: introduction to special issue. *Linguistics in Educations* (online). https://doi.org/10.1016/j.linged.2019.100758

Morita, E. (2019). Japanese two-year-olds' spontaneous participation in storytelling activities as social interaction. *Research on Children and Social Interaction*, 3(1–2), 65–91.

Nolan, A., Paatsch, L., and Scull, J. (2018). Video-based methodologies: the affordances of different viewpoints in understanding teachers' tacit knowledge of practice that supports young children's oral language. *International Journal of Research & Method in Education*, 41(5), 536–547

Pomerantz, A., and Fehr, B. J. (1997). Conversation analysis: an approach to the study of social action as sense making practices. In T. A van Dijk (ed.), *Discourse as Social Interaction. Discourse Studies: A Multidisciplinary Introduction* (2nd ed., pp. 64–91). London: Sage Publications.

Pursi, A. (2019). Play in adult-child interaction: institutional multi-party interaction and pedagogical practice in a toddler classroom. *Learning, Culture and Social Interaction*, 21, 136–150.

Sacks, H. (1972). On the analyzability of stories by children. In J. J. Gumperz and D. Hymes (eds.), *Directions in Sociolinguistics: The Ethnography of Communication* (pp. 325–345). New York: Rinehart & Winston.

Sacks, H. (1984). Notes on methodology. In J. M. Atkinson and J. Heritage (eds.), *Structures of Social Action: Studies in Conversation Analysis*. Cambridge: Cambridge University Press.

Sacks, H. (1995). *Lectures on Conversation, Volume 1 and 2*. Oxford: Blackwell.

Schegloff, E. A. (2007). *Sequence Organization in Interaction: A Primer in Conversation Analysis*. Cambridge: Cambridge University Press.

Schegloff, E. A., and Sacks, H. (1973). Opening up closings. *Semiotica*, 8, 289–327.

Searles, D. K. (2019). Positioning updates as relevant: an analysis of child-initiated updating in American and Canadian families. *Research on Children and Social Interaction*, 3(1–2). https://doi.org/10.1558/rcsi.37286

Sidnell, J. (2010). *Conversation Analysis: An Introduction*. Oxford: Wiley-Blackwell.

Sidnell, J., and Stivers, T. (2013). *The Handbook of Conversation Analysis*. Chichester: Wiley-Blackwell.

Sidnell, J. (2015). A conversation analytic approach to research on early childhood. In A. Farrell, S. L. Kagan, and K. M. Tisdall (eds.), *The SAGE Handbook of Early Childhood Research* (pp. 255–76). London: Sage Publications.

Sikveland, R., Kevoe-Feldman, H., and Stokoe, E. (2021). *Crisis Talk: Negotiating with Individuals in Crisis*. London: Routledge.

Stokoe, E (2011). Simulated interaction and communication skills training: the 'Conversation Analytic Roleplay Method'. In C. E. Antaki (ed.), *Applied Conversation Analysis: Changing Institutional Practices* (pp. 119–139). Basingstoke: Palgrave MacMillan.

Stokoe, E. (2013a). Overcoming barriers to mediation in intake calls to services: research-based strategies for mediators. *Negotiation Journal*, 29(3), 289–314.

Stokoe, E. (2013b). The (in)authenticity of simulated talk: comparing role-played and actual conversation and the implications for communication training. *Research on Language and Social Interaction*, 46(2), 1–21.

Stokoe, E. (2014). The Conversation Analytic Role-play Method (CARM): A method for training communication skills as an alternative to simulated role-play. *Research on Language and Social Interaction*, 47(3), 255–265.

Stokoe, E., and Edwards, D. (2008) 'Did you have permission to smash your neighbour's door?' Silly questions and their answers in police-suspect interrogations, *Discourse Studies*, 10(1), 89–111.

Stokoe, E., Sikveland, R. O., and Symonds, J. (2016). Calling the GP surgery: patient burden, patient satisfaction, and implications for training. *British Journal of General Practice*, 66(652): e779–e785.

Takada, A., and Kawashima, M. (2017). Relating with an unborn baby: expectant mothers socializing their toddlers in Japanese families. In A. Bateman and A. Church (eds.), *Children's Knowledge-in-Interaction: Studies in Conversation Analysis*. Singapore: Springer.

Theobald, M. (ed.). (2017). *Friendship and Peer Culture in Multilingual Settings. Sociological Studies of Children and Youth, Volume 21*. Bingley: Emerald Publishing.

Theobald, M., and Kultti, A. (2012). Investigating child participation in the everyday talk of a teacher. *Contemporary Issues in Early Childhood*, 13(3), 210–225.

Whalen, M. R. (1995). Working towards play: complexity in children's fantasy activities. *Language in Society*, 24(3), 315–348.

Wootton, A. J. (2006). Children's practices and their connections with 'mind'. *Discourse Studies*, 8(1), 191–198.

PART I

Talk as Social Action

1 Conversation Analysis for Early Childhood Teachers

AMELIA CHURCH, AMANDA BATEMAN, AND SUSAN DANBY

Introduction

The aim of this chapter is to introduce teachers to the methodology of conversation analysis (CA); to explain what conversation analysis is, how CA research is undertaken and key concepts used, and to illustrate why a CA approach provides a useful resource to reflect on teaching practices in early childhood education. This introduction to CA provides a foundation for readers to engage with the chapters that follow, as all Handbook authors are using this approach to unpack and understand talk among children, or between children and early childhood professionals.

Conversation analysis is one of many approaches used to investigate teaching and learning interactions. Different methods and methodologies provide different lenses on how we talk with young children. The lens we choose determines what we see or find, creating particular resources to inform our practice (Danby, 2002). The case we are making in this chapter – and through the evidence illustrated in the Handbook as a whole – is that research using the methods of CA allows us to see the mechanisms of interaction, and to see the interactional details of pedagogy. These details are particularly useful when applying recommended systematic approaches to teaching and learning such as *notice, recognize, and respond* (Carr, Lee, & Jones, 2004). Paying close attention to *how* we notice, recognize, and respond allows us to unpack teaching practices and offers insight into the practical achievement of concepts such as scaffolding (Wood, Bruner, & Ross, 1976), guided participation (Rogoff, 2003) and sustained, shared thinking (Siraj, Kingston, & Melhuish, 2015).

Early childhood education is increasingly adopting a sociocultural approach, changing the ways we think about traditional 'teaching and learning' in more formal educational systems. Contemporary early childhood education encourages us to view infants, toddlers, and young children as competent and capable citizens who make a valuable contribution to their own learning. Curriculum *frameworks* have become increasingly popular in establishing learning outcomes for children from birth to adolescence. Frameworks offer guidance for learning in ways that take notice of the specific social and cultural contexts of children and teachers, often recommending a sociocultural approach to support children's disposition for lifelong learning. The implementation of framework principles and practices, however, can be elusive. Using CA research to illustrate the everyday implementation of curriculum frameworks can fill in these details of how we engage in productive interactions with children. Essentially, the methods of CA provide accessible and transparent materials to reflect on the practices of learning and teaching in early childhood education and care (ECEC) (see Bateman & Church, 2017a; Church & Bateman, 2020).

What Is Conversation Analysis?

Conversation analysis is a wholly empirical methodological approach to understanding social actions, to provide 'an inductive, micro-analytic, and predominantly qualitative method for studying human social interactions' (Hoey & Kendrick, 2017, p. 151). CA is used to study how people make sense of one another, and how this sense-making is on display for participants (and analysts) in talk-in-interaction. 'Talk-in-interaction' is the term that conversation analysts often use to refer to the range of verbal, nonverbal, kinetic, and haptic resources people use to communicate and collaboratively achieve intersubjectivity (i.e.to arrive at some shared understanding). These terms, and other key analytic concepts used in CA research, are explained throughout this chapter.

The methodology and methods of CA emerged from the discipline of sociology at the University of California in the 1960s. It is here that Harvey Sacks began his development of a research methodology that became known as CA, and his legacy is one of being the founder of CA. He worked closely with colleagues Emmanuel Schegloff and Gail Jefferson to study how people interacted with each other and the mechanisms used to structure these interactions. Sacks, influenced by Harold Garfinkel's work in ethnomethodology (the study of social interaction to see how people make sense of the world in orderly ways), started to pay very close attention to talk-in-interaction when researching telephone calls to a helpline. His primary interest was in how people organize social action rather than from a primary interest in language per se. In studying social actions, Sacks was able to show that deliberate and systematic features of 'mundane' everyday talk allowed people to *do* particular things and achieve particular actions (illustrated in the publication of his original lectures from the 1970s; Sacks, 1995). Sacks, Schegloff, and Jefferson (1974) were able to specify the rules of interaction, showing how people take turns in everyday conversation: one turn at a time, one turn after another, and in a sequence of contingent turns. This ground-breaking paper was the first time that the systematic structure of conversation had been explained, identifying that speakers orient to these rules in order to make sense of one another.

Up until the 1960s, research in sociology had explored social practices as defined by particular categories (e.g. race, gender, age) and linguists mostly used hypothetical examples of talk to explain the usage of language. Sacks, Schegloff, and Jefferson were pioneers in demonstrating how social actions are achieved through language, and that these social actions have ordered, predictable, and rule-governed patterns of use. Harvey Sacks was interested in the talk of young children insofar as it provided insights into how people go about managing social actions, given that children are also participants in social interaction from birth. For example, his original work shows how children navigate restricted speaker rights (e.g., using the phrase 'You know what?' prompts an adult to respond 'What?', which then gives the child an opportunity to say something; see Sacks, 1995, volume I, p. 256). He also wrote about how children construct stories (Sacks, 1972) and rules of games (1995, volume I, p. 363), and the skills required in learning how to lie (Sacks, 1995, volume 1, p. 565). More detailed discussions on the history and approach of CA are provided elsewhere in relation to ontology (Heritage, 1984a); key principles (Hoey & Kendrick, 2017; Sidnell, 2010; Sidnell & Stivers, 2012); practical guides (Lester & O'Reilly, 2019; Psathas, 1995; ten Have, 2007); classroom interaction (Edwards-Groves & Davidson, 2017; Gardner, 2012, 2019; Mushin, Gardner, & Gourlay, 2021); and early childhood education (for example, Bateman, 2015; Burdelski & Howard, 2020; Butler, 2008; Church, 2009; Danby & Baker, 1998; Theobald, 2016).

Conversation analysis aligns with sociocultural learning theories that currently underpin and shape teaching practice throughout the world. From a CA perspective, the social and collaborative practices enacted by children and teachers are both the vehicle for and constitutive of learning. Rather than just focusing on either what the teacher *or* the child does, CA's core concern is with the co-construction and choreography of social practices (see Goodwin, 2017). By paying close attention to how turns at talk are related to one another, this emergent approach to understanding the social world – now known as conversation analysis – has provided insights about communication that have deepened our understanding of human interaction. Speakers themselves use talk-in-interaction as a way of doing things and making sense of one another, so conversation analysts pay attention to the same things speakers pay attention to (pauses, gesture, word choice, intonation, hesitations, and so on) to see how human sociality is achieved (see Enfield, 2017).

How Is Conversation Analysis 'Done'?

Conversation analysis aims to understand real interaction, usually captured through video or audio recordings. Rather than observing children in laboratory settings, observations are made in everyday settings such as early learning centres. Children and educators are not asked to respond to surveys, participate in interviews, or complete standardized tests, but rather to allow researchers to be present in the setting, to observe typical daily practices, and capture these practices on video. Recognizing the observer's paradox (Labov, 1972) – the notion that the researcher's presence can change the nature of the behaviour observed – researchers typically spend extended periods of time at their chosen research location, as ethnographers do, to mitigate the effect of introducing a researcher and their video camera to the early childhood setting. As CA is concerned with capturing interactional practices *in situ*, these video recordings serve as reliable documentation of the types of interaction that take place – at that time, with those participants, in that place.

Recording everyday interactions allows a study of these interactions through repeated reviewing of the recorded data to see how speakers make sense of one another (Sacks, 1984a) and to see what speakers do, rather than what we *think* they do (Stokoe, 2013). Video recording is preferred to capture the embodied features of talk-in-interaction (see Mondada, 2018), especially when exploring interactions with infants and toddlers. Features such as gesture, eye gaze, and body position are regarded as just as important as talk in the co-production of social interaction. Rather than labelling embodied features of social interaction as generally 'non-verbal', CA is interested in how specific embodied gestures are intertwined with verbal features of interaction; video footage allows the researcher to re-visit how this is achieved in the observed interactions.

After the researcher has made a series of recordings in the same setting, CA requires very detailed transcription of the video observations (see Jefferson, 2004). To this end, conversation analysts study the video recordings for sequences of interaction, to identify practices that may reoccur, providing a collection of a particular phenomenon (Butler, 2008; Church, 2009), or alternatively a single case that illustrates how local social order is done (Bateman, 2021; Danby, 2002; Schegloff, 1987). Approaching the task of transcribing video-recorded interactions with Sacks' attitude of 'unmotivated looking' (Hoey & Kendrick, 2017; Schegloff, 1996), the goal is to identify what the participants themselves orient to in the interaction.

Transcription and Analysis

The transcript includes the identity of the speaker (usually a pseudonym) of each turn, what was said, how the interaction was produced (i.e. through intonation, emphasis, speed, and volume), and the length of pauses within and between turns. Overlapping speech is marked in the transcript, and the use and timing of accompanying gestures or direction of eye gaze can be included. Laughing is captured by depicting the syllables (e.g. 'heh huh huh') (Hepburn & Bolden, 2017), and voice quality (e.g. creaky voice, smiling voice) is noted where noticeably different from other turns at talk. The intonational contour (falling or rising tone of voice) is marked at the completion of each turn, as it can indicate the trajectory of the turn and determine what comes next. This recognition is important as, for example, a flat tone at the end of a turn may indicate that the speaker is not yet finished or stretching out a syllable may invite children to complete the turn (e.g. an oral cloze). Even audible in-breaths and out-breaths are included in the transcripts, as these may be meaningful in the ongoing interaction.

One reason for capturing all this detail when transcribing is to see what might be meaningful to the speakers themselves, rather than what the analyst decides to look for. Transcription cannot capture the full complexity of talk-in-interaction, and what is transcribed in itself is an analytic decision about what matters most in the interaction (see Ochs, 1979). But transcribing the talk-in-interaction, and paying very close attention to the features of talk while transcribing, supports the 'unmotivated looking' and noticing central to the methods of CA. Through listening, re-listening – and ideally discussing the data with other analysts – the process of transcription enables the researcher to identify patterns and repeated phenomena in the interaction that reveal what it is that the participants are doing in the interaction (Sacks, 1995; Sidnell, 2010).

Furthermore, CA methods are accessible to non-experts. As conversation analysts provide transcripts of the recorded data – and video is becoming increasingly accessible in research publications (e.g. Burdelski, 2020) – others have access to the original observations. The process of the analysis is transparent, because conversation analysts must detail the evidence in the talk itself to illustrate any claims about what children know or what teachers do. Transparency of the original video data through the detailed transcription and analysis provides reliability of findings in CA research 'because others could look at what I had studied, and make of it what they could, if they wanted to be able to disagree with me' (Sacks, 1995, volume I, p. 622).

What Are Key Concepts in Conversation Analysis?

Once naturalistic (everyday) recordings are captured, and while transcribing these interactions in great detail, conversation analysts ask, 'why this, in this way, right now?' (Seedhouse, 2005, p. 251). The CA microanalytic transcription process offers opportunities to investigate how each turn builds on the prior turn of others to co-create sequences of interaction. As the researcher transcribes what was said and done by the participants in the video recording, the **turn-taking** between the participants becomes visible. By paying close attention to what each speaker does, we can see in detail how a conversation is co-produced through these turns of talk in everyday teacher-child interactions. For example, the following brief Extract 1.1 from a transcript of a recorded interaction between a four-year-old child (marked as CHD) and a teacher (marked as TCH) during a walk through a Welsh cemetery (Bateman & Waters, 2013: see Extract 3.1d in Bateman, Chapter 3, this volume) shows who spoke first (the child's question), then who replied (the teacher's explanation), and then the response to that reply (the child's receipt of understanding).

Extract 1.1

```
01 CHD: ↑why do they ↑put .hhh thems ↓a::rrows on top↓=
02 TCH: =they're not ↓a::rrows↓ >darlin< they're called
03      ↓gra::ve- uh=↓gra::ve stones where they write
04      the na:me of the↓per:son↑
05 CHD: >°↓ah↓° <
```

The **sequences of actions** that are visible in turns at talk provide an ongoing display for speakers of how their talk is received by others (see Kidwell, this volume; Kendrick et al., 2020). This preoccupation with what speakers are *doing* in conversation (Sacks, 1984b), is a helpful way to understand interaction as a series of actions.

The most basic sequence of actions is co-produced through **adjacency pairs**, where one turn (the **first pair part**) sets up an expectation for a particular type of next turn (a **second pair part**). For example, a first pair part shaped as a question should be followed with a second pair part in the shape of an answer. Likewise, a first pair part invitation should be responded to in a second pair part that accepts or declines the invitation. For example, a first pair part request for information (either by a child or a teacher) should be followed by a second pair part that provides the requested information, and so on. Schegloff and Sacks (1973, p. 298) explain that this basic sequence provides an in-built mechanism for monitoring understanding:

> What two utterances produced by different speakers can do that one utterance cannot do is: by an adjacently positioned second, a speaker can show that he understood what a prior aimed at, and that he is willing to go along with that. Also, by virtue of the occurrence of an adjacently produced second, the doer of a first can see that what he intended was indeed understood, and that it was or was not accepted.

In CA research, we see that even very young children demonstrate an understanding of the interactional obligation set up by a first pair part, and may, for example, demand an answer from their mother if none is provided (Keel, 2016; see also Kidwell, 2012, and this volume). The sequences of turns at talk provide researchers – and teachers – with immediately available data on what children are paying attention to, how they understand questions, instructions, or explanations by what they do next. It is this 'nextness' of conversation that displays speakers' understanding of the prior talk; every next turn provides the vehicle for intersubjectivity (shared understanding). In other words, we can see how others understand each other from what they do next.

Where there is an alternative for types of second pair parts – for example, an invitation can be accepted or declined – one is typically **preferred** (done immediately, briefly, and to the point; e.g., accepting an invitation without delay) and the other is **dispreferred** (delayed and includes some sort of account as to why the preferred action is not done; e.g. declining an invitation after a pause, and explaining why the invitation cannot be accepted) (Pomerantz, 1984). This action does not mean psychologically preferred (i.e. what the speaker wants) but rather is linguistically the most straightforward next action. So pervasive is this organizing principle of talk-in-interaction that people typically treat pauses of more than 0.3 seconds as a clue that a dispreferred action is coming next, because dispreferred actions are prefaced by some sort of delay. This **preference organization** is one of the mechanisms that contributes to the efficiency and progressivity of interaction (Stivers & Robinson, 2006). Children, parents, and teachers are sensitive to these organizing principles of talk-in-interaction, and the immediate context always determines the preferred next action.

Every turn is understood in relation to the surrounding turns at talk, and the '**conditional relevance**' (Schegloff, 1968) determines what might be the most relevant next action at any given point. In other words, 'the position of an utterance in a sequence is criterial to understanding what a turn at talk is doing' (Clift, 2016, p. 65). To help unpack this point, we return to the example above where the teacher's turn in lines 2–4 ('they're not ↓a::rrows↓ >darlin< they're called gra::ve- uh=↓gra::ve stones where they write the na:me of the↓per:son↓') treats the child's question as a request for information and provides a relevant next action explaining what the gravestones are for. We can see that the teacher's response *is* the relevant next action – a fitting second pair part – by what the child does next: the receipt token 'ah' (see Heritage, 1984b) demonstrates a shift in the child's understanding that the arrows on top (the gravestones) mark the name of the person who is buried there.

With each turn orienting to the prior turn(s), this in-built and highly efficient system is used to identify and resolve problems in talk-in-interaction. Defined as **repair**, speakers can at any point revise their own speech or query the meaning of another, either directly or, more commonly, by flagging some sort of trouble (e.g. '*what?*', '*huh?*'; see Drew, 1997; Kitzinger, 2012). The rules of turn-taking enable confirmation checks at every point; where misunderstanding occurs, speakers can move immediately to repair the problem. Returning to our brief example (Extract 1.1), we see that the teacher manages repair at the beginning of the turn when explaining the function of gravestones:

```
01 CHD: ↑why do they ↑put .hhh thems ↓a::rrows on top↓=
02 TCH: =they're not ↓a::rrows↓ >darlin< they're called
03      ↓gra::ve- uh=↓gra::ve stones where they write the
04      na:me of the↓per:son↑
05 CHD: >°↓ah↓° <
```

The teacher **self-repairs** in her own turn (↓gra::ve- uh=↓gra::ve stones), the sort of self-revision that is common in conversation, where speakers fix or revise their talk within their own turn. **Other-initiated repair** seeks clarification of the prior turn by another person, usually providing an opportunity for the other speaker to fix whatever the trouble source might have been. In the example above, we see **other-initiated repair**, where the recipient (the teacher) identifies a repairable and goes ahead to fix it themselves (repairing the incorrect 'arrows' to correct 'gravestones'). The way in which teachers do repair is important, because sensitivity is needed to support children's continuing contributions to the ongoing interaction. CA's interest in how repair is achieved can be very useful in unravelling the ways in which approaches to feedback can be tailored to the individual needs of each child.

Teachers are constantly shaping their talk to accommodate the level of understanding of the various children they interact with throughout the day, in what CA calls **recipient design**. In everyday life we try to avoid telling people what they already know, and shape the way we talk to meet the specific characteristics of the people with whom we are interacting. For example, early childhood teachers address parents in a particular way when they report news of the child's daily accomplishments, which differs from how they interact with the children themselves, and speak differently again when they are socialising with friends. The ways in which we design our talk for specific recipients is key in teacher practice, where we are given the task of extending children's knowledge whilst supporting their holistic wellbeing. Here the importance of knowing the child you are working with is imperative to building on their existing knowledge and extending their thinking in ways that are interesting for them. For this reason, talking with a group of children can be challenging, given the different knowledge and abilities of the recipients.

Difference in knowledge states can be described as the **epistemic status** of speakers (i.e. what each person knows; see Mushin & Gardner, Chapter 7, this volume). When the teacher asks the child a (recipient-designed) question, the child will demonstrate their knowledge (or lack thereof) in their second pair part response. Education research often identifies three-part sequences in classroom interactions which consist of initiation-response-evaluation (Mehan, 1979), where the teacher usually produces a question (initiation), the child provides an answer, or best guess (response), and the teacher then evaluates the answer by providing some kind of feedback (evaluation). Within these sequences, then, is a display of what children understood the question to mean, and a display of their knowledge in the response they provide. In CA research we see how a teacher's third turn can move beyond evaluation and expand on children's responses in order to build learning trajectories (Lee, 2007; McHoul, 1978; Waring, 2015). CA's treatment of sequences of turn at talk enable us to understand the collaborative exchanges between children and teachers that support learning.

In essence, conversation provides a type of assessment-in-interaction, where children's knowledge and sense-making are on display in each subsequent turn at talk. Paying close attention to how these turns at talk unfold provides teachers with insights into the collaborative work of talk-in-interaction. Importantly for early childhood teachers, the CA approach equips us with an awareness that every interaction is made up of *sequences* of actions. Our turns as teachers are significant when we consider how we might respond to children's interests in ways that extend and support their learning. Through watching video footage of teacher-child interactions and transcribing them to clearly mark out the turn-taking evident within the sequence of action, we gain access to the orderly ways in which children and teachers achieve effective pedagogy in interaction. Essentially, we can see how teaching and learning is managed through turns at talk.

Why Is Conversation Analysis Useful for Early Childhood Education?

Through the CA process of collecting video footage of everyday interactions between children and early childhood teachers and engaging in the transcription process, paying attention to each turn at talk, we can see how it is that speakers make sense of one another by what is done in each next turn. This sense-making – made by the participants – is available to onlookers, be they analysts or teachers paying close attention to the interactional practices of pedagogy. This entirely data-driven, empirical focus of CA lends itself to research in early childhood education, because we can see what both the teachers and the children are doing to collaboratively construct teaching and learning interactions.

The fact that the original data and analysis is on display in CA research means that the method can be used as a vehicle for applied studies and professional learning. Current work by Elizabeth Stokoe and her colleagues at Loughborough University has ' ... demonstrated to great effect how useful the methods of CA are for communication ... ' training for police, mediators, medical receptionists, and university admissions staff. Specifically, they developed the Conversation Analytic Role-play Method (CARM; see www.carmtraining.org), and have found that practitioners gain a deeper understanding of the interactional practices of their workplaces if they are supported to find the practices themselves, by exploring the sequential organization of talk (Stokoe, 2013, 2014b; Stokoe & Sikveland, 2017). Professional learning, in the form of reflection on practice that is directly informed by the details of practice, is relevant and constructive for current early childhood teachers (see Church & Bateman, 2019, 2020). Using evidence from CA research enables teachers to re-visit the mechanisms of learning interactions that enable children to contribute their ideas, explore meaning, and extend concepts.

Conversation analysis's approach to interaction as an entirely collaborative activity makes it a useful methodology for understanding the children's role in the active co-construction of learning activities. Recognizing that all parties shape the context of the ongoing interaction means that CA is compatible with early childhood's concern with children's rights (Theobald, 2019) in that it does not privilege the contributions of particular speakers (i.e. limiting analysis to what the teacher does). A CA approach considers how *all* members of a group negotiate and co-construct opportunities to participate – including how exclusion might be done. The methods of CA emphasize the interdependence of talk, illustrating that each turn at talk is contingent on what other speakers do, or do not do.

Given that CA underscores the inherently collaborative and cooperative nature of talk-in-interaction, this research methodology implicitly pays attention to children's agency and competence. Practitioners and researchers in early childhood education are necessarily concerned with listening to children's voices and the essential contributions they make. Early childhood research seeks to involve children as active co-researchers (Clark, 2017; Danby & Farrell, 2004; Mason & Watson, 2014; Mukherji & Albon, 2018), to understand children's culture from a child's point of view (Clark & Moss, 2001; Corsaro, 2017) and recognize children as agents in constructing the social context of early learning environments (James & Prout, 1997). Because CA is interested in emic perspectives – that is, the *participants'* own attention towards the ongoing activity – it aligns with research and educational policy that positions children as capable and agentive in interactions in early learning environments.

This emic orientation also allows us to detail children's own practices, to see how it is that they order and interact in the local social context, and demonstrate their interests to others. Researchers in early childhood education are *not* members of the group they seek to understand; even experienced early childhood practitioners cannot claim to see the world from the perspective of a three-year-old child. CA research does not make assumptions about practice or categorize actions from the analyst's point of view, but instead seeks to describe participants' own methods for managing interactions with others. The video recordings, detailed transcription, and analysis enable phenomena relevant to children's own lives to appear.

As summarized by Kidwell, 'the matter of what children "mean" or "intend" by their actions might seem to pose problems for researchers of children's early communication. CA provides a unique and effective tool set for finding and evidencing their concerns, goals and motivations in interaction' (Kidwell, 2012, p. 518).

Conclusion

This chapter has outlined what CA is, how it is done, and its usefulness for early childhood education praxis. The methods of CA give an apparatus to explain the *how* of pedagogy in different contexts. The chapters in this Handbook can be described as 'applied CA', in that they explore practices in education settings, as a type of institutional practice (see Antaki, 2011; Drew & Heritage, 1992; Heritage & Clayman, 2010), and consider the implications of interactional practices for the work of teaching and learning. This type of insight is not possible through recollection alone, because we do not remember all the details of talk. It is close analysis that uncovers which of these details are important when talking with children – for example, pausing at opportune moments to allow children time to think and shape their response, designing questions in particular formats that prompt exploration of a concept, or extending topics in ways that are contingent on children's own interest and knowledge.

Through understanding the systematic ways in which social interaction is achieved, CA can provide a magnifying tool to explore in detail the pedagogical practices that we engage in with infants, toddlers, and young children in our everyday interactions. CA allows us to hit the 'pause' button to explore in detail what children know and to reflect on how we might respond to their knowledge in ways that align with their interests. Through detailed transcriptions of child-teacher interactions, we see what children do in constructing social action, and also see their understanding of – and active contribution to – the social rules of educational settings, the peer-initiated and designed rules of play. We see children's conceptual knowledge on display, visible through unfolding turns at talk. As social beings, we rarely consider just how it is that we manage to navigate multiple social interactions throughout our daily lives. We tend to underestimate how complex social worlds are. We move from one activity to the next with little consideration of how each turn at talk and gesture we perform adds to our own socialization and the socialization of others. CA transcription and analysis affords the luxury of such pause and reflection, as we seek to understand the interactions that build our social worlds.

References

Antaki, C. (2011). Six kinds of applied conversation analysis. In C. Antaki (ed.), *Applied Conversation Analysis: Intervention and Change in Institutional Talk* (pp. 1–4). Basingstoke: Palgrave Macmillan.

Bateman, A. (2013). Responding to children's answers: questions embedded in the social context of early childhood education. *Early Years*, 33(2), 275–289.

Bateman, A. (2015). *Conversation Analysis and Early Childhood Education: The Co-Production of Knowledge and Relationships*. London: Ashgate/Routledge.

Bateman, A. (2017). Hearing children's voices through a conversation analysis approach. *International Journal of Early Years Education*, 25(1), 1–16.

Bateman, A. (2021). Teacher responses to toddler crying in the New Zealand outdoor environment. *Journal of Pragmatics*, 175(2), 81–93.

Bateman, A., and Church, A. (2017a). *Children's Knowledge-in-Interaction: Studies in Conversation Analysis*. Singapore: Springer.

Bateman, A., and Church, A. (2017b). Children's use of objects in an early years playground. *European Early Childhood Education Research Association Journal*, 25(1), 55–71.

Bateman, A., Hohepa, M., and Bennett, T. (2017). Indigenizing outdoor play in New Zealand: a conversation analysis approach. In T. Waller, E. Arlemalm-Hagser, E. B. H. Sandseter, L. Lee-Hammond, K. Lekies, and S. Wyver (eds.), *SAGE Handbook of Outdoor Play and Learning* (pp. 530–542). London: Sage Publications.

Björk-Willén, P., and Cromdal, J. (2009). When education seeps into 'free play': how preschool children accomplish multilingual education. *Journal of Pragmatics*, 41(8), 555–577.

Burdelski, M. (2020). Teacher compassionate touch in a Japanese preschool. *Social Interaction. Video-Based Studies of Human Sociality*, 3(1). https://doi.org/10.7146/si.v3i1.120248

Burdelski, M., and Howard, K. M. (2020). *Language Socialization in Classrooms: Culture, Interaction and Language Development*. Cambridge: Cambridge University Press.

Carr, M., Lee, W., & Jones, C. (2004). *An Introduction to Kei Tua o te Pae: He Whakamōhiotanga ki Kei Tua o te Pae* (Book 1). Auckland: Learning Media.

Church, A., and Bateman, A. (2019). Methodology and professional development: CARM for early childhood education. *Journal of Pragmatics*, 143(1), 242–254.

Church, A., and Bateman, A. (2020). Conversation Analytic Role-play Method (CARM) for teacher training. *Teacher Development*, 24(5), 652–668. https://doi.org/10.1080/13664530.2020.1820371

Clark, A. (2017). *Listening to young children: A guide to understanding and using the mosaic approach*, Third Edition. London: National Children's Bureau.

Clark, A., and Moss, P. (2001). *Listening to Young Children: The Mosaic Approach*. London: National Children's Bureau.

Clift, R. (2016). *Conversation Analysis*. Cambridge: Cambridge University Press.

Corsaro, W. (2017). *The Sociology of Childhood*. London: Sage Publications.

Danby, S. (2002). The communicative competence of young children. *Australian Journal of Early Childhood*, 27(3), 25–30.

Danby, S., and Baker, C. (1998). 'What's the problem?' – Restoring social order in the preschool classroom. In I. Hutchby and J. Moran-Ellis (eds.), *Children and Social Competence: Arenas of Action* (pp. 157–186). London: Falmer Press.

Danby, S., and Farrell, A. (2004). Accounting for young children's competence in educational research: new perspectives on research ethics. *Australian Educational Researcher*, 31(3), 35–50.

Drew, P. (1997). 'Open' class repair initiators in response to sequential sources of troubles in conversation. *Journal of Pragmatics*, 28, 69–101.

Drew, P., and Heritage, J. (eds.). (1992). *Talk at Work: Interaction in Institutional Settings*. Cambridge: Cambridge University Press.

Edwards-Groves, C., and Davidson, C. (2017). *Becoming a Meaning Maker: Talk and Interaction in the Dialogic Classroom*. Newtown: Primary English Teaching Association Australia.

Enfield, N. J. (2017). *How We Talk: The Inner Workings of Conversation*. New York, NY: Basic Books.

Fitzgerald, R., and Housley, W. (eds.). (2015). *Advances in Membership Categorisation Analysis*. London: Sage Publications.

Gardner, R. (2012). Conversation analysis in the classroom context. In J. Sidnell and T. Stivers (eds.), *The Handbook of Conversation Analysis* (pp. 593–611). Hoboken, NJ: Wiley.

Gardner, R. (2019). Classroom interaction research: the state of the art. *Research on Language and Social Interaction*, 52(3), 212–226.

Goodwin, C. (2017). *Co-Operative Action*. Cambridge: Cambridge University Press.

Hepburn, A., and Bolden, G. B. (2017). *Transcribing for Social Research*. London: Sage Publications.

Heritage, J. (1984a) *Garfinkel and Ethnomethodology*. Cambridge: Polity Press.

Heritage, J. (1984b) A change-of-state token and aspects of its sequential placement. In J. M. Atkinson and J. Heritage (eds.), *Structures of Social Action* (pp. 299–347). Cambridge: Cambridge University Press.

Heritage, J., and Clayman, S. (2010). *Talk in Action: Interactions, Identities, and Institutions*. Chichester: Wiley-Blackwell.

Hoey, E. M., and Kendrick, K. H. (2017). Conversation analysis. In A. M. B. de Groot and P. Hagoort (eds.), *Research Methods in Psycholinguistics: A Practical Guide* (pp. 151–173). Chichester: Wiley-Blackwell.

Houen, S. Danby, S., Farrell, A., and Thorpe, K. (2016). 'I wonder...' formulations in teacher-child interactions. *International Journal of Early Childhood*, 48(3), 259–276.

Houen, S., Danby, S., Farrell, A., and Thorpe, K. (2019). Adopting an unknowing stance in teacher–child interactions through 'I wonder...' formulations. *Classroom Discourse*, 10(2), 151–167. https://doi.org/10.1080/19463014.2018.1518251

James, A., and Prout, A. (eds.). (1997). *Constructing and Reconstructing Childhood: Contemporary Issues in the Sociological Study of Childhood*. London: Falmer Press.

Jefferson, G. (2004). Glossary of transcript symbols with an introduction. In G. H. Lerner (ed.), *Conversation Analysis: Studies from the First Generation*, (pp. 13–31). Amsterdam/Philadelphia: John Benjamins.

Keel, S. (2016). *Socialization: Parent-Child Interaction in Everyday Life*. New York, NY: Routledge.

Kendrick, K. H., Brown, P., Dingemanse, M., Floyd, S., Gipper, S., Hayano, K., Hoey, E., Hoymann, G., Manrique, E., Rossi, G., and Levinson, S. C. (2020). Sequence organization: a universal infrastructure for social action. *Journal of Pragmatics*, 168, 119–138.

Kidwell, M. (2012). Interaction among children. In J. Sidnell and T. Stivers (eds.), *The Handbook of Conversation Analysis*, (pp. 511–532). Hoboken, NJ: Wiley-Blackwell.

Kitzinger, C. (2012). Repair. In J. Sidnell and T. Stivers (eds.), *The Handbook of Conversation Analysis*, (pp. 229–256). Hoboken, NJ: Wiley-Blackwell.

Labov, W. (1972). *Sociolinguistic Patterns*. Philadelphia, PA: University of Pennsylvania.

Lee, Y-A. (2007). Third turn position in teacher talk: contingency and the work of teaching. *Journal of Pragmatics*, 39(6), 1204–1230.

Lester, N., and O'Reilly, M. (2019). *Applied Conversation Analysis*. Thousand Oaks, California, CA: Sage Publications.

McHoul, A. W. (1978). The organization of turns at formal talk in the classroom. *Language in Society*, 7(2), 183–213.

Mason, J., and Watson E. (2014). Researching children: research on, with, and by children. In A. Ben-Arieh, F. Casas, I. Frønes, and J. Korbin (eds.), *Handbook of Child Well-Being*. Dordrecht: Springer.

Mehan, H. (1979). *Learning Lessons: Social Organisation in the Classroom*. Cambridge, MA: Harvard University Press.

Mondada, L. (2018). Multiple temporalities of language and body in interaction: challenges for transcribing multimodality, *Research on Language and Social Interaction*, 51(1), 85–106.

Mori, J., and Zuengler, J. (2008). Conversation analysis and talk-in-interaction in classrooms. In M. Martin-Jones, A. M. de Mejia, and N. H. Hornberger (eds.), *Encyclopedia of Language and Education (2nd ed.,)*, vol. 3. London: Springer.

Mukherji, P., and Albon, D. (2018). *Research Methods in Early Childhood: An Introductory Guide*. Los Angeles, CA: Sage Publications.

Mushin, I., Gardner, R., and Gourlay, C. (2021). *Effective Task Instructions in the First Year of Schooling: What Teachers and Children Do*. London: Routledge.

Ochs, E. (1979). Transcription as theory. In E. Ochs and B. Schieffelin (eds.), *Developmental Pragmatics*. New York, NY: Academic Press.

Pomerantz, A. (1984). Agreeing and disagreeing with assessments: some features of preferred/dispreferred turn shapes. In J. M. Atkinson and J. Heritage (eds.), *Structures of Social Action: Studies in Conversation Analysis*, (pp. 57–101). Cambridge: Cambridge University Press.

Pomerantz, A., and Fehr, B. J. (1997). Conversation analysis: an approach to the study of social action as sense making practices. In T. A. van Dijk (ed.), *Discourse as Social Interaction. Discourse Studies: A Multidisciplinary Introduction* (2nd ed., pp. 64–91). London: Sage Publications.

Psathas, G. (1995). *Conversation Analysis: The Study of Talk-in-Interaction*. London: Sage Publications.

Rogoff, B. (2003). *The Cultural Nature of Human Development*. Oxford: Oxford University Press.

Sacks, H. (1972). On the analyzability of stories by children. In J. J. Gumperz and D. Hymes (eds.), *Directions in Sociolinguistics: The Ethnography of Communication*. New York, NY: Holt, Rinehart, and Winston.

Sacks, H. (1984a). Notes on methodology. In J. M. Atkinson and J. Heritage (eds.), *Structures of Social Action*, (pp. 21–27). Cambridge: Cambridge University Press.

Sacks, H. (1984b). On doing 'being ordinary'. In J. M. Atkinson and J. Heritage (eds.), *Structures of Social Action: Studies in Conversation Analysis*. Cambridge: Cambridge University Press.

Sacks, H. (1995). *Lectures on Conversation* (vols. I and II). Oxford: Blackwell.

Sacks, H., Schegloff, E. A., and Jefferson, G. (1974). A simplest systematics for the organization of turn-taking for conversation. *Language*, 50(4), 696–735.

Schegloff, E. A. (1968). Sequencing in conversational openings. *American Anthropologist*, 70(6), 1075–1095.

Schegloff, E. A. (1987). Analyzing single episodes of interaction: an exercise in conversation analysis. *Social Psychology Quarterly*, 50(2), 101–114.

Schegloff, E. A. (1996). Confirming allusions: toward an empirical account of action. *American Journal of Sociology*, 102, 161–216.

Schegloff, E. A. (2007). *Sequence Organization in Interaction: A Primer in Conversation Analysis*. Cambridge: Cambridge University Press.

Schegloff, E. A., and Sacks, H. (1973). Opening up closings. *Semiotica*, 8, 289–327.

Seedhouse, P. (2005). Conversation analysis as research methodology. In K. Richards and P. Seedhouse (eds.), *Applying Conversation Analysis*. London: Palgrave Macmillan.

Sidnell, J. (2010). *Conversation Analysis: An Introduction*. Oxford: Wiley-Blackwell.

Sidnell, J. (2012). Basic conversation analytic methods. In J. Sidnell and T. Stivers (eds.), *The Handbook of Conversation Analysis*, (pp. 77–99). Hoboken, NJ: Wiley-Blackwell.

Sidnell, J., and Stivers, T. (eds.). (2012). *The Handbook of Conversation Analysis*. Hoboken, NJ: Wiley-Blackwell.

Siraj, I., Kingston, D., and Melhuish, E. (2015). *Assessing Quality in Early Childhood Education and Care. Sustained Shared Thinking and Emotional Wellbeing (SSTEW) Scale for 2–5 Year-Olds Provision*. London: UCL and IOE Press.

Stivers, T., and Robinson, J. (2006). A preference for progressivity in interaction. *Language in Society*, 35(3), 367–392.

Stokoe, E. (2013). The (in)authenticity of simulated talk: comparing role-played and actual interaction and the implications for communication training. *Research on Language and Social Interaction*, 46(2): 165–185.

Stokoe, E. (2014a). 'The science of analysing conversations, second by second'. [Video]. www.youtube.com/watch?v=MtOG5PK8xDA [last accessed 9 December 2021].

Stokoe, E. (2014b). The Conversation Analytic Role-play Method (CARM): a method for training communication skills as an alternative to simulated role-play. *Research on Language and Social Interaction*, 47(3), 255–265.

Stokoe, E., Sikveland, R. (2017). The Conversation Analytic Role-play Method: simulation, endogenous impact and interactional nudges. In V. Fors, T. O'Dell, and Pink, S. (eds.), *Theoretical Scholarship and Applied Practice*, (pp. 73–96). Oxford: Berghahn Books.

ten Have, P. (2007) *Doing Conversation Analysis: A Practical Guide (2nd edition)*. London: Sage.

Theobald, M. (ed.). (2016). *Friendship and Peer Culture in Multilingual Settings*. Bingley: Emerald Publishing.

Theobald, M. (2019). UN Convention on the Rights of the Child: 'Where are we at in recognising children's rights in early childhood, three decades on …?'. *International Journal of Early Childhood*, 51(3), 251–257.

Theobald, M., and Danby, S. (2020). Children's competence and wellbeing in sensitive research: when video-stimulated accounts lead to dispute. In J. Lamerichs, S. Danby, A. Bateman, and S. Ekberg (eds.), *Children and Mental Health Talk: Perspectives on Social Competence*, (pp.137–166). Basingstoke: Palgrave Macmillan.

Waring, H. Z. (2015). *Theorizing Pedagogical Interaction: Insights from Conversation Analysis*. London: Routledge.

Wood, D. J., Bruner, J. S., and Ross, G. (1976). The role of tutoring in problem solving. *Journal of Child Psychiatry and Psychology*, 17(2), 89–100. https://doi.org/10.1111/j.1469-7610.1976.tb00381.x

2 | Sequences

MARDI KIDWELL

Introduction

A 'sequence' in interaction describes the relationship between two or more actors' coordinated, communicative actions with one another: an exchange of utterances, gazes, and/or facial expressions, for example. In the most basic terms, it is the call and response that organizes human communication (and that of other animals, too; Levinson, 2006). Another way to think about it is, in interaction, when one person does or says something, it sets up and constrains what another can do in response. This action by one and response by another is an action unit known as an 'adjacency pair'; two paired actions produced by different participants that 'fit' together: question and answer; complaint and solution; offer and acceptance; and so on (Schegloff and Sacks, 1973). Humans use these action pair units as building blocks to make longer sequences of action that are used to carry out all manner of human communicative business: requesting, complaining, appreciating, arguing, agreeing, joking, storytelling and so on. As Schegloff writes, 'Sequences are the vehicle for getting some activity accomplished' in interaction (2007, p. 2).

A question to ask is, where does the capacity to form sequences come from? Indeed, where does the capacity for interaction come from? From birth, infants are attracted to the faces and eyes of others; they spend a good deal of time looking at faces and eyes (Meltzoff & Moore, 1993). Also from birth, infants exhibit the ability to imitate facial expressions such as blinking eyes and tongue protrusions (Meltzoff & Moore, 1977). These innate abilities and attractions to other humans, especially their faces, are the foundation for the 'back and forth' that characterizes early caregiver-infant interaction (Bateson, 1975). In the first few weeks after birth, infants begin to produce vocalizations that – different from crying – are described as coos and murmurs, which elicit responses from caregivers (Oller, 2000). These vocal exchanges resemble conversations in their back-and-forth nature and are considered to be the early basis of turn-taking (Bateson, 1975; Trevarthen, 1998). It has been argued that these sorts of behaviours, and their emergence at birth, or shortly thereafter, are evidence of the innateness of the human propensity for interaction, and later, language, which Levinson has called the 'interaction engine' (Levinson, 2006).

Adults, of course, encourage infant participation in these early vocal and emotional exchanges, and provide scaffolding for their extension and elaboration (Snow et al., 1979). Their efforts to engage infants include tickling, foot wiggling, making funny faces, and showing and offering objects. These early interactions are based on shared experiences at first initiated by the adult: the adult and child experience an event or handling of an object together and make affective contributions about the experience with smiling, laughter, and emotion-laden vocalizations. Later, at about nine months, the child herself will begin to direct caregivers' attention to objects and events in the environment, both as requests for things she wants, but also to share attention and jointly appreciate happenings that have drawn the child's interest. This development marks a shift from interaction that is primarily 'dyadic' to interaction that is 'triadic', which is termed 'joint attention' in developmental psychology.

Tomasello (1999) notes a developmental ordering in the 9–15-month age range of particular behaviours based on the desire of young children to share experiences with others, particularly their efforts to get others to attend to and jointly appreciate objects and events in their environment. Children first begin to show objects at about 9 months of age; then at about 11–14 months, they begin to follow the gaze and pointing of others, and to check their responses to novel, frightening, and ambiguous objects (which is termed, 'social referencing'; Campos and Stenberg, 1981); and at about 13–15 months, they begin to point for imperative, and then declarative, purposes (Tomasello, 1999, p. 64–65). Indeed, children's facility with establishing and entering into joint attentional episodes is widely held to enable such uniquely human capacities as language. Moreover, the very ability to attend with others is believed to be founded on an innate and developing understanding of others' intentionality, that is, an understanding as to what, out of a host of possibilities, another is attending to and, most essentially, for what purposes (cf. Bruner, 1995; Jones and Zimmerman, 2003; Tomasello, 1999). One of the earliest predictors of autism, which is indicated by social impairments in the ability to recognize affect and motive in others, is lack of interest in entering into joint attention exchanges with an adult as typically developing children do by the end of their first year (Baron-Cohen, 1993; Osterling & Dawson, 1994). Indeed, as an early intervention technique for children with autism, parents and teachers are encouraged to engage them in joint attention activities, such as interesting them in a toy by holding it close to their face and using an excited tone of voice to get them to shift their gaze between the object and the person (Scherzt & Odom, 2007; see Sterponi and Yu, Chapter 17, this volume for discussion of neurodiversity).

The ability to share attention with others is foundational for interaction. For participants to interact, to construct sequences *about something*, requires that they are able to attend to one another, discern the relevant objects of one another's attentional focus, and implement their own lines of action by reference to what has grasped the attention of the other. Researchers of child development and early childhood education have identified a number of activities that engage this ability in young children as the basis for the development of higher order social and cognitive skills. Caregivers and young children regularly direct one another's attention to objects in their environments, and adults use the occasion to name the object, comment on some quality or feature of the object, or retrieve it for the child (Estigarribia & Clarke, 2007; Jones & Zimmerman, 2007; Kidwell & Zimmerman, 2007). Such activities are integral to language learning and learning about the environment, both its physical and social features.

Storybook reading is one such activity in which caregivers and young children develop a routine of shared looking at the pictures contained within books. As children are developing their language skills, caregivers use the activity to elicit naming (Ninio and Bruner, 1978) and discussion of story characters and events. This provides a basis for literacy development as well as learning to think about 'others' minds', that is, the motives, desires, and emotional states that story characters represent.

The joint attentional character of learning has been recognized as a feature of education that can be exploited to enhance learning. In line with Vygotsky's concept of a zone of proximal development, learning entails the ability to share a common point of reference and mutually coordinate attention with another toward that point of reference (Mundy & Newell, 2007, p. 269). The concept of 'active learning' is founded on a philosophy that children learn by directly experiencing objects, people, and events in a social context, one in which children's self-initiated explorations are guided by an adult who is responsive to their inquiries (Hohmann et al., 1995). These inquiries, and their social basis, can be optimized for learning as studies from a variety of child-centred pedagogies advocate (Cabelle et al., 2011; Church & Bateman, 2019; Joplin, 1981).

In this chapter, I examine how children in the one- to two-and-a-half-year age range initiate sequences of action with 'object presentations' based on their emerging joint attention capacities, sequences that can be expanded upon by adults in ways that facilitate children's repeated practice with social skills that in and of itself is a form of learning (i.e. about interaction), but that also leads to learning about the objects and people in their environment. The data are drawn from a large corpus of children's video-recorded, naturally occurring interaction in two different American preschool centres.

Sequences of Social Actions

For anyone who has experience with children between one- to two-and-a-half-years of age, the sort of activity under investigation here will be familiar: a child approaches another, usually an adult, with arm outstretched and object in hand; the other then produces a response, very often an identification of the object ('That's a bear"), an appreciation ('Oh wow!'), an appreciation plus an identification ('Wow! A bear!'), and/or an identification that expresses a social-relational feature of the object (e.g. 'That's your shoe' or 'You've got Bert'). In other words, the adult treats the child's action as a particular sort of *social action*, a 'show', that requires a particular sort of fitted response: a naming and/or appreciation of the object. Sometimes, the child brings the object to the adult's hand, a 'give', which the adult might respond to in the same manner as a 'show', but the 'give' also allows for other responses by the adult. For example, the adult might simply say 'thank you'. Alternatively, the adult might shake the object for the child, have it make a sound (as with a toy animal), incorporate it into a pretend routine (as in pretending to nibble on plastic food), or demonstrate something about its physical features (as in showing how its arms move).

These object presentation interactions with children, especially in the younger age range, can be fleeting, an exchange of but two or three turns, but they are significant in that (1) they are prolific, (2) they are motivated by children's natural curiosity about the objects in their environments, (3) they represent children's early efforts at engaging others in interaction that is *about* something, and (4) they are easily extended by adults in ways that invite children's attention to the social, relational, and physical aspects of objects. In other words, they provide ideal natural learning opportunities for children that adults can be alert to, support, and extend.

Making Action Recognizable

In Case 2.1, we see a fairly simple and short exchange between a child who is just a little more than one year of age and an adult. This example invites us to inspect how it is that the adult recognizes that the child seeks to engage her and what she (the adult) should do in response.

Case 2.1: Shoe: A Three-Part 'Proof Procedure' for Mutual Understanding (Intersubjectivity)

Julieta, 14 months, picks up her shoes and runs across the room with them toward the cameraperson, Sarah. As she gets closer to Sarah (not visible in the camera view), she raises one shoe to be in Sarah's line of sight. As she comes to a halt in front of Sarah, she is gazing at her and holding the shoe mid-air (Figure 2.1).

Julieta's action (approach, gaze, hold an object to be in another's line of sight) mobilizes Sarah's attention to the object, but *what for*? Sarah could simply look at the object and treat Julieta's action as merely making something perceptually available to her. But she treats it as requiring more. She treats it as an initiating *social* action, a move that requires a fitted response from her in the manner described above.

Extract 2.1a

```
01  J:  ((approaches Sarah holding up shoe and gazing
        at her))
02  S:  That's your shoe.
03  J:  ((lowers shoe))
```

We see in the transcript in Extract 2.1a that Julieta's action in line 1 initiates an object identification from Sarah in line 2 ('That's your shoe'), which includes a social-relational feature that links the object to Julieta via ownership ('*your* shoe'). That this response is acceptable to the child is indicated by what she does next: she lowers the shoe, removing it as an object of further attention.

These three lines of interaction provide an example of what Schegloff and Sacks (1973) called a 'three-part proof procedure', whereby participants

Figure 2.1. Julieta approaches Sarah to show her shoes to her.

make visible their understandings of one another's actions over the course of three turns: the first action by Julieta projects a response; the response that Sarah produces demonstrates her understanding of what Julieta is seeking; and finally, when Julieta lowers the object, she shows Sarah that her response was acceptable (in contrast, e.g. to continuing to hold up the object or moving it closer to Sarah). This latter action by Julieta implicitly confirms Sarah's understanding of what Julieta was after in presenting the object to her (Wootton, 1994).

In many such object presentation interactions, the interaction is brief, consisting of only three turns, but they may also be extended by the child in a way that links multiple related actions into a longer sequence. In Extract 2.1a, Julieta does not walk away upon lowering the object (thus terminating the interaction); rather, she continues to gaze at Sarah and then raises the shoe in her other hand. This is a second initiating action, and it also elicits a response from Sarah:

Extract 2.1b

```
04  J:  ((holding gaze toward S, raises other shoe))
05  S:  Those are your shoe:s.
06  J:  ((J lowers the second shoe, smiles, removes her
        gaze from S, and walks away))
```

In Extract 2.1b, Sarah identifies the second object as associated with the first by using the plural ('Those are your shoe:s.'), and, again, she connects the object(s) to Julieta via ownership ('your'). Put another way, Sarah might have responded with 'That's a shoe', and then again, 'That's a shoe', but she doesn't. The plural identifies Julieta's two actions as related, and the possessive form personally relates the objects to her. This may seem unremarkable, but in an environment in which conflicts over objects are prolific, and children are in the throes of learning about the social-relational features of objects, including 'ownership' (e.g. 'She had it first'; 'That's his. He brought it from home.'), this is one way that children not only learn what objects are called, but that other aspects about them (such as whose they are) are important as well. We again see the three-part proof procedure at work that let's Sarah know her response has been accepted: Julieta lowers the shoe, smiles, removes her gaze from Sarah, and walks away. These last actions by Julieta not only close the sequence and terminate the interaction, but positively evaluate the adult's response and their exchange with a smile.

In Case 2.1, we see a 'no problem' interaction. The three-part proof procedure allows child and caregiver alike to make visible their understandings of one another's actions in an ongoing fashion and to update and revise what they are doing as necessary. For children in the early stages of language use, this is a significant resource for maintaining the intersubjectivity of their actions with others and, as we see, it allows for the chain-like expansion of interaction by the child who can continue to produce initiating actions that prompt a response from the other.

Sometimes, however, it is not clear what a child intends when she approaches an adult with an object in hand, and the adult may misunderstand. But such 'failures' are a training ground for children in the work of making their actions recognizable. As we see in the next case, a child can make visible what he means by *not* accepting the adult's response, which has the effect of a repair initiation. In this case, we see an adult, with a revised understanding of what the child intends with his object presentation, modify her actions toward him.

Establishing and Maintaining Intersubjectivity

Case 2.2: Airplane: Making a Misunderstanding Visible

In Case 2.2, Freddy, 20 months of age, approaches a seated caregiver, Susan, with arm outstretched and a toy airplane in hand, calling out his word for the object: 'Ayeen!' '<u>AY</u>:een!' His utterance and embodied actions topicalize the object for her attention, but again, for what? Susan, in response, has stretched her arm out as if ready to accept the object into her hand. If Freddy intends this object presentation as a 'give', rather than a show as in Case 2.1, this is the proper response. But, in the manner of the proof procedure described above, the child turns his body away just before the caregiver can grasp the object. This is not the response he was after (Extract 2.2a).

Extract 2.2a

```
01    F:    *Ayeen! (.2) AY:een! ((*approaching S
            holding out
            toy airplane toward her))
02    S:    ((S reaches outstretched hand toward
            object))
03    F:    ((F turns body away from S, 'saving'
            object from her grasp))
```

The interaction might end here, but Susan, seeing that her response has been rejected, tries a revised tactic to bring the child back into the interaction. She produces an initiating action that invites him to show her the object, and offers an appreciation of it at line 4 (Extract 2.2b):

Extract 2.2b

```
04  S:  Let's see that airplane. *Wow! Look at that!
        ((*leans in close
        to look at object))
05  F:  ((F brings close so S can look at it))
06      he he he ((giggling, smiling))
07  S:  (                   ) that airplane.
08  F:  nyeah!
```

In Case 2.2, the caregiver is now in the role of producing an action that requires a response from the child at line 4. At lines 5 and 6, the child moves the object back into view for Susan and, taking up her appreciation of the object ('Wow! Look at that!'), giggles and smiles in response (Figure 2.2).

It is hard to hear what Susan says at line 7, but now with both adult and child looking closely at the object, Susan produces another utterance that again projects a response from the child. He replies with an affirmative-sounding vocalization ('nyeah!') as if he has heard her utterance as an assessment or question inviting agreement.

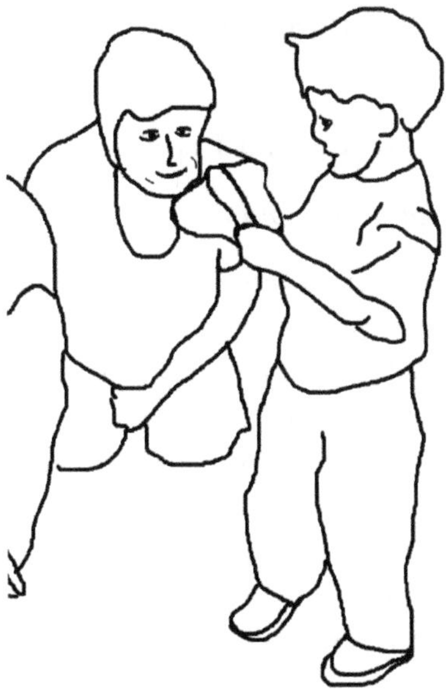

Figure 2.2. Susan and Freddy jointly appreciate the toy airplane.

In Case 2.2, the caregiver revises her course of action from one in which she was ready to accept the object as a 'give' to one that is more fitted to a 'show' action. Freddy's willingness to subsequently engage with her, in the manner of the proof procedure, confirms that she is now on the right track with the interaction: jointly appreciating the object. But after this moment of heightened shared attention and joint appreciation of the object, the adult leans back and the interaction is over as the child walks away.

The situation of 'heightened shared attention', itself an interactional accomplishment between adult and child (i.e. one that may require that participants revise their understandings and actions toward the other), creates the opportunity for 'joint appreciation': the joint valuing of an object via verbal and embodied (e.g. smiling) positive assessment and shared visual attention. Interestingly, researchers of joint attention in other animals, particularly primates, note that, while other species may direct or follow the attention of their conspecifics or their human caretakers, it is primarily to request food or other desired objects, or (in the case of gaze following) to find out if there is something of interest that the other has located (e.g. a food source or predator). The directing or sharing of attention to 'appreciate' is, it seems, a uniquely human behaviour, one that is the foundation for another uniquely human predisposition, namely, that of intensive teaching and learning (Tomasello, 1999). In addition to allowing for the appreciation of objects, heightened shared attention allows for the extension of sequences of action in which adults can bring to children's attention features and affordances of objects that allow for their further exploration.

Creating a Frame of Heightened Shared Attention for Learning

Case 2.3: Airplane Wheels: Modelling an Object's Affordances

In a continuation of Case 2.2, a few moments later, Freddy, still holding the airplane in one hand, picks up a toy car in the other hand. Then he sees Susan extend her hand toward him (she is pointing at the toy car he is holding), but he puts the toy airplane in it (Extract 2.3, line 2). This is a move that allows him to rid himself of one object in preparation to play with another, the toy car, on a toy parking structure in front of him. His object presentation of the airplane is different from his earlier presentation. He does not say the object's name in the manner of trying to draw attention to it, and, having put it in Susan's hand, he turns away from her ready to turn his attention to the new object:

Extract 2.3

```
01  S:  ((S extends hand and points to toy car in F's
        hand))
02  F:  ((F puts toy airplane into S's hand, turns to
        walk away))
03  S:  Let's see. *Oooh look at that. ((* looks closely
        at object))
04      (.2)
05      ↑Freddy.
06      (1.0)
07      ((F turns his head/gaze toward S))
08  S:  Freddy look! ((S is swiping the airplane across
        the floor))
09      (1.5) ((S moves object close to F's hand))
10      Watch! ((does swiping motion across floor
        again))
11      ((moves object close to F's hand))
12  F:  ((F turns away without taking object))
13  S:  ((S turns away, setting toy airplane near F))
```

Clearly, Freddy means his action at line 2 as a 'give' and does not intend further interaction with Susan. But the caregiver uses the opportunity to try to re-engage Freddy. Susan, taking the object into her hand and bringing it close to her eyes (line 3), verbally frames her action as one of joint attention ('Let's see'), and she produces an object appreciation ('Oooh look at that'). Still, Freddy keeps his focus on the toy parking structure. Susan, in 'pursuit' of a response to her initiating action, calls for his attention at line 5 ('↑Freddy'). When he turns toward her, she directs him to 'look' (line 8): she is swiping the toy airplane across the floor, showing him that it has wheels. Then she tries to get him to take the object (line 9), but he doesn't. She swipes the object across the floor again, directing him to 'watch' (line 10), and again tries to get him to take the object (line 11), but he turns away and she turns away, setting the toy airplane near him. The interaction has ended for the moment.

Susan's various efforts to engage the child's attention toward the object were effective, but he did not reciprocate the actions that she modelled for him. Yet, a moment later, Freddy picks up the object and, while Susan is looking across the room (i.e. no longer engaged with him), he attempts to roll it along the play parking structure. While the adult may not have been successful at engaging Freddy in joint play and exploration of the object, she did engage his attention (via multiple efforts), enabling him to see what she was doing. Thus, her actions, in an exemplary Vygotskian fashion, provide support for the child to try out an exploration on his own, using the context of their shared engagement with the object across the prior two interactions as a basis for his independent effort.

In short, the adult builds off the child's initiating actions in both Cases 2.2 and 2.3 – his object presentations – to try to sustain his attention toward, and create interest in, the toy airplane and its affordances. This 'interest' is one that cuts across the two 'mini' interactions he has with her thus far, making of the object a sort of 'common ground' that provides for subsequent explorations, individual and joint. He presents the object to her again a few moments later.

Case 2.4: Airplane Propeller: Getting a Child to Engage in Joint Exploration

In Case 2.4, Freddy approaches Susan with the object (the airplane) for the third time. She is looking away and he says the object's name to summon her attention to it. This takes several efforts before she turns to him and takes hold of the object in line 4. She immediately tries to draw him into interaction with questions about the object (Extract 2.4, lines 4 and 5):

Extract 2.4

```
01  F:  Ayeen!* Ayeen!* ((*S shifts gaze to F; * S looks
        away))
02      (.2)
03      Ayin! *Ayeen! ((*S shifts gaze to F))
04  S:  *↑Where* ((*takes hold of object; *F turns
        away))
05      You got the propeller?
06      *Look. Here. ((*begins twirling the propeller))
07      (.2)
08  F:  ((F turns back to look at object))
09  S:  *Look ↑Freddy. (.5) Propeller. ((*twirling
        propeller))
10      16 seconds/ ((F and S take turns twirling the
        propeller as they smile and look at the object))
```

Freddy, however, apparently means the object presentation as a 'give' in this third presentation of the object, because when the adult accepts it, he turns away (line 4). But, as in the other cases, Susan seeks to draw him back. Receiving no responses to her questions, she seeks to re-engage him at line 6 with a directive aimed at his visual attention ('Look'), and a word that solicits visual inspection ('He̲re'; Goodwin, 1987). At the same time, she begins twirling the propeller. Freddy turns back to her and now, with his attention on the object and her manipulation of it, she demonstrates how it works while seeking to maintain his attention with verbal actions ('Look ↑Freddy. (.5) Propellor'). Together, they take turns twirling the propeller for some 16 seconds – a relatively long spate of shared mutual attention and activity for this child.

In Case 2.4, the adult successfully sustains the child's attention to her demonstration through her manipulation of the object and verbal attention-recruiting actions, and further, gets him to participate in a joint exploration of the object. For several seconds, Freddy and Susan look intently at the airplane as they manipulate the propeller, engaging in smiles and making appreciative utterances (not shown in the transcript). This in and of itself creates an interesting and inviting situation for other children. Kelly, another 20-month-old child, approaches and takes a turn at moving the propeller. Thus, the 'attractiveness' of the object and its affordances is made visible and enticing by Freddy and Susan's actions, creating an opportunity for another child to join in and explore.

Teacher-Child Explorations Attract 'Bystanders'

That one person's attention to something can attract the attention of another is a fairly commonplace fact (e.g. passersby stopping to ask someone looking through binoculars aimed at a tree what they are looking at). The human inclination to follow others' attentional direction (part of the constellation of joint attention behaviours emerging in the 9–15-month age-range discussed above) means that for young children in a preschool setting, teachers' success in engaging one child in exploration can work to engage other children.

Case 2.5: Airplane Propeller 2: Another Child Joins In

In Case 2.5, Kelly looks for several seconds in the direction of Freddy and Susan as they explore the toy airplane together and then she approaches them (Extract 2.5):

Extract 2.5 (a few moments later in the interaction from Extract 2.4)

```
11        ((S is modelling twirling the propeller for F))
12  K:    ((Approaches F and S))
13  F:    ((F turns to walk away))
14  K:    ((K moves in closer, reaches hand out and twirls
          propellor))
15  S:    (See.)
16  K:    ((K grasps object and tries to take it))
17  S:    *I think- I think this is Freddy's?= ((*S holds
          onto object))
18        =*Freddy you want this? ((*S extending object to
          F; K's gaze follows object)
```

At just the point that Kelly reaches Freddy and Susan's interaction huddle, Freddy turns and walks away, creating an opportunity for Kelly to explore the toy airplane with Susan unimpeded – or so it would seem. Kelly twirls the propeller for a second or two, but then she tries to take hold of it. Children's attraction to objects that other children are engaged with, and their conflicts over objects, are prolific in this age range (Hay and Ross, 1982). As mentioned above, the object-rich environment of the preschool is a natural training ground for children to learn not just about the properties and affordances of objects, but also about the norms that govern the possession of objects. Adults in the preschool setting routinely intervene in children's conflicts over objects with accounts that articulate these norms, as in, 'she had it first', 'he brought it from home', or 'you've had it long enough and it's time to give someone else a turn'. In this case, Susan simply states, 'I think this is Freddy's' (an account for denying Kelly the object; line 17), and there is no conflict (Freddy has turned away from the object, but the adult may be trying to avert a conflict should Freddy turn his attention back). However, the interaction exposes Kelly to the rather nuanced standards regarding object possession and object use such that, while some objects may be looked at and touched, they may not be taken into one's own hands because, as in this case, another child has a priority entitlement to them.

Recommendations for Practice

In an object-rich environment such as a preschool, young children have the opportunity to engage in exploration of a variety of object types, including those made for children (play items) and those not (food items, articles of clothing, utensils for eating, furniture, and so on), and they use these objects to engage others in interaction. This creates opportunities for social learning. That is, children's curiosity, explorations, and 'discoveries' extend not only to their material surroundings, but also to the people in their surroundings. Objects in this regard might be thought of as 'bridging devices' in the manner described by Erving Goffman (1963). Goffman meant the bridging device as an object that strangers who otherwise have no reason to interact could nonetheless do so by means of an object: asking for a cigarette, offering a match, complimenting someone's scarf, and so on. It has also been recognized that somewhat older children use objects as a basis for entering into play with their peers, that is, as 'access rituals' (Bateman & Church, 2017; Corsaro, 1979). It seems, too, that for those with limited language resources – and perhaps for the traveller in a foreign country as much as for a very young child – the presentation of an object is a very expedient resource for making interaction happen, providing for an optimal, natural learning context.

In summary, from the previous section:

- Interaction relies on the ability of participants to share attention with one another and to recognize *for what purpose* our attention is being called for.
- For young children, joint/shared attention engagements involving the presentation of an object allow them to practise interaction fundamentals such as making recognizable to another what is meant with a particular configuration of behaviour(s): in the cases examined here, what a child intends with arm outstretched and object in hand, and what the adult should do in response (Take the object, or just look at it and offer an appreciation?).
- Making action recognizable makes use of a three-part proof procedure that is part of the unfolding sequence of initiating and responding actions that allows for troubles to be identified and remedied after each responding action, or, otherwise be allowed to stand as acceptable.
- Child and adult can extend interaction by producing new action pair units, setting up a context in which children's attention can be directed to features and affordances of an object: What is the object called? How does it move? What are its parts? Who does it belong to? Children can be encouraged to explore the object in concert with the adult or on their own.

These observations lend themselves to a set of recommendations for educational practice:

- Teachers of young preschool children can learn to recognize children's efforts to engage them, and to be sensitive to the differentiated types of engagement that children are seeking.

- Teachers can be alert to the various forms of curiosity that motivate children in these interactions (curiosity toward objects, toward people, and towards social interaction), and use these occasions to engage children in extended sequences of action that support and encourage children's explorations.
- Children's attention for such explorations, and interaction itself, entails 'work'. Through embodied and verbal actions, and manipulations of an object, teachers can work to initiate and sustain children's interest in and attention to the interaction and the object at its centre.
- Teachers can become skilled in the techniques of drawing and sustaining children's engagement in interaction and managing their attention to gain from the learning opportunities these interactions afford.

While the children in this study have many years to go before they will join a formal classroom, these recommendations are ones that derive from pedagogical philosophies from early learning contexts through grade school and beyond. They are based on our natural human propensities to interact and can be cultivated to encourage and make the most of the moments of heightened shared attention which provide the optimal context for social learning.

References

Baron-Cohen, S. 1993. *Autism*. New York, NY: Oxford University Press.

Bateman, A., and Church, A. (2017). Children's use of objects in an early years playground. *European Early Childhood Education Research Journal*, 25(1), 55–71. https://doi.org/10.1080/1350293X.2016.1266221

Bateson, M. C. (1975). Mother-infant exchanges: the epigenesis of conversational interaction. *Annals of the New York Academy of Sciences*, 263, 101–113.

Bruner, J. 1995. Introduction. In: C. Moore, and P. Dunham (eds.), *Joint Attention: Its Origins and Role in Development*. Mahwah, NJ: Erlbaum.

Cabell, S. Q., Justice, L. M., Piasta, S. B., Curenton, S. M., Wiggins, A., Turnbull, K. P., and Petscher, Y. (2011). The impact of teacher responsivity education on preschoolers' language and literacy skills. *American Journal of Speech-Language Pathology* (online). https://doi.org/10.1044/1058-0360(2011/10-0104)

Campos, J. J., and Stenberg, C. R. (1981). Perception, appraisal and emotion: the onset of social referencing. In M. E. Lamb, and L.R. Sherrod (eds.), *Infant Social Cognition*, (pp. 273–314). London: Routledge.

Church, A., and Bateman, A. (2019). Children's right to participate: how can teachers extend child-initiated learning sequences? *International Journal of Early Childhood*, 51(3), 265–281.

Corsaro, W. A. 1979. 'We're friends right?': children's use of access rituals in a nursery school. *Language in Society*, 8(3), 315–336.

Estigarribia, B., and Clark, E. V. (2007). Getting and maintaining attention in talk to young children. *Journal of Child Language*, 34(4), 799–814.

Goffman, E. (1963). *Behavior in Public Places*. Doncaster: Free Press.

Hay, D. F., and Ross, H. S. (1982). The social nature of early conflict. *Child Development*, 53, 105–113.

Hohmann, M., Weikart, D. P., and Epstein, A. S. (1995). *Educating Young Children: Active Learning Practices for Preschool and Child Care Programs*. Ypsilanti, MI: High/Scope Press.

Jones, S. E., and Zimmerman, D. H. (2003). A child's point and the achievement of intentionality. *Gesture*, 3(2), 155–185.

Joplin, L. (1981). On defining experiential education. *Journal of Experiential Education*, 4(1), 17–20.

Kidwell, M., and Zimmerman, D. H. (2007). Joint attention as action. *Journal of Pragmatics*, 39(3), 592–611.

Levinson, S. C. (2006). On the human 'interactional engine'. In N. J. Enfield, and S. C. Levinson. *Roots of Human Sociality*. New York: Berg.

Meltzoff, A. N., and Moore, M. K. (1977). Imitation of facial and manual gestures by human neonates. *Science*, 198, 75–78.

Meltzoff, A. N., and Moore, M. K. (1993). Why faces are special to infants – On connecting the attraction of faces and infants' ability for imitation and cross-modal processing. In *Developmental Neurocognition: Speech and Face Processing in the First Year of Life*, (pp. 211–225). Dordrecht: Springer.

Mundy, P., and Newell, L. (2007). Attention, joint attention, and social cognition. *Current Directions in Psychological Science*, 16(5), 269–274.

Ninio, A., and Bruner, J. (1978). The achievement and antecedents of labelling. *Journal of Child Language*, 5(1), 1–15.

Oller, D. K. (2000). *The Emergence of the Speech Capacity*. Mahwah, NJ: Lawrence Erlbaum Associates Publishers.

Osterling, J., and Dawson, G. (1994). Early recognition of children with autism: a study of first birthday home videotapes. *Journal of Autism and Developmental Disorders*, 24(3), 247–257.

Schegloff, E. A. (2007). *Sequence Organization in Interaction: A Primer in Conversation Analysis I* (vol. 1). Cambridge: Cambridge University Press.

Schegloff, E. A., & Sacks, H. (1973). Opening up closings. *Semiotica*, 8(4), 289–327.

Snow, C. E., De Blauw, A., and Van Roosmalen, G. (1979). Talking and playing with babies: the role of ideologies of child-rearing. *Before Speech: The Beginning of Interpersonal Communication* (pp. 269–288). Cambridge: Cambridge University Press.

Tomasello, M. (1999). *The Cultural Origins of Human Cognition*. Cambridge, MA: Harvard University Press.

Trevarthen, C. (1998). The concept and foundations of infant intersubjectivity. *Intersubjective Communication and Emotion in Early Ontogeny*, 15, 46.

Wootton, A. J. (1994). Object transfer, intersubjectivity and third position repair: early developmental observations of one child. *Journal of Child Language*, 21(3), 543–564.

3 | Participation

AMANDA BATEMAN

Introduction

In many countries, there is increasing provision of early childhood studies and early childhood education programmes at degree level. Participating in such studies opens up a world to theoretical perspectives and approaches to working with children, enabling graduates to become an educated and skilful workforce. The best of these programmes offer clear links between theoretical influence on early childhood policy and, importantly, practice. These important philosophical understandings underpin our early childhood teaching, yet even with years of professional practice and knowledge, many of us may find ourselves in a situation with a child where we feel that things had not really worked out as we had hoped. The aim of this chapter is to unpack in great detail, what we might 'do' as early childhood teachers to support children's learning and, more specifically, what our participation might look like in everyday situations with children. To begin this chapter, a review of early theories of interaction will be discussed in order to provide some context, before moving on to illustrate the practices of participation in the most local sense.

Socio-Cultural Theories

A socio-cultural approach considers the social and cultural context of the child and recognizes that each child will learn in their own unique way. The work of socio-cultural theorists such as Vygotsky, Bruner, and Rogoff are often taught at various levels of early childhood education and care (ECEC) professional qualifications where metaphors are used to explain the concepts of these theories. One example is the metaphor of a 'zone of proximal development' (ZPD) (Vygotsky, 1962) – a space between what a child can do unassisted and what they can achieve with the assistance of a more experienced other. An important aspect of the ZPD is that the 'zone' is occupied by two (or more) people, emphasizing it as a social space for learning. Within this social learning zone, there is typically one person who is a 'more experienced other', and this person assists the less knowledgeable in their learning. Of importance here is that the 'more knowledgeable other' does not have to be a person who is older than the child, just someone who is more knowledgeable in the temporal context of the learning. This latter point is important in ECEC, where all children are perceived as competent and capable members of society, as it acknowledges that even the youngest children can bring knowledge to a situation where they can help contribute to another's understanding.

Other metaphors within theories of children's early learning from a socio-cultural perspective include 'scaffolding' (Wood, Bruner, & Ross, 1976) children's learning. The scaffolding metaphor, mostly accredited to Bruner, represents the 'process that enables a child or novice to solve a problem, carry out a task or achieve a goal which would be beyond his unassisted efforts' (Wood, Bruner, & Ross, 1976, p. 90). The scaffolding here refers to the structure that the more experienced other sets in place to help focus the child or novice's learning trajectory. This metaphor is similar to Vygotsky's ZPD as it requires knowledge asymmetry – one person knowing more than the other – and knowledge being co-constructed between those people in a social space. One way that we can better understand these metaphors and their connection to one another is to consider the ZPD as the space in which we build the scaffolding to structure the child's understanding.

Both the ZPD and scaffolding have similarities to Rogoff's guided participation (Rogoff, 2003). Rogoff's work has given more emphasis to the cultural aspect of socio-cultural theory concerning children's knowledge as a response to what she believed to be an overemphasis on research that too often explored the knowledge and understanding of white middle class children (Rogoff, 1990). The ways in which children and their caregivers participate together in culturally relevant ways has shed light on 'the organized and common practices of particular communities in which children live' where 'Guided participation involves the structuring of children's activities and the offering of well-placed pointers' (Rogoff, 1990, p. 110–111). As such, guided participation can be viewed as similar to scaffolding, in that both practices suggest that adults structure a specific trajectory to a learning activity, eliminating distractions and focusing on what will be achievable for the child in the temporal activity at hand.

Considering these theories together, we can see that a change in knowledge state within the ZPD (Vygotsky, 1962) is interactively shaped by teachers and children in partnership, where the more knowledgeable other structures the scaffolding (Wood, Bruner, & Ross, 1976) from one level of knowledge to the next through guided participation in culturally relevant ways (Rogoff,

2003). These theories give us valuable knowledge regarding pedagogical interactions and the importance of teacher participation in the process of children's learning, underpinning our practice as early childhood teachers. We now turn to early childhood education literature to explore further how we might implement such rich socio-cultural theory in our practice.

Early Childhood Education Guidance on Participation

So far, we have explored socio-cultural theories around teacher-child interactions which help support our understanding of how learning is a collaborative, social process where our role as early childhood teachers is integral to children's learning. We also recognize how challenging it can be to practically implement such theories in everyday practice whilst working within early childhood curricula frameworks – we know from the theorists that our participation is important, but *how* do we actually construct scaffolding and guide participation in the ZPD? An important point to consider is how some early childhood curricula make explicit links to the role of the teacher and socio-cultural theories, such as the New Zealand early childhood curriculum Te Whāriki:

> This curriculum emphasizes the critical role of socially and culturally mediated learning and of reciprocal and responsive relationships … [where] children learn through collaboration with adults and peers, through guided participation.
>
> (Ministry of Education [MoE], 1996, p. 9)

Help and guidance can be found in ECEC resources created to support curriculum implementation, such as the New Zealand early childhood exemplars, *Kei Tua o te Pae* (Carr, Lee, & Jones, 2004–2009). *Kei Tua o te Pae* are a series of books which provide examples of best practice to help teachers understand their role in strengthening children's understandings. Of importance to this chapter on 'participation' is Book 1 of *Kei Tua o te Pae* which introduces the concept of notice, recognizes, and respond, a systematic process for engaging in learning moments with children of all ages. These three processes can be viewed as *progressive filters*, building systematically from noticing a possible learning moment whilst observing children, recognizing the potential to explore the moment in pedagogical ways, and responding to the moment in ways that support learning. 'Teachers notice a great deal as they work with children, and they recognise some of what they notice as "learning". They will respond to a selection of what they recognise' (Carr, Lee, & Jones, 2004, p. 6).

Within this process, noticing and recognizing can be viewed as internal observations that identify potential learning, where '[t]he difference between noticing and recognising is the application of professional expertise and judgments' (Carr, Lee, & Jones, 2004). Once we have noticed and recognise a learning opportunity, we then respond – often moving closer to the child/ren and starting a conversation with them about their immediate focus of interest. The ways in which teachers respond to children's contributions is key to scaffolding their learning and is an important interactional turn in the sequence of scaffolding (Koole & Elbers, 2014) where the children's displays of competence are made noticeable (Theobald, 2019). Responding to a child's interests through a conscious and deliberate change in our physical location to be closer to the child marks the opening of our participation into the ongoing activity as a co-participant in the learning experience. It is argued here that this responding part of the progressive filter needs further exploration though, as teachers are often unsure of how to enter into an ongoing activity owned by children, and what we 'do' once we have entered into that space, or 'zone'. Some guidance around what our participation might look like can be planned when considering what children themselves are working on in that space.

Children's working theories are identified as a combination of knowledge, skills, and attitudes, where 'Working theories become increasingly useful for making sense of the world, for giving the child control over what happens, for problem solving, and for further learning' (MoE, 1996, p. 44). In order to support children to engage in working theories about their world, teachers have to be able to notice, recognize, and respond to children's interests and provide opportunities for children to participate in the exploration of their environment. Through providing such support, teachers encourage children's disposition to learn – a life-long attribute that motivates children to initiate and engage in learning enquiry in environments subsequent to early childhood education settings and throughout their lives. Questions are an essential pedagogical tool in early childhood pedagogy, where teachers are encouraged to pose interesting open-ended questions to support and extend young children's working theories about the world. However, as O'Reilly & Lester (Chapter 16, this volume) identify, although open-ended questions are recommended to be used to prompt children's talk in various professions '[practitioners] rarely critically address what constitutes an open question or challenge the circumstances in which these might be less effective than closed questions'. The everyday conversations between children and teachers, therefore, need to be explored in detail to reveal the teachers' role in initiating and maintaining their participation in pedagogical moments through questions. Such detailed analysis of everyday interactions between children and early childhood teachers help to shed light on how pedagogical moments support children's working theories, embedded within everyday social interactions.

Participation Frameworks

Participation frameworks (Goffman, 1981) refer to the way people interact together to co-produce interactional spaces for various purposes, where each participant is categorized as having a specific role, such as Animator, Author, Principal, and Figure etc. Interactional spaces are typically framed around a point of interest, or mutual engagement on a particular focus (Goffman, 1961, 1963). Goffman's categorization of members in a participation framework has been addressed by Goodwin and Goodwin (2004); they have shown that members bring with them their cultural, moral, and social values and experiences in competent ways in the co-production of a framework. Goodwin & Goodwin' s (2004) work offers us a more socio-cultural approach to understanding participation in activities with others, resonating with the work of Rogoff in educational contexts. Participation frameworks can be co-produced through the way we position our bodies when we interact with others, where gaze as well as gesture is essential in the co-production of the framework (Goodwin & Goodwin, 2004; Goodwin, 2006) as well as with our talk.

Through exploring social interaction as participation frameworks, we can analyse how we as ECEC teachers and children use our talk and gesture to co-produce pedagogical episodes around points of shared interest. Such an approach acknowledges children as competent and capable participants in the frameworks through their multi-modal, cultural, and linguistic contributions (Goodwin & Goodwin, 2004). When a participation framework has been initiated, it is likely to change as members leave and others join. A participation framework is maintained as we tie our talk and bodily positioning to the prior talk and gesture of others, sometimes in a process that has been termed an 'F-formation' (see Figure 3.1)

> An F-formation arises whenever two or more people sustain a spatial and orientational relationship in which the space between them is one to which they have equal, direct, and exclusive access ... It provides a means by which the participants can maintain differential access to one another and it facilitates the maintenance of a common focus of attention.
>
> (Kendon, 1990a, p. 209)

Figure 3.1 An F-formation for shared attention.

Kendon (1990a) suggests that people initiate a frame for close spatial proximity through greeting each other at first, then maintaining the frame through subsequent conversation. The spatial proximity between the participants is important here, as participants use the same space as others in close proximity, 'orienting their bodies in such a way that each of them has an easy, direct, and equal access to every other participant's transactional segment' (Kendon, 1990b, p. 239).

Here, we are interested in how participation frameworks for pedagogical purposes are initiated and maintained – how we as ECEC teachers 'do' participation in practical terms. When thinking about what the ZPD might look like in practice, we can consider participation frameworks as a physical positioning of our bodies as we show our interest in participating with children. For example, we can observe (notice) that two or more children might be co-producing a participation framework through a shared interest by their bodily positioning displays, where they are visible as being together and orienting to the same focus of attention (see Church & Moore, Chapter 19, this volume for an example of marbles as a central focus for a participation framework). Our role as early childhood teachers is to work out whether what we are observing is recognizable (recognize) as a learning moment that we could/should participate in (respond to), asserting ourselves as part of that participation framework. It might seem an easy project, to enter into a participation framework with a child simply by approaching them when we see they are demonstrating an interest in something, but here we are reminded of another theory proposed by Csikszentmihalyi (1990) termed 'flow', a vivid state of concentration and focus where mastery of a task is independently conquered. Our initiation of a participation framework with this engaged child will undoubtedly break their 'flow' and so disrupt an important learning opportunity.

So how *do* early childhood teachers initiate or become a member of a participation framework with children? The examples now given in the next part of this chapter aim to shed some light on the practical issues of how we might initiate and maintain participation frameworks for pedagogy, with some examples of practice to help unpack these challenges.

Participation Frameworks in Early Childhood Education

Excerpts of real-life everyday interactions between teachers and young children within a range of early learning environments will now be explored using conversation analysis to demonstrate what the role of the early years teacher might look like when participating with children in everyday practice to support and extend learning. Examples of the skilful ways in which teachers and children participate in the 'zone of proximal development' to 'scaffold' learning through 'guided participation' in verbal and non-verbal turn-taking will be demonstrated with excerpts of real-time footage. Through this exploration, we will be able to see how and when we might initiate and maintain participation frameworks for pedagogy in our everyday practice with children.

Initiating Participation Frameworks for Enquiry: Opening an Interaction through Noticings to Mobilize a Topic

The first extract in this section is intentionally very brief to familiarize the reader with a conversation analysis style of transcript. It documents a brief interaction between an ECEC teacher (Tim) and a four-year-old child Annie (ANE) as they walk through a woodland area in New Zealand. In Extract 3.1a, we see Tim opening up (initiating) an interaction with Annie by orienting his talk to a feature of the physical environment (a defensive trench embedded in the woodland area) and offering some knowledge about it. To accomplish this action, Tim not only makes the feature noticeable with his talk, but also with his body as he stops in front of it, physically framing the feature as a main focus of interest and prompting Annie to also draw her attention to it.

Extract 3.1a Teacher making an environmental noticing (Bateman & Waters, 2013)

```
01  TIM:  this is a ↓defensive tre:nch↓ ((stops in front
02        of the feature))
03  ANE:  look it has a door on it↓ (1.5) on the ↓si::de
```

The lines of transcription here demonstrate how orienting verbally and physically to an environmental feature can initiate a participation framework for knowledge exchange, through a 'common focus of attention' (Kendon, 1990a, p. 209) that prompts each person to offer some knowledge around the feature being talked into significance (Goodwin, 2007). Tim's verbal opening strategy in a first pair part (FPP) here could have set up a framework of learning where he is the more knowledgeable – an 'I know it, you don't' (Enfield, 2011, p. 307) type format – where he is presented as the more knowledgeable other who would guide learning about the feature. When we look at Annie's second pair part (SPP) response though, she also makes a noticing about the feature, framing herself as a competent and knowledgeable co-participant in her reply (Theobald, 2019). Although this interaction is very brief, we can see through the turns of talk that each person contributes noticings about the environmental feature in their co-construction of knowledge.

The practice of initiating participation frameworks with children to stimulate knowledge exchange is also seen in the following extracts taken from a New Zealand project investigating children's play after the earthquakes in Christchurch in 2010 and 2011. In Extract 3.1b, we see the teacher, Pauline (PLN) using a similar technique as Tim in Extract 3.1a, as she makes an environmental noticing to prompt talk with the four-year-old children Sienna (SIE) and Myla (MLA) while they are out on a walk. During their walk, the children and teachers comment on the broken environment – in Extract 3.1b they have found a broken wall just outside their preschool and stop to look at it. What we will focus on here is how Pauline uses the verbal utterance 'I wonder' to open the participation framework, and how it is responded to by the children in their subsequent replies.

Extract 3.1b Teacher making an environmental noticing (Bateman, Danby, & Howard, 2013)

```
01  PLN:  I wonder how it got like ↑tha::t↑
02  SIE:  It was the ↓fence↓of it↓=
03  MYL:                                =no it was the
04        ea::rthquake
```

The teacher's use of the utterance 'I wonder' has been found to be a deliberately designed turn of talk to elicit children's knowledge on a specific topic in everyday interactions between children and ECEC teachers (Houen, Danby, Farell, & Thorpe, 2016). When teachers use 'I wonder' formulations, they frame themselves as the less knowledgeable other, providing opportunities for children to offer their knowledge about the topic (Houen, Danby, Farell, & Thorpe, 2018). We can tell whether or not this 'I wonder' formulation works to elicit children's working theories by looking at how the children respond in their turns of talk that immediately follow. Here we can see that each child offers some working knowledge about the feature, that it was a fence (Sienna – line 2) and that it was the earthquake that damaged it (Myla – line 3). The initiation of such participation frameworks elicits the children's working theories about environmental features, where they can make sense of their world that has changed considerably due to the impact of the earthquake.

In the first two extracts we have seen how teachers can initiate participation frameworks through making environmental noticings which invite the child to enter into a participation framework, rather than approaching a child at play and inadvertently disrupting their *flow* (Csikszentmihalyi, 1990). We now look at how children can initiate participation frameworks with teachers, also through orienting to their immediate environment to draw attention to a shared focus of interest. What is interesting in children's initiation of participation frameworks is the structure of the utterance, as the following extracts (3.1c, 3.1d, 3.1e) show that children are more likely to formulate their openings in the shape of a question. To begin, we look at two examples taken from a project in Wales exploring conversations in the outdoor environment. The following two extracts (3.1c and 3.1d) demonstrate how children are just as competent in opening up participation frameworks for pedagogical purposes as teachers are. The following two extracts involve the primary school teacher (TCH) and child (CHD).

Extract 3.1c Child making an environmental noticing (Bateman & Waters, 2013)

```
01   CHD:   what's↑ that ↓arr:ow thingy:↓
02          (0.8)
03   TCH:   ↓they're↓- ↑that's the ce:metery where they
04          bu:ry people↓
05   CHD:   ↓ahh↓
```

Extract 3.1d Child making an environmental noticing (Bateman & Waters, 2013)

```
01  CHD:   ↑why do they ↑put .hhh thems ↓a::rrows on top↓=
02  TCH:          =there not ↓a::rrows↓ >darlin< they're called
03                ↓gra::ve- uh=↓gra::ve stones where they write the
04                na:me of the ↓per:son↑
05  CHD:   >°↓ah↓° <
```

In both of these extracts we see the child approaching the teacher with a question, the teacher responding with an answer, and the child responding in a third turn with a demonstration that their knowledge about the topic has changed with their verbal 'ah' (Heritage, 1984). These examples illustrate children's awareness of how to engage in pedagogical transitions of knowledge in orderly and systematic ways (Theobald, 2019). Conversation analysis tells us that when a FPP asks a question, a SPP is required to *respond* in the form of an answer (Sacks, Schegloff, & Jefferson, 1974 – also see Chapter 1), and also that children tend to have restricted rights to talk (Sacks, 1992). So, what we tend to see is children initiating interactions with adults through the form of a question, as this requires the adult to respond with an answer (Sacks, 1992), therefore successfully initiating an interaction. We can see this happening here, and in the subsequent Extract and 3.1e. Of primary importance here is how we as ECEC teachers *notice* children's questions and *recognize* them as an initiation of a participation framework for pedagogical purposes. We can then *respond* to children's questions in ways that support knowledge exchange and exploration in intentional ways (Theobald, 2019).

For the final example of children's competence in initiating a participation framework through a question about the environment, we return to the scenario of the teacher, Tim (TIM) and the defensive trench. A four-year-old child, Kyba (KBA) draws Tim's attention back to the environmental feature, as Tim and Annie move away from the trench.

Extract 3.1e Child making an environmental noticing (Bateman & Waters, 2013)

```
13  KBA:  what- what is that for- what is that↓ ((points to
14        trench))
15  TIM:  that's the de↑fensive tr↑ench↓
16  KBA:  and what=do they ↑do::↓
17  TIM:  well it was dug out so you could get up here but
18        only very slo:wly (0.6) so if some ↑enemies were
```

```
coming (1.0) then they could stop the enemies (0.7)
before they got up the hill: (0.7) and you could
fight back
```

In Extract 3.1e, we notice once again that the child – in this instance Kyba – has initiated contact with the teacher through the use of a question. Tim's first response is to give the requested knowledge in a short and simple reply, simply naming the feature (line 15). Kyba then demonstrates that he has more interest in the feature, as he asks a second question (line 16) and so Tim responds again, this time with an extended explanation (lines 17–21). The orderly way that this interaction is managed between teacher and child demonstrates what scaffolding in the ZPD (Vygotsky, 1962) might look like in practice, where this space is co-produced by the child showing an interest and the teacher responding with knowledge shaped for Kyba's level of understanding (Theobald, 2019). The ways in which participants shape their talk for maximum understanding by the recipient is termed 'recipient design' in conversation analysis, defined as 'an orientation and sensitivity to the particular other(s) who are the coparticipants' (Sacks, Schegloff, & Jefferson, 1974, p. 727). As early childhood teachers, we aim for maximum intersubjectivity (shared understanding) with children, as we know that this is essential in the process of pedagogical interaction. Being aware of how children might use their turns at talk to initiate participation frameworks for learning offers insight into how early childhood teachers might 'hear' children's contributions differently and respond in ways that speak to the child's specific level of understanding.

An important point to make here is that, although these first excerpts of interaction are not examples of sustained conversations, as recommended by the EPPE study (Siraj-Blatchford, Sylva, Muttock, Gilden, & Bell, 2002) there is clear evidence of knowledge exchange, and most importantly, *attuned* responses from the teacher. In Extracts 3.1c, 3.1d, and 3.1e, the child competently initiates a participation framework with the teacher to gain knowledge about a topic they are interested in, and the teacher responds in ways that frame the child as competent of understanding the level of knowledge they provide making a ZPD visible. It is important to consider whether intentionally sustaining a conversation with a child is within the child's interest, and to critically reflect on the learning supported by an extended, but not necessarily expansive, sequence of talk. In other words, *depth* of knowledge is better than sustaining superficial talk over a linear amount of time.

To explore the issues discussed in this first section in more detail, we now move from how participation frameworks are initiated by teacher and child, to examples of interaction that demonstrate scaffolding and guided participation in everyday teacher-child talk.

Scaffolding Participation Frameworks through Guided Participation within the Zone of Proximal Development

The first extract in this section is taken from a research project investigating children's early literacy and narrative. The interaction involves the ECEC teacher sitting at a table with a group of children who are telling stories using storytelling shells – seashells with characters printed on. One of the children (RAM) has selected a number of shells from the pile and is having a turn at making up a story. We see that the teacher (KIM) prompts her to contribute turns at talk, beginning at line 1 which follows a significant pause in the telling. This interaction offers an example of what guided participation might look like within the ZPD, where the teacher guides the child to contribute, scaffolding the telling of certain aspects of the story.

Extract 3.2a Teacher prompts during a storytelling (Bateman & Carr, 2017)

```
01  KIM:  →  ↑>yip< and then w=what happened when he
02           found the i::sland↓
03           (1.2)
04  RAM:     he found trea:sure
05  KIM:     he found trea:sure↓
Some lines omitted
06  KIM:  →  what happened the::n
07           (1.5)
08  RAM:     >then the< (0.6) other pirate ↑fou:nd it.
09  KIM:  →  (.HHH) (0.8) and what happened the::n
10           (2.2)
11  RAM:     the pirate was loo:king for it
12           (1.0)
13  KIM:     a::nd
14           (0.8)
15  RAM:     then they live ha:ppily ever after=↑the
             e:nd.
```

Early childhood education research tells us that early storytelling is an enjoyable way for young children to engage in early literacy (Schaughency, Suggate, & Reese, 2017) and conversation analysis tells us that storying requires skilful ability to understand the sequences of talk involved in holding the floor over multiple turns and making the story interesting for the recipient (Mandelbaum, 2013; see also Filipi in Chapter 9 of this volume). Responding to children's early storytelling in ways that prompt their tellings has been found to support the contributions of bilingual children in linguistically diverse settings (Theobald, 2019). We therefore know that offering opportunities for children to tell stories in early childhood is important – but how might ECEC teachers maximize potential learning opportunities during storytelling activities?

Of specific interest here is how the conversational strategy of 'what happened' scaffolds children's contributions to storytelling by paying specific attention to the positioning of the utterance in the transcript. In the ensuing lines of talk, we see turn-taking by each participant, which might look more like a conversational structure than a usual storytelling format where the storyteller speaks over several lines of talk. To prompt further contribution from the child so that a storytelling structure is more visible, the teacher Kim uses 'what happened?' as an open-ended question several times (lines 1, 6, and 9). Questions require an answer (Sacks, Schegloff, & Jefferson, 1974) and so 'what happened' works to prompt further contribution from the teller in the shape of an answer. Asking 'what happened when he found the island' (line 1) requires the child to contribute further to the storyline, with a specific focus on what a pirate might do when he reaches an island, and so the question scaffolds (Wood, Bruner, & Ross, 1976) the trajectory of the child's answer and guides a specific kind of participation (Rogoff, 2003). In line 6, the teacher asks more broadly 'what happened then', which is followed by a significant pause (line 7) which we might attribute to 'think time' (Rowe, 1986) and a further contribution that adds to the storyline through the introduction of another pirate character (line 8). The extract here maps out the turns of talk that co-produce the early storytelling activity, helping us to consider the role of the ECEC teacher in scaffolding children's early tellings through carefully prompting contributions from the children.

In the next extract (3.2b), the ECEC teacher (SHA) is sitting at the edge of a large outdoor sandpit in the EC centre. Two four-year-old children Frank (FNK) and Levi (LVI) have created a large hole in the sand and are pouring water into it, attempting to make a pool, but the water keeps sinking into the sand. The teacher uses her professional vision (Goodwin, 1994) to notice,

Figure 3.1 An F-formation for shared attention.

recognize, and respond to the interests of Levi and Frank. As with Extract 3.2a, we see the teacher beginning the interaction with 'what's happened', an open-ended question that affords opportunity for a range of answers, co-producing a participation framework for pedagogical exploration.

Extract 3.2b Scaffolding working theories (Bateman, 2013)

01 SHA: → ↑what's happened↑ (0.6) ↑where's the water gone↓
02 FNK: ↓gone↓ ((*holds palms of hands out to sides*))
03 (2.9)
04 LVI: it' s not **work**ing↓ ((*runs to get more water*))
Some lines omitted
05 LVI: ((*pours another bowl of water into sand*))
06 SHA: → now ↑watch what happens when you pour the water↓
07 → ↑what happens↓ ((*holds palm of hand out*))
08 (1.7)
09 LVI: $it's- it's ↓go::ne↓$
10 SHA: it's gone but where's it ↑gone↓
11 LVI: I (think) it's gone ↑**un**:der↓
12 SHA: it's gone under (0.6) under **where**↓
13 LVI: under the ↑**ho**:le↓
14 SHA: under the ↑ho:le↓
15 LVI: the:re ((*points to the hole*))
16 SHA: what=do=you- why do you think it's gone under
17 the hole↓
18 LVI: (er) (1.0) because it ↑sunked↓ [do=you=see-]
19 SHA: [it **sunk**]

LVI: do you see the hole (0.6) it's went through ↑**that**
hole↓

The initiation of a participation framework for enquiry is mobilized though the 'what happened' question (line 1) as the ECEC teacher prompts the children to contribute their understanding about the current problem they are encountering – the water sinking into the sand rather than gathering in a pool. Rather than give the children an explanation of what is happening, this open-ended question offers an opportunity for the children to articulate a working theory about what they believe might be happening. The children both contribute a response and pour more water into the hole and the teacher once again uses 'what happened' to prompt further discussion (lines 2–7), as with Extract 3.2a, leaving a pause in time (line 8) for the children to respond (Rowe, 1986).

We can see evidence of scaffolding as the teacher narrows the line of enquiry, specifically asking 'where's it gone' (line 10) and 'under where' (line 12) so that the exploration is not too broad for the child that they cannot find a solution. Guided participation (Rogoff, 2003) and scaffolding (Wood, Bruner, & Ross, 1976) can be seen here, as the teacher offers guidance to the child around how to approach the problem in specific ways that scaffold the trajectory of their learning. When teachers notice, recognize, and respond to children's interests in such ways, the line of enquiry can be supported in ways that extend children's working theories about the world.

Another significant aspect of this interaction regarding how it supports scaffolding and guided participation is the physical positioning of the teacher. In Figure 3.1 we see how the teacher sits at the edge of the sandpit so that her gaze is at the same level as the children's, with her body facing them, making a circle around the object of interest (the hole). Through this close physical proximity, the teacher and children are 'orienting their bodies in such a way that each of them has an easy, direct, and equal access to every other participant's transactional segment' (Kendon, 1990b, p. 239). This physical positioning is as key to the co-production of the participation framework for pedagogical exploration as the talk – further demonstrated in the final extended sequence below (Extract 3.2c).

The prior excerpts have demonstrated how participation frameworks can be initiated and maintained using specific verbal resources. We now focus more specifically on non-verbal interaction where participation frameworks can be co-produced nonverbally, where 'a conversation is not really the context of the utterance; a physically elaborated, nonlinguistic undertaking is, one in which nonlinguistic events may have the floor'

(Goffman, 1981, p. 141). Within the physical positioning of bodies, ECEC teachers and children work together pedagogically, where the theoretical ZPD materializes into a physical space or 'zone' (Bateman, 2021). The following extract segments together make a longer interaction (see citated article for full transcript) of a group of four-year-old children and their teacher exploring a protected woodland reserve in New Zealand. The images that accompany the extracts demonstrate the interactions are mainly physical, and usually initiated by the children asking for some physical assistance from the ECEC teacher. The first image – Figure 3.2 – shows how the ECEC teacher, Tim (TIM), positions his body across the ditch to act as a physical resource for the children's transition from one side to the other.

With the teacher positioning his body in such a way, he makes himself available to the surrounding children, evident in what happens in the extract that follows. Here, Cloe (CLO) moves within close physical proximity of the teacher and lifts her arms up towards him (Figure 3.3) as she asks him to copy the movement he has just engaged in with another child, lifting over the ditch. Two other children, Sam (SAM) and Kora (KOR), and a second teacher (TCH) are also present.

Figure 3.2 Physical proximity for participation frameworks.

Figure 3.3 Teacher body position.

Extract 3.2c Visible participation frameworks (Bateman & Waters, 2018)

```
CLO:  Tim (0.4) c- (0.6) can [you do¿-
SAM:                         [can't=get=me=mud-monster
TIM:  ((lifts boy up and lowers him gently into the pit))
TCH:  [hah hah
SAM:  [argh::::
CLO:  [can you do that to me¿
TIM:  ((continues lowering boy))
CLO:  can you do that to me¿ Tim? ((reaches arms out))
TIM:  ((holds Cloe's hands and lifts her up then lowers
      her into the pit))
```

In this interaction, Tim's physical stance has made him available to Cloe, who approaches and asks him to swing her across the ditch – again in a question format that initiates the participation framework. The extract demonstrates how, when teachers are interacting with many children in one space, children may need to repeat their question before it is responded to, competently initiating what is termed as 'self-repair' in conversation analysis (Schegloff, 1992). Tim's response to this question is physical as he grasps both of the child's hands and swings Cloe across the ditch safely. Through their close physical positioning we can see them as participating together in an interaction to make a framework for doing a particular activity.

Following the teacher holding both hands firmly to cross Cloe over the ditch, she approaches him again, and this time he responds by just offering her one hand, where she has to do the majority of the work independently (Figure 3.4).

```
11 CLO: ((holds hand out towards Tim)) do that agai::n
12 TIM: ((takes Cloe's hand))
13 KOR: do I get a pa::ss;
14 CLO: ((jumps across holding Tim's hand))
15 TIM: ((left hand reaches to Kora which she receives with
16       both hands))
17       [((Kora swings across holding Tim's hand))
18 CLO: [do that again;
19 KOR: ((lands and Tim takes his left hand away from her))
20 CLO: do that ag[ain;
21 KOR:           [wow
22       ((Cloe swings across holding Tim's hand)).
```

This time, the teacher and child work together in this physical space, where Cloe contributes more fully to the interaction as she jumps and holds just one of Tim's hands, demonstrating willingness to participate through multi-modal means (Goodwin & Goodwin, 2000). The participation

Figure 3.4 Cloe initiating contact and the teacher responding and scaffolding the crossing.

framework here is co-constructed through collaborative actions of mutual engagement (Goffman, 1981) centred around an environment feature. This happens a few more times until the teacher suggests to Cloe that she try to cross independently, noticing, recognizing, and responding to her individual interests and scaffolding her independence. It is when teachers shape their responses accurately to the level of the child's ability that scaffolding can occur.

TIM: you might need to try getting over your↑self Cloe;
(0.5) then you won't even ↑need me to be here.
CLO: ((*walks towards a tree growing out of the ditch*))
TCH: >probably across there if you **hold** on to the tree¿<
( ) >↓climb in through the trees . you might be
able to get across **this** one<) ((*points to a tree*))
CLO: ((*holds on to the trees across the ditch. Looks back*
and smiles at teacher))
TCH: well ↑**done** Cloe.
CLO: **Tim** (0.1) I holded on to the ↑**tree:.**
TIM: **Wow** good job Cloe now you don't need ↑me:.

At the end of this interaction, we see Cloe taking on the teacher's challenge to cross alone, where the second teacher (lines 26–28) offers guided participation about how she might achieve this. The sequences of action here demonstrate how important physical proximity and bodily position are in the co-production of participation frameworks for pedagogical purposes, as Cloe starts off tentatively grasping the teacher with both hands as he moves her, then with a single hand, and then independently (Figure 3.5). Early childhood teachers need to be aware of their physical bodily positioning when engaging in scaffolding interactions with children, as this is as important as their verbal contributions in supporting and extending learning.

Figure 3.5 Cloe crossing the ditch unassisted.

Recommendations for Practice

Through this exploration, the chapter brings together contemporary socio-cultural approaches to early years teaching and ethnomethodology's concern with the practical achievement of participation to explain how participation frameworks provide a useful lens for understanding the interaction between children and teachers. Participation frameworks allow us to see how engagement is enacted as practical concern. The following recommendations are given for practice:

- Teachers and children are both capable of initiating a participation framework for pedagogical purposes.
- When children initiate participation frameworks with teachers using questions, teachers need to notice, recognize, and respond to their interests through recipient design, as each child will have a specific level of knowledge; this is how we can ensure that the information we give is not above the child's level, which would cause anxiety, or not challenging enough, which could result in boredom/withdrawal.
- Physical positioning of the body is equally as important as verbal turn-taking in the co-production of participation frameworks for pedagogical purposes.
- Guided participation and scaffolding require teachers to listen to children's contributions and respond specifically to what they just did or said in their immediately prior turn.
- Participation frameworks for pedagogical purposes can be brief and are more concerned with the depth of knowledge than the length of the interaction.

References

Bateman, A. (2013). Responding to children's answers: questions embedded in the social context of early childhood education. *Early Years*, 33(2), 275–289.

Bateman, A. (2021). Teacher responses to toddler crying in the New Zealand outdoor environment. *Journal of Pragmatics*, 175, 81–93.

Bateman, A., and Carr, M. (2017). Pursuing a telling: managing a multi-unit turn in children's storytelling. In A. Bateman and A. Church (eds.), *Children and Knowledge: Studies in Conversation Analysis* (pp. 91–110). Singapore: Springer.

Bateman, A., Danby, S., and Howard, J. (2013). Living in a broken world: how young children's well-being is supported through playing out their earthquake experiences. *International Journal of Play*, 2(3), 202–219.

Bateman, A., and Waters, J. (2013). Asymmetries of knowledge between children and teachers on a New Zealand bush walk. *Australian Journal of Communication*, 40(2), 19–32.

Bateman, A., and Waters, J. (2018). Risk-taking in the New Zealand bush: issues of resilience and wellbeing. *Asia Pacific Journal of Research in ECE*, 12(2), 7–29.

Carr, M., Lee, W., and Jones, C. (2004–2009). *Kei tua o te pae: Assessment for Learning: Early Childhood Exemplars*. Wellington: Learning Media.

Carr, M., Lee, W., and Jones, C. (2004). *An Introduction to Kei Tua o te Pae: He Whakamōhiotanga ki Kei Tua o te Pae (Book 1)*. Wellington: Learning Media.

Csikszentmihalyi, M. (1990). Literacy and Intrinsic Motivation. *Daedalus*, 119(2), 115–140.

Enfield, N. J. (2011). Sources of asymmetry in human interaction: enchrony, status, knowledge and agency. In T. Stivers, L. Mondada, and J. Steensig (eds.), *The Morality of Knowledge in Conversation* (pp. 285–312). Cambridge: Cambridge University Press.

Goffman, E. (1961). *Encounters: Two Studies in the Sociology of Interaction*. Indianapolis, IN: Bobbs-Merrill.

Goffman, E. (1963). *Behavior in Public Places: Notes on the Social Organization of Gatherings*. New York, NY: Free Press.

Goffman, E. (1981). *Forms of Talk*. Pennsylvania, PA: University of Pennsylvania Press.

Goodwin, C. (1994). Professional vision. *American Anthropologist*, 96(3), 606–633.

Goodwin, M. H. (2006). Participation, affect, and trajectory in family directive/response sequences. *Text & Talk*, 26(4/5), 513–541.

Goodwin, M. H. (2007). Participation and embodied action in preadolescent girls' assessment activity. *Research on Language and Social Interaction*, 40(4), 353–375. https://doi.org/10.1080/08351810701471344

Goodwin, M. H., and Goodwin, C. (2000). Emotion within situated activity. In A. Duranti (ed.), *Linguistic Anthropology: A Reader*(pp. 239–257). Oxford: Blackwell.

Goodwin, M.H., and Goodwin, C. (2004). Participation. In A. Duranti (ed.), *A Companion to Linguistic Anthropology (pp.* 222–243). Oxford: Blackwell.

Heritage, J. (1984). A change-of-state token and aspects of its sequential placement. In J. M. Atkinson and J. Heritage (eds.), *Structures of Social Action* (pp. 299–345). Cambridge: Cambridge University Press.

Houen, S., Danby, S., Farrell, A., and Thorpe, K. (2016). 'I wonder what you know … ' teachers designing requests for factual information. *Teaching and Teacher Education*, 59, 68–78. https://doi.org/10.1016/j.tate.2016.02.002

Houen, S., Danby, S., Farrell, A., and Thorpe, K. (2018). Adopting an unknowing stance in teacher–child interactions through 'I wonder…' formulations. *Classroom Discourse*, 10(2), 1–17. https://doi.org/10.1080/19463014.2018.1518251

Kendon, A. (1990a). Spatial organization in social encounters: the F-formation system. In A. Kendon (ed.), *Conducting Interaction: Patterns of Behavior in Focused Encounters* (pp. 209–238). Cambridge: Cambridge University Press.

Kendon, A. (1990b). Behavioral foundations for the process of frame-attunement in face-to-face interaction. In A. Kendon (ed.), *Conducting Interaction: Patterns of Behavior in Focused Encounters* (pp. 239–262). Cambridge: Cambridge University Press.

Koole, T., and Elbers, E. (2014). Responsiveness in teacher explanations: a conversation analytic perspective on scaffolding. *Linguistic & Education*, 26, 57–69.

Mandelbaum, J. (2013). Storytelling in conversation. In J. Sidnell and T. Stivers (eds.), *Handbook of Conversation Analysis* (pp. 492–508). Cambridge: Cambridge University Press.

Ministry of Education. (1996). *Te Whāriki: He Whāriki mātauranga mō ngā mokopuna ō Aotearoa: Early Childhood Curriculum*. Wellington, New Zealand: Learning Media.

Rogoff, B. (1990). *Apprenticeship in Thinking: Cognitive Development in Social Context*. Oxford; Oxford University Press.

Rogoff, B. (2003). *The Cultural Nature of Human Development*. Oxford: Oxford University Press.

Rowe, M. B. (1986). Wait time: slowing down may be a way of speeding up. *Journal of Teacher Education*, 37(1), 43–50.

Sacks, H. (1992). *Lectures on Conversation* (vols. I & II). Oxford: Blackwell.

Sacks, H., Schegloff, E. A., and Jefferson, G. (1974). A simplest systematics for the organisation of turn-taking for conversation. *Language*, 50, 696–735.

Schaughency, E., Suggate, S., and Reese, E. (2017). Links between early oral narrative and decoding skills and later reading in a New Zealand sample. *Australian Journal of Learning Difficulties*, 22, 109–132. https://doi.org/10.1080/19404158.2017.1399914

Schegloff, E. A. (1992). Repair after next turn: the last structurally provided defense of intersubjectivity in conversation. *The American Journal of Sociology*, 97(5), 1295–1345.

Siraj-Blatchford, I., Sylva, K., Muttock. S., Gilden, R., and Bell, D. (2002). *Researching Effective Pedagogy in the Early Years. DfES Research Report 365*. London: HMSO.

Theobald, M. (2019). Scaffolding storytelling and participation with a bilingual child in a culturally and linguistically diverse preschool in Australia. *Research on Children and Social Interaction*, 3(1–2), 224–247.

Vygotsky, L. (1962). *Thought and Language*. Cambridge, MA: MIT Press.

Waters, J., and Bateman, A. (2013). Revealing the interactional features of learning and teaching moments in outdoor activity. *European Early Childhood Education Research Journal*, 21(2), 1–13.

Wood, D. J., Bruner, J. S., and Ross, G. (1976). The role of tutoring in problem solving. *Journal of Child Psychiatry and Psychology*, 17(2), 89–100. https://doi.org/10.1111/j.1469-7610.1976.tb00381.x

4 | Embodiment

FRIEDERIKE KERN

Introduction

In recent years, embodiment has attracted increasing attention in research on social interaction (Goodwin, 2000; Goodwin & Cekaite, 2018; Mondada, 2019; Streeck, Goodwin, & LeBaron, 2011), as well as in the area of cognitive science (Rambusch & Ziemke, 2005; Wilson & Foglia, 2017). Expanding the perspective from speech to other modalities, embodiment refers to bodily behaviour comprising all aspects of speech – verbal and paraverbal (speech rhythm, voice melody, emphatic stress, or other vocal features) – as well as body posture and orientation, hand movements, and gaze. This shift in paradigm has resulted in an exploration of the impact of embodiment on cognitive theory, and in a more systematic inclusion of embodiment in the analysis of social interaction. Research in cognitive science increasingly acknowledges the role of the physical body in cognition, with the aim of integrating the reciprocal effect of bodily based perception and thinking (Wilson & Foglia, 2017). Meanwhile studies in conversation analysis have persuasively demonstrated how people use their bodies and hands to create meaning and manage social interaction in situ, thus revealing the interactive work accomplished by resources such as touch, gesture, and body orientation (C. Goodwin, 2000, 2013; M. Goodwin, 2007).

This chapter will first introduce the key term of embodiment both in cognitive science theory and in research on social interaction in the area of ethnomethodology and conversation analysis (EMCA). It will then provide insight into the role of embodiment in emerging intersubjectivity and language acquisition in infancy and early childhood, and subsequently discuss how the body can be employed in interactions with children to gain and direct attention, to invite participation, to display and manage affect and to provide emotional support, as well as to gain access to and demonstrate an understanding of objects and concepts in learning and teaching situations. The content of this chapter is arranged as follows: An introduction to the concept of embodiment will be provided both from a cognitive science and from an EMCA perspective. The discussion will then provide a state-of-the-art review of EMCA studies on embodiment in the area of early childhood interaction, illustrating these by providing two transcribed examples and, finally, discussing possible implications for the practices of childhood educators.

Key Concepts: Embodiment in Cognitive Science and in Interaction Studies

'Embodiment' is widely used as a key notion in the two scientific fields of cognitive science and EMCA. While CA-informed research during the last decade has intensively studied the role of embodiment in shared understanding and meaning-making in natural interactions, the term has also become increasingly widespread in cognitive theory. Accordingly, studies have either investigated experimentally how the body may be connected to, and indeed influence, the way we think, or have explored the many ways in which participants use their bodies to establish and perform joint actions in situated social interactions. Thus, two major perspectives on embodiment can be identified, asking the following questions: What role does it play for the mind, and how is it embedded in social interaction.

As divergent as the two approaches may be, both have gained much of their motivation to pay more attention to the body as a source of knowledge and human sociality from the work of Merleau-Ponty (1962) and his concept of intercorporeality. Merleau-Ponty refers to the philosophical theory of phenomenology, as developed by the German philosopher Edmund Husserl, according to which all knowledge is derived from our direct bodily experience of and interaction with the world.[1] Although the concept of intercorporeality is rather radical in that it assumes that the body exists only in relation to other bodies, it provides a new foundation for a theory of intersubjectivity, i.e., how two individuals come to share their minds. With regard to Merleau-Ponty, intersubjectivity is deeply rooted in the ability of bodies to be involved in joint actions. This is central to the first interactions between an infant and a caregiver, as studies in developmental psychology have demonstrated. In this respect, the reciprocity of infants' and parents' motor patterns in moments of social interaction are considered as early

[1] Similarly, phenomenology is also a starting point in contemporary gesture theory: 'As we perform practical actions with our hands, by touching, feeling, grasping and handling the world around us, gestures emerge as a by-product that may help us in "making sense of the world at hand"' (Streeck, 2009, p. 8).

forms of intersubjectivity (Trevarthan, 1998), and newborns already adjust their leg movements to the caregivers' articulation, thus interpersonally coordinating their own movements with the adult's speech (Condon & Sander, 1974). The ability to recognize others as having similar perceptions and emotions is grounded in the skill of infants to imitate body movements and even facial expressions (Meltzoff, 2007). Embodied interpersonal coordination in terms of temporal alignment of bodily behaviour is thus a central feature of social interaction (Condon & Ogston, 1971). At the same time, such alignments are prerequisites of social cooperation, which – from the perspective of childhood interaction – 'are important for fostering the development of skills and creative exploration of the world' (Goodwin & Cekaite, 2018, p. 20).

Studies in childhood interaction provide more evidence for the conclusion that intersubjectivity originates in bodies rather than in minds. Even very young children are able not only to use embodiment as a resource for communication, but also to observe other people's active bodies to infer their possible knowledge and expected next action. For example, children may show a caregiver the part of their body that hurts, or they may point to objects they desire, thus deploying embodied resources as 'answers' (Kidwell, 2011, p. 272). Children also display their ability to infer from other people's observed behaviour to their state of knowledge in the various ways they attempt to affect adults' inferential process. They might, for instance, try to get away from a scene of conflict, conceal incriminating objects, or provide misleading answers (ibid.). Thus, children attend to and employ embodiment as a resource for 'reading' other people's minds, in order to carry out their own embodied actions.

The Brain and the Body: Embodiment in Cognitive Science

Human cognition is deeply rooted in the body's interactions with its physical surroundings (Gallagher, 2009). The understanding that our bodies play a vital role in the way we conceptualize the world has led to the development of an 'embodied cognition' framework in cognitive science. In contrast to more traditional cognitive theory, this framework does not view the brain as the only source of cognition, thus acknowledging the growing evidence that cognition is at least partly rooted in the physical body (Wilson & Foglia, 2017, p. 1). The framework essentially builds on the phenomenological belief that our cognitive abilities are grounded in the features we have, such as our eyes, hands, or legs, because they shape how we experience the world around us. Cognition always involves acting with a body, and thinking is not possible without it. Consequently, embodiment is not seen as just another stimulus on otherwise disembodied cognitive processes but is conceptualized as being part of them, having considerably more impact on the mind than being a mere input-output device (Rambusch & Ziemke, 2005). The role of perception is emphasized, and, as a consequence, cognition, perception, and action are seen to be essentially intertwined with each other (Wilson & Foglia, 2017). Additionally, as our bodies are entangled with the environment they are situated in, the environment also provides important clues for perception and thus has an impact on cognition as well (Goodwin, 2013).

Interesting examples for the entwinement of mind, body, and environment come from animal behaviour and robotics, or linguistics (Wilson & Golonka, 2013). For example, it is claimed that our bodies shape many of the metaphors we use, by at the same time influencing how we think about abstract categories (ibid.). For example, the metaphor HAPPY IS UP originates in the observation that happy people have more upright body positions than sad people; accordingly, SAD IS DOWN is another metaphor (Lakoff & Johnson, 1981). The spatial concepts the metaphors employ, i.e. 'up' and 'down', are grounded in our upright stance, direction of motion, and field of view. The same holds for other spatial concepts like 'in front of' or 'back': creatures with different fields of view (e.g. horses), or with long and flat bodies, may have very different notions of them, or maybe none at all (Wilson & Foglia, 2017, p. 7).

Within the field of cognitive science, growing attention has also been paid to embodiment in the area of learning theories and educational research. In this regard, Rambusch & Ziemke (2005) argue that a better understanding of human learning and cognition can be achieved when the body's involvement in social interaction in general, and tool use in particular, is studied more closely. However, the authors also point out that embodied cognition is in many regards a social process, not just a cognitive one. Conversely, it is assumed that social processes like embodied mimicry and imitation are essential for establishing and maintaining social relations and communication, and additionally have functions for cognitive processes: through imitation, children are directed towards specific aspects of the environment and thus learn about sequences of goals, actions, and results (Call & Carpenter, 2002, p. 223). Furthermore, embodiment in the form of intrapersonal synchronization of intermodal resources (i.e. using emphatic stress in the voice and a gesture simultaneously) helps to transmit information by lightening the cognitive load for the interactive partner. For example, caregivers of three-month-old infants were found to synchronize their speech with bodily actions, thus providing audible as well as visual input to the children (Nomikou & Rohlfing, 2011), and such simultaneous use of embodied and vocal signals in interactions with infants has been linked to vocabulary acquisition in early childhood (Gogathe & Bahrich, 2001; Nomikou et al., 2017).

Finally, gestures are generally considered to be evidence for the assumption that language and cognition are not only mental but are also in part physical, or 'bodily' (Hostetter & Alibali, 2008), and that gesturing not only serves communicative functions but also seems to help speakers to think (Roth, 2002). Speakers use their hands to express their ideas (Goldin-Meadow, 2003), and children's gesturing may contribute to their success when solving a maths problem (Goldin-Meadow et al., 2009). Gestures may thus be a powerful 'learning resource' (Alibali & Nathan, 2012; Gerofsky, 2012).

In sum, even though there are different understandings of embodied cognition, most approaches share the view that it spans the brain, body, and environment (Wilson & Foglia, 2017). Important implications can be drawn from this for educational practice and research. Furthermore, while the studies referred to above provide stimulating results on the connection between body and mind, they also make it very clear that moments of embodied behaviour are always situated in and thus related to an interactive environment. Thus, embodied cognition is a fundamentally social process, and studying social interactions oriented towards learning and teaching may thus shed more light on how both are mutually achieved through embodiment (Rambusch & Ziemke, 2005).

Embodiment in Social Interaction

In contrast to cognitive science, most CA-informed research takes a different approach to embodiment, by focusing on how it shapes actions and creates meaning in ongoing processes of social interaction. While paraverbal behaviour (speech rhythm, voice melody, emphatic stress, or other vocal features) has been included in the analysis of social interaction for some time, the interest in bodily conduct, including gesture, touch, and body position, is rather new. It is argued that actions are not organized within talk alone 'but are instead constructed through the simultaneous use of multiple semiotic resources' (Streeck, Goodwin, & LeBaron, 2011, p. 1), which include the body, as well as materials and objects provided by the surrounding environment. The widespread shift from a simple focus on talk to a more holistic and multimodal view of communication and social interaction thus arises from the premise that social actions are being performed with a body that is situated in a social and material environment.

While there is a vast amount of research on embodiment in the area of EMCA, some attention has been given to its function in establishing a participation framework in which participants organize themselves and the available semiotic resources to build mutual reference and meaning-making (Goodwin, 2000; see also Bateman, Chapter 3, this volume). An embodied participation framework is established and maintained when participants use gaze, pointing gestures, and body position to highlight visible structures in the environment, which can then become a shared focus of interest (Goodwin, 2013).

Embodiment is also an important resource for establishing shared understanding, and for displaying as well as assessing understanding. While verbal forms of manifestation of understanding comprise reformulations (Kern, 2020), continuers, and acknowledgement tokens like 'uh huh' or 'ah' (Heritage, 1984; Schegloff, 1982), embodied forms include nodding/nods, facial expressions, and specific body postures (Mondada, 2011). Particularly interesting cases are interactions in which experts, such as teachers, guide apprentices into new forms of skilled behaviour. For example, in clinical training sessions, dentists assess their students' claims of understanding in part by virtue of their embodied action: students do not simply produce an acknowledgement token during or after a dentist's instruction, but also use their bodies to display their continuous attention, interest, and understanding during instruction (Hindmarsh et al., 2011). Likewise, teachers rely on bodily conduct to evaluate the students' understanding with respect to relevant professional standards (Zemel & Koschmann, 2014). Indeed, the students' embodied actions may be the only resource for the teachers to assess their ongoing understanding of the matter at hand. It is not so different in teaching and learning situations with children, as will be outlined below.

Embodiment in Childhood Interactions

Research on embodiment in childhood interactions in the area of EMCA has focused on a variety of social settings and themes, among them the embodied guiding of children's bodies into shared participation frameworks for joint activities (Cekaite, 2015, 2016; M. Goodwin, 2007; Goodwin & Cekaite, 2013), the intertwining of family members' bodies when engaging in affective intimacy (M. Goodwin, 2017), embodied ways of socializing children into appropriate bodily conduct through or during instruction

(Burdelski, 2012; Cekaite, 2015, 2016; de Léon, 2011; Tulbert & M. Goodwin, 2011), and the role of embodiment in making material and objects accessible to students in learning interactions (Jakonen, 2015; Kääntä & Piirainen-Marsh, 2013; Kern, 2018).

With regard to forms of embodiment, much attention has been drawn to the use of touch. As touch provides a kinaesthetic form of mutual perception and monitoring, it provides a sensory resource for socializing children into culturally appropriate forms of behaviour (Goodwin & Cekaite, 2018, p. 65). For example, touch can be used as a form of intervention and social control in adults' directives to children, when requesting the performance of everyday tasks and activities, such as brushing one's teeth, or going to bed (Cekaite, 2015; M. Goodwin & Cekaite, 2013; Tulbert & M. Goodwin, 2011), as a way to guide children into the correct bodily postures for culture-specific, embodied politeness routines (Burdelski, 2012), or to adjust their bodily conduct into socially acceptable forms while talking to their parents in a public situation (Kern, 2018b).

The goal of this chapter is to demonstrate the purposes of embodiment in interactions: to establish a shared focus for joint attention, to display and share affects and emotions, and to organize learning material as mutually accessible for the participants' further exploration. Even though the functions may not always be clear-cut, and embodiment may serve more than one purpose at a time, it is the aim of this chapter to demonstrate their relevance for language socialization (see Burdelski, Chapter 6, this volume) and socio-emotional development.

Establishing Joint Attention and Mutual Monitoring through Embodiment

One research focus is on how embodied resources are used for the situated construction of shared interaction spaces, in order to establish mutual perception and orientation towards an object of joint attention. In this regard, embodied resources have been found to be important in play situations (Goodwin, 2000), in routine grooming activities, such as brushing one's teeth, or combing one's hair (Tulbert & Goodwin, 2011), or in institutional learning interactions (Bateman & Roberts, 2018; Jakonen, 2015; Käänta & Piirainen-Marsh, 2013; Kern, 2018a). With young children, establishing and sustaining a participation framework for joint attention and mutual monitoring is a vital prerequisite for language acquisition, situated learning, and social-cognitive development (Tomasello & Carpenter, 2008). In particular, gaze and pointing gestures are important embodied resources for guiding a child's attention towards an object that can subsequently become the shared focus of interest. The ability to share gaze is said to be critical for establishing reference, supporting early word learning and further language development (Mundy et al., 2017), and pointing gestures further help to identify an object that can then be labelled or talked about (Filipi, 2009). Both resources are used systematically in interactions with infants and young children to establish reference within a shared participation framework (Mundy et al., 2017).

Thus, in the context of early childhood education, gaze and pointing gestures are key devices with which children's attention is guided towards possible objects of shared interest and which children themselves use from an early age to direct caregivers' attention to objects. Additionally, the use of touch has increasingly attracted attention in research on childhood interaction. Indeed, participation also relies on the establishment and maintenance of *interactional space*, which includes the spatial arrangements of bodies in relation to one another (Kendon, 2010). Such spatial arrangements (also analysed in terms of *participation frameworks*, cf. Goodwin 2000; see also Bateman, Chapter 3, this volume) facilitate mutual perception and orientation during face-to-face interactions, and touch can be a way to establish and sustain a spatial arrangement in which the bodies are mutually perceived and monitored not only visually but also kinaesthetically (Cekaite, 2016).

To illustrate how touch and other embodied resources are used to guide a child back manually into a shared participation framework, the following Extract 4.1 shows how a mother employs touch in interaction with her four-year-old son when he starts walking away from her. She uses her left hand to stop him, while at the same time pointing at a spot on the floor with her right hand, thus indicating where she wants him to sit. Her manual guiding and pointing is accompanied by a verbal instruction (line 17) and an account of why she wants him to sit down again.

Extract 4.1

```
11   MO:    was hast du denn mit karina gerade gemacht, ¤
            what did you just do with karina
     CH:    ein hund,(1.0)
            a dog
            der der der |so
            that that that like
                         |((raises and lifts his right arm
            with
                              closed fingers))
```

((walks to table))

Figure 4.1

[uhm
MO: [|bleibst du mal da.
stay there
-> |*((stops child with left hand on thigh*
| *while pointing to cushion))*
-> dann kann ich dich besser
sehen.
then I can see you more clearly
CH: *((walks backwards, turns around, looks at the cushion))*
MO: *((repeats pointing gesture to cushion))*
CH: *((walks |to the cushion, puts fingers of both hands together))*
|SO::;
like this

The extract illustrates how embodied resources may be employed to gain control and manage children's participation in joint activities (Cekaite, 2016). However, even if touch is applied in a regulating way, it may signal affect and care towards the child, which Extract 4.1 also shows.

Sharing Affect and Emotions through Embodiment

Embodiment also has important functions in showing and regulating emotions and affect in social interactions, especially for humans in close relationships, such as members of a family. Embodiment creates various conditions for being together intimately and sharing mutual affect and emotions, thus playing an important role in the co-construction of sociality (M. Goodwin, 2017). As embodiment provides rich opportunities to 'participate haptically in a shared experience' (Goodwin & Cekaite, 2018, p. 182), family members rely on many different practices of 'tactile intercorporeality', such as hugs, grooming, or shared play with hands or faces, to form intimate social relationships with one another (M. Goodwin, 2017). Relying on a broad range of forms of touch, such embodied practices of tactile intercorporeality often occur as care work and are employed to perform many different forms of action, for example reconciliation, play, comforting, and joint celebrations of achievements (Goodwin & Cekaite, 2018). For example, varied forms of tactile engagement (touch, hugs, grooming, cuddling) serve as remedial actions to hostile or aggressive acts, thus restoring feelings of mutual affection in family interactions, (Goodwin, 2017, p. 78f.). Through 'embodied shepherding' (Cekaite, 2010), an adult may control a child's body through some kind of 'tactile intervention' (ibid.: p. 7) and, at the same time, scaffold the child's movements towards a specific action, thereby accomplishing an embodied directive. However, aggravated affective engagements also show in the ways parents perform directives towards their children. By employing embodied forms like a firm grip or arm-pulling, parents upgrade their directives or requests to disciplining the child in cases of non-compliance (Goodwin & Cekaite, 2018, p. 73f). In contrast, touch is also used to relieve children from stress and provide comfort, which may happen in more formal educational settings as well (Burdelski, 2020).

Children themselves use embodied action, such as emphatic stress, body positioning, gaze, and facial expression, during storytelling, to display affective stance towards the activity of storytelling itself, and in order to prompt embodied emotional responses from the recipients, who thereby display their affective engagement with the story (Bateman, 2020). When engaged in conversation, peers may use body positioning and gesture (as well as talk) to show their friendship but also to display feelings of disgust and contempt towards each other, using bodily disalignment to create a close spatial formation between two participants that excludes a third one (M. Goodwin, 2007). Physical stance is thus not just a sign of an inner state but also a visible public practice – with consequences for the further development of the ongoing activity (Goodwin & Cekaite, 2018).

Embodiment in Formal Educational Settings

Every community has the task of educating new and culturally competent members, and providing them with relevant forms of knowledge and skills. Cooperative action lies at the heart of this transformation process (Goodwin, 2018). While bodies are 'shaped by being and interacting in the world'

(Cekaite, 2015, p. 153), children are socialized into appropriate bodily conduct through ongoing practices and actions (Burdelski, 2012; Kern, 2018b). While embodied socialization into new skills happens to a great extent in active family life (see Goodwin & Cekaite, 2018, chapter 11 for an overview), we will now turn to educational settings and consider the role embodiment plays in organizing a learning situation.

Gaze, touch, or pointing are employed to establish joint attention to classroom material, which then becomes an object of learning and thus a resource for further action (Jakonen, 2015; Kääntä & Piirainen-Marsh, 2013). For example, peers in a physics classroom employ manual guiding as a resource to enable their visual and physical access to objects and classroom materials; it also provides a powerful resource for upgrading prior instructions, which then become more compelling, and therefore more difficult to resist. Furthermore, arranging children's bodies may be employed as an embodied resource to give access to and achieve understanding of a learning object that becomes salient during a play activity. Dalgren (2017) describes how a preschool teacher moves a child's body around on a seesaw in order to make the seesaw move or bring it to a stop. With these embodied actions, the teacher provides access to the physical concepts of equilibrium and gravity, thereby following Swedish preschool pedagogic practice by intertwining learning, play, and care.

With regard to the organization of the learning situation, children's embodied signs of attention and understanding provide important clues for teachers. For example, students' embodied behaviour can be taken as a visible indication of their being engaged and paying attention during a lesson, and gaze, head movement, and body posture may provide evidence for ongoing understanding: Students orienting visually and kinaesthetically to the teacher during an informational or instructional sequence were able to later successfully complete a task, in contrast to those who had not exhibited such embodied attention (Gardner & Mushin, 2017; Mushin & Gardiner, Chapter 7, this volume).

Additional functions of embodied actions, such as the handling of objects and the manual guidance of students through touch, gaze, and pointing, have been highlighted in research. For example, during digital classroom activities, nine-year-olds use the embodied action of blocking their peer's hand and even sweeping it away with their own when collaboratively working on a tablet, thereby claiming or sustaining their turn at handling the tablet (Jakonen & Niemi, 2020). While blocking is thus a manual practice with which a peer's attempt to gain access to the digital device can be controlled, it may at the same time be a resource for displaying intimacy and affect. A block extending from a short swift of the hand to a gentle hold of the wrist transforms into a jointly accomplished activity when the peer whose hand is blocked does not move it away. An extended gentle hold thus provides children with the opportunity to signal reciprocal intimacy and responsiveness.[2]

Manual guiding is a powerful resource for socializing children into appropriate forms of bodily conduct. Japanese preschool teachers have been found to deploy touch and manual guidance to help children adopt expected body postures, thereby socializing them into politeness routines that comprise linguistic as well as embodied resources (Burdelski, 2010). Parents use similar resources to limit their children's nonverbal behaviour when it seems to them to be situationally inappropriate (Kern, 2018).

Finally, the twofold role of embodiment in (1) establishing a close participation framework and (2) the teaching of abstract concepts, is illustrated in the following excerpt in which a teacher observes a first grader during his attempt to write a two-syllable word (*springen – jump*) on the blackboard. When he stops, the teacher approaches him from behind, asking him what he would like to write down. Step by step, she builds up a close embodied participation framework with which she tries to help him solve the spelling problem.

Extract 4.2

TEA: was möchtest du schreiben,= milan?
what do you want to write milan
MI: springe:n.
jump
TEA: hm_hm, dann wolln wir ma lesen.
then let's read it
MI: ʃ ʃ:::pʁ::
TEA: lies mir mal die (.) e:rste,
read to me the first
[(0.8) das erste]<
the first
MI: [ʃp ʃ:pʁI:::N]
ʃpʀiːŋ,
TEA: ʃPʀIːŋ,

[2] The students' embodied practices were found to be in stark contrast to adults' explicit verbal requests ('let me see') with which they coordinate their collaborative work on a shared mobile phone (Thorne et al., 2015).

```
MI:    [(ŋ)::ɛ:]
TEA:   [und wie müsst jetzt guck mich ma an]
       and how would you now look at me
       ((touches MI by the shoulders
               and turns him slowly around))
```

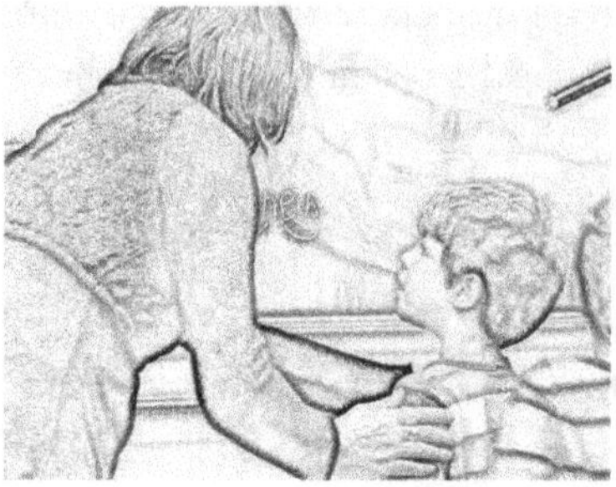

Figure 4.2

```
MI:    n_n
```

Figure 4.3

```
TEA:   ʃpʁiːŋ, (-)
```

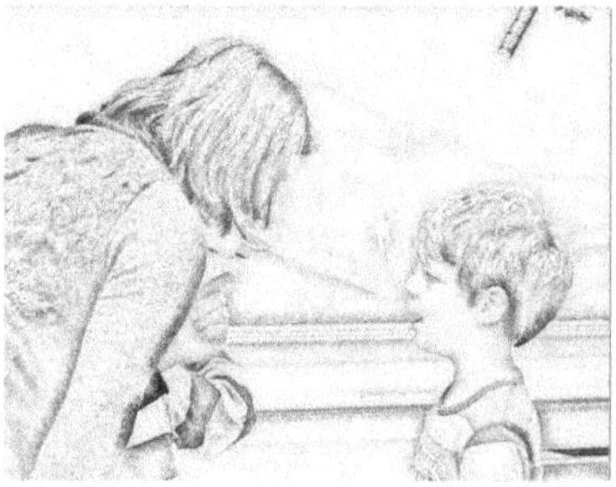

Figure 4.4

```
       und wie gehts dann weiter;
       and what now
MI:    n::œ:::n:
TEA:   'ʃprin 'nɛn?
MI:    ʃpʁɪŋ'ən;
TEA:   spring? (1.5)
       jump
```

Figure 4.5

```
          ((touches MI with
            index finger at
            shoulder))
          wie heißt der zweite teil,
          what is the second part
          [spring,]=
           jump
     MI:  [°spring°] (1.0)
            jump
          seil springen, (0.5)
          rope skipping
```

Figure 4.6

```
     TEA: ja [(.)] ʔə_ʔə      ]
     MI:  [°seil springen°] (2.0)
          rope skipping
     TEA: ((kneels in front of him))
           wir klatschen mal
          let's clap
     TEA: 'ʃpʁɪŋ (1.0)'gɛn (1.2)
          ((both clap their hands))
     TEA: nochmal (0.5)
          once more
     MI:  'ʃpʁɪŋ (1.0)'gɛn
```

((*both clap their hands*))
MI: häh?
TEA: so: (1.1)
right

First, the teacher moves the child, Mike, gently by the shoulders, thus performing a 'body twist' (Cekaite, 2010), so that they stand opposite each other at a close distance. While still holding the boy, the teacher kneels down in front of him. By getting down to his level she increases intimacy while asking him to clap hands with her. She then produces the word in two clearly audible syllables while clapping her hands twice right in front of his face, asking him further to join her, which he dutifully does. They both clap their hands in near-perfect synchrony with each other. The teacher thus uses embodiment not only to build a close, haptically tangible participation framework but also in an attempt to teach the boy the abstract concept of a syllable through the shared synchronized activity of clapping the (number of) syllables together.[3] While she succeeds in skilfully building a joint participation framework in which she has the boy's undivided attention, this cannot be said unreservedly about her attempt to teach him how to syllabify words, because this is, for some children, an extremely difficult concept to grasp. For example, when Mike first says 'rope' for 'the second part' he thereby demonstrates that he has not yet grasped the idea that the word 'springen' itself has parts. However, equally importantly, by speaking the word and clapping with it, the teacher turns a spoken (and written) word into an object that can be investigated in terms of its formal features, besides its semantic meaning. Turning words into 'cognitive artifacts' (Goodwin 1994, p. 615) is an important initial step in the direction of regarding words as objects with formal properties. Achieving this can be viewed as a milestone for the acquisition of writing skills.

Recommendations for Practice

This chapter has highlighted the important role of the body for cognition as well as for social interaction, and has demonstrated its importance in family interactions, in kindergartens and schools, during lessons or play sessions, and for adult-child interactions as well as for peer interactions. What are the practical implications that can be drawn from this research?

[3] This is a common practice in German classrooms because it is considered to be a successful way of teaching children how to split words into syllables.

- Build pedagogical practices on the presumption that
  - mind and body are intertwined in complex ways
  - using the body may help to understand objects and concepts
  - embodied forms such as touch, gaze, and gesture can be used systematically to gain children's attention and maintain it during an interaction.
- Employ touch and other forms of bodily guidance as a completement to verbal instructions about everyday activities.
- Encourage children to use embodied resources when, for example, telling a story or solving a maths or language problem, to foster their understanding of narrative structure and abstract concepts.
- Use embodied resources to support children's understanding of such structures and concepts.

References

Alibali, M., and Nathan M. (2012). Embodiment in mathematics teaching and learning: evidence from learners' and teachers' gestures. *Journal of the Learning Sciences*, 21(2), 247–286.

Bateman, A., and Roberts P. (2018). Morality at play: pretend play in five-year-old children. *Research on Children and Social Interaction*, 2(2), 195–212.

Bateman, M. (2020). Young children's affective stance through embodied displays of emotion during tellings. *Text & Talk*, 40(5), 653–668.

Burdelski, M. (2012). Language socialization and politeness routines. In A. Duranti, E. Ochs, and B. Schiefferlin (eds.), *The Handbook of Language Socialization* (pp. 275–295). Chichester: Wiley-Blackwell.

Burdelski, M. (2020). Teacher compassionate touch in a Japanese preschool. Social interaction. *Video-Based Studies of Human Sociality*, 3(1). https://doi.org/10.7146/si.v3i1.120248

Call, J., and Carpenter, M. (2002).Three sources of information in social learning. In K. Dautenhahn (ed.), *Complex Adaptive Systems. Imitation in Animals and Artifacts* (pp. 211–228). Cambridge, MA: MIT Press.

Cekaite, A. (2010). Shepherding the child: embodied directive sequences in parent–child interactions. *Text & Talk*, 30(1), 1–25.

Cekaite, A. (2015). The coordination of talk and touch in adults' directives to children: touch and social control. *Research on Language and Social Interaction*, 48(2), 152–175.

Cekaite, A. (2016). Touch as social control: haptic organization of attention in adult-child interactions. *Journal of Pragmatics*, 92, 30–42.

Condon, W. S., and Ogston, W. D. (1971). Speech and body motion synchrony of speaker-hearer. In D. L. Horton and J. Henkings (eds.), *Perception of Language* (pp. 150–173). Columbus, OH: Merill.

Condon, W. S., and Sander, L. W. (1974). Neonate movement is synchronized with adult speech: interactional participation and language acquisition. *Science*, 183, 99–101.

Dalgren, S. (2017). Questions and answers, a seesaw and embodied action: how a preschool teacher and children accomplish educational practice. In A. Bateman and A. Church (eds.), *Children's Knowledge-in-Interaction. Studies in Conversation Analysis (pp. 37–56)*. Singapore: Springer.

Filipi, A. (2009). *Toddler and Parent Interaction: The Organisation of Gaze, Pointing, and Vocalisation*. Amsterdam: John Benjamins.

Gallagher, S. (2009). Philosophical antecedents to situated cognition. In P. Robbins and M. Aydede, (eds.), *The Cambridge Handbook of Situated Cognition*. Cambridge: Cambridge University Press.

Gardner, R., and Mushin, I. (2017). Epistemic trajectories in the classroom: how children respond to informing sequences. In A. Bateman and A. Church (eds.), *Children's Knowledge-in-Interaction. Studies in Conversation Analysis* (pp. 13–36). Singapore: Springer.

Gerofsky, S. (2012). Mathematical learning and gesture: character viewpoint and observer viewpoint in students' gestured graphs of functions. In J.-M. Coletta and M. Guidetti (eds.), *Gesture and Multimodal Development* (pp. 199–220). Amsterdam: John Benjamins.

Gogathe, L. J., and Bahrick, L. E. (2001). Intersensory redundancy and 7-month-old infants' memory for arbitrary syllable-object relations. *Infancy*, 2(2), 219–231.

Goldin-Meadow, S. (2003). *Hearing Gesture: How Our Hands Help Us Think*. Cambridge, MA: Harvard University Press.

Goldin-Meadow, S., Cook, S. W., and Mitchell, Z. A. (2009). Gesturing gives children new ideas about math. *Psychological Science*, 20(3), 267–272.

Goodwin, C. (1994). Professional vision. *American Anthropologist*, 96(3), 606–633.

Goodwin, C. (2000). Action and embodiment within situated human interaction. *Journal of Pragmatics*, 32(10), 1489–1522.

Goodwin, C. (2013). The co-operative, transformative organization of human action and knowledge. *Journal of Pragmatics*, 46(1), 8–23.

Goodwin, C. (2018). *Co-operative action*. Cambridge: Cambridge University Press.

Goodwin, M. H. (2007). Participation and embodiment in preadolescent girls' assessment activity. *Research on Language and Social Interaction*, 40(4), 353–375.

Goodwin, M. H. (2017). Haptic sociality: the embodied interactive constitution of intimacy through touch. In C. Meyer, J. Streeck, and S. Jordan (eds.), *Intercorporeality. Emerging Socialities in Interaction* (pp. 73–102). Oxford: Oxford University Press.

Goodwin, M. H., and Cekaite, A. (2013). Calibration in directive/response sequences in family interaction. *Journal of Pragmatics*, 46, 122–138.

Goodwin, M. H., and Cekaite, A. (2018). *Embodied Family Interaction. Practices of Control, Care, and Mundane Activities*. London, New York: Routledge.

Heritage, J. (1984). A change-of-state-token and aspects of its sequential placement. In J. Atkinson and J. Heritage (eds.), *Structures of Social Action. Studies in Conversation Analysis (pp. 219–248)*. Cambridge: Cambridge University Press.

Hindmarsh, J., Reynolds, P., and Dunne, S. (2011). Exhibiting understanding: the body in apprenticeship. *Journal of Pragmatics*, 43, 289–503.

Hostetter, A., and Alibali, M. (2008). Visible embodiment: gestures as simulated actions. *Psychonomic Bulletin & Review*, 15(3), 495–514.

Jakonen, T. (2015). Handling knowledge: using classroom materials to construct and interpret information requests. *Journal of Pragmatics*, 89, 100–112.

Jakonen, T., and Niemi, K. (2020). Managing participation and turn-taking in children's digital activities: touch in blocking a peer's hand. *Social Interaction. Video-Based Studies of Human Sociality*, 3(1). https://doi.org/10.7146/si.v3i1.120250

Kääntä, L., and Piirainen-Marsh, A. (2013). Manual guiding in peer group interaction: a resource for organizing a practical classroom task. *Research on Language and Social Interaction*, 46(4), 322–343.

Kendon A. (2010). Spacing and orientation in co-present interaction. In A. Esposito, N. Campbell, C. Vogel, A. Hussain, and A. Nijholt (eds.), *Development of Multimodal Interfaces: Active Listening and Synchrony. Lecture Notes in Computer Science, vol. 5967*. Springer, Berlin, Heidelberg. https://doi.org/10.1007/978-3-642-12397-9_1

Kern, F. (2018a). Clapping hands with the teacher. What synchronization reveals about learning. *Journal of Pragmatics*, 125, 28–42.

Kern, F. (2018b). Mastering the body. Correcting bodily conduct in adult-child interaction. *Research on Children and Social Interaction*, 2(2), 213–234.

Kern F. (2020). Interactional and multimodal resources in children's game explanations. *Research on Children and Social Interaction*, 4(1), 7–27.

Kidwell, M. (2011). Epistemics and embodiment in the interaction with very young children. In T. Stivers, L. Mondada, and J. Steensig (eds.), *The Morality of Knowledge in Conversation* (pp. 257–283). Cambridge: Cambridge University Press.

Lakoff, G., and Johnson, M. (1981). *Metaphors We Live By*. Chicago, IL: University of Chicago Press.

Meltzoff, A. (2007). 'Like me': a foundation for social cognition. *Developmental Science*, 10(1), 126–134.

Merleau-Ponty, M. (1962). *Phenomenology of Perception*. London: Routledge.

Mondada, L. (2011). Understanding as an embodied, situated and sequential achievement in interaction. *Journal of Pragmatics*, 43(2), 542–552.

Mondada, L. (2019). Challenges of multimodality: language and the body in social interaction. *Journal of Sociolinguistics*, 20(3), 336–366.

Mundy, P., Block, J., Delgado, C., Pomares, Y., Hecke, A.V., and Parlade, M. A. (2007). Individual differences and the development of joint attention. *Child Development*, 78(3), 938–954.

Nomikou, I., and Rohlfing, K. (2011). Language does something: body action and language in maternal input to three-month-olds. *IEEE Transactions on Autonomous Mental Development*, 3(2), 113–128.

Nomikou, I., Koke, M., and Rohlfing, K. (2017). Verbs in mothers' input to six-month-olds: synchrony between presentation, meaning and actions is related to later verb acquisition. *Brain Sciences*, 7(5), 52. https://doi.org/10.3390/brainsci7050052

Rambusch, J., and Ziemke, T. (2005). The role of embodiment in situated learning. In B. G. Bara, L. Barsalou, and M. Bucciarelli (eds.), *Proceedings of the 27th Annual Conference of the Cognitive Science Society* (pp. 1113–1118). Mahwah, NJ: Erlbaum.

Roth, W.-M. (2002). Gestures: their role in teaching and learning. *Review of Educational Research*, 71, 365–392.

Streeck, J. (2009). Gesturecraft. *The manufacture of meaning*. Amsterdam: Benjamins.

Streeck, J., Goodwin, C., and LeBaron, C. (2011). Embodied interaction in the material world: an introduction. In J. Streeck, C. Goodwin, and C. LeBaron (eds.), *Embodied Interaction. Language and Body in the Material World* (pp. 1–26). Cambridge: Cambridge University Press.

Thorne, S. L., Hellermann, J., Jones, A., and Lester, D. (2015). Interactional practices and artifact orientation in mobile augmented reality game play. *Psychology Journal*, 13(2–3), 259–286.

Tomasello, M., and Carpenter, M. (2007). Shared intentionality. *Developmental Science*, 10(1), 121–125.

Trevarthan, C. (1998). The concept and foundations of infant intersubjectivity. In S. Braten (ed.), *Intersubjective Communication and Emotion in Early Ontogeny (pp.* 15–46). Cambridge: Cambridge University Press.

Tulbert, E., and Goodwin, M. H. (2011). Choreographies of attention. Multimodality in a routine activity. In J. Streeck, C. Goodwin, and C. LeBaron (eds.), *Embodied Interaction. Language and Body in the Material World* (pp. 79–92). Cambridge: Cambridge University Press.

Wilson, R. A., and Foglia, L. (2017). Embodied cognition. *Stanford Encyclopedia of Philosophy Website*. Last modified 8 December 2015. Accessed 1 October 2020. Available at: plato.stanford.edu/entries/embodied-cognition

Wilson. A., and Golonka, S. (2013). Embodied cognition is not what you think it is. *Frontiers in Psychology* (online). https://doi.org/10.3389/fpsyg.2013.00058

Zemel, A., and Koschmann, T. (2014). 'Put your finger right in here': learnability and instructed experience. *Discourse Studies*, 6(2), 163–183.

5 | Emotion

ASTA CEKAITE

Introduction

According to a social perspective of emotions, emotions are conceptualized as interactionally manifested, situated in and shaped by cultural practices (Demuth, 2012; Goodwin, Cekaite, & Goodwin, 2012). In interactions, emotional expressions constitute social acts that indicate one's orientation towards some phenomena or actions: for instance, being angry, sad, or upset about something (Goodwin et al., 2012). Accordingly, emotional expressions emerge in the turn-by-turn environment of a social encounter; they involve a combination of language and bodily resources (facial expression, body posture, touch, gaze, gestures). Emotional expressions in everyday interactions are closely intertwined with the participants' moral expectations and broader cultural norms; and both children and adults are held responsible – accountable – for their own emotional conduct, how and when they express their emotions, and how they interpret the other's emotions. Emotional expressions have culturally dependent content, and therefore emotional development and emotion socialization are inextricably related. Accordingly, children's emotional development is part of dynamic socialization processes.

Emotion Socialization through Talk and Embodied Actions

Socialization, including emotion socialization, is situated in recurrent practices of various communities – family, early childhood education, and children's peer group, among others. Community members use talk and nonverbal resources to sanction, ignore, or discipline each other's emotional expressions, and in the process, they practise and learn to indicate and interpret others' emotional expressions according to socioculturally valid norms and expectations, that is, they participate in socialization processes (Ochs & Schieffelin, 2012; Burdelski, Chapter 6, this volume; Takada, Chapter 21, this volume). By participating in social interaction with close and caring adults and peers, children can 'share their personal experience of the world with others, including "being with" others in intimacy, isolation, loneliness, fear, awe, and love' (Stern, 1985, p. 182). Such participation is important to be able to understand one's own, as well as others', emotional experiences. In these ways, and especially, through engagement in talk and embodied actions that deal with feelings in close social relations, children can engage with, explore, and learn shared cultural concepts. Notably, such concepts, including those that cover emotional experiences such as being 'angry', 'upset', 'glad', 'happy', or 'disappointed', can differ widely across cultures and socio-economic groups. Therefore, social interaction within particular sociocultural contexts has an influence 'on the perception and classification' of affective experiences (Dunn, 2003). In various cultural contexts, caregivers – parents and teachers – engage children in talk about their own and others' feelings (Ahn, 2010; Burdelski, 2013; Cekaite, 2013). The characteristic features of this talk are dependent on the normative expectations and communicative practices related to what constitutes appropriate emotional expression and actions. For instance, in Western contexts, children are encouraged and expected to verbalize their negative emotional experiences through talk, e.g. in conflict situations telling the other children to 'stop' or that they are upset or scared (Cekaite, 2020). So-called emotion narrativity and emotion talk are preferred and practised (Kusserow, 2004). Embodied expression of negative emotions, such as anger and sadness, are to be curbed and verbal messages used instead (Ahn, 2010; Kyratzis & Köymen, 2020).

When children's language is growing, they can themselves engage in using language in their expression of intimacy and connectedness in their social relations. Starting at the age of two to three, these capacities markedly increase. Children in their spontaneous talk, even in rudimentary narratives, explore, wonder, and talk about others' and their own feelings, why they do things in specific ways, especially in relation to being upset or hurt (Dunn, 2003).

Children's verbal and nonverbal participation in social interaction with caregivers – parents, preschool teachers, and educators – influences their skills in *emotion regulation* that includes behaviours 'that serve to modulate, inhibit, and enhance emotional experiences and expressions' (Calkins & Hill, 2007, p. 229). Emotion regulation is not individual and limited to self-contained management of one's own emotions; rather, it is a social process that involves the development of socio-cognitive abilities to manage one's own emotions and to influence the emotions of others, in ways that meet children's own and their co-participants' social and emotional needs

(Calkins & Hill, 2007; Dunn, 2003). These skills and processes are inextricably linked to children's communicative abilities to influence the other person's behaviour and manage their close social relations. They involve children's abilities to upscale or downscale their negative emotions, to show affection, empathy, and compassion towards others, to explain their own feelings, and to procure comfort or assistance, and in various ways influence the feelings and social practices of those around them.

Emotion and Early Childhood Education

Children's development of emotional competence is a part of teachers' professional responsibilities, implicitly or explicitly outlined in local and national educational policies (e.g. Preschool Curriculum, 2019). However, children's emotional development has been largely studied in mother-child relationships. Children's emotions as a part of preschool practices are a growing area of knowledge development (Bergnehr & Cekaite, 2018; Denham et al., 2012; Jools & Elfer, 2013). In that educators have institutional obligations to create conducive conditions for children's wellbeing in early childhood education settings, one significant area of research examines the management of children's negative emotions, and specifically, anger or distress. Children's distress in conflictual situations is usually a part of conflict resolution, mediated by teachers who also scaffold children's appropriate participation (Ahn, 2010; Bateman, 2015; Cekaite & Ekström, 2019; Moore, 2020; see also Church & Moore, Chapter 19, this volume). Children's disputes and arguments that are accompanied by expressions of, for instance, anger, sulkiness, or sadness, constitute a crucial focus of teachers' and peer group's concerns (Danby & Theobald, 2012). Teachers encourage and teach children to verbalize and explain their feelings instead of crying and yelling (Ahn, 2010; Kyratzis, & Köymen, 2010). To mediate in children's conflict, and restore the social ambience, they scaffold children's apologies, teaching children concrete acts of prosocial, empathetic conduct, such as verbal and bodily apologies (hugs, sharing of toys) (Björk-Willén, 2018; Burdelski, 2013; Danby & Baker 1998; Kampf & Blum-Kulka, 2007).

Research on children's crying shows that although crying usually indicates distress or trouble, the social meaning of crying is multifaceted. As an expression of distress, it has a normative value; teachers treat children's crying in different ways depending on its causes (Hsuenh & Tobin 2003; Ahn, 2016; Hilppö et al., 2019; Holm Kvist, 2018; Lipponen et al., 2018;

Moore, 2020). Educators' responses can be fashioned as disciplining of children's distress (Holm Kvist, 2018), playful diversion (Pursi, 2019), or compassionate soothing embraces (Cekaite & Holm Kvist, 2017). Teacher responses can also differ in relation to the cultural context. For instance, as documented in a cross-cultural study of teacher responses to children's peer play conflict crying, in a Japanese, and in a Swedish, preschool, teachers typically started investigation in order to figure out the events that precipitated crying, but children were provided with different opportunities to narrate their version of the events by themselves or to quickly confirm the teacher's understanding of the conflict. The teachers then used this information to socialize children's conduct towards each other (Burdelski, 2020; Cekaite, 2020; Cekaite & Burdelski, 2021). Moreover, the cause and extent of crying were important for teachers' normative evaluation of whether children's distress was a valid and adequate emotional state of being 'sad' or was problematic behaviour, such as being 'grumpy' (Holm Kvist, 2018; see also Kyratzis & Köymen, 2020).

Laughter, Humour, and Positive Emotions in Teacher-Child Social Interactions

Positive emotions, which can be expressed as laughter, smiling, and joking, feature prominently in young children's social interactions, both in their peer group and with adults. Positive emotions manifest close alignment between the community members and therefore generate conditions conducive to children's wellbeing. The expression of shared humour and laughter is important to the quality of social relations in that reciprocation of positive emotions is a part of emotion sharing (Tomasello, 2019); in other words, laughter is important for strengthening of close social relationships. Even very young children, at 18 months of age, notice various types of incongruences and are able to present these as joking events to the members of their community with whom they may share understanding of social routines (Dunn, 2003). As children get older, verbal joking becomes more elaborate, and conventionalized jokes become a part of children's social repertoires. It has been shown (in an ethnographic study of children and emotions in Swedish preschools), however, that laughter is not necessarily shared between children and preschool teachers (Andrén & Cekaite, 2017). Rather, as a part of emotion regulation, teachers acknowledged children's positive emotions by responding with smiling, or neutral talk, but they did not manifest a similar degree of emotional involvement in child-initiated joking. Teachers acknowledged children's laughter invitation by deploying a downgraded emotional expression (Cekaite & Andrén, 2019). This suggests that children and preschool teachers constructed emotional worlds that were unique for their age group.

Emotions in Teaching Strategies

Teaching practices are also characterized by emotional expressions, for instance, in situations, when students'/children's work is evaluated. Emotional stances are used to manifest and emphasize a particular teaching message. For instance, teachers can use various emotional stances in performing a story character during book reading or story telling for young children (Cekaite & Björk Willen, 2018; Bateman, 2020) and in organizing young children's own literacy practices, for instance, in children's peer reading (Johnson, 2017; Kyratzis, 2017). Children's expressions of positive emotions during academic work are important in that a child's social identity as a successful and academically eager student can be interpreted by teachers as an indication of the child's academic maturity and willingness to learn (Cekaite, 2012). Positive evaluation (e.g. praise) is used by teachers not only in the evaluation of children's performance of learning tasks, but also in gender socialization. For instance, in Japanese preschools, *kawaii* (a characteristic of being 'cute') is associated with being a girl, and is evaluated positively when girls' embodied and verbal conduct conforms to these gendered normative expectations (Burdelski & Mitsuhashi, 2010).

In all, previous research on children and emotions in preschools shows that there is a variety of practices that teachers use in emotion socialization. Such practices involve explicit emotion training activities and programmes, where children are explicitly taught how to deal with specific emotions, how to be a good friend, how to resolve conflict, etc. Other important interactional templates where children's emotional competences are at the core of teachers' work are less explicit. Nevertheless, they are of great importance in that they involve spontaneous everyday interactions that are inextricably related to children's socialization into normatively relevant emotional expressions and actions. By using detailed exploration of daily practices, and paying attention to children's meaning-making, researchers and teachers can discern successful and unsuccessful practices and suggest ways in which teachers can organize their work.

Teacher Responses to Children's Distress: Emotion and Moral Socialization

Educators' Investigation and Disciplining Responses during Peer Play Crying

Children's crying is a rather frequent occurrence during a day in preschool. It can occur for different reasons: it can arise during conflict situations, recurrent between younger children during play. Children's crying can also arise in situations of noncompliance in response to teachers' directives and instructions. In that children's crying and other displays of distress constitute a disturbance in preschool practice, it is a part of educators' institutional responsibilities to resolve the situation of distress, restore social ambience, and sustain (or re-introduce) institutional activity. Children's crying indicates distress and requires a response from co-present teachers and children. Crying and responses to crying constitute situations for emotion and moral socialization, where the participants, teachers, and children can show empathy and compassion. Responses to crying can also involve clarification of rules concerning how the rules have been broken.

In Extracts 5.1a–b, three boys, including Gustav and Henrik (3 years old), get into conflict while playing together in a play bed (a preassigned play area) because they cannot share the play space. As Henrik starts crying, two preschool teachers respond (lines 1, 3). As is common in early childhood educational contexts in Sweden (Cekaite & Burdelski, 2021), Teacher 2 responds to the child's crying by asking an open-ended question and starts an investigation by inquiring 'how are you doing'.

Extract 5.1a

1	Teacher 2:	***Gu****stav! hur går det?* Gustav! how are you doing?
2	Teacher 2:	*((tells T1 about conflict))*
3	Teacher 1:	*så-. det är inte ok****ej*** *Gustav.* so. it's not OK Gustav.
4		*((carries Gustav out of the room))*
5	Gustav:	hhehh hhheh hhhEEEHH
6	Teacher 1:	*nä det är inte ok****ej*** *att slåss med kompisar.* no it is not OK to fight with your buddies.
7		*då får man inte vara* ***med*** *å leka. (.)* if you do so, you're not allowed to be here

8 *så* ***är*** *det.*
and play. that's the way it is.

9 *((sits with Gustav in adjacent room))*

10 Gustav: HHEEHHH HHEEEHH HHEEEH

11 Teacher 1: *då kan vi sitta lite* ***här*** *istället.*
in that case we can sit here for a while.

12 Gustav: *NÄ::::::::: HHEHH HHEEH*
NO HHEHH HHEEH

13 Teacher 1: *vad* ***va****r det som* ***hä****nde?*
what was it that happened?

14 Gustav: HHEEHHH HHEEEHH HHEEEH HHEEEH

15 Teacher 1: *på samma sätt som när Henrik* ***slo****g dig*
in the same way as Henrik hit you before

16 *i byggis innan. (.)*
in the block area.

17 *det var* ***så*** *du gjorde mot* ***He****nrik nu.*
what you did to Henrik now was the same.

Gustav does not respond to Teacher 2's request for information at the beginning of Extract 5.1a, so – as was common in these conflict crying situations – the teacher physically removes the child (Gustav, who was the instigator of the fight between the boys) from the conflict space (lines 3–4). Even though Gustav starts crying loudly (line 5), the teacher addresses the conflict situation with a disciplining negative assessment 'it's not OK Gustav' and spells out several non-negotiable rules: 'no it is not OK to fight with your buddies. If you do so, you're not allowed to be here and play. That's the way it is'. The teacher carries the boy into the adjacent room and sits with him on the sofa, explaining the consequences of his actions: 'in that case we can sit here for a while', line 11). This mild admonition highlights for the child his accountability for his inappropriate action. Notably, the teacher uses a complex explanatory format: the social rules, formulated as statements that do prevent any kind of negotiation or noncompliance, are supported with justifications. These statements spell out and explain the link between one's actions and their normative consequences. In this way, the teacher is able to causally connect and clarify the normative assessment of emotionally and morally charged actions and the neutral institutional rule that informs the negative assessment of these actions.

However, Gustav continues to loudly protest by crying (line 12). In response, the teacher re-initiates investigation, asking the child an open-ended question that invites him to articulate his version of events: 'what was it that happened?' (see Cekaite & Burdelski, 2021). By using questions, the teacher provides the child with interactional opportunities to tell his own version of problematic events. Rather than ascribing responsibility for an untoward action, he asks Gustav neutrally what happened (line 13). When Gustav continues crying, the teacher yet again offers a normative explanation that contextualizes and draws a concrete causal parallel between untoward actions, negative emotions, and their consequences. He uses concrete, everyday examples to foster the child's perspective-taking: 'in the same way as Henrik hit you before in the block area. What you did to Henrik now was the same' (lines 15–17). The child's heightened emotional display of crying prompts the teacher to action, responding attentively to the child in ways that try to re-establish emotional equilibrium. This is done in several steps: first the teacher offers opportunities to discuss the problem ('what happened') and then by providing rules (line 15 onwards).

Extract 5.1b

18	Gustav:	*NÄ:::Ä:: jag vill le:::ka.* no:: I want to play:::.
19	Teacher 1:	*ja du kan få gå **in** där om en stund igen.* yes you can go there in a while again.
20	Gustav:	*nä men Henrik-. Henrik sitter på **min** säng.* no but Henrik. Henrik is sitting in my bed.
21	Teacher 1:	*men (.) det är ju inte **din** säng.* but it's not your bed you know.
22		*Henrik och Oscar är också **med** i din lek.* Henrik and Oscar are playing in your game.
23		*eller i **er** lek. ni leker till**sa**mmans.* or in your (plr.) play. you play together.
24		*då får dom **också** vara i sängen.* therefore they can sit in the bed too.
25	Gustav:	*nä:::* no::: *((tries to leave teacher's lap))*

26	Teacher 1:	*men då kanske du ska göra något* ***an****nat*
		but in that case maybe you'll have to
27		do *vännen (.) om du inte klarar* **av** *att leka*
		something else if you cannot play together
28		*med dom* ***an****dra.*
		with the others.
29	Gustav:	*NÄ:Ä::*
		no::: *((tries to get away))*
31	Teacher 1:	*för det är inte-.*
		because it is not-
32		*det är inte* **du** *som bestämmer.*
		it is not you (sng.) who decides.
33		*ni bestämmer till****sa****mmans.*
		you (plr.) decide together.

As Gustav continues resisting, the teacher spells out future consequences of his persistent distressed refusals. He states a premise that needs to be fulfilled if the child is to continue playing with his peers: 'but in that case maybe you'll have to do something else if you cannot play together with the others' and yet again states the communal rule of sharing and playing together when in the preschool: 'because it is not-. It is not you (sng.) who decides. You (plr.) decide together' (lines 26–28; 31–33). Throughout, the child's crying and refusals occasion the teacher's repeated explanations of rules (Reynolds, 2006). Providing rules as a response to an upgraded emotional display can be viewed as particularly removed from emotion. Rule statements can be seen as objective and not attached to negative or positive emotions, and they may be used as a strategy to defuse the emotional situation. The rules transcend the current situation of play and regulate how to use, i.e. share play space and property according to the normative expectations concerning solidarity and empathetic understanding of the other (Preschool Curriculum, 2019). Notably, the teacher not only disciplines the child, manages the boy's bodily position and conduct, but also responds to the child's distress by soothing and holding the boy closely in his lap. In multiple ways, a single episode of responding to the child's distress is transformed into a complex emotional and moral universe, where key cultural concepts and the social consequences of one's negative emotional expressions are invoked and engaged with.

Educators' Comforting Responses to Children's Injuries and Distress

Responses to children's distress vary according to the causes of crying. Studies of social interaction in preschool settings show that distress occasioned by various kinds of injury and pain commonly receive empathetic responses by the preschool teachers (Bateman, 2015; Cekaite and Holm Kvist, 2017; Pursi, 2019). Various soothing actions – comforting talk, touch, handing play objects – can be used to provide an empathetic response. Notably, between younger preschool children (2–4-year-olds), soothing responses to distress are not necessarily accepted. Previous studies show that young children do not readily accept peer empathetic actions, although children of this age have been shown to express empathy towards their peers (Dunn, 2003; Kidwell, 2013). In many cases, the preschool teacher is chosen as a relevant soother (Holm Kvist and Cekaite, 2021). This preference places a considerable responsibility on preschool teachers to serve as the main soother. Crying sounds in children's conversation with the teacher, the institutional and moral authority, can be used as a communicative resource.

In Extract 5.2a, Zeinab, a three-year-old Somali girl (with limited knowledge of Swedish) hurts her hand when Marina (4.5-year-old Romani girl) pushes her during their play. Zeinab starts crying and Marina immediately examines Zeinab's injury, responding to the peer's distress with an attempt of an empathetic soothing act (lines 1–2). However, the peer's comforting response to her injury is not accepted. Rather, Zeinab refuses Marina's assistance with a conventionalized objection 'stop' (line 3).

Extract 5.2a

1	Zeinab:	A:: A A A::
2	Marina:	*((touches Zeinab's hand))*
3	Zeinab:	STOP! *((gets her hand free))*
4	Marina:	*nä men det är inte så sto:r.* no but it's not so bi:g.
5		*SPRING SPRING SPRING!* run run run! *((guides Zeinab to researcher))*
6	Zeinab:	*hello! **ti**tta.* hello! look. ((pleading, to researcher))
7	Researcher:	*ja. ska du göra så**hä**r. gå till teacher* yes. you'll do like this. go to teacher.

Marina mitigates the severity of the injury ('but it's not so big') then guides Zeinab to the adult instead, urging her to run to the researcher (lines 4–5). In such a way, the children deflect responsibility to deal with the injury and distress and assign this responsibility to the adult (lines 4–5); the researcher redirects the child to the teacher who is nearby (line 7). CA transcripts aim to capture crying as it is produced (see Hepburn, 2004), so Zeinab's approach to the teacher that follows (line 9), is the sound of her crying.

Extract 5.2b

8	Zeinab:	*((goes to teacher, shows her hand))*
9		hello hheh hheh hheh
10	Teacher:	Zeinab. *((looks at child's palm))*
11	Zeinab:	hheh hhehh
12	Teacher:	*gjorde du dig* ***illa****?* did you hurt yourself?
13	Zeinab:	hheh hhehh
14	Teacher:	*ja:: på handen blev det?* yes does it happen on your hand?
15	Zeinab:	*((stops crying))*
16	Teacher:	*det är* ***här*** *ja.* yes it is here. *((touches Zeinab's palm))*
17	Zeinab:	e::y!
18	Teacher:	*ne:j! oh* ***nej****! oj! sår blev det.* no:! oh no! ai! it's a wound. *((empathetic))*
19	Teacher:	*((blows at Zeinab's palm))*
20		*vad kan vi* ***göra*** *Zeinab?* what can we do Zeinab?
21	Zeinab:	um!
22	Teacher:	*vill du ha en* ***plå****ster?* do you want a band aid?
23	Zeinab:	*((nods))*
24	Teacher:	*ska jag hämta en plåster?* shall I fetch a band aid?
25	Zeinab:	*((gets up))*
26	Teacher:	*ska du följa* ***med*** *i? vi går in och* are you going inside with me?
27		*hämtar plåster bara.* we'll just go inside and fetch a band aid.

Notably, the child's distress crying is not an outburst, not an uncontrollable expression of negative emotion. Rather, Zeinab uses distress to communicate when she summons the adult's attention (lines 8–9; 11; 13). As Zeinab's language proficiency in Swedish is still limited, distress sounds combined with a visual display of her injured hand and a summons ('hello') allows her both to attract the teacher's attention, and to indicate the reason for her summons. Here, the child publicly calibrates and modulates her crying, stopping crying or increasing it depending on her interlocutor. For instance, Zeinab restarts and increases crying when the teacher approaches and asks her about her injury ('did you hurt yourself', line 12). When the teacher starts paying attention to Zeinab's injury, 'investigating' the incident, Zeinab stops crying (lines 14–15). The teacher's responses comprise several actions: the teacher is empathetic, caring, and instructive. She responds to Zeinab's exclamation ('e::y') with empathetic talk and embodied soothing, blowing on Zeinab's hand. She also engages Zeinab, who has limited knowledge of Swedish, in an informal language lesson. The teacher uses elaborate vocabulary, repeating the key concept 'band aid' in several full sentences; her Yes/No questions require only minimal verbal responses, and allow Zeinab to participate in the conversation. Although the girl responds mostly with embodied actions (lines 21, 23, 25), the teacher is able to scaffold and extend her participation in managing the distress.

Narrating, Explaining, and Discussing Emotions: Teachers' and Young Children's Tellings about Negative Emotions and Disconcerting Events

Emotion terms and emotionally charged actions constitute a part of children's everyday interactions and play. Children at a certain age start talking about feelings in order to explore the meaning of various social situations and emotions (Dunn, 2003); one's own feelings and those of one's peers become a focus of attention during the peer group and teacher-child spontaneous narratives. Such narratives and 'emotion talk' generally centre around children's negative emotions that are manifested in concrete events. Among young children, self-initiated emotion narratives have a simple discursive organization and teachers' conversational support and scaffolding can provide an interactional template for a more complex exploration. It is by talking about the child's actions and emotional experiences that these experiences can be connected to and interpreted within the framework of sociocultural norms of feelings.

In Extract 5.3, we examine a spontaneous conversation that evolves between four-year-old boys (a group of friends who just had a minor fight) and their preschool teacher. As Sawan, in a sad voice and with a sad facial expression, tells the teacher 'he hits me' (line 1), and lightly hits a wall with his head, the teacher tells him to stop hitting himself, but he does not stop (line 3), and the teacher initiates an investigation about the causes of his emotional state (Cekaite and Burdelski, 2021).

Extract 5.3a

1	Sawan:	*han slår mig.* he hits me. *((sad, looks down, hits his head))*
2	Teacher:	nej du ska inte ***slå*** på dig heller Sawan. no you shouldn't hit yourself either Sawan.
3	Sawan:	*((hits himself))*
4	Teacher:	*är du **ar**g på nånting Sawan?* are you angry at something Sawan?
5	Sawan:	*((softly nods))*
6	Teacher:	*är du **le**dsen för nånting?* are you sad about something?
7	Sawan:	*((hits his head))*
8	Teacher:	*jag kan **se** på dig att* I can see on you
9		*du inte är riktig **gla**d.* that you're not really happy.
10		*vad **ä**r det för nånting?* what is it?
11	Amir:	*han vill **gå** till pa- hans pappa.* he wants to go to da- his dad. *((points at Sawan))*
12	Teacher:	*längtar du efter **pa**ppa? **gö**r du det?* do you long for your dad? do you?
13		*det kan man ju göra.* one can do that of course.
14		*det **få**r man göra.* one is allowed to.

The teacher interprets Sawan's facial expression and hitting actions as indicative of his negative feelings towards some focus of concern. Her questions 'are you angry at something Sawan' and 'are you sad about something' (lines 4, 6) connect causally the boy's actions to a reason that the teacher aims to reveal. The teacher's responses are in line with the institutional responsibilities to care and create conditions for children's wellbeing (e.g. Preschool Curriculum, 2018; see also O'Reilly & Lester, Chapter 16, this volume). The child's negative stance becomes a focus of concern that the boy is asked to talk about; he is positioned as accountable to explain what has occasioned his negative emotions (Cekaite, 2013; Evaldsson & Melander Bowden, 2020). Sequentially, emotion talk is as a collaborative telling that evolves with the assistance of an adult's, here, teacher's, questions (Burdelski & Evaldsson, 2019; Morita, 2019). Sawan, the main participant, offers only limited verbal responses to the teacher. It is his peers who volunteer explanations, e.g. 'he wants to go to da- his dad' (line 11). The teacher immediately interprets and expands rudimentary explanations by connecting the child's emotional experiences to concrete events; 'do you long after your dad. Do you. One can do that of course. One is allowed to' (lines 12–14). By using so called 'emotion labels', the teacher verbalizes and validates the child's feelings and experiences (cf. Dunn, 2003).

Extract 5.3b

15	Sawan:	*nej min pappa hämtar inte* ***mig****.*
		no my dad will not collect me.
		((hits his head))
16	Teacher:	*nej. vem hämtar dig i****dag*** *då?*
		no. who is going to collect you today?
17	Sawan:	*((hits his head))*
18	Teacher:	*är det* ***ma****mma? vad fint.*
		is it your mom? how nice.
19		*men det var* ***pa****ppa som lämnade dig då?*
		but it was your dad who brought you then?
20	Sawan:	mh.
21	Teacher:	m:h.
22	Sawan:	*((stops hitting himself))*
23	Teacher:	*är dina- dina* ***sto****ra syskon*
		are your your older siblings
24		*är de* ***he****mma nu Sawan eller går de i* ***sko****la?*
		are they at home now Sawan or do they go to school?
25	Sawan:	*de går till skola.*
		they go to school.

Sawan is still self-harming when he responds to the teacher by objecting and saying that his dad will not collect him from preschool (line 15). The teacher is modelling their conversation as an emotion narrative that is shaped in line with a common interpretative framework for children's upset in a preschool, namely, children being distressed because they long for their parents. In such cases, it is a sadness that can be definitely remedied when the parent collects the child. Notably, it is the teacher who scaffolds the child's emotional telling by modelling it to address the issues that are of pertinence to the boy (lines 18, 19, 23), and in such a way is able to distract the boy from his mild self-harming. She does not need to use controlling touch (Bergnéhr & Cekaite, 2018; Kern, 2018), but she is able to redirect the child from negative emotional conduct (line 23–24) to collaboratively addressing the sensitive issues that are relevant for understanding what is causing the child's distress. As is demonstrated in this episode, together with the teacher, several children engage in discourse about feelings. They discuss what brought about the child's negative emotions, articulate and examine the possible causes and the possible impact on the wellbeing of their peers. Although the children's actions are not necessarily active attempts to ameliorate the peer's distress, when guided by the teacher, they are collaboratively engaged in social interaction where they have opportunities to show empathy, affiliation, and intimate knowledge about their friends.

Using Emotions in Literacy Teaching: Organizing 'Enchantment' in Storytelling

Embodied displays of emotional stances have been shown to serve as interactional resources in the organization of teaching encounters, such as storytelling and other forms of literacy training practices (Johnson, 2017; Kyratzis, 2017; Cekaite & Björk-Willén, 2018). Storytelling is an emotionally charged practice that can assist children in making sense of the events in the world and their own experiences. It can contribute to children's development of understanding the story, events, actions, and motives of characters, as well as the teller's and audience's responses (Goodwin, 1990; Ochs & Capps, 2001). Storytelling for and with children can be organized so as to create a situation where young children together with teachers can immerse themselves in early literacy by cooperating in aesthetic experiences and affective evaluation of story characters and events. The story format and the teachers' embodied choreography of the telling can invite the children to experience and to participate in the telling, and in such a way engage them in a jointly entertaining and 'enchanting' activity. The teachers can exploit several embodied features in the telling and, together with the children, configure affectively marked performance of various characters and their actions, and engage the child audience into attentive listening.

Affective Dramatizations, Multiple Voices, and Embodied Stances

In storytelling, embodied emotional expressions can be configured to express various emotions, such as fear, sadness, or happiness. Teachers can use their body orientation, and so called 'lighthouse gaze' (Cekaite & Björk-Willén, 2018) when they turn their head to gaze at each child in turn, shifting their observant gaze to look at and notice the entire children's group. In doing so, they express and mediate their emotional expressions to the child audience and can share a specific emotion with the children. Dramatization of various story characters can be used by teachers to captivate the audience. The teachers vividly perform emotionally charged dramatizations and play out story events and dialogues by using multiple affectively charged voices, capitalizing on their full dramatic power. By changing voices and facial expressions, the teachers not only perform various characters, but also enact the teller's commentary upon the story actions. In such ways, they invite the child audience's emotional participation in the story (Cekaite & Björk-Willén, 2018).

In Extract 5.4, the teacher reads a well-known fairy tale *Little Red Riding Hood (LRRH)* for a small group of three-year-olds. They sit on the sofa, cosily tucked in, children seated on both side of the teacher. During the telling, the teacher utilizes different voices, dramatic changes in pitch (from low to high), and intonation while telling the story.

Extract 5.4

```
1   Teacher:   'vem äh det'.
               'who is it?'.
2              ((changes voice))
               ropade farmor- eller mormor.
               calls grandma or grandma.
3              ((gazes at children to right))(0.2)
4              'det är jag Rödluvan'.
               'it is me LRRH'.
5              ((changes voice))
               svarade vargen.
               the wolf answered.
6              ((changes voice))
               'kom in kom in Rödluvan'.
```

```
        come in come in LRRH.
7       ((changes voice))
        sa mormor och vargen.
        said grandma and the wolf
8       han öppnade dörren och sprang in.
        he opened the door and ran inside.
```

Figure 5.1

```
9   Lilly:    ((Figure 5.1, raises her hands, opens
              her mouth, 'scared' face))
10  Teacher:  Och
              And
```

Figure 5.2

((Figure 5.2, raises one hand, 'scared' face, looks at children to her right))
11 *och åt upp* ***he****la mormor.*
and he ate grandma all up.
((turns to children on her left side, 'scared' facial expression))

The teacher in her telling has come to a point where dramatic suspense is built up: she sets up a dialogue between the wolf and grandmother by animating their voices. She acts as an animator who talks on behalf of another party (Björk-Willén & Aronsson, 2014). The teacher performs the wolf, grandma, and the narrator's commentary by using typical 'in character' voices and builds up suspense (lines 1–11). When the teacher narrates the exciting and scary event, saying that wolf 'opened the door and ran inside oh' (line 8), one of the girls, Lilly, performs the emotion of 'being frightened': she covers her open mouth with her hand, hiding a 'scared' facial expression, Figure 5.1, line 9). Lilly's embodied emotional display predicts that some frightening events are imminent in the story. The teacher immediately takes up and repeats Lilly's embodied enactment of being 'frightened' as she adopts a similar facial expression and gestures (Figure 5.2). Simultaneously, she narrates the main, dramatic, event of the plot: the wolf eating up the grandmother (line 11). Together, the child and the teacher establish and show their emotional expression towards the events in the story.

The teacher's actions are multifaceted: her narrative performance is not only informative about the story, but is also emotionally charged, and distributed across the children's audience. Several messages are combined in this educational activity. The teacher uses a 'lighthouse' gaze (Cekaite & Björk-Willén, 2018), turning to look and observe the children on either side of her. Her 'lighthouse' gaze and facial expression monitor the children's attention and mediate her emotional expression: she publicly displays the 'frightened' emotional expression – which originated in Lilly's performance – to the other children (lines 9; 11). In this way, the teacher publicly shows that she shares the child's emotion and makes it possible for the other children to observe this mutual reading of the book.

In all, the performance of the text of the story becomes a lived interactional template for the children to understand the social events, and their emotional and moral consequences. In this sense, emotionally charged performances of traditional stories can be seen as cultural artefacts that demonstrate what it is to be human in that embodied emotional expressions visualize the concepts of good and bad for the engrossed and 'enchanted' audience. In such a way, teacher-organized activities that encourage emotional engagement can be linked to moral work with children.

Recommendations for Practice

Teachers spend a considerable amount of time with children and in large peer groups, where they educate children and show care in emotionally laden caregiving tasks. In many ways, they work to create conditions for children's wellbeing. Therefore, interactional research can provide a ground for a greater understanding of how teachers can take part in children's emotional development and emotion socialization. Understanding how emotionally charged events are handled in different ways in various cultural contexts and with children of different ages can make it possible to discover methods for organizing these practices so that teachers can adequately address children's emotional competences. Overall, by using a broad range of interactional strategies, teachers are able to give children tools to express and regulate emotions and act as competent members of a community, both in the peer group and with adults. From the analyses of everyday interactions in preschools presented in this chapter, I identify some key suggestions for early childhood educators:

- Observe, identify, and evaluate successful and unsuccessful verbal and embodied practices employed when responding to children's anger, sadness, irritation, or fear. Pay attention both to the educators' as well as children's actions.
- Help children to infer causes of negative emotions and their consequences to others. In doing so, clarify how children's actions and emotional conduct are related to the normative rules, values, and expectations concerning solidarity and others' wellbeing.
- Teach by talking and enacting the social meanings and appropriate versus inappropriate uses of various emotions. In doing so, take a point of departure in concrete, daily situations characterizing children's everyday life and concerns.
- Provide children with explicit rule statements and summary of the rules in order to mitigate an emotionally charged situation. In peer conflicts, this type of strategy – providing a summary of the rules – can defuse negatively charged situations and assist in regulating the child's emotions.

- It is important to attend to children's positive emotional expressions, to actively pursue the sharing of positive emotions with and between children, and to assist children in discovering various ways of showing affiliation and support to others.

References

Ahn, J. (2010). 'I'm not scared of anything!' Emotion as social power in children's worlds. *Childhood*, 17, 94–112.

Ahn, J. (2016). 'Don't Cry, You're Not a Baby!': emotion, role and hierarchy in Korean language socialisation practice. *Children & Society*, 30, 12–24.

Andrén, M., and Cekaite, A. (2016). Don't laugh! Socialization of laughter and smiling in pre-school and school settings. In A. Bateman & A. Church (eds.), *Children's Knowledge-in-Interaction: Studies in Conversation Analysis* (pp. 127–147). Singapore: Springer.

Bateman, A. (2015). *Conversation Analysis and Early Childhood Education. The Co-production of Knowledge and Relationships*. Surrey: Ashgate Publishing.

Bateman, A. (2020). Young children's affective stance through embodied displays of emotion during tellings. *Text & Talk*, 40, 643–668.

Bergnéhr, D., and Cekaite, A. (2018). The forms and functions of touch in a Swedish preschool. *International Journal of Early Education*, 26, 312–331.

Björk-Willén, P. (2018). Learning to apologize: moral socialization as an interactional practice in preschool. *Research on Children and Social Interaction*, 2(2), 177–194.

Björk-Willén, P., and Aronsson, K. (2014). Preschoolers' 'animation' of computer games. *Mind Culture and Activity*, 21, 316–318.

Burdelski, M. (2010). Socializing politeness routines: action, other-orientation, and embodiment in a Japanese preschool. *Journal of Pragmatics* 42, 1606–1621.

Burdelski, M. (2013). 'I'm sorry, flower'. Socializing apology, relationships, and empathy in Japan. *Pragmatics and Society*, 4(1), 54–81.

Burdelski, M. (2020). 'Say can I borrow it': teachers and children managing peer conflict in a Japanese preschool. *Linguistics and Education*, 59, 100728.

Burdelski, M. and Evaldsson, A-C. (2019). Young children's multimodal and collaborative tellings in family and preschool interaction. *Research on Children and Social Interaction*, 3, 1–5.

Burdelski, M., and Mitsuhashi, K. (2010). 'She thinks you're *kawaii*': socializing affect, gender and relationships in a Japanese preschool. *Language in Society*, 39, 65–93.

Calkins, S., and Hill, A. (2007). Caregiver influences on emerging emotion regulation. In J. Gross (ed.), *Handbook of Emotion Regulation* (pp. 229–248). New York, NY: Guilford Press.

Cekaite, A. (2012). Affective stances in teacher-student interactions: language, embodiment, and willingness to learn. *Language in Society*, 41, 641–670.

Cekaite, A. (2013). Socializing emotionally and morally appropriate peer group conduct through classroom discourse. *Linguistics and Education*, 24(4), 511–522.

Cekaite, A. (2020). Triadic conflict mediation and perspective taking in a Swedish preschool. *Linguistics and Education*, 59(2), 100753.

Cekaite, A., and Andrén, M. (2019). Children's laughter and emotion sharing with peers and adults in the preschool. *Frontiers in Psychology*, 10, 852.

Cekaite, A., and Björk-Wilén, P. (2018). Enchantment in storytelling: co-operation and participation in children's aesthetic experience. *Linguistics and Education*, 48, 52–60.

Cekaite, A., and Burdelski, M. (2021). Crying and crying responses: a cross-cultural exploration of pragmatic socialization in a Swedish and Japanese preschool. *Journal of Pragmatics* (online). https://doi.org/10.1016/J.PRAGMA.2021.03.012

Cekaite, A., and Ekström, A. (2019). Emotion socialization in teacher-child interactions: teacher responses to children's negative emotions. *Frontiers in Psychology*, 10, 185.

Cekaite, A., and Holm Kvist, M. (2017). The comforting touch. Tactile intimacy and touch in managing children's distress. *Research on Language and Social Interaction*, 50, 109–127.

Curriculum for the Preschool, Lpfö 2018. Available at: www.skolverket.se/publikationsserier/styrdokument/2019/curriculum-for-the-preschool-lpfo-18 [last accessed 12 December 2021].

Danby, S., and Baker, C. (1998). 'What's the problem?': restoring social order in the preschool classroom. In I. Hutchby and J. Moran-Ellis (eds.), *Children and Social Competence: Arenas of Action* (pp. 157–186). London: Falmer.

Danby, S., and Theobald, M. (2012). *Disputes in Everyday Life: Social and Moral Orders of Children and Young People*. New York, NY: Emerald.

Demuth, C. (2012). Socializing infants toward a cultural understanding of expressing negative affect. A Bakhtinian informed discursive psychology approach. *Mind, Culture and Activity*, 20(1), 1–23.

Denham, S., Bassett, H., and Zinsser, K. (2012). Early childhood teachers as socializers of young children's emotional competence. *Early Childhood Educational Journal*, 40(3), 137–143.

Du Bois, J., and Kärkkäinen, E. (2012). Taking a stance on emotion: affect, sequence, and intersubjectivity in dialogic interaction. *Text & Talk*, 32(4), 433–451.

Dunn, J. (2003). *Emotional Development in Early Childhood: A Social Relational Perspective*. In R. Davidson, S. Scherer, and H. Goldsmith (eds.), *Handbook of Affective Sciences* (pp. 332–346). Oxford: Oxford University Press.

Evaldsson, A-C., and Melander Bowden, H. (2020). Co-constructing a child as disorderly: moral character work in narrative accounts of upsetting experiences. *Text & Talk*, 40, 599–622.

Goodwin, M. H. (1990). *He-Said-She-Said.* Bloomington, IN: Indiana University Press.

Goodwin, M., Cekaite, A., Goodwin, C. (2012). Emotion as stance. In A. Peräkylä and M. Sorjonen (eds.), *Emotion in Interaction* (pp. 16–41). Oxford: Oxford University Press.

Hepburn, A. (2004). Crying: Notes on description, transcription, and interaction. *Research on Language and Social Interaction*, 37(3), 251–290.

Hilppö, J., Rajala, A., and Lipponen, L. (2019). Compassion in children's peer cultures. In G. Barton and S. Garvis (eds.), *Compassion and Empathy in Educational Context* (pp. 79–95). Basingstoke: Palgrave Macmillan.

Holm Kvist, M. (2018). Children's crying in play conflicts. A locus for moral and emotional socialization. *Research on Children and Social Interaction*, 2, 153–176.

Holm Kvist, M., and Cekaite, A. (2021). Emotion socialization – compassion or non-engagement – in young children's responses to peer distress. *Language, Culture, and Social Interaction* (online). https://doi.org/10.1016/j.lcsi.2020.100462

Hsuenh, Y., and Tobin, J. (2003). Chinese early educators' perspectives on dealing with a crying child. *Journal of Early Childhood Research*, 1(1), 73–94.

Johnson, S. J. (2017). Multimodality and footing in peer correction in reading picture books. *Linguistics and Education*, 41, 20–34.

Jools, P., and Elfer, P. (2013). The emotional complexity of attachment interactions in nursery. *European Early Childhood Education Research Journal*, 21(4), 553–567.

Kampf, Z., and Blum-Kulka, S. (2007). Do children apologize to each other? Apology events in young Israeli peer discourse. *Journal of Politeness Research Language Behaviour Culture*, 3(1), 11–37.

Kern, F. (2018). Mastering the body: correcting bodily conduct in adult–child interaction. *Research on Children and Social Interaction*, 2, 213–234.

Kidwell, M. (2013). Interaction among children. In J. Sidnell and T. Stivers (eds.), *The Handbook of Conversation Analysis* (pp. 511–532). Chichester: Wiley Blackwell.

Kusserow, A. (2004). *American Individualisms: Child Rearing and Social Class in Three Neighborhoods.* New York, NY: Palgrave Macmillan.

Kyratzis, A. (2001). Emotion talk in preschool same-sex friendship groups: fluidity over time and context. *Early Education and Development*, 12, 359–92.

Kyratzis, A. (2017). Peer ecologies for learning how to read: exhibiting reading, orchestrating participation, and learning over time in bilingual Mexican-American preschoolers' play enactments of reading to a peer. *Linguistics and Education*, 41, 7–19.

Kyratzis, A., and Köymen, B. (2020). Morality-in-interaction: toddlers' recyclings of institutional discourses of feeling during peer disputes in daycare. *Text & Talk*, 40(5), 623–642.

Lipponen, L., Rajala, A., and Hilppö, J. (2018). Compassion and emotional worlds in early childhood education. In C. Pascal, T. Bertram, and M. Veisson (eds.), *Early Childhood Education and Change in Diverse Cultural Contexts* (pp. 168–178). New York, NY: Routledge.

Moore, E. (2020). 'Be friends with all the children': friendship, group membership, and conflict management in a Russian preschool. *Linguistics and Education*, 59, 10074. https://doi.org/10.1016/j.linged.2019.06.003

Morita, E. (2019). Japanese two-year-olds' spontaneous participation in storytelling activities as social interaction. *Research on Children and Social Interaction*, 3, 65–91.

Ochs, E., and Capps. L. (2001). *Living Narrative: Creating Lives in Everyday Storytelling*. London: Harvard University Press.

Ochs, E., and Schieffelin, B. (2012). The theory of language socialization. In A. Duranti, E. Ochs, and B. Schieffelin (eds.), *The Handbook of Language Socialization* (pp. 1–22). Chichester: Wiley Blackwell.

Pursi, A. (2019). Play in adult-child interaction: institutional multi-party interaction and pedagogical practice in a toddler classroom. *Learning, Culture and Social Interaction*, 21, 136–150.

Reynolds, E. (2006). *Guiding Young Children: A Child-centered Approach* (4th ed.). Mountain View, CA: Mayfield.

Stern, D. (1985). *The Interpersonal World of the Infant*. New York, NY: Basic Books.

Tomasello, M. (2019). *Becoming Human: A Theory of Human Ontogeny*. Cambridge, MA: Harvard University Press.

6 | Socialization

MATTHEW BURDELSKI

Introduction

Early childhood education is a fundamental and dynamic site for fostering children's acquisition of knowledge and skills in tandem with their development as social beings. These intertwined aspects of learning occur through a process of socialization in which children acquire language along with institutional and cultural norms. The theory of *language socialization* (e.g. Ochs & Schieffelin, 1984, 2011) describes this dual process as 'socialization through the use of language and socialization to use language' (Schieffelin & Ochs, 1986, p. 163). It proposes that as children acquire the ability to understand and engage in interaction, they become familiar with ways of thinking, feeling, and acting that are characteristic of other group and community members. With its disciplinary roots in linguistic anthropology, language socialization shares a number of methodological and theoretical concerns with the field of conversation analysis (CA). Both camps are committed to examining how participants use talk and other communicative resources (e.g. gestures, facial expressions) to perform *social actions* (Atkinson & Heritage, 1984) and display *affective stances* in interaction (M. H. Goodwin, Cekaite, & C. Goodwin, 2012). While these two concepts will be discussed below, in general, social action refers to what speakers 'do' with talk and other communicative resources (e.g. make an apology, perform a request), whereas affective stance refers to the feelings, attitudes, or emotions they express towards their interlocutors and/or the focus of their talk (e.g. 'I'm fond of X'; 'Ugh, this is so difficult!'). In comparison to CA, language socialization is also centrally concerned with how social actions and stances *index* (Ochs, 1990; Silverstein, 1976) meanings related to identity and institutions (meso-level) and culture and society (macro-level). While the notion of index was originally discussed by Peirce (1955) as the relationship between a 'sign' and what the sign points to or indicates in the environment (e.g. smoke indicates fire), it was later argued by linguists to be applicable to *linguistic* signs, such as what the pronouns 'I' and 'you' or

Thank you to the editors and outsider reviewer who provided helpful feedback on this chapter.

the adverbs 'today' and 'here' refer to in any given discourse, which vary from one context to the other (e.g. Lyons, 1981). Moreover, the notion of index was also broadened by the linguistic anthropologist Michael Silverstein (1976) to include *social* indexes, or the ways that language can evoke socio-cultural meanings. For example, *tu* and *vous* in French or honorific markers in Korean and Japanese may point to the relationship (e.g. status differential, hierarchy) between the speaker and addressee. Social indexes include not only linguistic resources but also a wide range of paralinguistic (e.g. voice quality) and non-linguistic phenomena (e.g. gesture, facial expression), such as when a child 'makes a face' at another child to tease or taunt him or her.

There is a growing body of research in CA that examines ways in which discursive, institutional, and cultural meanings are brought into being in various settings (Antaki & Widdicombe, 1998; Stivers, Mondada, & Steensig, 2011), including within early childhood education (Bateman & Kern, 2018). However, there are few studies that attempt to bridge these two domains of inquiry in ways that can shed light on early childhood education (Burdelski, 2021). As Kimura, Malabarba, and Hall (2018) have recently argued, research utilizing CA in educational settings needs to pay more attention to how 'institutional, curricular, and temporal contexts within which a particular moment is situated to better understand local actions and sequences' (p. 13). Language socialization, with its interest in multiple levels of social context (e.g. *micro*, *meso*, and *macro*; see The Douglas Fir Group, 2016), can greatly assist us in this project. It can also go beyond the CA agenda by probing the cultural norms (e.g. morality, ideology) that are simultaneously informed by and constitutive of teachers' and children's talk.

This chapter approaches the topic of how adults in early childhood educational settings talk to children by examining the discursive, institutional, and cultural meanings that permeate teachers' everyday talk. Focusing on triadic *participation frameworks* (Bateman, Chapter 3, this volume; Goffman, 1981) of peer conflict mediated by teachers (Burdelski & Cekaite, 2020; Church & Moore, Chapter 19, this volume; Moore & Burdelski, 2020), it analyses two practices that have been extensively observed across preschools in various societies: (1) directives on what to say to peers, and (2) replaying the speech of a third-party peer. It will be argued that these practices are important vehicles for encouraging children to use and respond to talk as social action, and to use talk to display affective stance, which will be elaborated in the next section. Then, following an analysis of extracts from naturally occurring interaction of my own and others' research (micro level), it relates the findings to socialization into identity, institutional rules, and ideology (meso and macro levels), and suggests some pedagogical implications.

Talk as Social Action and Affective Stance

As mentioned above, both CA and language socialization are concerned with the ways that talk is deployed in the service of performing social actions and displaying affective stances in interaction. The CA notion of social action, which resonates with the earlier *speech act theory* (Austin, 1962; Searle, 1969), broadly refers to goal-directed communicative acts (e.g., apology, request, praise, complaint, invitation, report) (see Atkinson & Heritage, 1984). In comparison to speech act theory, however, where verbal/written acts (i.e. speech acts) were typically treated in isolation from their context or made up to illustrate a point, CA proposes that social actions must be examined in conversational data within turns at talk and the larger sequences in which they are embedded and emerge. Moreover, it views that what any utterance is performing as a social action is not only determined by the speaker, but also negotiated by the recipient who responds and, in the process, can display an understanding of what the utterance was 'doing' at that moment. For example, while an utterance such as 'It's hot in here', can be heard in a number of ways (e.g. as a request to open the window or as a complaint), how the recipient responds *co-constructs* (Jacoby & Ochs, 1995) the utterance as a specific kind of social action. While language socialization research is in alignment with this co-constructive view of social action, of central empirical concern for those examining interaction with children is showing *how* children are socialized to 'use' talk to perform social action, and to 'hear' an utterance, as well as to 'see' non-verbal behaviour, as social action. That is, for example, how does a child learn to use the phrase 'please X' as a request, and learn to interpret another's facial expression as a rejection? There is an array of practices for encouraging children to do so and various dyadic, triadic, and multiparty arrangements in which socialization occurs.

In terms of learning to use talk to perform social action, in my research on Japanese socialization (Burdelski, 2011), I have frequently observed how in triadic interaction parents and preschool teachers encourage young children what to say to others by providing them with a given expression followed by directives to say the expression to the third party, or what I refer to as *prompting* (e.g. Say 'thank you'). Japanese adults frequently use prompting to encourage children to use language to perform the social actions of appreciation, offers, requests, and apologies, and to provide answers to personal questions (e.g. child's name or age).

This practice of directing a child what to say (i.e. prompting) can be considered in relation to Goffman's (1981) notion of *participation frameworks*, which consists of complex *speakers* and *hearers* (C. Goodwin, 2007). Essentially, by providing a child with a linguistic expression accompanied by a directive to say it to another person, there are two 'speaker' roles associated with the utterance: the adult is the *author* (i.e. one who comes up with the words), and the child is its proposed animator (i.e. one who voices those words). One could relate this to movie actors, who animate the words that another person (i.e. screenwriter) has written for them.

In addition to performing their own social actions, children also learn to 'hear' others' talk as social action and then respond appropriately. In my research, for instance, I examined an extended episode of triadic interaction among a mother, her two-year-old daughter, and a four-year-old boy at a neighbourhood library (Burdelski, 2015). When the boy accidently knocked one of the books off the table and then declared aloud, 'Something fell' (*nanka ochita*), the girl's mother immediately repeated the boy's utterance to her as reported speech, 'He said it fell (*ochita tte*)', and then proceeded to orient the girl's body towards the book on the floor in encouraging her to hear this utterance as a request to pick it up. In this episode, the shape of the utterance and what it was 'doing' can be explicated as follows: a declarative is used to describe a state of affairs as 'Something fell', but should be heard as a request to 'Pick it up'. In this example, similar to a person dropping her own handkerchief on the ground and a bystander saying, 'You've dropped your handkerchief', here, by encouraging the girl to pick up the book, the mother positioned her as its current 'owner' who had an obligation and responsibility to pick up the book since she had originally taken it off the shelf so it was temporarily *her* book. The child's carrying out of the parent's directive required no verbal participation by the child, but rather non-verbal participation that entailed performing a social action with her body and the object. Thus, in some cases, social actions can be done silently through gesture and embodied action.

Talk (and non-verbal behaviours) not only performs social action but also displays stance, such as affective stance, which refers to the interactional display of 'mood, attitude, feeling and disposition, as well as degrees of emotional intensity vis-à-vis some focus of concern' (Ochs, 1996, p. 410). Ochs and Schieffelin (1989) proposed two categories for analysing the verbal expression of affect in interaction: *affect specifiers* and *affect intensifiers* (see also Burdelski, 2019). On the one hand, affect specifiers indicate the affective orientation of an utterance, such as lexical items (e.g. yummy, disgusting) and certain suffixes (e.g. X-*chan* in Japanese implying 'little X' or 'sweet X' for people, animals, and some objects). On the other hand, affect intensifiers modulate the affective strength of an utterance, such as adverbs (e.g. 'unbelievably handsome'), repetition (e.g. 'She's cute, she's cute'), and voice quality (e.g. saying something loudly may index a heightened affective stance). Importantly, any utterance can deploy both affect specifiers and affect intensifiers (e.g. saying 'I love you' in a loud voice or with an affectionate voice quality). Thus, for language socialization researchers, of central importance is to examine *how* children are socialized not only to feel towards others (including objects and animals) and about themselves (Moore, 2020), but also to 'use' talk to display affective stance. In prior research, I and a colleague examined how Japanese preschool teachers frequently used the word *kawaii* 'cute, adorable' with children to display a positive affective stance towards objects and children's appearances and actions, and how preschool children (mainly girls) used *kawaii* with peers (Burdelski & Mitsuhashi, 2010)

In sum, the process of language socialization thus entails acquiring language to interpret and perform social actions and display affective stances (socialization *to use* language). It also entails acquiring a familiarity with institutional and cultural norms (socialization *through* the use of language). An important setting in which this dynamic can be observed and considered in early childhood education settings is *peer conflict* (Church & Moore, Chapter 19, this volume), which for many preschool teachers takes up a significant portion of their daily attention and efforts. In what follows, I detail how talk is a vehicle of socialization by paying specific attention to social action and affective stance.

Data Analysis: Directives

In various situations, teachers attune children to use language as social action by deploying *directives* on what to say to peers (i.e. prompting). Directives refer to a communicative act of social control in which 'one participant *tells* another to do something' (Craven & Potter, 2010, p. 420). They are constructed with various turn formats, such as imperatives (e.g. 'Open the window!'), interrogatives (e.g. 'Would you be able to open the widow?'), and declaratives (e.g. 'I would like you to open the window'), and some formats such as imperatives are more linguistically 'forceful' and 'direct' (Ervin-Tripp, 1976). From an interactional perspective, when speakers use utterances to perform directives, it positions themselves 'as highly entitled to direct the recipient's behavior' (Drew & Couper-Kuhlen, 2014, p. 14). Thus, directives are often observed in interaction between participants where there is asymmetrical power and authority, such as parent-child (Goodwin & Cekaite, 2013; Takada, 2013; Chapter 21, this volume) and teacher-student (He, 2000). Specifically, directives - on what to say (or what not to say) and how to say it - have been observed in the reparatory phase of peer conflict mediation (Burdelski & Cekaite, 2020). They are aimed at attuning children to use talk as both *social action* and *affective stance*. Both of these dimensions (talk as social action and stance) will be examined next.

Attuning Children to Use Talk as Social Action

In mediating peer conflict, teachers often issue directives to children on what to say (i.e. prompts), such as *apologies* (Björk-Willén, 2018; Burdelski, 2010) and *requests* (Kryatzis & Köymen, 2020; LeMaster, 2020). These directives either provide the child with the expected utterance (e.g. 'Say sorry') or urge the child to come up with the expected utterance on his or her own (e.g. 'Do you have something to say?'). In talking to young children (e.g. two- and three-year-olds), teachers often provide the expected utterance accompanied by a directive to repeat it (i.e. *elicited imitation*; Burdelski, 2011; Hood & Schieffelin, 1978).

Apologizing

An illustration of a teacher using a prompt to encourage two children to produce an apology expression ('I'm sorry') is Extract 6.1 from a Swedish preschool (Björk-Willén, 2018). Just prior to the extract, while mediating in peer conflict between two girls (Lisa and Sally) in which Lisa admitted to having pinched Sally, a teacher has been told different versions of how the conflict started. Having heard the children's accounts, the teacher directs Lisa to apologize to Sally.

Extract 6.1 Swedish preschool (Björk-Willén, 2018, p. 182)

```
5→   TEA:   kan du säga förlåt till Sally=
            Can you say 'I'm sorry' to Sally?
            looks at Lisa
6    LIS:   =förlåt Sally
            I'm sorry, Sally.
7    SAL:   sits on the floor with her hands hiding her
            eyes
8    TEA:   hörde du Sally
            Did you hear, Sally?
```

9 SAL: ***nods still hiding her eyes with her hands***
10→ TEA: *ska du säga förlåt också*
Can you also say 'I'm sorry'.
11 SAL: *FÖRLÅ:T*
I'm sorry.

As shown in lines 5 and 10, the teacher issues directives to the girls, one at a time, to produce an apology expression. More specifically, she provides the expression ('I'm sorry') accompanied by a directive to repeat it, using a *modal interrogative* ('Can you say'). These directives encourage the children's reciprocation of apologies. In comparison, research in a Japanese school (Burdelski, 2010) has also observed the use of prompting to encourage children to produce apology expressions; however, instead of reciprocating the apologies, teachers often urged the addressee of the apology to respond with a verbal acknowledgement (*ii yo* 'It's okay'). The reciprocation of apologies indexes both children as blameable for acts that led to the conflict, whereas an asymmetrical apology indexes only one child as blameable. In terms of socialization to use language, we see preschool teachers in various societies prompting children to say fixed linguistic expressions (e.g. 'I'm sorry'), to perform the social action of apology in resolving peer conflict.

As mentioned above, verbal directives index the speaker (teacher) as having entitlement to direct the addressee's (child's) action (Drew & Couper-Kuhlen, 2014). From a relational perspective, they also index the addressee as having little or no entitlement to decide his or her next action: Following a teacher directive, the child is expected to comply. Yet, children do not always comply. As we know, children may refuse, ignore, or display non-understanding of what to do next. In such cases, teachers in various societies often extend the sequence through further directives and other practices until the child complies (see M. H. Goodwin & Cekaite, 2013; Takada, Chapter 21, this volume, on family interaction). This is illustrated in Extract 6.2 from a United States preschool.

Prior to Extract 6.2, Theresa – an ESL learner who does not yet speak English well – has pulled another girl's (Amy) pigtails. The teacher has reprimanded her (e.g. 'Don't pull hair, Theresa!') and explained the consequences of Theresa's action (e.g. 'It hurts when you pull hair'). At line 27, we see the teacher direct Theresa to produce an apology expression to Amy.

Extract 6.2 United States preschool (LeMaster, 2020, p. 4).

```
27→   TEA:   Can you tell her 'sorry'?
28→          Say, 'Sorry'
29     THE:   tugs lightly at her own hair, then at Amy's
              pigtail
lines skipped
36→   TEA:   Theresa! You tell Amy 'sorry'.
lines skipped
43     TEA:   Theresa!
44     THE:   looks up at teacher's face
45→   TEA:   Say sorry!
46     THE:   Sorry
              softly, looking at Amy
47     TEA:   Okay.
```

When Theresa does not animate the teacher's apology expression – she continues to engage in the reprimanded behaviour (albeit, as shown in line 29, 'lightly' on her own hair and then on her peer's pigtails, possibly as a demonstration of understanding on what she is *not* supposed to do) – the teacher extends the directive sequence. Previous research has often observed that a recipient's non-compliance with a directive is followed by an upgraded directive, or one that is on the surface more linguistically 'direct' and pragmatically 'forceful' than the one that came before it (e.g. Craven & Potter, 2010). This is similar to what we observe here. Although the teacher's initial directive to say an apology expression is formatted as a modal interrogative (line 27: 'Can you tell her sorry?') – similar to the Swedish data presented in Extract 6.1, line 5 – in subsequent turns she upgrades her directives to imperative forms, such as 'Say sorry!' (lines 28, 36, and 45). This directive sequence is brought to closure when Theresa complies by animating the apology expression to Amy, to which the teacher responds with 'Okay' (i.e. *sequence closing third*; Schegloff, 2007) that is a minimal but positive acknowledgement of Theresa's compliance with the directive. This example sheds light on the observation that in encouraging children to use language to perform social action, teachers often have to expend a great deal of effort, such as repeating their prompts, when children do not immediately comply. This effort may be required when issuing directives to very young children and children who are second language learners, who may have trouble understanding the teacher's talk.

Requesting

In addition to expressions of apology, teachers use talk in ways that encourage children to perform *requests*. Requests are a social action in which 'one participant *asks* the recipient to perform a specific activity or asks for the transfer of an object from one place or person to another' (Curl & Drew, 2008, p. 136), and they include a range of sub-types, such as requests for permission, clarification, information, or advice. Prior to Extract 6.3, a girl (Mao: 2 years, 5 months) has attempted to surreptitiously pick up a toy (a tunnel from a train set) off the floor of a play area. This action was noticed by a nearby boy (Hamid: 2 years, 1 month) – a second language speaker of Japanese with low ability to speak the language – who begins chasing after her while crying. As we join their interaction, a teacher has come up to Mao and put her hands around her to stop Mao from running away with the toy.

Extract 6.3 Japanese preschool (Burdelski, 2020, p. 4).

3→ TEA: *ka:shi:te: tte yuu no ga saki desho:::::*
First you say, "Can I borrow it (lit. lend it)," right?
stops MAO and turns her toward HAM
4 HAM: ***crying***
5 MAO: *ka:shi:te.=*
Can I borrow it (lit. Lend it).
6 HAM: ***crying***

As shown in line 3, while turning Mao's body towards Hamid, the teacher issues a directive to Mao to say a request expression (line 3: 'First you say can I borrow it [lit. lend it], right?'). This expression ('Can I borrow it [lit. lend it]') is a permission request for *object transfer* (Takada & Endo, 2015). In the teacher's directive, the request expression is accompanied by a reported speech frame ('First you say …'). At the end of this directive, the teacher uses the pragmatic particle *ne* (similar to an English tag-question, 'right?'), which indexes a shared understanding (i.e. *epistemic status*; Heritage, 2012) of what to say in this situation. That is, through her prompt, the teacher positions Mao as being familiar with this expression, and just needing a gentle reminder of what to say in this context. Her directive indexes not only the absence of the request in the child's conduct, but also a sequential relation between talk and action: the request needs to be produced *before* taking the object. Directives to perform such requests were often observed in this Japanese preschool, such as when a child had encroached upon another's game or play space without seeking permission first (e.g. *nosete tte* 'Say, can I ride'; *irete tte* 'Say, can I enter [your game]').

As observed above, in mediating peer conflict, early education teachers often issue directives to children on what to say to peers. The directive format ranges from imperatives (e.g. 'You must say sorry') to interrogatives ('Can you tell him you're sorry?'); a combination of formats may be used when children do not comply. These directives are an important means for encouraging children *to use* language as social action, such as making apologies and requests in managing peer conflict. Such prompts can also socialize children to avoid peer conflict. For instance, when a child makes a request for a toy instead of taking it away, this potentially pre-empts conflict.

Attuning Children to Use Talk as Affective Stance

In addition to performing social action, teachers encourage children to use language to display *affective stance*. As mentioned above, affective stance refers to emotional intensity, disposition, mood, attitude, or feeling regarding a focal concern (Ochs, 1996; see also M. H. Goodwin, Cekaite, & C. Goodwin, 2007). While affective stance is on a gradient of positive to negative, in situations of conflict teachers often treat children's talk and other acts as having displayed a negative affective stance, and encourage them to instead display a positive affective stance, as illustrated in Extract 6.4.

In a Japanese preschool (Burdelski, unpublished data), two girls (Kana, 3 years, 3 months and Hina, 3 years, 2 months) had been playing together when Hina picked up one of two balls that Kana had accidentally dropped on the floor and began to walk away with it, leading to Kana yelling a claim of possession ('IT'S MINE:::!' *KANA NO:::!*). In response, a nearby teacher (TE1) urged the girls to each hold one ball (rather than two balls), and took one of the balls away from Hina. We join the interaction when another teacher (TE2), who had been an observer until now, addresses Kana (line 1) about her verbal conduct, which she cast as being very negative towards Hina.

Extract 6.4 Japanese preschool (Burdelski, unpublished data)

```
1    TE2:   sonna okora[nai] de.
            Don't get so angry.
2    TE1:              [so ] so [so so.
                   Right, right, right, right.
3    TE2:                       [yasashiku yuu no.
                     Say it nicely.
```

```
4     TE2:   shiwa yosete okoro[nai de.
             Don't get angry with a scowl.
5     TE1:             [(shiwa)
                       scowl
6     KAN:             [datte (   )
                       But (   )
7     TE2:   kawaii o[kao de (   )
              (   ) with a cute face.
8     KAN:            [datte [mottechatta n da mon.
             But, it's that she took it from me.
9     TE1:                   [°soo yo::::::°
                         That's right.
10→   TE2:   un, dakara mottekanai de tte.
             Mm, so say, "Don't take it away."
             high pitched, soft voice
```

Figure 6.1 Teacher-2 tilts head to side.

```
11→          [so]re Kana na no yo tte ieba ii no.
             You should say, "That's mine".
             high pitched, soft voice; tilts head to side
12    TE1:   [un]
             Mm.
13    TE2:   sonna okonnai [no.
             Don't get so angry.
14    TE1:                 [soo yo::::
                            That's right.
```

As shown in line 1, teacher-2 upbraids Kana for her yelling 'IT'S MINE!' by issuing a directive to her on what *not* to do ('Don't get so angry'). Similar to other research on peer conflict in preschool (Moore, 2020), with this directive the teacher interprets the child's communicative behaviour as having expressed a negative affective stance of 'anger' (i.e., *cultural gloss*; Burdelski, 2015; Ochs & Schieffelin, 1995). She continues by issuing directives to Kana to speak 'nicely' (line 3), to not 'scowl' (line 4), and to speak with a 'cute face' (line 5). When Kana responds by providing an account for her own yelling (line 8: 'But it's that she took it from me'), the teacher issues two directives to Kana on what to say as an alternative. In the first, she provides Kana with an expression aimed at prohibiting Hina's action (line 10: 'Say don't take it away'). In the second, she reformulates Kana's prior claim of ownership (line 11: 'You should say, that's mine'). Both of these expressions can be heard as requests for object transfer (i.e., to return the ball), and they are produced in a soft tone. Similar to the notion that requesting is often a 'sensitive' or 'delicate' communicative practice (i.e., a *dispreferred* action; Schegloff, 2007), here the teacher uses a high-pitched voice in producing these expressions, which demonstrates how to 'soften' or mitigate them in a way that indexes a positive affective stance (e.g. being 'cute,' speaking 'nicely' as in lines 3 and 7). In addition, in the second directive (line 11), the teacher tilts her head to the side (Figure 6.1), which demonstrates in an embodied way how to soften the request – tilting the head to the side is often viewed as a sign of 'cuteness' in Japan, especially for girls. Sequentially, having come *after* the child's yelling her claim of ownership ('IT'S MINE!'), the teacher's directives operate on the child's prior talk to her peer as 'problematic'. In this way, the teacher's talk simultaneously performs the social action of *correction*. Specifically, the teacher's utterances can be characterized as *exposed correction*, in which correcting another's talk becomes 'the current interactional business' (Jefferson, 1987, p. 90). Here, this correction is aimed especially at the child's original tone of voice, loudness, and facial expression. In response to the teacher, Kana neither overtly accepts or rejects the teacher's suggestions, which is not treated as a problem here as Kana is ostensibly not expected to repeat them now but when encountering a similar situation in the future.

In comparison to Extracts 6.1 to 6.3, in Extract 6.4 the teacher's directives were aimed at a child's talk in ways that encouraged her to replace a negative affective stance (i.e. anger) with a positive affective stance (i.e. speaking nicely and with a cute face). Previously we have observed that teachers' directives on what to say can become extended when the child does not comply (Extract 6.2). Here, the extension is also related to the child's non-compliance, but in a different way: Kana 'talks back' to the teacher by providing an account for why she yelled at Hina (line 8: 'But it's that she took it from me'). In this extended sequence, the teacher's directives are aimed not only at *what* to say, but also *how* and *how not to* speak, which conveys to the child how to avoid displaying a negative affective stance through talk, prosody, and facial expression. Thus, we see that in encouraging children to use language to perform social action, teachers also instruct children how to use language to display specific affective stances. This is an example of socialization on how to use language, as well as how not to use language, aimed at the affective and emotional aspects of language use.

Replaying the Talk of a Third Party

In mediating peer conflict, a second teacher practice that has been observed is replaying the talk of a third party (e.g. 'He's asking you to stop'; 'She says she wants it back'). Such replayings can take the form of *reported speech* (e.g. Holt & Clift, 2007), or an utterance utilizing verbs or other (grammatical, lexicon, prosodic) markers of quoting talk such as 'say' (e.g. 'He said', 'She asked'). Here, replayings are limited to a specific kind of embedded speaker (i.e. third party) and sequential position (i.e. following a turn by a child that implicates the opponent's next action). In replaying the talk of a third party, the role of 'speaker', in Goffman's (1981) sense, can be described as having several sub-roles: the caregiver is the 'animator' of the embedded talk and the third-party child is positioned as its 'author'. We often observe teachers replaying children's *requests* to peers, which take various turn formats such as imperatives and declaratives, as discussed earlier.

A teacher's replaying of a third party's request for permission is illustrated in Extract 6.5 from a Japanese preschool (Burdelski, 2020).

Extract 6.5 Japanese preschool (Burdelski, 2020, p. 4)

```
3    TEA:   ka:shi:te: tte yuu no ga saki desho:::::
            First you say, "Can I borrow it" [lit. lend
            it]," right?
            stops MAO and turns her toward HAM
4    HAM:   crying
5    MAO:   ka:shi:te.=
            Can I borrow it [lit. Lend it].
6    HAM:   crying
```

```
7→    TEA:    kashite da tte.
              She said, "Can I borrow it [lit. lend it]".
              takes toy out of MAO's hands
8     HAM:    (nn)
              takes toy out of TEA's hands
9     TEA:    dame na no?
              It's no good?
```

When Mao utters the expected expression of request to Hamid (line 5), Hamid continues to cry (line 6). In response, the teacher replays Mao's request to him as direct reported speech (line 7: 'She said, "Can I borrow it"'). In Japanese interaction with young children there is a tendency to replay others' speech as direct reported speech ('She said, "Can I borrow it"'), rather than as indirect reported speech ("She's asking you if she can borrow it"), but in other societies we might observe the opposite (see Extract 6.6 from a Swedish preschool). Such replayings are often found in sequential contexts where one child has initiated a social action (i.e. *first pair part*) and the addressed child has not immediately produced a relevant response (i.e. *second pair part*). In this way, replaying a third party's utterance encourages the addressed child to 'hear' (i.e. listen to and display their understanding of) the original utterance as a social action by producing an expected response (i.e. a *conditionally relevant response*; Schegloff, 2007), such as by either granting or rejecting the request. When Hamid responds to the teacher's reported speech by producing an inaudible utterance while taking away the toy that is now in the hands of the teacher (line 8), the teacher displays her understanding of Hamid's behaviour as rejecting Mao's request (line 9: 'It's no good?'). In this way, teachers' replayings urge the addressed child to perform a next action, but leave it to him or her to figure out the next relevant action and thus can position the child as having an entitlement to choose how to respond. Thus, we could say that replayings provide the child with a good deal of agency, by positioning him or her as competent and capable of making their own decisions on how to respond, which may contribute to their own socialization of using and responding to language as social action.

In addition to requests for permission, we frequently observe teachers replaying children's requests for *action* to peers that were in the form of a *prohibitive* (e.g. 'She's asking you to stop doing X') or desire/*need statement* (e.g. Ervin-Tripp, 1976) in Extract 6.6 from a Swedish preschool (Cekaite, 2020). Just prior to the extract, a peer conflict has erupted in a room where no teachers were present. When a boy (Miran, 4 years) had pulled on the back of another boy's shirt (Johnie, 3 years 5 months) causing him to fall down on the sofa, Johnie cried and then reported what happened to a teacher who responded by comforting him. The extract continues from there.

Extract 6.6 Swedish preschool (Cekaite, 2020, p. 4).

15 TEA: *gillar inte du det?*
Don't you like that?
16 JOH: ***shakes his head 'no'***
17 TEA: *nä, ibland kan jag också tycka att jag*
18 *inte vill att nån drar i linnen så här.*
No, sometimes I also think that I don't want anybody pulling on my shirt like this.
19 JOH: Uhhuhhu
20 TEA: *så. då kan man säga'nej det gör jag inte'*
OK. Then you can say 'no I don't (want to)'
21 JOH: *det gör jog inte:.*
I do:n't (want to).
whining voice
22 TEA: *ja bra::.*
Yes goo::d.
turns skipped
41→ TEA: *miran? förstår du vad johnie menade? han vill inte att du ska dra i tröjan.*
Miran? Do you understand what Johnie meant? He does not want you to pull his shirt.
demonstrates pulling
42 MIR: *looks down*
43 TEA: *tänker du på det då?*
So, are you thinking about this?
44 MIR: ***nods slightly***

After confirming with Johnie that he does not like having his shirt pulled on (lines 15–16), the teacher directs him to state his wishes (line 20: 'Then you can say "no I don't [want to]"'), which Johnie complies with by repeating the given expression. This expression of desire, which utilizes a negative formulation ('I don't [want to]'), can be heard as a request for action to the opponent: to refrain from pulling on Johnie's shirt. Following more talk (omitted here), the teacher invokes earlier talk in the sequence by replaying Johnie's expression of desire to Miran (line 41: 'He does not want you to pull his shirt'). In comparison to Extract 6.5 above, here the teacher's replaying is not framed with an explicit reported speech marker such as 'say' or 'ask' ('He does not want you to pull his shirt'), and is prefaced with a confirmation question to Miran (line 41: 'Do you understand what Johnie meant?'). Although Johnie's desire was expressed earlier in the sequence, the teacher replays Johnie's statement to encourage Miran to produce the relevant next action (i.e. to refrain from pulling on Johnie's shirt) but leaves it to him to figure out what that next action is. This replaying positions the addressee (Miran) as not being entitled to decide his next action, but instead as being able to figure out what he should do next: he is expected to comply with the embedded request (i.e. to stop pulling Johnie's shirt). When Miran responds to this replaying by putting his head down, the teacher treats this action as a relevant one with her confirmation question (line 43: 'So are you thinking about this?'). Thus, as we have also seen before (Extract 6.5, line 9), when children respond to teachers' replayings, teachers often *gloss* children's responses, including their non-verbal acts, as relevant ones. As mentioned earlier, this practice affords space for the child to make his or her own decision about what to do next as a competent social member in ways that contribute to an ability to use language and respond with social action.

Discussion: Socialization to Use Language and Socialization through Language

The preceding section has examined processes of socialization in settings of early childhood education by focusing on how children learn to use and respond to language as social action and use language to display affective stance. It has examined teachers' use of two central practices within episodes of mediating peer conflict, namely (1) directives on what to say to peers, and (2) replaying a third-party peer's talk. It has highlighted ways in which adults' talk, including their linguistic resources (e.g. formulaic expressions, verbs of speaking, quotative particles) and discursive practices (e.g. directives), is a central modality through which this socialization occurs. Qualitative data analysis from various early childhood education settings across the globe shows how these two practices share a capability to embed talk *within* talk, or social action *within* social action (Burdelski, 2015), such as an apology expression *within* a teacher's directive or a request expression within a teacher's replaying (itself a directive for action).

It can be argued that these two practices are important in many early childhood education settings for encouraging young children to use and understand talk as social action, and to use talk as affective stance, in ways that are fundamental to their acquisition of communicative skills and their development as social beings. This analysis of *socialization to use language* – including what to (not) say and how (not) to speak – allows for a discursively grounded discussion of another key aspect of language socialization: *socialization through the use of language*.

Socialization *through* language includes learning to understand and use language as an index of institutionally situated and culturally meaningful realties, among them identities and institutional rules (i.e. meso level of social context). In terms of identity, according to Ochs (1993), linguistic resources *directly* index stances and social actions, and stances and social actions in turn *indirectly* index identities, such as roles (e.g. speaker and addressee, teacher and student) and relationships (e.g. kinship, friendship). In mediating peer conflict, by using specific linguistic resources in their talk to perform the social action of directing children what to say, teachers indirectly index children's roles in the conflict activity, such as 'culprit' (e.g. animator of apology expression) and 'victim' (e.g. addressee of apology), without explicitly naming those identities or assigning blame. Moreover, in prompting children what to say and replaying other's talk, teachers are shaping children's next expected action while at the same time indexing them as having a particular identity: one who is competent and capable to carry out a next action.

This use of talk to directly index social action also indirectly indexes children's relationships to each other. For instance, as illustrated in a Japanese preschool (Extract 6.3), in issuing a directive to a child to perform the request expression *kashite* 'Can I borrow it [lit. lend it]' – an expression that is used with family members and close acquaintances but not with superiors or strangers (Hill et al., 1986) – the teacher indirectly indexed the children as close and familiar peers, thus fostering their relationship.

In relation to institutional rules, in issuing directives to children on what to say and replaying the talk of other peers, teachers evoked ways of being and acting in the preschool that are rooted in morality (e.g. 'good' vs. 'not good'), such as physically harming others ('not good'), asking for an object that is ostensibly in use by another ('good'), or yelling at another child who conveys that she or he does not want to be yelled at ('not good').

Teachers' talk also socializes children into ideologies (e.g. beliefs, values) of the societies, communities, or groups in which early childhood education settings reside (i.e. macro level). Some of these ideologies, particularly within post-modern industrial and democratic societies, include having agency to make one's own decisions, learning to take others' perspectives and recognizing their entitlements (e.g. to play with toys without having them taken away), as well as individual rights, needs, and desires. Socialization in early childhood education thus entails both the individual and the group, where tensions may arise between a need to promote children's autonomy and independence on the one hand and a need to encourage their conformity and adherence to group norms in resolving and avoiding conflict on the other hand.

Recommendations for Practice

The preceding analysis and discussion suggest the following pedagogical implications for the ways teachers talk with children in settings of early childhood education.

- Children may need explicit instruction on what to say, what not to say, how to speak, and how not to speak to peers. In providing this instruction, teachers might reflect upon whether it would be more useful to provide the child with the expected expression (e.g. 'Say, sorry'), or urge the child to come up with the expression on his or her own (e.g. 'What do you say')? As a guideline, with younger children (e.g. aged two to three) and less proficient second language learners, it might be beneficial to provide the expected expression, whereas for older children (aged three and above) it might be better to urge them to come up with the expression on their own.
- Children may require the replaying of the talk of third-party peers. In replaying this talk, teachers need to be aware that they are urging the child to perform a next action, but are positioning the child as competent to figure out what the next action should be. For this reason, in comparison to directives on what to say (especially those in which the teacher provides the expression: 'Say, I'm sorry'), such replayings may be more demanding for younger children than older children to respond to with a next relevant social action, which positions them as agents who have a choice in the next action such as accepting or refusing another child's request.
- Following a teacher prompt or replaying, when children ignore, refuse, or display non-understanding of the social action made relevant through

this talk, teachers might find it necessary to expend energy and time by repeating or reformulating their talk multiple times until children respond with a next relevant social action that displays their understanding of that talk.

- Finally, as early childhood education is a foundation of linguistic and social development, teachers should be aware that their talk provides valuable linguistic 'input' that not only promotes children's language acquisition, but also socializes cultural norms and expectations of how to interact with peers.

References

Antaki, C., and Widdicombe, S. (eds.). (1998). *Identities in Talk*. London: Sage Publications.

Atkinson, J. M., and Heritage, J. (eds.). (1984). *Structures of Social Action: Studies in Conversation Analysis*. Cambridge: Cambridge University Press.

Austin, J. L. (1962). *How to Do Things with Words*. Oxford: Oxford University Press.

Bateman, A., and Kern, F. (2018). Childhood interaction: establishing, maintaining and changing the moral order. *Research on Children and Social Interaction*, 2(2), 147–152.

Björk-Willén, P. (2018). Learning to apologize: moral socialisation as an interactional practice in preschool. *Research on Children and Social Interaction*, 2(2), 177–194.

Burdelski, M. (2010). Socializing politeness routines: action, other-orientation, and embodiment in a Japanese preschool. *Journal of Pragmatics*, 42(6), 1606–1621.

Burdelski, M. (2011). Language socialisation and politeness routines. In A. Duranti, E. Ochs, and B.B. Schieffelin (eds.), *The Handbook of Language Socialisation* (pp. 275–295). Malden, MA: Wiley-Blackwell.

Burdelski, M. (2015). Reported speech as cultural gloss and directive: socializing norms of speaking and acting in Japanese caregiver-child triadic interaction. *Text & Talk*, 35(5), 575–595.

Burdelski, M. (2019). Emotion and affective stance in language socialization. In S. E. Pritzker, J. Fenigsen, and J. M. Wilce (eds.), *The Routledge Handbook of Language and Emotion* (pp. 28–48). London: Routledge.

Burdelski, M. (2020). 'Say can I borrow it': teachers and children managing peer conflict in a Japanese preschool. *Linguistics and Education*, 59, 1–11.

Burdelski, M. (2021). Classroom socialisation: repair and correction in Japanese as a heritage language. *Classroom Discourse*, 12(3), 255–279.

Burdelski, M., and Cekaite, A. (2020). Control touch in caregiver-child interaction: embodied organization in triadic medication of peer conflict. In A. Cekaite and L. Mondada (eds.), *Touch in Social Interaction: Touch, Language and Body* (pp. 103–123). London: Routledge.

Burdelski, M., and Mitsuhashi, K. (2010). 'She thinks you're *kawaii*': socializing affect, gender, and relationships in a Japanese preschool. *Language in Society*, 39(1), 65–93.

Cekaite, A. (2020). Triadic conflict mediation as socialisation into perspective taking in Swedish preschools. *Linguistics and Education*, 59, 1–9.

Craven, A., and Potter, J. (2010). Directives: entitlement and contingency in action. *Discourse Studies*, 12(4), 419–442.

Curl, T. S., and Drew, P. (2008). Contingency and action: a comparison of two forms of requesting. *Research on Language and Social Interaction*, 41(2), 129–153.

The Douglas Fir Group (2016). A transdisciplinary framework for SLA in a multilingual world. *The Modern Language Journal*, 100(S1), 19–47.

Drew, P., and Couper-Kuhlen, E. (eds.). (2014). *Requesting in Social Interaction*. Amsterdam: John Benjamins.

Ervin-Tripp, S. (1976). 'Is Sybil there?' The structure of some American English directives. *Language in Society*, 5, 25–66.

Goffman, E. (1981). *Forms of Talk*. Philadelphia, PA: University of Pennsylvania.

Goodwin, C. (2007). Interactive footing. In E. Holt and R. Clift (eds.), *Reporting Talk: Reported Speech in Interaction* (pp. 16–46). Cambridge: Cambridge University Press.

Goodwin, M. H. and Cekaite, A. (2013). Calibration in directive/response sequences in family interaction. *Journal of Pragmatics*, 46(1), 122–138.

Goodwin, M. H., Cekaite, A., and Goodwin, C. (2012). Emotion as stance. In M-L Sorjonen and A. Perakyla (eds.), *Emotion in Interaction* (pp. 16–41). Oxford: Oxford University Press.

He, A. W. (2000). Grammatical and sequential organization of teachers' directives. *Linguistics and Education*, 11(2), 119–140.

Heritage, J. (2012). Epistemics in action: action formation and territories of knowledge. *Research on Language and Social Interaction*, 45(1), 1–29.

Hill, B., Ide, S., Ikuta, S., Kawasaki, A., and Ogino. T. (1986). Universals of linguistic politeness: quantitative evidence from Japanese and American English. *Journal of Pragmatics*, 10, 347–371.

Holt, E., and Clift, R. (eds.). (2007). *Reporting Talk: Reported Speech in Interaction*. Cambridge: Cambridge University Press.

Hood, L., and Schieffelin, B. B. (1978). Elicited imitation in two cultural contexts. *Quarterly Newsletter of the Institute for Comparative Human Development*, 2(1), 4–12.

Jacoby, S., and Ochs, E. (1995). Co-construction: an introduction. *Research on Language and Social Interaction*, 28(3), 171–183.

Jefferson, G. (1987). On exposed and embedded correction in conversation. In G. Button and J. R. E. Lee (eds.), *Talk and Social Organization* (pp. 86–100). Clevedon, Bristol: Multilingual Matters.

Kimura, D., Malabarba, T., and Hall, J. K. (2018). Data collection considerations for classroom interaction research: a conversation analytic perspective. *Classroom Discourse*, 9(3), 185–204.

Kryatzis, A., and Köymen, B. (2020). Morality-in-interaction: toddlers' recyclings of institutional discourses of feeling during peer disputes in daycare. *Text & Talk*, 40(5), 623–642.

LeMaster, B. (2020). 'Theresa! Don't pull her hair! You'll hurt her!': peer intervention and embodiment in U.S. preschools. *Linguistics and Education*, 59, 1–8.

Lyons, J. (1981). *Language and Linguistics: An Introduction*. Cambridge: Cambridge University Press.

Moore, E. (2020). 'Be friends with all the children': friendship, group membership, and conflict management in a Russian preschool. *Linguistics and Education*, 59, 1–12.

Moore, E., and Burdelski, M. (2020). Peer conflict and language socialisation in preschool: introduction to special issue. *Linguistics and Education*, 59, 1–6.

Ochs, E. (1990). Indexicality and socialisation. In J. W. Stigler, R. A. Shweder, and G. Herdt (eds.), *Cultural Psychology: Essays on Comparatives Human Development* (pp. 287–308). Cambridge: Cambridge University Press.

Ochs, E. (1993). Constructing social identity: a language socialisation perspective. *Research on Language and Social Interaction*, 26(3), 287–306.

Ochs, E. (1996). Linguistic resources for socializing humanity. In J. J. Gumperz and S. C. Levinson (eds.), *Rethinking Linguistic Relativity* (pp. 407–437). Cambridge: Cambridge University Press.

Ochs, E., and Schieffelin, B. B. (1984). Language socialisation: three developmental stories. In R. A. Shweder and R. A. Levine (eds.), *Culture Theory: Essays on Mind, Self, and Emotion*. Cambridge: Cambridge University Press.

Ochs, E., and Schieffelin, B. B. (1989). Language has a heart. *Text*, 9(1), 7–25.

Ochs, E., and Schieffelin, B. B. (2011). The theory of language socialisation. In A. Duranti, E. Ochs, and B. B. Schieffelin (eds.), *The Handbook of Language Socialisation* (pp. 1–21). Malden, MA: Wiley Blackwell.

Peirce, C. (1955). *Philosophical Writings of Peirce: Selected and Edited with an Introduction by J. Buchler*. New York, NY: Dover.

Schegloff, E. A. (2007). *Sequence Organization in Interaction: A Primer in Conversation Analysis*. Cambridge: Cambridge University Press.

Schieffelin, B. B., and Ochs, E. (1986). Language socialisation. *Annual Review of Anthropology*, 15(1), 163–246.

Searle, J. R. (1969). *Speech Acts: An Essay in the Philosophy of Language*. Cambridge: Cambridge University Press.

Silverstein, M. (1976). Shifters, linguistic categories and cultural description. In K. H. Basso and Henry A. Selby (eds.), *Meaning in Anthropology* (pp. 11–55). Albuquerque, NM: University of New Mexico Press.

Stivers, T., Mondada, L., and Steensig, J. (eds.). (2011). *The Morality of Knowledge in Conversation*. Cambridge: Cambridge University Press.

Takada, A. (2013). Generating morality in directive sequences: distinctive strategies for developing communicative competence in Japanese caregiver-child interactions. *Language & Communication*, 33, 420–438.

Takada, A., and Endo, T. (2015). Object transfer in request-accept sequence in Japanese caregiver-child interaction. *Journal of Pragmatics*, 82, 52–66.

7 | Epistemics

ILANA MUSHIN AND ROD GARDNER

Introduction

The term *epistemics* is now commonly used in ethnomethodology and conversation analysis (EMCA) to refer to the ways that participants in conversation attend to knowledge claims, and how these are asserted, contested, and defended in their contributions to the unfolding interaction (Heritage, 2012a, p. 370). The study of epistemics builds on longstanding observations that coherent talk and mutual understandings are only possible if participants are able to recognize and anticipate each other's knowledge with respect to what is being talked about (e.g. Clark, 1996; Tomasello, 2008). Under this interpretation, the management of knowledge is seen not only to be about what participants *actually* know, but also how they frame their own and the perceived others' knowledge with respect to authority over who has the primary rights to this knowledge. For example, while you and I might both know that I won the lottery recently, in the presence of another person, typically I will be the one authorized to tell the story of my prize, and I will be the one authorized to talk about how I feel about it. That is, typically, people are authorized to talk about their own direct experience and internal thought processes, but not automatically authorized to talk about other's direct experiences and internal thought processes. Participants in conversation thus recognize that not only do they come to the conversation knowing different things, resulting in asymmetries of knowledge, but that these asymmetries also extend to authority to talk about knowledge.

The study of epistemics in early childhood education recognizes that the practice of teaching is fundamentally about the management of epistemic asymmetries. Children attain new knowledge about the curriculum, classroom procedures, and ways of behaving in accordance with institutional requirements, usually from their teachers. Teachers are authorized within the institutional context of the school to be the providers and arbiters of this knowledge. This is not to say that children do not have agency over their own knowledge. Indeed, child-centred approaches to early childhood education views children's existing knowledge as a resource to be drawn on (e.g. Bateman, 2015; Bateman & Carr, 2017). However, it is recognized that in order to learn, students must be able to manage these asymmetries, recognizing what they do or do not know about the task at hand, and adopting strategies to resolve knowledge differences. Epistemics thus provides a lens through which researchers of classroom interaction can explore the ways in which teachers and students constitute their roles and manage learning environments (e.g. Gardner & Mushin, 2013, 2017; Jakonen & Morton, 2015; Kern & Ohlhus, 2017; Koole, 2010; Sert & Walsh, 2013). In this way, studies of epistemics in classroom interaction contribute new understanding of intersections between classroom management (including what Bernstein (2003) called 'regulative' discourse) and the teaching and learning objects of lessons (including what Bernstein (2003) called 'instructive' discourse).

In this chapter we first present a summary of research on epistemics in conversation analysis (CA) and early childhood education contexts before illustrating the ways in which knowledge asymmetries are managed by teachers and students in an Australian Prep class (the first year of school – typically for children turning five by June in that calendar year) to accomplish a complex task. Through this example we are able to show that the attribution of epistemic authority is locally managed and negotiated.

Epistemics in Conversation, Education, and Early Childhood Education

The management of knowledge in conversation can be understood primarily as one in which participants display a *stance* towards what they say that indicates how they have understood the relative relationships between all participants and the knowledge at hand (e.g. Heritage, 2012b; Mushin, 2001). This stance may be commensurate with the actual *status* of knowledge that a participant has, i.e. what they actually know, but it need not be. For example, participants may claim to lack knowledge that they actually have, when another participant is attributed a more primary claim to that knowledge, for example when someone talks about a child to that child's parent (e.g. Heritage & Raymond, 2005; Raymond & Heritage, 2006; Stivers et al., 2011).

Knowledge asymmetries exist not only in access to knowledge, but also authority over that knowledge. This has its linguistic roots in Labov & Fanshel's (1977) work on knowledge asymmetries in therapeutic talk (where the therapist has institutional expertise and the patient has expertise about their own experienced life), and in Kamio's (1997) pragmatic approach that focused on speakers interpretations of 'territories' of knowledge (what

Labov & Fanshel 1977 called an 'epistemic domain'), and the impact this had on the choice of linguistic structures, according to what is being talked about and participants' perceptions of who has primary rights to know.

Some aspects of language that teachers and children use are sensitive to epistemic factors. These include the choice of response tokens like *oh* (Heritage, 1984) and *right* (Gardner, 2007), which display the receipt of knowledge as prompting a 'change of state' from not knowing to knowing (in the case of *oh*), or recognizing connections to some information that has been articulated earlier (in the case of *right*). The use of evidential and epistemic constructions (e.g. adverbs like *apparently* and *obviously*, modals like *must* and *might*, quotation and epistemic phrases like *I think*) that display knowledge as (un)certain or (un)reliable (e.g. Kärkkäinen, 2003; Mushin, 2013) are another way that language expresses epistemic meanings. Language can therefore be used as a tool for educators to identify epistemic stances and to monitor learning in the classroom. As we show in the next section, children in early years education already show competence in utilizing at least some of these linguistic strategies for displaying epistemic stances in much the same way as has been described for adult talk.

This observation is consistent with the CA work to date on children's interactional competence which shows that by the time they start school, children are already highly competent social actors in turn-taking, orientation to sequential organization (e.g. knowing that their questions should be answered), and the accomplishment of recognizable social actions, such as offers or requests (e.g. Filipi, 2009, 2018; Kidwell & Zimmerman, 2007; Wootton, 2005 for very young children). Recent work examining epistemically relevant actions have focused on the ways in which young children answer questions (Filipi, 2018; Stivers et al., 2018), or the way in which children display an understanding of the status of direct perception as an indicator of having knowledge (Kidwell, 2011). However, there has been little work to date on how the management of knowledge asymmetries may apply in interactions involving young children, let alone in the context of early childhood education.

Of particular relevance to educators are the ways in which knowledge asymmetries affect the interpretation of utterances as requests for information (i.e. questions) or declarations of information (i.e. statements that inform). As Heritage (2012a) demonstrates for ordinary conversation, the attribution of knowledge in terms of speakers' epistemic domains influences the ways that utterances made with declarative (e.g. You are hungry) or interrogative (e.g. Are you hungry?) syntax may be understood as informing or questioning, even though declaratives are normally understood to be informing/making statements while interrogative syntax is normally understood as signalling that something is a question. We can see this epistemic asymmetry at play in Extract 7.1, from our corpus of Australian classes in the first year of formal schooling, where the teacher, Mrs Bathurst,[1] has just provided information to the whole class about the activity they are about to undertake.

Extract 7.1

```
1   Mrs Bat:     You:r jo:b. (0.3) fi:rst jo:b. (.)
                 *^On the ba:ck
                 *turns booklet
2                of the boo:klet.* (0.7) *You're going to
                 wri:te
                 around----------*       *points to back of
3                your na:me.*
                 booklet----*
5                (0.9)
6   Mrs Bat:->   What's your fi:rst job?
7   Childr:->    Write/Name/Write your name
8   Mrs Bat:     Wri:te your *na:me. E:xcellent.*
                             *puts booklet down-*
```

In line 1/2, Mrs Bathurst presents the first step in a multistep task involving the use of booklets (... *first job ... on the back of the booklet you're going to write your name*). As Mrs Bathurst is the teacher who has assigned this activity for the class, and therefore knows all of the steps that make up the task, her declarative syntax utterance is heard as an informing.

In line 6, Mrs Bathurst begins an initiation-response-evaluation (IRE) sequence (Mehan, 1979),[2] with an interrogative *what's your first job?* As she was the one who had just told the students what the first job was, the answer lies within her epistemic domain. This interrogative is not a request for information but rather a check of the children's' understanding of the first task step. As a result, the children's chorus of responses, summarized in line 7, are not treated as updating the teacher's knowledge of the '*first job*', and her response in the third turn includes an assessment (*excellent*) rather than an indication of a change of knowledge state (cf. Heritage, 1984).

Extract 7.1 also illustrates another principle concern of epistemic management in classroom interaction – the distinction first observed in Sacks

[1] Names of teachers and children have been changed for anonymity.

[2] IREs are common sequences in classrooms, whereby a teacher asks a question, one or more students answer, and the teacher evaluates the answer by accepting it, praising it, probing for more information, or rejecting it.

(1992, vol. 2, pp. 252–253) from a lecture given in 1970, between *claims* and *exhibitions* (or *demonstrations*) of understanding. According to Sacks (1992), a speaker's claim to understand does not necessarily mean that that person has actually understood. Evidence for understanding comes from demonstrations such as the novel application of understanding by recipients. Under this interpretation, the students' choral responses in line 7 (*write your name*), that merely parrot the teacher's framing of the instruction only display *claims* of understanding. Demonstrations of understanding in this instance would come from observing whether the children do actually write their names on the booklet as the first step in the activity sequence – something that is not done until later in the class (cf. Gardner & Mushin, 2017; Koole, 2010).

Epistemics, as outlined so far, provides researchers with a framework for understanding why participants structure their contributions in interaction in the ways that they do. This points to a central goal of analysis, namely to account for the occurrence of an utterance at a particular point in the unfolding talk, and emerging out of something in the prior talk. However, as we have shown here, knowledge management in classrooms is a central feature of schools as institutions, and there is an emerging interest among EMCA scholars on understanding epistemics in its role in supporting teaching and learning (recent examples include Bateman, 2015; Bateman & Church, 2017; Eskildsen & Majlesi, 2018; Heller, 2017; Jakonen & Morton, 2015; Kern & Ohlhus, 2017; Kunitz, 2018; Michalovich & Netz, 2018; Sert, 2013; Sert & Walsh, 2013). However, aside from Bateman (2015) and the collection of chapters in Bateman & Church (2017), this research has focused on older learners – in upper primary school, secondary school, and adult education classrooms – leaving much still to be discovered about how younger children and their teachers manage knowledge in classroom interaction.

Epistemic Management and Procedural Understanding: An Analysis of Epistemic Management

In the extended extract we have chosen, there is a wide range of ways in which knowledge and knowledge asymmetries are managed. The teacher introduces a detailed set of instructions for an activity that is preparatory for further work they will be doing later in the week. They will have to cut out two pictures of penguins, one with a capital 'A', and one with a lower case 'a', but they will need to follow six steps in a precise order. Yet, as Garfinkel

(1967) explained, no matter how carefully instructions are set out, they remain essentially incomplete and inevitably ambiguous. So, teachers often have to remind students what to do while they are engaged in the activity, and children may help each other, or observe and copy what other children are doing. Sometimes children will also dispute what they are supposed to be doing. The extended extract thus provides a rich environment through which we can illustrate how epistemics are managed by teachers and children, both during the time when the instructions are first given, and later when the children are engaged in the task.

The data come from a larger study of classroom interaction in the first year of formal schooling in Australia (the 'Prep' year) supported by the Australia Research Council (ARC DP150100113) called 'Talking knowledge, doing learning'. The data collected for this study consists of over eighty hours of video-recorded lessons in three public schools in Queensland. We used two or three cameras in each classroom and each child wore a Zoom H1 recorder in a pouch during the recording. In this way we were able to capture not only more than one angle or section of the classroom on video, but we were also able to hear what each child was saying. Our EMCA methods allow for insights on the effectiveness or otherwise of procedural instructions, how tasks are accomplished successfully, and what appear to be barriers to success in real-time classroom interaction (Mushin, Gardner, & Gourlay, 2022).

We selected the 'Penguins' task to illustrate how epistemics can be seen in the data as relevant to interpreting what the teacher and students do. This is a complex activity which follows immediately after the instructions were presented during 'carpet time' to the whole class. The task is to cut out pictures of two penguins on the first page of a six-page stapled booklet in preparation for a subsequent literacy activity. The multiple steps arise because before the children cut out the penguin, they need to write their names on the worksheet, and on a paper bag, and then they need to rip off the first page of the worksheet to make the scissor work easier. Next, they will colour in the penguins, and finally put the penguins in a paper bag.

Epistemics during Activity Instructions

We present the full set of instructions in Extract 7.2 to show the careful, staged way in which the teacher told them what they had to do, and consider the evidence for how different students attended to these instructions, and the epistemic dynamics of the interaction. We then focus on five students who were sitting at the same table while doing the activity – Annie, Ember, Hadlee, Naia, and Atini – and show how an analysis in terms of epistemic management reveals how epistemics in the classroom is not simply a matter of who knows what, but crucially, how this knowledge is negotiated moment by moment as they engage in the task.

Extract 7.2

```
1   Mrs Bat:   You:r jo:b. (0.3) fi:rst jo:b. (.)
               *^On the ba:ck of
               *turns booklet
2              the boo:klet.* (0.7) *You're going to
               wri:te your
               around-------*       *points to back of
               booklet--
3              na:me.*
               ------*
4              (0.9)
5   Mrs Bat:   What's your fi:rst job?
6   Childr:    Write/Name/Write your name
7   Mrs Bat:   Wri:te your *na:me. E:xcellent. (0.3)
               Your se:cond job
                           *puts booklet down------------
               -----------------
8              You're go*ing to get a pa:per ^ba:g.
               ---------*picks up paper bag and shows it
               to class
9   Annie:     Hm?
               ->
10  Mrs Bat:   What do you think you're gonna put ˇo:n:
               the
11             *paper ba:g.
    Annie      *raises her hand
12             *(0.5)
               *teacher points at Annie
13  Annie:     Um: your name?
14             (0.2)
15  Mrs Bat:   You:r na:me. *So you gotta wri:te your name
               how many
                            *holds up two fingers to
               class-------
16             ti:mes.
               -------
```

17 Childr: Two
---
18 Mrs Bat: Two:* ti::mes. (0.5) [O:n your boo:klet?
o:n the
----*
19 Annie: [Whah?
20 Mrs Bat: ba::ck? (0.7) and o:n your ba:g.
21 Mrs Bat: Once you've written your na:me, (0.3)
toda:y, (.)
22 <a:ll we are do:ing> (0.2) is the
<fi::rst> pa:ge.
23 (0.4)
24 Mrs Bat: So o:nce you've done your na:me, you're
going to::,
25 (0.4) r:ip off the fi:rst pa:ge,
26 Annie: Hm?
27 (1.2)
28 Annie: [^Ho:w.]
29 Mrs Bat: [*and the:n,*]
pretends to rip off the first page
30 (0.6)
31 Mrs Bat: I wo:n't do it cause this is (oh-) (0.4)
this will be
32 someone's booklet so they won't >have to
do: it<.
33 *(0.5)*
rips off the first page
34 Mrs Bat: Like tha:t.
35 (0.6)
36 Annie: Oh.
37 Mrs Bat: M'kay? Just rips off.
38 (0.2)
39 Mrs Bat: Okay?
40 (0.4)
41 Mrs Bat: I'm gonna ri:p off the first pa:ge, (0.4)
*and then
*circles
42 you're going to cu:t, ju:st the pe:ngui*n
ou:t.
the penguin picture with index finger--*
43 (0.5)

44 Mrs Bat: Don't worry about the wri:ting, that's all go:ing i:n
45 the bi:n. (0.2) *You're gonna cu:t out your pe:nguin,*
circles penguin with index finger---
46 *(0.2) o:n the dotted li::nes, (1.3)* and the:n you're
runs finger along dotted line----
47 going to co:lour i:n your pe:nguin, (1.5) *O:nce you've
*picks up
48 co:loured i:n your pe:nguin, you're go:ing to pu:t it,
paper bag to show the class----------->
(holds up paper bag until the end of extract)
49 (0.7)
50 Luisa: in there.
51 (0.2)
52 Mrs Bat: i:n your ba:g, which has your na::me on it.
53 (0.6)
54 Mrs Bat: And that's a:ll we're doing toda:y.

At the start of the extract, the class are seated on the floor facing the teacher, roughly in rows. Annie and Naia are next to each other in the front row, with Annie right in front of the teacher. Hadlee and Ember are in the middle rows and Atini is near the back.

The teacher tells the class that their first task is to write their names on the back of the booklet, which she holds up for them to see. She follows this with an immediate understanding check, 'What's your first job?' Several children, including Annie and Naia (but not Hadlee, Atini, and Ember) call out a range of responses, 'write', 'name', 'write your name' (line 6).

Next, she switches the booklet for a paper bag, announcing the 'second job', that they are going to get a paper bag. At line 9 Annie calls out 'Hm?', which is an 'open class repair initiator' (Drew, 1997), which is used to assert that you have *not* understood something. While Annie is the only child to vocalize a lack of understanding, the teacher, rather than respond solely to Annie, holds up the paper bag and addresses the whole class to announce the next task step. Rather than tell the children what to do, she attempts to get them to display their understanding by asking a question, 'What do you think you're going to put on the paper bag?' (line 10/11). In response, Annie raises her hand, is selected by the teacher, and she says, 'Um, your name?' (line 13), which the teacher accepts. Note that the teacher has provided these first two instructions in a careful and staged way. Writing their names on their work is routine, but writing their names twice would be unusual. This class occurred near the end of the school year, so the teacher knew the class well, and she is showing sensitivity to what she knows the children know, and that what they are being asked to do is new. The teacher now reinforces these two instructions with another question: 'So you gotta write your name how many times?' (line 15/16), further helping them by holding up two fingers. This is an example of how gesture can also be used in epistemic management in the classroom, by providing a non-verbal clue to the answer. Given the saliency of the gestural clue, a lot of the children call out 'two'. Annie then calls out what sounds like 'What?', suggesting the non-routine nature of writing one's name twice.

The third job, presented in line 24/25, is for the children to rip off the first page of the booklet.[3] The teacher simulates ripping the first page of the booklet she is holding and appears to be moving on with the next instruction but is prompted by Annie's 'how' question in line 28 to actually rip the first page off to fully demonstrate what is required. Mrs Bathurst responds to Annie's question by not shifting to the next instruction, but rather to making the ripping instruction clearer. This shows her sensitivity to not only monitoring epistemic status, but also her responsibility to ensure they have enough information to undertake the activity. Her demonstration of ripping is done with eyes gazing at Annie, who had prompted the question, but with the booklet and ripping action in full view of the whole class. In this way she doubly addresses Annie's particular concern while at the same time addresses other possible non-understandings of what 'ripping' the page means for this activity (St. John & Cromdal, 2016).

The fourth job is to cut out the penguins. Mrs Bathurst demonstrates this by tracing her finger around the dotted line that the children will follow with their scissors. She does this twice and includes additional information that they will not have to worry about the parts of the page that have writing on it. As there are no displays of non-understanding (or understanding), she moves straight on to the fifth job which is to colour in the penguins. There is no accompanying demonstration or specification of how the

[3] Although it is not made explicit during the instructions, it becomes apparent during the activity itself that the teacher's rationale for this ordering of ripping before cutting is to make the fine motor skills activity of cutting easier.

children are to accomplish this, indicative that colouring is a familiar activity. The final job is to put the two cut-out penguins in the paper bag and for this, Mrs Bathurst picks up a paper bag and utters a designedly incomplete 'Once you've coloured in your penguin you're going to-' which provides a space for children to demonstrate their understanding of what is to be done in the final step of the activity (Koshik, 2002; Margutti, 2010). Only one child, Luisa, attempts to complete the utterance ('in there' at line 50, gazing at the paper bag). Mrs Bathurst looks at Luisa while she completes the instruction 'in your bag which has your name on it'. While Luisa's response is accurate in that it picks out the paper bag as the unspecified location, Mrs Bathurst's reformulation additionally includes a reminder that the bag is to have a name written on it. In this way the teacher has again drawn attention to a part of the activity that is novel for the children – that they will need to write their name on a paper bag as part of an activity involving worksheets in a booklet (with which they are familiar).

In summary, Extract 7.2 has shown how the teacher presents this six-step activity with planned formulations that present task steps as known or knowable to the children (e.g. the use of teacher routines such as the IRE format in lines 10–15 and the designedly incomplete utterance in line 48), evidence that the teacher is taking children's epistemic status into account. It also illustrates how the teacher modified her plan in response to children's' claims of understanding or non-understanding, which is evidence that she is monitoring for signs of epistemic status.

We have focused so far on Annie's verbal turns in this extract as evidence for her epistemic status. However verbal contributions are only one way of displaying how one is engaging with the knowledge. Annie is the most vocal of the children by far, and her contributions provide clear displays of her engagement with learning – in this case learning about how the task is to be accomplished. In addition to these verbal contributions, Annie also shows a wide range of non-verbal attention behaviours, including following the teacher's focus with her gaze for joint attention (Kidwell & Zimmerman, 2007) and maintaining a forward-leaning posture. She has also bid for and answered a question correctly and joined in choral answers. While less vocal than Annie, Hadlee and Naia also maintain their attention on what the teacher is showing them, with Naia also leaning forward throughout these instructions.

In contrast with these children, Atini is showing very different attention behaviours. At the start of the extract he is gazing at the teacher, but when she checks what their first job is (line 5), he is making sounds into his voice recorder (i.e. the device provided by the researchers to capture children's talk), and he continues to gaze at the boys around him and to make noises into his voice recorder again, so he is distracted through most of the first two instructions. This extended distraction would suggest that he is likely to have missed information about what to do in these first two steps, so if that is the case, he will need to find other paths to the knowledge he needs later if he is to start the task successfully. When Mrs Bathurst comes to the instruction to rip off the first page (line 24–25), Atini is thoroughly distracted, which will turn out to be consequential. Atini also fidgets a lot, does not look at the teacher, except when she says 'You're going to rip off the first page', but he continues to interact with the boy next to him, including when the teacher actually demonstrates ripping off the first page, and when she says, 'You're going to cut just the penguin out' (line 42). For the rest of the instructions, Atini's gaze is on the teacher.

Ember is also distracted, but in different ways. When they are told to write their names on the back of the booklet, she is gazing at the teacher, but her eyes are not moving, so she is not following the subtle shifts to where her attention needs to be. A potentially more serious distraction occurs when they are told to write their name on the back of the paper bag. She is looking behind her at Atini and the other boy making noises into their voice recorders. The consequences of this distraction can again be tested by seeing whether she knows she needs to write her name on the paper bag when she is doing the activity. Ember is back to attending when the teacher announces, and demonstrates, ripping off the first page; she is leaning forward, tilting her head to the left for a more direct line of sight to the teacher. Just after the teacher rips off the page, Ember opens her mouth a little, and her head tilts up slightly: two subtle embodied attention gestures. The timing of these coordinated movements suggests she is actively attending to this instruction, although she has given no indication at this stage of whether she has understood the instructions or not.

Following Extract 7.2, Mrs Bathurst spends about forty seconds telling them what they will be doing for this project later in the week, before returning to a summary of the instructions for the task just prior to handing out booklets and the children taking their places at tables to begin the activity. This summary is provided in Extract 7.3, which directly follows on from the explanation of the rest of the project during the week.

Extract 7.3

```
1   Mrs Bat:   But today, a:ll you're doing is writing
               your na:me,
2              (0.6) Seamus, and cu:tting, ripping off the
               fro:nt
3              pa:ge, and doing your two letter A:s.
```

```
4   Mrs Bat:   Okay? That's it.
5              (0.3)
6   Mrs Bat:   That's a:ll you're doing toda:y.
7   Mrs Bat:   Alri:ght.
```

The teacher's summary is disrupted by some behaviour management, when she calls out Seamus' name. This may have affected her summary, because just after this she mentions 'cutting, ripping off the front page', which are in the opposite order from when she first gave the instructions. She also does not mention writing their names twice, nor does she remind them to put the cut-out penguins in the paper bag. This deviation from the first, detailed set of instructions will also have its consequences. Atini's gaze is back on the teacher during the summary, and he has shifted away from the boy he was interacting with earlier. So, what he has heard is that they need to cut first, then rip. He also says, after the summary, 'I can't cut the penguin out', which demonstrates that he knows what he is being asked to do, even though he claims to lack the skills to do it.

To compare the five children: Annie, Hadlee, and Naia's attention behaviours were exemplary, with Annie displaying the most active engagement through her verbal contributions. Ember's attention wandered, at times focusing on the teacher, at other times watching children in the classroom. Atini was very distracted for much of the time, but did attend intermittently, most notably during the summary at the end. If the varying attention behaviours of these three children is to predict their understanding of the task, then we would expect Annie, Hadlee, and Naia to be successful in the task, but Ember and Atini to run into some problems.

Epistemics while Doing the Activity

We have so far seen how *epistemic status* (the actual knowledge that someone has or does not have) is managed by teachers and children during the delivery of procedural instructions. We saw that while in theory all the children have equal access to the information they need to accomplish the activity, their variable attention behaviours suggest there will be differences in what they actually know as they start to do the activity. In this section we show how analysis of interaction in terms of *epistemic stances* taken by participants provides useful insights into how epistemic authority is negotiated and managed in the classroom. The examples we present in this section show how the teacher is maintained as the person with higher epistemic authority, but that within the peer group, children assume epistemic authority, or are granted epistemic authority by their classmates.

The extract we have selected (Extract 7.4 below) comes 35 seconds after the recording of the five children attempting the task started. The recording begins after they have sat at their table, and each child has a booklet. Extract 7.4 illustrates a number of ways that differences in knowledge are managed through the assumption and allocation of epistemic authority over knowledge of how to accomplish the six-step task correctly. The main focus is on the ordering of the third job (ripping) and the fourth job (cutting).

Extract 7.4

```
27   Ember:   H:ow do I: rip ˘this.
28            (1.2)
29   Annie:   >Lemme do it<
30            (2.6)
31   Atini:   OI YOU CA:N'T RI:P IT ˘FI:RST.
32            (0.7)
33   Annie:   >^She already done her ^na:me.<
34            (0.3)
35   Annie:   Did you do your name on [your ba:g¿
36   Naia:                            [^YOU'RE NOT
              ALLOWED^ break it.
37   Annie:   Wait-
38            (0.8)
39   Atini:   [You have to [rip- (.) y'have to r:ip] i:t.
40   Ember:                [I do it on that one (though),]
41   Naia:    Yes:.
42            (0.6)
43   Annie:   Yes you do::¿
44            (0.4)
45   Atini:   ^NO:::;^
46            (0.4)
```

Extract 7.4 begins with Ember's claim not to know how to rip the page off. The formulation of the question suggests that Ember knows that she has to rip off the first page, and she had been gazing at the teacher during the demonstration of this. However, ripping pages off booklets may be something they do not usually do, so she asks the other children for help. Annie is sitting next to Ember. Annie says, 'Lemme do it' (line 29). Annie thus assumes a more knowledgeable epistemic stance, authorizing herself to be the one to assist Ember. Ember shows acceptance that this knowledge is within Annie's epistemic domain because she allows Annie to do the ripping for her.

During this time (the silence in line 30), Atini looks over at the two girls to his right, and shouts out, 'Oi, you can't rip it first' (line 31). This, remember, reflects the order of the two steps of ripping and cutting in the summary we showed in Extract 7.3 (when Atini was paying attention), but not in the first delivery of the instructions (when Atini was not paying attention). Annie responds to him by saying, 'She's already done her name', further demonstrating her knowledge of the ordering of activity steps as originally articulated by the teacher. In saying this, Annie is positively asserting her knowledgable stance, providing evidence for Atini that she knows the order of the task steps. She also then checks with Ember whether she has written her name on the paper bag, which even further reinforces her claims to epistemic authority over the ordering of steps, before Annie turns from Ember to Atini, and says 'Yes you do'. It seems she sees Atini as still trying to tell Ember not to rip off the first page.[4]

So, Annie has done three things to bolster her epistemic claims since Atini challenged her epistemic authority by claiming a different ordering of activity steps. In this time, Naia has also verbally displayed support for Annie's position.[5] Atini however maintains his own epistemic claim with a loud 'No' in line 45.

Extract 7.5 shows the continuation of this dispute. While we can see that both Annie and Atini are 'correct' in terms of claiming to know the order of steps from what they heard from the teacher, neither of them has yet expressed this explicitly.

Extract 7.5

```
47  Annie:   Yih ^have^ to:. Miss Bathurst [ri-
48  Atini:                                 [^YOU HAVE TO
             <CU:T
49           THE:SE^ FI::R:ST.>
50           (0.9)
51  Annie:   [Miss Bathurst said ]rip-
52  Naia:    [NO:                ]YOU HAFTA C:U:T (I:N:).
```

[4] We skip a close analysis of Naia's interaction with Atini in lines 36, 39, and 41 which we take to be Atini correcting Naia's 'You're not allowed break it' (line 36) with 'You have to rip it' (line 39). Annie's 'yes you do' appears to support Naia's position.

[5] Just prior to the time of this extract, Naia had left the table to check with Mrs Bathurst that she was up to the third step, having written her name twice as instructed. So Mrs Bathurst has just confirmed with Naia that the next step is to rip her page off.

```
53   Atini:   [^N o : : :, ^]
54            (1.0)
55   Atini:   ^You hafta cut the penguins <fi::r::st>.
56   Naia:    No::
57   Hadlee:  <˘No::::o>?=
58   Atini:   =[Ye:::s>?=
59   Naia:    =[(You hafta)
60   Naia:    No:::?
61   Atini:   Miss Bathurst said, ay X.
62   X:       (          )
63            (0.5)
64   Atini:   ·hhh ^You hafta cut the penguin^ <fi::r:st>.
65            (1.4)
66   Annie:   Stop- fighti:ng:.
```

Extract 7.5 shows a shift in epistemic stances of both Annie and Atini as they tussle for epistemic authority in the face of competing claims to know. In line 48 Annie says 'you have to', and then mentions the teacher by name (lines 47 and 51). So, Annie has gone from assuming epistemic authority without reference to her original source of knowledge to being explicit about how she knows – it lies with the teacher. Atini however continues to hold his position that the cutting step precedes the ripping. He holds this even though both Naia (line 56) and Hadlee (line 57) align with Annie's stance that the correct order is ripping then cutting. At line 61 Atini, like Annie, also refers to the teacher as the original source of information, thus presenting his evidence for his knowledge as on equal footing with Annie's. The dispute is only resolved when the teacher herself passes the table a few moments later, and sees that Atini is cutting out the penguins without having ripped off the first page. She admonishes him with, 'What were you told to do. You were told to rip it off so it's easier to cut'. She then rips off Atini's first page. Naia says, 'See?', and Hadlee says, 'Yeah', to which Atini responds (to Hadlee), 'You're mean'. Note that Ember, the one child in this group who claimed a lack of knowledge with respect to this activity, does not engage at all in this dispute.

This short exchange between five children engaged in the same task shows us a range of ways that children manage their respective knowledge statuses, and apparent differences in what they know with respect to what has been instructed. We see a child (Annie) who has been the most active in making sure she understands the instructions while they are on the carpet, assume a position of epistemic authority that is granted by all but one of the other children (Atini). Her authority is such that Ember accepts her help.[6] Atini's intermittent attention during the instructions meant that his knowledge of the order of ripping and cutting came from the teacher's final summary in which she had reversed the order. We know however that this was not the order she intended because she confirms that ripping comes before cutting when she comes by the table (and adds a reason why – so it is easier to cut out the penguins).

The dispute emerges because both Annie and Atini assume a knowledgeable epistemic stance and both are able to cite the teacher as the original (and reliable) source of this knowledge in order to support their claims to know, but their knowledge claims are contradictory. The extent to which Atini holds his position is evidence of the degree to which these children in their first year of school hold the teacher as the ultimate epistemic authority.

Recommendations for Practice

The intricate and ever-changing ways in which knowledge is managed in classrooms is evident from the extracts from the Penguins activity. If classrooms are – above all – about learning in all its facets and complexity, then the management of knowledge is a fundamental aspect of a classroom's business. Classrooms are also rich and complex social milieus, and a teacher's job, to say the least, is highly challenging: it borders on the impossible for a teacher to follow everything that is occurring in a classroom. As we have seen, there will inevitably be misunderstandings and misconstruals by teachers and children. A scenario where the teacher provides all the information the students need to successfully engage in an activity (or any other learning situation) without further prompting, and where all the students agree on what they need to do, is not the real world of the classroom.

The tracking of knowledge management and epistemic trajectories in the short extracts above shows us some of the ways that teachers and children orient to knowledge, and that what happens in classrooms is a lot more

[6] Other strategies we observed being used by these children in this activity to gain knowledge they perceived as lacking (i.e. taking a K- epistemic stance) included Atini looking at Hadlee writing his name on his paper bag, and then doing so himself, i.e. copying another child, and Naia leaving the table and checking with the teacher what to do next, i.e. appealing to the teacher for help or confirmation.

complex than a unidirectional transmission of knowledge from the teacher (the knower) to the students (the non-knowers). These examples suggest the following for early childhood educators:

- Knowledge is not simply accumulated, but is understood, partially understood, and misunderstood; it is reviewed, revised, and disputed. Knowledge builds on other knowledge. Children in their first year of schooling already have many of the skills of orienting to what they should already know, and using strategies for acquiring knowledge not only from the teacher during teacher-led phases of the lesson, but also from each other.
- The formulation of instructions matters (as it does for all teaching). We saw how carefully Mrs Bathurst – who knew her class well – constructed her instructions based on her awareness of what the children already knew or had done before. When it came to steps in the activity that were unusual or new for the children, she took particular care to ensure the steps were understandable
- No matter how carefully instructions are presented, they are inevitably incomplete and to some degree ambiguous.
- Distractions can disrupt the formulation of instructions. Interruptions (e.g. for behaviour management) are inevitable in the complex social milieu of classrooms, but teachers can be mindful that these interruptions may affect the intelligibility or completeness of instructions.
- If children are not listening and watching, that is, not paying attention, then the best constructed instructions will be missed or misunderstood.
- Children display signs of listening or paying attention, and teachers can look for these clues. Other than providing (correct) answers to prompts from the teacher, there are other subtler signs of attention: active gaze following the teacher's focus of attention, forward body posture, shifting position for a better line of sight to the teacher. *Inattention* is when children look away for extended periods, fidget with other objects, or talk with each other.
- Given that instructions are often incomplete, there are other ways to provide necessary details. The teacher (and teacher aides or parent helpers) can be available for children to appeal directly to during an activity to check their understanding of what to do, or be reminded of what they have forgotten.
- Peer-to-peer interactions can also be an effective teaching support. But evidence from EMCA research show us that the ultimate epistemic authority in early learning environments lies with the teacher.

References

Bateman, A. (2015). *Conversation Analysis and Early Childhood Education: The Co-production of Knowledge and Relationships*. Farnham: Ashgate Publishing Company.

Bateman, A., and Carr, M. (2017). Pursuing a telling: managing a multi-unit turn in children's storytelling. In A. Bateman and A. Church (eds.), *Children's Knowledge-in-Interaction* (pp. 91–109). Singapore: Springer. https://doi.org/10.1007/978-981-10-1703-2_6

Bateman, A., and Church, A. (eds.) (2017). *Children's Knowledge-in-Interaction: Studies in Conversation Analysis*. Singapore: Springer.

Bernstein, B. (ed.) (2003). *Class, Codes and Control. Volume 4: Structuring of Pedagogic Discourse*. New York, NY: Routledge.

Clark, H. H. (1996). *Using Language*. Cambridge: Cambridge University Press.

Drew, P. (1997). 'Open' class repair initiators in response to sequential sources of troubles in conversation. Journal of Pragmatics, 28, 69–101.

Eskildsen, S., and Majlesi, A. (2018). Learnables and teachables in second language talk. *The Modern Language Journal*, 102(S1), 3–10.

Filipi, A. (2009). *Toddler and Parent Interaction: The Organisation of Gaze, Pointing and Vocalisation* (vol. 192). Amsterdam: John Benjamins. https://doi.org/10.1075/pbns.192

Filipi, A. (2018). Making knowing visible: tracking the development of the response token yes in second turn position. In S. Pekarek Doehler, J. Wagner, and E. González-Martínez (eds.), *Longitudinal Studies on the Organization of Social Interaction* (pp. 39–66). Basingstoke: Palgrave Macmillan. https://doi.org/10.1057/978-1-137-57007-9_2J.M

Gardner, R. (2007). The right connections: acknowledging epistemic progression in talk. *Language in Society*, 36(3). https://doi.org/10.1017/S0047404507070169

Gardner, R., and Mushin, I. (2013). Teachers telling: informings in an early years classroom. *Australian Journal of Communication*, 40(2), 63–81.

Gardner, R., and Mushin, I. (2017). Epistemic trajectories in the classroom: how children respond in informing sequences. In A. Bateman and A. Church (eds.), *Children's Knowledge-in-Interaction* (pp. 13–36). Singapore: Springer. https://doi.org/10.1007/978–981-10–1703-2_2

Garfinkel, H. (1967). *Studies in Ethnomethodology*. Englewood Cliffs, NJ: Prentice-Hall.

Heller, V. (2017). Managing knowledge claims in classroom discourse: the public construction of a homogeneous epistemic status. *Classroom Discourse*, 8(2), 156–174. https://doi.org/10.1080/19463014.2017.1328699

Heritage, J. (1984). A change-of-state token and aspects of its sequential placement. In M. Atkinson & J. Heritage (eds.), *Structures of Social Action: Studies in Conversation Analysis* (pp. 299–345). Cambridge: Cambridge University Press.

Heritage, J. (2012a). Epistemics in action: action formation and territories of knowledge. *Research on Language & Social Interaction*, 45(1), 1–29. https://doi.org/10.1080/08351813.2012.646684

Heritage, J. (2012b). The epistemic engine: sequence organization and territories of knowledge. *Research on Language & Social Interaction*, 45(1), 30–52. https://doi.org/10.1080/08351813.2012.646685

Heritage, J. (2012c). Epistemics in conversation. In J. Sidnell and T. Stivers (eds.), *The Handbook of Conversation Analysis* (pp. 370–394). Chichester: John Wiley & Sons, Ltd. https://doi.org/10.1002/9781118325001.ch18

Heritage, J., and Raymond, G. (2005). The terms of agreement: indexing epistemic authority and subordination in talk-in-interaction. *Social Psychology Quarterly*, 68(1), 15–38. https://doi.org/10.1177/019027250506800103

Jakonen, T., and Morton, T. (2015). Epistemic search sequences in peer interaction in a content-based language classroom. *Applied Linguistics*, 36(1), 73–94. https://doi.org/10.1093/applin/amt031

Kamio, A. (1997). *Territory of Information* (vol. 48). Amsterdam: John Benjamins. https://doi.org/10.1075/pbns.48

Kärkkäinen, E. (2003). *Epistemic Stance in English Conversation: A Description of Its Interactional Functions, with a Focus on I Think*. Amsterdam: John Benjamins.

Kern, F., and Ohlhus, S. (2017). Editorial to special issue 'The social organisation of learning in classroom interaction and beyond.' *Classroom Discourse*, 8(2), 95–98. https://doi.org/10.1080/19463014.2017.1328702

Kidwell, M. (2011). Epistemics and embodiment in the interactions of very young children. In T. Stivers, J. Steensig, & L. Mondada (eds.), *The Morality of Knowledge in Conversation* (pp. 257–282). Cambridge: Cambridge University Press.

Kidwell, M., and Zimmerman, D. H. (2007). Joint attention as action. *Journal of Pragmatics*, 39(3), 592–611. https://doi.org/10.1016/j.pragma.2006.07.012

Koole, T. (2010). Displays of epistemic access: student responses to teacher explanations. *Research on Language and Social Interaction*, 43(2), 183–209.

Koshik, I. (2002). Designedly incomplete utterances: a pedagogical practice for eliciting knowledge displays in error correction sequences. *Research on Language & Social Interaction*, 35(3), 277–309. https://doi.org/10.1207/S15327973RLSI3503_2

Kunitz, S. (2018). Collaborative attention work on gender agreement in Italian as a foreign language. *The Modern Language Journal*, 102, 64–81.

Labov, W., and Fanshel, D. (1977). *Therapeutic Discourse: Psychotherapy as Conversation*. New York, NY: Academic Press.

Margutti, P. (2010). On designedly incomplete utterances: what counts as learning for teachers and students in primary classroom interaction. *Research on Language & Social Interaction*, 43(4), 315–345. https://doi.org/10.1080/08351813.2010.497629

Mehan, H. (1979). *Learning Lessons: Social Organization in the Classroom*. Cambridge, MA: Harvard University Press. https://doi.org/10.4159/harvard.9780674420106

Michalovich, A., and Netz, H. (2018). Tag-naxon? (Tag-Right?) in instructional talk: opening or blocking learning opportunities. *Journal of Pragmatics*, 137, 57–75. https://doi.org/10.1016/j.pragma.2018.09.006

Mushin, I. (2001). *Evidentiality and Epistemological Stance Narrative Retelling*. Amsterdam: John Benjamins.

Mushin, I. (2013). Making knowledge visible in discourse: implications for the study of linguistic evidentiality. *Discourse Studies*, 15(5), 627–645.

Mushin, I., Gardner, R., & Gourlay, C. (2022). *Effective Task Instruction in the First Year of School: What Teachers and Children Do*. Abingdon: Routledge.

Raymond, G., and Heritage, J. (2006). The epistemics of social relations: owning grandchildren. *Language in Society*, 35(5), 677–705. https://doi.org/10.1017/S0047404506060325

Sacks, H. (1992). *Lectures on Conversation: Volumes I & II*. Oxford: Blackwell.

Sert, O. (2013). 'Epistemic status check' as an interactional phenomenon in instructed learning settings. *Journal of Pragmatics*, 45(1), 13–28. https://doi.org/10.1016/j.pragma.2012.10.005

Sert, O., and Walsh, S. (2013). The interactional management of claims of insufficient knowledge in English language classrooms. *Language and Education*, 27(6), 542–565. https://doi.org/10.1080/09500782.2012.739174

St. John, O., and Cromdal, J. (2016). Crafting instructions collaboratively: student questions and dual addressivity in classroom task instructions. *Discourse Processes*, 53(4), 252–279. https://doi.org/10.1080/0163853X.2015.1038128

Stivers, T., Mondada, L., and Steensig, J. (eds.). (2011). *The Morality of Knowledge in Conversation*. Cambridge: Cambridge University Press. https://doi.org/10.1017/CBO9780511921674

Stivers, T., Sidnell, J., and Bergen, C. (2018). Children's responses to questions in peer interaction: a window into the ontogenesis of interactional competence. *Journal of Pragmatics*, 124, 14–30. https://doi.org/10.1016/j.pragma.2017.11.013

Tomasello, M. (2008). *Origins of Human Communication*. Cambridge, MA: MIT Press.

Wootton, A. J. (2005). *Interaction and the Development of Mind*. Cambridge: Cambridge University Press.

PART II

Pedagogy in Interaction

8 | Literacy

MARJOLEIN I. DEUNK, MYRTE N. GOSEN, FRANS HIDDINK, AND JAN BERENST

Introduction

Literacy is one of the most important cultural tools in most contemporary societies. Learning to read and write is therefore central to the curriculum of primary education. Before formal literacy learning, young children already demonstrate their orientation towards the existence, features, use and usefulness of written language, taken together in the broad concept of *emergent literacy* (Teale & Sulzby, 1986). In a recent review, Teale, Whittingham, and Hoffman (2020) noticed how the umbrella terms *emergent literacy*, *early literacy*, and *beginning reading* were used to describe literacy practices and literacy environments of children in the preschool period until third grade. They also noted an increased emphasis on literacy development within sociocultural contexts, highlighting the presence of literacy in children's natural environments alongside more formal educational activities in order to stimulate literacy development. We choose to use the term *emergent literacy* to emphasize the developmental stage where children become increasingly aware of literacy, in interaction with texts and adults or other children. This rather informal knowledge about literacy forms an important basis for later formal reading and writing instruction and literacy development (e.g. Bus, IJzendoorn, & Pellegrini, 1995; Mol & Bus, 2011; Sénéchal & LeFevre, 2002).

Parents, caregivers, and early childhood educators play an important role in stimulating children's emergent literacy by orienting them to written text, from a very young age. Through their interactions, adults help children to make sense of the world, which in many cultures contains a salient linguistic landscape. Children may get oriented to (adult's engagement with) written text through shared reading and (role) play with peers, but also through more everyday events like noticing print on food packaging at the breakfast table, observing parents scrolling on their smartphones, and reading aloud during digital technology use (e.g. Davidson et al., 2020; Duke & Purcell-Gates, 2003; Neumann, Hood, & Ford, 2013).

These interactions with children around written language may arise spontaneously or intentionally. Intervention studies like that of Reese et al.

(2010) have shown that interventions targeting parental skills are found to be effective in enriching parent-child interactions relevant for literacy development. Besides interactions with adults, other children may also be a resource to develop aspects of narratives (Cekaite et al., 2014; Ninio & Snow, 1996) and to develop individual writer's identities (Kissel et al., 2011). This chapter aims at constructing recommendations for early childhood professionals to recognize and elicit meaningful teacher-child and peer interactions around written text and thereby adding to the emergent literacy development of young children. Accordingly, this chapter discusses three interactional environments in educational settings in which children are oriented to aspects of emergent literacy: everyday interactions around text, shared picture book reading, and collaborative writing. The affordances of these settings are illustrated by analysing how aspects of literacy interactively come about in preschool and kindergarten.

Everyday Literacy Events

In many contemporary societies, print is omnipresent and ever-present, so children are exposed to environmental print from early on. For educational purposes, instances of environmental print are increased, for example through letters on toys or word walls and other literacy displays in (pre-school) classrooms. Both adults and young children are found to refer to environmental print, thereby highlighting it as a certain type of visual information, different from pictures. Because of the natural occurrence of print in the daily environment of children, its role in emergent literacy development is a matter-of-course.

Being tuned in to children's spontaneous attention to written text will help early childhood educators to engage them in meaningful literacy interactions, orienting them to the meanings and purposes of literacy (Haas Dyson, 1995). Although this may lead to very short, fleeting snippets of interaction, the value of these moments cannot be underestimated because of the authentic context, following the child's focus and interest.

However, research has shown that young (two- to four-year-old) children's spontaneous, child-initiated orientation to text in preschool classrooms is rare (Deunk, 2009). Therefore, early childhood educators can incorporate their own authentic adult acts of reading and writing, like administration, into the curriculum, thereby creating opportunities for meaningful interaction about text.

Figure 8.1 HEMA colouring pencil.

Child-Initiated Orientation to Environmental Print

The recognition of print and understanding its uses and functions is a gradual process. The perspectives of the literate adult and the young child that has hardly any experience with literacy may be so different that it is hard to imagine how a child in that early stage of development may see the world. Through interactions with children, early childhood educators may get more insight in the literacy knowledge a child has acquired at a certain point in time. An example of how interaction with children can help literate adults appreciate a child's perspective is given in Extract 8.1.

Extract 8.1 features Raoul (3 years; 6 months), who focuses on the print on a colouring pencil, which reads the store brand name (see Figure 8.1). Raoul's orientation shows that he recognizes letters as a special type of visual information, knows that these letters in combination have meaning and can be read, and knows that others have the skills to do so.

Extract 8.1 Colouring pencil [RAO, Raoul (3;6), MEL, Melanie (2;4), TEA, Diana (teaching assistant)]

1		RAO:	hm colour	hm kleur
2		MEL:	blue	blauw
3		TEA:	yes there you've got ↑light blue melanie, well done	ja daar heb je ↑lichtblauw melanie, goed zo
...				
6	→	RAO:	this is another (light), look	dis nog een (licht), kijk
7		RAO:	(1.7) ((holds up pencil))	(1.7) ((houdt het potlood omhoog))
8		RAO:	look ((leans over to Diana))	kijk ((leunt naar Diana))
9			(1.1)	(1.1)
10		RAO:	look ((leans closer to Diana))	kijk ((leunt dichter naar Diana))
11		TEA:	that's purple	dat is paars
12	→	RAO:	look ((points at text at pencil))	kijk ((wijst naar de tekst op het potlood))

13			(1.0)	(1.0)
14	→	TEA:	yes it says- it says hema ((points at text))	ja daar staat- daar staat hema ((wijst naar de tekst))
15		RAO:	hema?	hema?
16		TEA:	hema	hema
17		RAO:	yes?	ja?
18		TEA:	yes	ja
19		RAO:	have (bought)?	heb e koch?

(Source: Deunk, 2009)

At first, teaching assistant Diana does not recognize Raoul's focus on print and thinks Raoul is interested in the colour, in line with the topic of conversation somewhat earlier ('that's purple', line 11). However, Raoul persists ('look', line 12) and manages to use Diana's expertise, being a literate adult, to crack the code and read the print for him ('it says hema', line 14). Of special interest is Raoul's perseverance: when Diana focuses on the colour instead of the text, Raoul initiates a repair sequence, to fix the misunderstanding (lines 10–14), followed by a confirmation sequence (lines 15–18), also initiated by him.

Explicating Expert Acts of Literacy

Just like environmental print is naturally part of children's daily environment, so are people in their surroundings performing acts of reading and writing. Throughout the day, literate people read different types of text, ranging from environmental text to text messages, headlines, instructions, and newspapers and books. Also, writing is a common practice for literate people, ranging from scribbling a note to typing a text message, signing a card, making a grocery list, and keeping a diary. Part of emergent literacy is that children become aware of literate experts performing these frequent acts of reading and writing, and develop an understanding of their relevance.

Because reading and writing is so self-evident to people who have learned to do so, the act of reading and writing in everyday life often goes unnoticed. Yet, explicating this offers great opportunities for making written text and all its features salient to young children. Early childhood educators can help children increase their awareness and understanding through engaging with them in interactions during these expert acts of literacy. In Extract 8.2, early childhood educator Molly engages with a couple of children in conversation about different characteristics of text and writing during a free drawing activity. This extract illustrates attention for different aspects of emergent literacy: the concrete act of name writing, and the use of writing, in this case to indicate ownership.

Extract 8.2 The functions of writing [KIM, Kimberly (3;6), KIR, Kirsten (2;6), TEA Molly (early childhood educator)]

			A couple of children are drawing. Molly sits with them at the table.	Een paar kinderen tekenen. Molly zit bij hen aan tafel.
1		TEA:	do I need to write something on it kimberly?	moet ik er nog wat opschrijven kimberly?
2			(0.7)	(0.7)
3		TEA:	yes?	ja?
4			(0.6)	(0.6)
5		KIR:	no mine	nee mijne
6			(0.5)	(0.5)
7		TEA:	((to kimberly)) what shall I write on it then?	((tegen kimberly)) wat zal ik er op schrijven dan?
8			(0.4)	(0.4)
9		TEA:	what shall I write on it?	wat zal ik er opschrijven?
10		KIM:	(3.7) ((points to the paper))	(3.7) ((wijst naar het papier))
11		TEA:	there? write there? and what shall I write?	daar? daar schrijven? en wat zal ik schrijven?
12			(2.2)	(2.2)
13		KIR:	[mine	[mijn
14	→	TEA:	((to kimberly)) [write kimberly? so everyone knows it's yours?	((tegen kimberly)) [kimberly schrijven? zodat iedereen weet dat die van jou is?
15		TEA:	((to kimberly)) [yes?	((tegen kimberly)) [ja?
16		KIR:	[my	[mij
17		TEA:	well done. it's that one isn't it?	goed zo. is die he?

18			(2.1)	(2.1)
19		KIR:	mine too:::	mijne oo::k
20		TEA:	do I have to write (on) yours too?	moet ik w- (op) die van jou schrijven
21			(1.6)	(1.6)
22		KIR:	nthis [with this ((points to text on kimberly's drawing))	nditte [met ditte ((wijst naar de tekst op kimberly's tekening))
23	→	TEA:	[says k:::imberly.	[staat k::imberly.
24			(0.8)	(0.8)
25	→	TEA:	then e:::verybody knows it is kimberly's.	dan weet ie:::dereen dat ie van kimberly is.
...				
34		KIR:	me too!	ik ook!
35		TEA:	write something °too°?	°ook° wat schrijven?
36			(0.7)	(0.7)
37		TEA:	I'm going to write here	ga ik hier schrijven
38			(2.1)	(2.1)
39		TEA:	<kirsten:::>	<kirsten:::>
40			(0.7)	(0.7)
41		TEA:	it says kirsten	daar staat kirsten

(Source: Deunk, 2009)

In Extract 8.2, teacher Molly offers Kimberly her writing skills. Molly makes an effort to let Kimberly dictate what she should write (lines 1, 3, 7, 9, 11), to no avail. Even though Kimberly does not respond verbally, she is engaged in the interaction and does point to where she wants the text to be written. Molly then suggests she could write Kimberly's name on the drawing (line 14), a common practice in early childhood classrooms in order to keep track of authorship and to make sure children take their own products home. Interestingly, Molly adds *why* this would be useful ('So everyone knows it's yours?', line 14), adding to the knowledgebase on the use and functions of writing. She does so again in line 25, when talking to Kirsten, who persists in making use of Molly's writing skills as well (lines 5, 13, 16, 19). Just as Raoul in Extract 8.1, Kirsten (line 22) is also oriented to Molly's *reading* skills in addition to her *writing* skills. When writing Kirsten's name, Molly explicitly orients Kirsten to the act of name writing by verbally accompanying the activity before ('I'm going to write here', line

37), during ('kirsten:::', line 39), and after ('it says Kirsten', line 41) writing the name.

This type of free drawing activity creates opportunities for interactions about different aspects of emergent literacy, like the concrete act of writing and the indication of ownership. In literate societies, written text has authority, which is an important characteristic because it influences decisions in everyday life. Therefore, gaining understanding of the status of text over oral information is important for the emergent literate child. Of course, for children, the legal consequences of having something 'put in writing' are not relevant, but understanding the higher status of written text is. In Extract 8.2, Molly emphasized twice that once the name is written on the drawing, ownership is publicly established ('so everyone knows it's yours', line 14, and 'then everybody knows it is kimberly's', line 25), implicitly also making clear that contesting ownership will be harder from then on. These kinds of interactions, which also take place during other activities in pre-school environments such as book loan activities (Deunk, Berenst, & de Glopper, 2013) and pretend play (Morrow & Tracy, 2005), contribute to children's growing understanding of the use and status of text in the literate world they live in.

Shared Book Reading

Shared book reading is one of the most studied environments in relation to children's language and literacy development (e.g. Bus, Van IJzendoorn, & Pellegrini, 1995; Mol & Bus, 2011; Payne, Whitehurst, & Angell, 1994; Sénéchal & LeFevre, 2002), especially when children are actively involved in interactions during shared reading (e.g. Huebner & Meltzoff, 2005; Mol et al., 2008). Adults may assist children in understanding written language by means of reading aloud the picture books, but also by adding comments, asking questions, and explaining potential difficult parts of the book or text. Individual picture books may differ in how easily they elicit complex interaction, also partly depending on contextual preconditions and individual characteristics, interests, and competences of the adult and the child (Muhinyi et al., 2019; Teale et al., 2020). Nevertheless, the importance of shared reading for emergent literacy is undisputed, and always worth highlighting, not only because of world knowledge being conveyed through books and social-emotional insights through its characters, but also because shared reading can lead to meaningful interactions about features of text and books. The remainder of this particular section will focus on how shared reading may establish meaningful interactions, centred around aspects of story structure and story understanding.

Talking about Story Structure

During shared picture book reading, kindergarten teachers pay attention to the structure of stories. A recurrent element that is discussed is the title of the book in relation to the rest of the book. Teachers display an orientation to the title as written text and use this moment in time to address the reading of and reflecting on the title as an important component in the activity of reading a book. In Extract 8.3, the teacher directs children's attention to the title as something that *can* be read, at the same time stressing that this is the *first* thing to be read.

Extract 8.3 The title of the book [KRI, Kris (6;2), RIC, Rick (6;2), TEA, Teacher]

1	→	TEA:	I will first tell what it says there on the cover	ik ga eerst even vertellen wat daar op de voorkant staat
2			(0.9)	(0.9)
3	→		because the cover is the title of the book, isn't it?	want de voorkant is de titel van het boek hè
4			(0.3)	(0.3)
5			and it says	en daar staat op
6			(0.3)	(0.3)
7		KRI:	mine=	van mij=
8		TEA:	=m-	=v-
9			(1.1)	(1.1)
10		RIC:	mine=	van mij=
11		TEA:	=mi:ne	=van: mij

Not only does the teacher show an orientation to the title of the book as written text that she is able to read, she also displays an orientation to the structure of stories and shared book reading, in which the title of the book is expressed as 'first' (line 1). These references to the logical ordering of book reading are also shown by Berenst (2006) and Clay (1991). They demonstrate how parents place emphasis on the start and ending of books, and how young children are oriented on the reading direction and the page turning in books. These and other 'book handling skills' of young children are also described in Lowe (2011) and Edwards (2014).

In Extract 8.4, the teacher also displays an orientation to the title as something you can read on the front of a book ('please have a look', line 20), but in this case she also underlines the title as revealing important information about the contents of the book. By asking for an explanation (Gosen, Berenst, & de Glopper, 2015a) for why the book is titled 'shhh', the children get oriented to the title as essential to the content of the story.

Extract 8.4 Providing explanations [DAN, Daniël (5;2), RIC, Rick (6;2), REB, Rebecca (5;11), DRI, Dries (5;7), TEA, teacher]

20	→	TEA:	please have a look	kijk maar eens eventjes
21			(0.9)	(0.9)
22		TEA:	<because the name of this book is ((finger to lips)) shhh>	<want dit boek heet dus ((vinger voor mond)) sssst>
23		RIC:	[who wrote it	[door wie is het geschreven
24	→	TEA:	[why ((shakes head)) I- why would the book- would the book be called this way	[waarom ((schudt hoofd)) ik- waarom zou het boek- zou het boek zo heten
25	→	RIC:	maybe someone is asleep	misschien slaapt er iemand
26		TEA:	·h °oh° [((looks around in circle))	·h °oh° [((kijkt kring rond)
27	→	DAN:	[or maybe there is a giant close by who wants to eat them	[of misschien is er een reus in de buurt die hun wil opeten
28		TEA:	((glances questioning from daniël to book))	((kijkt vragend van daniël naar boek))
29	→	REB:	(that you [therefore have to be silent)	(dat je [daarom stil moet zijn)
30		DRI:	[((stamps on floor)) boom boom [boom	[((stampt op de vloer)) doem doem [doem
31		TEA:	[what did you say rebecca I don't hear you	[wat zeg je rebecca ik versta het niet
32	→	REB:	that you therefore have to be silent [what daniël said	dat je daarom stil moet zijn [wat daniël zei
33		TEA:	[could be	[zou kunnen
		...		

69	→	RIC:	maybe that (.) little guy that says ssh [cause he sits (.) there	misschien zegt dat (.) mannetje wel sst [want hij zit (.) daar
70	→	TEA:	[well who knows, let's have a look	[nou wie weet we gaan eens even kijken

(Source: Gosen, 2012; Gosen, Berenst, & de Glopper, 2015a)

In this extract, the children make inferences on what the story will be about (lines 25, 27, 29, and 32) after the teacher initiated a request for explanations in line 24. At the same time, we see an example of Rick (line 23) orienting on another aspect around characteristics of a story: the author of the story. As in Extracts 8.1 and 8.2, he orients to the teacher as the one having the skills to read this information. However, the teacher is postponing his request to read the author's name, to maintain the focus on the request for explanations. She is collecting the children's contributions in lines 26, 28, and 33 without explicitly evaluating them. Rick then offers a contribution in line 69 in which he uses the cover page of the book as an information source, thereby orienting to story structure again. Once more, the teacher does not respond to his contribution by (dis)confirming his hypothesis as could be expected in conversation. Instead, she refrains from answering and directs the children's attention to the continuation of the book as the source of information for finding the answer together in the continuation of the shared reading (line 70) (see also Gosen, Berenst, & de Glopper 2013, 2015a, 2015b). This specifies the structure of books with content that is released page by page. At the same time, making predictions gives children the opportunity to lay the grounds for further understanding of the book content, which is addressed in the next section of this chapter.

Reflecting on Story Understanding

The previous two extracts were both derived from the beginning of a shared picture book reading session, while there are also ample instances of interaction during and after the reading. After reading a picture book, children are often invited to evaluate the (events of the) book that was just read (see also Berenst, 2006). During shared reading, teachers can create moments of interaction to discuss children's understanding of the story so far. An example of such an interaction is displayed in Extract 8.5. Here, teacher and children discuss the explanation for a book character's emotional state.

Extract 8.5 Understanding the story so far [RIC, Rick (6;2), KYR, Kyra (5;6), TEA, teacher]

232	→	TEA:	but why- why is he sad then	maar waarom- waarom is die dan verdrietig
233		RIC:	well becau[se he th-	nou om[dat-ie d-
234	→	KYR:	[because he could not have the [kite	[omdat hij niet de vlieger [mocht
235	→	TEA:	[((points at kyra))	[((wijst naar kyra))

(Source: Gosen, 2012; Gosen, Berenst, & de Glopper, 2015a)

Preceding this fragment of interaction, teacher and children have concluded that the main character of the book appears sad. Hereafter, the teacher asks the children to explain why this is the case. In providing this explanation, Kyra (line 234) shows that she understands the causal relationship between an earlier event in the book and the emotional state of the book character. Kyra thus shows that she is able to step back from the storyline and reflect on it as a reader. In this extract, the teacher evaluates her answer as correct by pointing at Kyra (line 235). This differs from the responses to possible explanations as shown in Extract 8.4, because there is now known information that is reflected upon (Gosen, Berenst, & de Glopper, 2015a). In this case, the teacher's feedback and request for explanation helps Kyra and the other children in the classroom to practise deriving meaning from texts, a skill that will increasingly be required at school.

Collaborative Writing

Apart from teachers and other adults, children also form a source for emergent literacy learning. For young children, emergent literacy is ideally embedded in meaningful play activities, since play is regarded by Vygotsky (1978, p. 103) as the *leading activity*. In peer interaction during play, children may construct all kinds of actions and activities such as reasoning and problem-solving (Hiddink, 2019a) but they may also display their orientation to literacy by constituting stories (Ninio & Snow, 1996). For instance, children may discuss different aspects that are associated with literacy, such as the role of protagonists and the logical event order and different forms of reflexivity (e.g. Cekaite et al., 2014).

Alongside these aspects in relation to emergent reading, peer interaction also contributes to children's writing. Conversations about each other's literate performances, like drawings, mark making, and texts, may stimulate *individual* children to reflect on their products and on their identity as literate beings (Coates & Coates, 2006; Kissel et al., 2011). Furthermore, interactions in the process of *collaborative writing*, may contribute to children's emergent writing development, as will be shown in this section.

Peer Interaction about Correctness

It is often reported that the practice of literacy seems to be reduced to decontextualized performances (e.g. Van Oers, 2007) without a clear idea about what is already apparent in children's emergent writing development. For instance, writing in kindergarten is often limited to an orientation to the alphabetic script, but by doing so, early childhood educators neglect how young children's writing emerges. To quote Sulzby, Teale, and Kamberelis (1989, p. 69): 'Most destructive, we think, is the assumption that children cannot write (that is cannot compose) until they have mastered the mechanics and that the only way they should write is through conventional orthography'. Berenst (2015) demonstrated that before young children are oriented to the alphabetic script, different kinds of writing aspects are already apparent in children's writing products.

As Extract 8.6 demonstrates, when children are oriented towards the alphabet, they mainly focus on discussing the correctness of orthography of words. In contrast to younger children (like Raoul in Extract 8.1), who are oriented on a word as a complete unit, these children are already oriented to the individual letters in a word and also in the order in which those letters should appear. Similarly to older children (Herder, Berenst, De Glopper, & Koole, 2018), young writers may recruit help from their peers. Here, Irene asks for help while writing the Dutch word 'vla' (in English, 'custard'), after she wrote the letter 'v'.

Extract 8.6 Recruiting help for letter writing [IRE, Irene; IMK, Imke; VIC, Victor; kindergartners aged 5–6 years].

1	→	IRE:	who wants to take a look what you write next to the v?	wie wil even kijken wat na de v je schrijft?
2		VIC:	I don't	ikkuh niet

3		IRE:	you ( ) ((looks at imke))	jij ( ) ((kijkt imke aan))
4			(1.2)	(1.2)
5	→	VIC:	what do you want to write then?	wat wil je dan schrijven?
6		IRE:	vla	vla
7		VIC:	oh give me that ((stands up and is unsuccessfully trying to get the paper))	oh geef maar ((staat op en probeert zonder succes het papier te pakken))
8			(0.4) ((walks to whiteboard))	(0.4) ((loopt naar schoolbord))
9	→	VIC:	the l and after that the letter a ((returns))	de l en daarna de letter a ((komt teruggelopen))
10		IRE:	((walks to the whiteboard and starts writing))	((loopt naar het schoolbord en gaat schrijven))

While Irene writes the first letter of the Dutch word 'vla' (in English, 'custard'), she invites others to check on the whiteboard what the next letter has to be (line 1). Although Victor refuses at first, after an insertion sequence in which Irene answers Victor's question about what she wants to write (lines 5–6), Victor tries to take the paper from Irene, but when this is not successful, he goes to check the word on the whiteboard and mentions the next two letters of custard (lines 7–9). This negotiation about the letter placement between young children demonstrates how they can initiate such interactions themselves. Moreover, it displays their disposition to write words correctly by recruiting help and by using available resources in the classroom.

The activity the children work on during Extract 8.6 is that of constructing a dinner menu as part of a Storyline Approach (Bell, Harkness, & White, 2006). The final product is displayed in Figure 8.2. During the construction of the product, the children did not discuss its formal text structure. However, Figure 8.2 illustrates children's un-explicated ideas about the formal text structure of a dinner menu. Their knowledge of dinner menus having three subsequent courses is reflected in their choice to write down the appetizer, main course, and dessert in the correct order from top to bottom. Moreover, they write the words from left to write and as separate units (see also Berenst, 2015). By doing so, they show their understanding of the spatial and sequential aspects of written language.

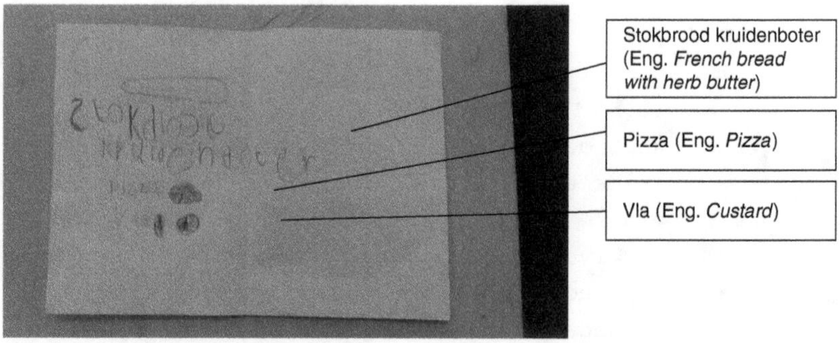

Figure 8.2 The children's dinner menu.

Peer Interaction about Appropriateness

Although young children in peer interaction during writing mainly discuss the correctness of orthography, on some occasions we observed children discussing *forms of appropriateness* before writing, as Extract 8.7 demonstrates. Here, children are going to write an invitation for guests of the party of a King.

Extract 8.7 Discussing forms of appropriateness [IRE, Irene; IMK, Imke; VIC, Victor; kindergartners aged 5–6 years]

1	→	IRE:	uhm:::: what are the names of the guests?	uhm:::: hoe heten de gasten?
2			(2.0)	(2.0)
3		IRE:	what?	hoe?
4	→	IMK:	what yes	hoe ja
5		IRE:	what- what ((places pencil on the paper))	hoe- hoe ((zet potlood op papier))
6	→	VIC:	with the letter what	met de letter hoe
7	→	IRE:	((writes down the letter w))	((schrijft de letter h op))
8			((in the continuation they discuss how to write the other letters and next words correctly, while irene writes))	((in het vervolg bespreken ze hoe ze de andere letters en volgende woorden correct opschrijven, terwijl irene schrijft))

Before they start writing, Irene raises the question about the names of the guests (line 1). By doing so, she displays her orientation to the formal structure of an invitation, namely that the first element is to whom it is addressed. After a pause, she reformulates her question (line 3). Her question is treated here by herself, by Imke, and by Victor as a proposal to write it down (lines 4–6), after which Irene starts writing it down (line 7).

Although we would expect that the answer to Irene's question (specifically the actual names of the guests) should be written down on an invitation, and not the question itself, this simple sequence of a proposal that is immediately agreed upon displays that the children have an idea about the entire speech activity (Levinson, 1992) 'inviting guests', as a sort of possible preliminary brainstorm, in which 'what are the names of the guests?' is a part of it, before writing the actual invitation. Even though young children may discuss forms of appropriateness, these discussions are scarce in peer interaction between young children, especially in contrast to older children in primary school, who more regularly collectively reflect on different kinds of appropriateness (Herder et al., 2018).

This might be an opportunity for teachers to explicitly discuss different kinds of writing aspects with children who show that they are already oriented to certain writing characteristics. Early childhood teachers are probably more aware than other adults in children's lives that the opportunities to demonstrate orientations to aspects of emergent writing are central to children's literacy development. Nevertheless, even for professionals, it may sometimes be difficult to respond contingently to their emergent literacy demonstrations. This is illustrated in Extract 8.8, which is part of the same activity as Extract 8.7. Here, the teacher joins the peer interaction.

Extract 8.8 Teacher's reorientation [IRE, Irene; IMK, Imke; kindergartners aged 5–6 years; TEA, Teacher]

1	→	TEA:	((comes walking with imke)) what do you want to know?	((komt aangelopen met imke)) wat wil je weten?
2	→	IRE:	what are the names of the guests?	hoe heten de gasten?
3		TEA:	what do you say?	wat zeg je?
4		IRE:	what are the names of the gue[sts?	hoe heten de gas[ten?
5	→	TEA:	[well, we don't know that, but I think that uh:: the king's chef is able to write it on the envelope himself	[nou, dat weten we niet, maar ik denk dat uh:: de kok van de koning dat zelf wel op de envelop kan schrijven
6			(0.2)	(0.2)

7	TEA:	but we ↑did discuss what we need to write down in it	maar we hebben het er ↑wel over gehad wat we er in moesten schrijven
8		(0.2)	(0.2)
9	TEA:	do you remember ((looks at the children))	weten jullie dat nog? ((kijkt rond))
10		(2.0)	(2.0)
11	TEA:	because there is the letter ((points to the whiteboard)) and it also says what we need to write down.	want daar hangt de brief ((wijst naar het bord)) en daar staat ook op wat we op moeten schrijven.

In line 1, the teacher asks the children what they want to know. In response, Irene repeats their question (line 2) that they already wrote down, demonstrating their orientation to the speech activity (Levinson, 1992) of 'inviting guests for a party' (and/or to the text structure of an invitation). After an insertion sequence (lines 3–4), the teacher's instruction as response (line 5 and following), in which she reorients the children to the preceding whole-class instruction on the content of the invitation, concludes the problem-solving interaction in an information-delivery format, as often in teacher interventions (e.g. Hiddink, 2019a, 2019b; Koole, 2012). Interestingly, the children's approach to writing the invitation is different to what they are *required* to do. This possible clash might explain why the teacher does not elaborate on the children's own orientation to this aspect of the product as part of their emergent writing. In any case, it emphasizes that in order to respond contingently in interaction it is important to notice and recognize children's literacy practices.

Recommendations for Practice

With this chapter, we aimed to emphasize the importance of interactions around reading, writing, and text with and among young children in order to stimulate their emergent literacy. We showed (a) how everyday classroom activities can provide opportunities for meaningful interaction about various aspects of literacy, (b) how the common literary practice of shared book reading creates opportunities to discuss story structure and story understanding, and (c) how children display and discuss productive literacy practices in peer interactions during meaningful activities that are elicited by teachers. From our analyses of the everyday interactions children in preschool and kindergarten classrooms take part in, we extract some key suggestions for early childhood educators:

- Treat and make books, reading, and writing an obvious, inevitable part of life. Besides creating reading spots with freely accessible books and regular shared reading sessions, this means initiating literacy stimulating interactions throughout the day, in a range of contexts.
- Plan educational activities, like shared reading or collaborative writing activities, to create contexts for enriched interaction about literacy. In addition, pay keen attention to children's spontaneous focus on aspects of literacy, and grasp the opportunity to elaborate with them on this.
- Be aware of every time you read and write in the presence of a child, even the most everyday moments of reading and writing. Try to use these moments to make your literacy act explicit and engage with children in conversation about it.
- Use shared reading interactions to move beyond a focus on new vocabulary. Rather, initiate more complex interactions about story structure and children's understanding of the story to prepare them for reading comprehension skills. Try to direct children's attention to the activity of reading together to find the answers instead of providing them with answers as a teacher.
- Be sensitive to what aspects, besides the alphabetic script, children themselves are already demonstrating during their (emergent) writing or in their writing products in order to strengthen these practices, by eliciting meaningful contexts in which collaborative writing is embedded.

References

Bell, S., Harkness, S., and White, G. (2006). *Storyline: Past, Present and Future*. Glasgow: University of Strathclyde.

Berenst, J. (2006). Metacommunicatieve praktijken van ouders in voorleesinteracties met kinderen. In H. Hoeken, B. Hendriks, and P. J. Schellens (eds.), *Studies in Taalbeheersing 2* (pp. 20–31). Assen: Van Gorcum.

Berenst, J. (2015). Ontluikende geletterdheid. In J. H. Loonstra, M. Mentink, and C. Rem (eds.), *Van baby tot kleuter. De veelzijdige en indrukwekkende ontwikkeling van kinderen van 0–4 jaar* (pp.179–221). Antwerpen/Apeldoorn: Garant Uitgevers.

Bus, A. G., IJzendoorn, M. H., and Pellegrini, A. D. (1995). Joint book reading makes for success in learning to read: a meta-analysis on intergenerational transmission of literacy. *Review of Educational Research*, 65(1), 1–21.

Cekaite, A., Blum-Kulka, S., Grøver, V., and Teubal, E. (eds.). (2014). *Children's Peer Talk: Learning from Each Other*. Cambridge: Cambridge University Press.

Clay, M. (1991). *Becoming Literate: The Construction of Inner Control*. Portsmouth, NH: Heinemann.

Coates, E., and Coates, A. (2006). Young children talking and drawing. *International Journal of Early Years Education*, 14(3), 221–241.

Davidson, C., Danby, S., Ekberg, S., and Thorpe, K. (2020). The interactional achievement of reading aloud by young children and parents during digital technology use. *Journal of Early Childhood Literacy* (online). https://doi.org/10.1177/1468798419896040

Deunk, M. I. (2009). *Discourse practices in preschool: young children's participation in everyday classroom activities* [doctoral thesis]. Groningen: University of Groningen.

Deunk, M. I., Berenst, J., and de Glopper, C. (2013). Home-school book sharing comes in many forms: a microanalysis of teacher-child interaction during the activity of borrowing a school book. *Journal of Early Childhood Literacy*, 13(2), 242–270.

Duke, N. K., and Purcell-Gates, V. (2003). Genres at home and at school: bridging the known to the new. *The Reading Teacher*, 57(1), 30–37.

Edwards, C. M. (2014), Maternal literacy practices and toddlers' emergency literacy skills. *Journal of Early Childhood Literacy*, 14(1), 53–79.

Gosen, M. N. (2012). *Tracing learning in interaction: an analysis of shared reading of picture books at kindergarten* [doctoral thesis]. Groningen: University of Groningen.

Gosen, M. N., Berenst, J., and de Glopper, K. (2013). The interactional structure of explanations during shared reading at kindergarten. *International Journal of Educational Research*, 62, 62–74.

Gosen, M. N., Berenst, J., and de Glopper, K. (2015a). Problem-solving during shared reading at kindergarten. *Classroom Discourse*, 6(3), 175–197.

Gosen, M. N., Berenst, J., and de Glopper, C. (2015b). Shared reading at kindergarten: understanding book content through participation. *Pragmatics and Society*, 6(3), 367–397.

Haas Dyson, A. (1995). Writing children. Reinventing the development of childhood literacy. *Written Communication*, 12(1), 4–46.

Herder, A., Berenst, J., De Glopper, K., and Koole, T. (2018). Reflective practices in collaborative writing of primary school students. *International Journal of Educational Research*, 90, 160–174.

Hiddink, F. C. (2019a). *Early childhood problem-solving interaction: young children's discourse during small-group work in primary school* [doctoral thesis]. Groningen: University of Groningen.

Hiddink, F. (2019b). Probleembesprekingen met samenwerkende kleuters. *Tijdschrift voor taalbeheersing*, 41(1), 89–103.

Huebner, C. E., and Meltzoff, A. N. (2005). Intervention to change parent-child reading style: a comparison of instructional methods. *Journal of Applied Developmental Psychology*, 26, 296–313.

Kissel, B., Hansen, J., Tower, H., and Lawrence, J. (2011). The influential interactions of pre-kindergarten writers. *Journal of Early Childhood Literacy*, 11(4), 425–452.

Koole, T. (2012). The epistemics of student problems: explaining mathematics in a multi-lingual class. *Journal of Pragmatics*, 44(13), 1902–1916

Levinson, S. (1992), Activity types and language. In P. Drew and J. Heritage (eds.), *Talk at Work: Interaction in Institutional Settings* (pp. 66–100). Cambridge: Cambridge University Press.

Lowe, V. (2011). 'Don't tell me all about it, just read it". In B. Kümmerling -Meibauer (ed.), *Emergent Literacy: Children's Books from 0–3*. Amsterdam/Philadelphia: John Benjamins.

Mol, S. E., and Bus, A. G. (2011). To read or not to read: a meta-analysis of print exposure from infancy to early adulthood. *Psychological Bulletin*, 137(2), 267–296.

Mol, S. E., Bus, A. G., de Jong, M. T., and Smeets, D. J. H. (2008). Added value of dialogic parent–child book readings: a meta-analysis. *Early Education and Development*, 19(1), 7–26.

Morrow, L. M., and Tracy, D. H. (2005). Instructional environments for language and learning: considerations for young children. In: J. Flood, D. Lapp, and S. Brice Heath (eds.), *Handbook of Research on Teaching Literacy Through the Communicative and Visual Arts* (pp. 485–495). Abingdon: Taylor and Francis.

Muhinyi, A., Hesketh, A., Stewart, A. J., and Rowland, C. F. (2020). Story choice matters for caregiver extra-textual talk during shared reading with preschoolers. *Journal of Child Language*, 47(3), 633–654.

Neumann, M. M., Hood, M., and Ford, R. (2013). Mother-child referencing of environmental print and its relationship with emergent literacy skills. *Early Education and Development*, 24(8), 1175–1193.

Ninio, A., and Snow, C.E. (1996). *Pragmatic Development*. Boulder, CO: Westview Press.

Payne, A. C., Whitehurst, G. J., and Angell, A. L. (1994). The role of home literacy environment in the development of language ability in preschool children from low-income families. *Early Childhood Research Quarterly*, 9(3–4), 427–440.

Reese, E., Sparks, A., and Leyva, D. (2010). A review of parent interventions for preschool children's language and emergent literacy. *Journal of Early Childhood Literacy*, 10(1), 97–117.

Sénéchal, M., and LeFevre, J. A. (2002). Parental involvement in the development of children's reading skill: a five-year longitudinal study. *Child Development*, 73(2), 445–460.

Sulzby, E., Teale, W. H., and Kamberelis, G. (1989). Emergent writing in the classroom: home and school connections. In D. S. Strickland and L. M. Morrow (eds.), *Emerging Literacy: Young Children Learn to Read and Write* (pp 63–79). Newark, NY: IRA.

Teale, W. H., and Sulzby, E. (1986). *Emergent Literacy: Writing and Reading*. Norwood, NJ: Ablex.

Teale, W. H., Whittingham, C. E., and Hoffman, E. B. (2020). Early literacy research, 2006–2015: a decade of measured progress. *Journal of Early Childhood Literacy*, 20(2), 169–222.

Van Oers, B. (2007). Helping young children to become literate: the relevance of narrative competence for developmental education. *European Early Childhood Education Research Journal*, 15(3), 299–312.

Vygotsky, L. S. (1978). *Mind in Society. The Development of Higher Psychological Processes*. Cambridge, MA: Harvard University Press.

9 | Storytelling

ANNA FILIPI

Introduction

People from all cultures tell stories. Stories are culturally bound (Bruner, 1986; Horsdal, 2012) but also have identifiable elements that are universal. It is through stories that people make sense of the world and of themselves (Barkhuizen, 2011). Through the opportunity to share experiences in storytelling, people also locate themselves and connect to others.

In all contexts, storytelling takes a central position and fulfils a number of purposes (or 'social projects'; Mandelbaum, 2012). In the case of children, one purpose is for children to experience pure enjoyment, which allows them to exercise their imagination through listening to, (re)telling, or following stories that are read to them (Bateman, 2020; Cekaite & Björk-Willén, 2018; Heller, 2019). Another purpose is to expose them to novel, vicarious experiences which enable the taking of another's perspective (Heller, 2019). The latter is essential to personal, social, and educational development, and is associated with development of socio-cognition in the field of developmental psychology (Nelson, 1996). A third purpose includes creating opportunities to build resilience and wellbeing in children through shared reports of traumatic events (Bateman & Danby, 2013; Bateman, Danby, & Howard, 2015), which, as the COVID-19 pandemic in 2020 and 2021 and environmental disasters have shown, are a reality, and unfortunately likely to increase. A fourth purpose of storytelling is to contribute to children's development of interactional and linguistic competence, and preparation for successful schooling in laying the foundations for literacy (Snow, Tabors, & Dickinson, 2001). Moreover, these competences also create confidence and skills for children to engage socially through knowing about and applying skills in initiating and sustaining storytelling with a range of others including their peers (e.g. Theobald, 2016; Theobald & Reynolds, 2015), family members (e.g. Blum-Kulka, 1990; McCabe & Peterson, 1991), family friends (e.g. Filipi, 2019), and teachers (e.g. Bateman & Carr, 2017; Theobald, 2019). Finally, and relatedly, are the opportunities provided through storytelling for building identity as children explore and play with social roles (e.g. Goodwin & Kyratzis, 2011; Theobald, 2019). Fundamental to each of these practices is social interaction.

Related to purpose is how storytelling takes shape as a genre. Children's exposure to – and experience of – a variety of genres is essential to the development of both their social interactional skills and their foundational success in schooling through early literacy and oracy practices. Language and interaction for schooling and socializing is provided through stories (and the discussions they generate) in children's books in print or on digital devices (e.g. Filipi, 2017a, 2019; Reese, 1995; Takada & Kawashima, 2019). Storytelling is also central to pretend play with adults and/or peers (e.g. Bateman, 2018; Filipi, 2022; Nicolopoulou, 2016; Snow, Tabors, & Dickinson, 2001) and in imaginative, spontaneous stories with peers and/or adults (e.g. Bateman, 2020; Theobald, 2019). Recounts of shared personal experiences (e.g. Burdelski, 2019; Farrant & Reese, 2000; Filipi, 2017b; Morita, 2019; Takagi, 2019) and updates of personal news (Reese & Brown, 2000; Searles, 2019) are other genres common in early childhood. All of these story genres begin in the home. They continue in early childhood settings and in the playground to provide children with rich experiences and potential opportunities for ongoing development as they create a foundation for schooling.

This chapter begins with an overview of research in conversation analysis (CA) that has explored the practices of storytelling. The ways in which the methods of CA are applied to understanding conversational storytelling are illustrated through analysis and discussion of three extracts representing two genres. One is an example of how storybook reading leads to second stories where the parent and child relate the events in the storybook to their own lives, while the other two are examples of recounts of personal events, thirteen months apart. These two latter examples reveal how children's storytelling develops over time. The analyses also show how a CA framing of research adds to our understanding of what children are actually able to do, and how, when they initiate or respond to invitations to shape storytelling. The chapter ends with suggestions of how this research has practical applications for teachers in their interactions with children, and in working with families.

Storytelling: Research Findings from the Perspectives of Conversation Analysis

Children's storytelling has been a focus of research activity since the late 1970s. Initially, attention was on the structural features of storytelling (Peterson & McCabe, 1983) which grew out of Labov and Waletsky's (1967) work on adult's oral stories; researchers therefore used the adults' practices as the norm for understanding children's stories. Heath's (1983) ethnographic studies in natural settings brought attention to the cultural differences in children's storytelling practices and provided a springboard for understanding the possible implications for literacy development in the alignment of these practices with the culture of schools. While approaches and analytical interests have since varied, interaction continues to be the primary focus of research in early storytelling. This is not surprising when the pivotal storytelling practices achieved through book reading, sharing of past or group experiences, pretend play, and spontaneous stories, are by their very nature highly interactive and social, irrespective of any purpose or project underlying the practice.

The study of storytelling in interactions with children from the perspective of CA is fairly recent, starting in the last decade (with Filipi, 2009, in describing the features of recounts of the day, and Radford & Mahon, 2010, on storybook reading with deaf children among the earliest), and culminating more recently in a collection of studies spanning storytelling in dyadic, multiparty, home, and preschool contexts, with adults and with peers (Burdelski & Evaldsson, 2019). This body of work has sought to draw attention to children's agency through their actions in interaction with adults and peers storytelling is produced collaboratively, and children participate in its creation and delivery. Each of these studies draws attention to the achievement of storytelling through a 'multimodal package' (Filipi, 2018a) that includes verbal and nonverbal resources.

Typically developing children, observed in western cultures, start to participate as co-tellers in pretend play as soon as they are producing single word utterances at the age of 1 year 3 months; Filipi, 2022). For example, they may point to a toy, vocalize, and look at the parent. This draws the attention of the parent who then responds. In this way conversation begins. Furthermore, children are engaging in talk elicited during storybook reading (Takada & Kawashima, 2019) and personal recounts from 1 year 6 months to 2 years where they are 'spotlighted speakers' (Burdelski, 2019) who are invited to share accounts of their everyday experiences (Burdelski, 2019; Engel, 1995; Filipi, 2017a, 2017b; Takagi, 2019). This is achieved through the highly supportive, scaffolded actions of the parent. However, there is also emerging evidence that even very young children are initiating stories rather than merely being solicited to respond. Heller (2019), for example, shows how a child aged 1 year 7 months engages in 'nonverbal discussion' by invoking absent characters and place. In essence this demonstrates the early interactional properties of decontextualized talk, so crucial for early literacy. Similarly, Filipi 2022 analyses how, through the actions of pointing and, often co-occurring vocalization, a child aged 1 year 3 months initiates pretend play, which is considered to be enacted storytelling (Nicolopoulou, 2016).

By the age of 2 years 2 months and before age 3, children are increasingly initiating stories and recruiting the assistance of others as they contribute to multi-party accounts through a range of verbal and non-verbal (Morita, 2019), and cultural resources including different languages (Evaldsson & Fernandes, 2019). Through these resources, they are able to elaborate the details of their experience or past actions (Takagi, 2019) and 'perform' stories that are highly tellable (Evaldsson & Fernandes, 2019), and elicit positive feedback or praise (Cekaite & Björk-Willén, 2018; Evaldsson & Fernandes, 2019; Takagi, 2019). In their storytelling, we know that children are sensitive to contextual details, because they display attendance to others and to what others know about an event (Morita, 2019).

From the age of 3 to 4 years, children are increasingly able to use linguistic resources to initiate or announce a story alongside embodied, non-linguistic resources (Filipi, 2019; Theobald, 2016). They also know how to link their own story to what is being spoken about; they monitor talk so that they can make a contribution and maintain the continued attention of their co-participants (Theobald & Reynolds, 2015); they also engage in extended talk where they hold the floor (Filipi, 2019; Searles, 2019). These are all important and recognizable features of storytelling. This means that by the age of 5 years, when children are ready to start school, most have developed the skills necessary (through the cumulative experience of interacting with a range of others) for them to be able to talk about their everyday experiences, create spontaneous stories, and engage in book-sharing discussions (Schick & Melzi, 2010). Above all, CA research shows us the interactional competences of children at very young ages and the complexity of their skills. These competences are uncovered through the micro-detailed attention of CA to both what is said, and also to *how* it is said and done through the body and voice in sequences of talk.

Examples of Early Storytelling

In the following section, two different conversational story genres from one parent-child dyad (Rosie aged 1 year 11 months, 2 years, and 3 years respectively, and her mother) will be briefly analysed. They are two recounts of a family event, one at 1 year 11 months and the other at 3 years (chosen because they provide insight into changes over a 13-month period) and a second story generated from a shared book reading activity. These samples have been selected because they shed light on: (1) the social and sequence structural qualities of early storytelling as displayed through the collaborative actions of parent and child as they unfold turn-by-turn; (2) the ways in which work on interactional (and therefore also language) skills is occasioned; and (3) the ways in which the stories are recognizable as stories. All three episodes occurred in the home. The data comes from a large collection in Australia, collected fortnightly for 30-minute sessions, which started when Rosie was 9 months and ended when she was aged 2 years. A further one-hour sample was collected when Rosie was aged 3 years. Transcription notations used in the extracts are consistent with each of the chapters in this volume, with the additions of the following from Filipi (2007) to convey nonverbal features: '–>' to indicate gaze, 'TU' to indicate turning towards, 'P–>' to indicate pointing to, and the curly bracket '{' to indicate the onset of a nonverbal action.

Second Stories through Shared Storybook Reading

In the first extract, we see the ways in which a second story is generated. Second stories are very common features of adults' conversational storytelling (Sacks, 1992) as speakers connect to each other socially through what is often the same or related experience. This is an important function of storytelling (Stokoe & Edwards, 2006). However, second stories must also display how they are related and relevant to the talk in the first story (Sacks, 1992; Sidnell, 2010).

This first story in Extract 9.1 is not told for an 'other'. The purpose of the story is derived from the opportunity it provides mother and child to share/reflect on a similar experience to the one arising out of the storybook reading. It provides the foundation for developing skills in reflecting on what members have in common with others, an important part of interactional and social competence.

Extract 9.1 Rosie at age 2 years

The mother is reading *Brown Bear* to Rosie who is sitting on her lap with the book in front of her. At the point of the story where the mother reads *i see a purple cat looking at me*, she looks down at Rosie who points to the picture of the cat; this launches a brief labelling sequence - *that's a cat isn't it?* - just prior to the cat story.

1 MOT: did we see a cat yesterday?
2 ROS: yeah!
3 (0.3)
4 MOT: and who ↑else did we see.=
5 ROS: =mm::?
6 (0.5)
7 MOT: we saw a- the cat.
8 >we saw< the MUmmy cat.
9 ROS: ↑yeah.
10 (0.4)
11 MOT: and the KItten¿
12 (0.2)
13 ROS: yeah.
14 MOT: and the baby- and the mummy cat¿
15 (1.0)
16 what did we give the cat to drink?
17 ROS: mm::?
18 MOT: what did we give the cat to drink?
19 ROS: °mm?°
20 (0.7)
21 MOT: can you remember?
22 ROS: milk.
23 MOT: milk.
24 good girl.
25 we gave her a little bit of milk on a plate
26 didn't we?
27 (1.0) ((Mother resumes reading - *purple cat*
28 *purple cat…*))

The story *Brown Bear* (Martin, 1994), is a favourite, and read often, so that Rosie is completely familiar with it. We note that this second story emerges seamlessly, aligning with the principle of the need for relevance of the story to the first (Sacks, 1992). It connects to the storybook through the character of the cat. As has been reported in previous research on narratives and conversational storytelling of children (e.g. Blum-Kulka, 1990; Engel, 1995; Filipi, 2009, 2017b, 2019; Rome-Flanders, Cronk, & Gourde, 1995; Wigglesworth & Stavans, 2001), the child's collaboration to co-tell is elicited through a series of wh- (lines 4, 16, 18) and yes/no questions (lines 1, 11, 14). These provide the details of the story: the time – yesterday; the characters – mummy and baby cat; the action – feeding them milk. Furthermore, three of these questions are designed as 'and' prefacing questions, a device that sustains the storytelling activity over a number of sequences (Heritage & Sorjonen, 1994) thereby connecting each question and answer to create an episode (Nevile, 2006). All these actions are also referred to as 'maternal elaborativeness' (Reese, Haden, & Fivush, 1993) because the mother prompts her child to provide the relevant features of the story step-by-step.

Rosie's responses are minimal – delivered mainly through a yes response as a direct answer or as a confirming action (lines 2, 9, 13), and an actual answer to an informing question *milk*. There is also evidence that she does not always understand the mother's question, for example through her repair initiating *mm?* in lines 5, 17, 19. These are potential difficulties that the mother orients to as she accommodates to the child by adjusting her questions through follow-up yes/no questions (to be discussed further below). In this way the child is supported in the co-creation of the story. Equally, there are signs that the mother also 'pushes' Rosie to complete an answer (see Filipi, 2017a). This is evident in the final three-part sequence – initiation, response, evaluation (Mehan, 1979), common in instructional talk, which begins in line 16 with a wh- question – *what did we give the cat to drink?* Rather than reformulating the question to a yes/no when Rosie initiates repair in her response turn, the mother repeats her question exactly in line 18. Furthermore, subsequent to Rosie's repeated repair initiation *mm?*, she counters with a *can/do you remember* recognition check (Schegloff, 1988; Shaw & Kitzinger, 2007; You, 2015). This is a device that speakers use to indicate that they have an expectation that their co-participant shares knowledge about a topic under discussion. The use of this device has also been described in pedagogical work in the classroom (Filipi, 2018a, 2018b), where teachers expect that students know the answer to their question as they have previously covered the topic. In a similar way, the mother's use of the recognition check coupled with her pursuit of the question, provide evidence that the mother expects the child to know the answer, and indeed Rosie's answer *milk*, shows that this was in fact the case.

The microdetails of these actions show how powerful such fine-grained analyses can be in exposing what the child can do (for example, respond immediately through repair initiation), and what the parent expects the child to be able to do, which influences actions to support the child in co-participation.

Recounting Personal Experience

Extract 9.2 provides an analysis of a recount of an event of the day. These recounts are commonplace in family interactions and start to appear just as the child is producing two-word utterances from the age of 1 year 6 months onwards (Filipi, 2009). As noted by Filipi (2017b), the purpose of these stories or tellings is to share everyday experiences, an important feature of children's social worlds played out in the family context. Additionally, when an outsider is present, an opportunity for the child to put on show what she knows or what she can do for others is created, which is also pervasive at this age (Filipi, 2009, 2017b). This makes the event newsworthy and tellable, an important principle of storytelling in general (Sacks, 1992; Sidnell, 2010).

As in the above extract, highly scaffolded questions of the adult (cf. Bateman & Carr, 2017; Filipi, 2017a, 2017b; Peterson & Jesso, 2008; Rome-Flanders, Cronk, & Gourde, 1995) are a feature of these early tellings. Through this feature the child is invited and supported to collaborate and 'shape the delivery of the story' (Lerner, 1992, p. 260) through minimal answers. This is often done for the benefit of someone who is present in the room but who does not know about the event (Filipi, 2017b). The story is therefore told for a particular audience or addressee.

Extract 9.2 Rosie at 1 year 11 months

```
Rosie is having a bath.

1   MOT:  so what did you do today,
          ((Rosie is dropping toys in the bath.))
2            (0.8)
3         °°you're a sausage aren't you.°°
4            (1.0)
5   MOT:  did you stay home with daddy today¿
6   ROS:  {yep.
          {((Face each other.))
7            (0.2)
8   MOT:  and what did {you and daddy do::,=
                       {((Rosie--->down.))
9            (0.2)
10  ROS:  ={mm?
           {((Rosie--->Mother.))
11           (0.3)
12  MOT:  {what did you do?
          {((Nods.))
13           (0.3)   ((Rosie--->down.))
14  ROS:  (um da::) (0.4){WATER!
                         {((Rosie--->Mother.))
```

```
15             (0.5)
16   MOT:   did you go into the water?
17   ROS:   yeah:::.
18   MOT:   where?
19             (0.4)
20   ROS:   {heh (              )
            {((Rosie--->down.))
21   MOT:   i $couldn't see any water in the ↑$poo::l?
22             (0.3)
23   ROS:   (               )
24             (0.2)
25   MOT:   where was the water,
26             (0.2)
27   ROS:   mm?
28             (0.3)
29   MOT:   hey?
30   ROS:   {my water!
            {((Rosie--->Mother.))
31   MOT:   it was your {wa::ter?
32   ROS:   ((Puts a toy in her mouth and vocalizes.))=
                        {((Rosie--->down.))
33   MOT:   =did you go for {a walk in the pram?
                            {((Rosie--->Mother.))
34             (0.4) ((Rosie----->down.))
35   ROS:   ((Continues vocalizing with toy in her mouth.))
36             (0.3)
37   MOT:   did you::?
38             (0.4)
39   ROS:   (((Continues to vocalize with the toy in her
            mouth, also shakes her head.))
40             (0.5)
41   MOT:   °°you're a little monkey aren't you¿°°
42             (0.6)
43          did you go for a walk in the pram with daddy?
44             (0.2)
45   ROS:   YE::P! °°one, two°° ((Yells.))
((Mother cleans her face and the talk turns to counting.))
…
```

The event or story being shared in this extract, which the mother knows about, concerns Rosie spending the day with her father and going for a walk in the pram. However, the specific details do not at first emerge in the structure of the mother's question. Instead, she starts by asking a completely open question through the information eliciting – *what did you do.* This is left unanswered as Rosie is intent on playing with the toys in the bath, an action which leads the mother to rephrase her question into a simpler yes/no question in line 5. This has the effect of narrowing the openness of the question – *did you stay home with daddy today?*

This same sequence format (reported in Filipi, 2017a, 2017b), a further example of which appears in lines 8 and 16, starts with an open question which is then followed up with a more explicit and narrowing yes/no question when an answer is not forthcoming. The question design not only accommodates to the child but also enables her to participate in shaping the story, evidence for which is visible through Rosie's confirming actions in lines 6, 17, and 45.

In the developmental literature (e.g. Aldridge & Wood, 1998), information-eliciting open questions have been shown to pose some challenge for children at this age, unlike yes/no questions which are the earliest question forms that are understood. This may be the case in Rosie's responses in lines 14 and 30, although the mother treats them as acceptable even if they are not contingently relevant next responses. In line 14, Rosie's answer is about water. The original story being pursued by the mother (i.e. a walk in the pram), is suspended as the mother questions Rosie about the water, noting that the play pool is empty. This action provides a display of the ways in which she creates an opportunity for Rosie to steer the conversation and to control its direction through her telling. After subsequent attempts to get Rosie to clarify what she is referring to – *where was the water* – through further clarification follow-ups in lines 29 and 31, she asks a yes/no question in line 33 – *did you go for a walk in the pram*? In receiving neither a reply nor signs of engagement from Rosie who continues to look down, she again pursues an answer in lines 37 and 43. This time, Rosie answers with an emphatic *yep*, and she quickly moves onto a counting activity, thereby ending the recount of the day's events.

An interesting feature of these early recounts is that they often fail to sustain the child's interest, and parents struggle to go beyond one question/answer/evaluation or acknowledgement sequence to build an episode, as is the case in Extract 9.1. Clearly though, parents see the value of engaging their children in these recounts. Indeed, as studies of older children at family meal times have shown (e.g. Blum-Kulka, 1990), these recounts become dinnertime sharing stories where parents routinely ask their children what they did during the day, even when the parent knows all or most of what transpired.

The last extract, Extract 9.3, also of a recount but from a year later, will be analysed from the perspective of visible changes both in the sequence structure, and in engagement and participation.

Extract 9.3 Rosie at age 3 years

Rosie and her mother are recounting a birthday party event they attended at the weekend, which is sparked off by the balloon received at the party. (From Filipi 2019, p. 132.)

```
1   MOT:   now where did you get that balloon from?
2              (1.5)
3          where did you get that balloon from?
4              (0.3)
5   ROS:   from {(0.5) ti::::lly.
                {((Runs towards Mother.))
6              (0.3)
7   MOT:   and (0.3) what- what was the special
8          occasion when we went to tilly's house=
9   ROS:   =you say it.
10             (0.3)
11  MOT:   huh huh (0.2) why do you want me to say it.
12  ROS:   i want {you to.
                  {((TU---→camera.))
13  MOT:   {but you know what it was (we sang a song.)
    ROS:   {((TU---→Mother.))
14             (0.3)
15  MOT:   what was the special song we sang,
16  ROS:   you say it.
17             (0.3)
18  MOT:   was it happy birthday?
19  ROS:   ((Nods.))
20  MOT:   and why did we sing happy birthday.
21  ROS:   (cause) it's tilly's birthday.
22  MOT:   yes.
23         and how old was tilly.
24             (0.5)
25  ROS:   three like me.
26  MOT:   three just like you. (0.3) yeah.
((Rosie resumes playing catchy with the balloon.))
```

In Extract 9.3, the telling is for the benefit of the researcher who is present and filming the interaction. It occurs in a space during balloon play so that play is temporarily suspended. As in the first two extracts, we note the same use of a series of questions. This time however, they are overwhelmingly wh- questions. In fact, there is only one yes/no question, in line 18, when trouble in understanding a keyword – *occasion* – seems to arise. There are also 'and' prefaced questions in lines 7, 20, and 23, which provide details of what, why, and the age of the birthday child. Noteworthy is that Rosie is able to successfully answer the mother's questions. There are two notable exceptions, her failure to respond to her mother's question in line 1, which can be explained by her focus on the balloon with which she has just been playing, and her response to the question in lines 7– and 8 – *you say it*, which is an answer but not the expected answer to the question. We note that it occurs in the slot where the repair-initiating *mm?* appeared at the earlier age of 1 year 11 months (see lines 10 and 27 in Extract 9.2) in response to a question that she could not answer, suggesting that Rosie has now expanded her response repertoire. Her *you say it* hands the floor back to the mother, who, however, resists the action through an ascription of knowledge – *but you know what it was* – and her follow-up – *what was the special song we sang* – when an answer is still not forthcoming. She finally produces the only yes/no question in the episode in line 18, when both of these actions fail to deliver an answer, and Rosie immediately produces an answer through an affirmative head nod. The extract thus provides a clear sense of the changes both in the need for the mother's level of support and the greater independence of Rosie in being able to supply actual propositional answers.

Recommendations for Practice

This chapter has described the practices surrounding early conversational storytelling, essential in helping children to build interactional, linguistic, and social competence. In the home, in the classroom, and in the playground, through children's picture storybook reading, spontaneous storytelling, in pretend play, and in conversation around the table or when someone outside the family is present, children share and reflect on events experienced, engage in imaginative play and story creation, and make connections between events depicted in picture books and similar events in their own lives. These practices provide an insight into both the socializing that occurs and the groundwork established for early literacy.

The three extracts in this chapter offered a small sample to show how children are supported to co-tell and create stories in ways that display what expectations they have of others in being invited to share and to co-tell a story, and what actions and resources they use to either adjust their expectations or to realize them as a result of monitoring the telling. This is true for both the mother and child in the extracts discussed. From an educational perspective, the actions of the mother are recognizable as scaffolding. They work in the same ways as teacher scaffolding described by Theobald (2019) in a preschool setting (see also Bateman, Chapter 3, this volume). She upped the ante (Bruner, 1986; Filipi, 2009) to extend Rosie's turns, based on what she knew Rosie was able to produce or could be 'pushed' to produce. To adopt a Vygotskian (Vygotsky, 1962) perspective, learning occurs when more knowledgeable others allow learners to bridge a gap with support from others. These actions were on display through the mother's use of the less supportive open and wh- questions, and more supportive and facilitating yes/no questions when expected answers were not forthcoming. As noted, these are now well-established findings both in the CA research and in developmental psychology. However, even though the mother was initiating the work in the samples presented here, what is noteworthy is how these actions were being responded to and therefore shaped, or indeed reshaped, through Rosie's own actions. This was illustrated through her displays of propositional or interactional understanding, and the ways in which she attempted to briefly take the story in a different direction as in Extract 9.2.

These findings have implications for the ways in which teachers can, and indeed do, engage and set up opportunities for storytelling to occur in the classroom, and for assessment of children's learning. Pedagogical applications for teachers to consider arising from CA research on storytelling are to:

- Create opportunities for children to initiate stories and recognize when children are in fact engaging in storytelling through the conversational resources they use, such as '*you know what?*', '*I know*', and elaborate on these as children grow older, to push them beyond and enrich their current repertoires.
- Communicate regularly with families to share specific skills and advice about how to invite children to tell both first and second stories and to explain their importance.
- Make children aware of the relevance of stories, and how to take and maintain the floor/contribute to stories in appropriate ways when adopting listener behaviours.

- Explicitly teach children how to initiate, develop, and conclude stories (i.e. pragmatic and interactional skills), through linguistic devices used to do this work, and assess these skills for both formative feedback purposes and for reporting to parents.
- Provide children with practice and resources to extend/elaborate their stories.
- Include a specific daily time and a physical space for storytelling in class; not just for reading but also for telling.
- Be aware that typically developing children start school with considerable skills and experience in storytelling but that there may be others who need further support.
- Invite children to respond to each other's stories.
- Record, transcribe, and analyse story sequences as part of self-evaluation to understand teachers' own practices in telling, inviting, and sharing stories with children.

References

Aldridge, M., and Wood, J. (1998). *Interviewing Children: A Guide for Child Care and Forensic Practitioners*. West Sussex: John Wiley.

Barkhuizen, G. (2011). Narrative knowledging in TESOL. *TESOL Quarterly*, 45(3), 391–414. Available from: www.jstor.org/stable/41307694

Bateman, A. (2018). Ventriloquism as early literacy practice: making meaning in pretend play. *Early Years*, 38(1), 68–85. https://doi.org/10.1080/09575146.2016.1254162

Bateman, A. (2020). Young children's affective stance through embodied displays of emotion during tellings. *Text & Talk*, 40(5), 643–668. https://doi.org/10.1515/text-2020-2077

Bateman, A., and Carr, M. (2017). Pursuing a telling: managing a multi-unit turn in children's storytelling. In A. Bateman and A. Church (eds.), *Children and Knowledge: Studies in Conversation Analysis* (pp. 91–110). Singapore: Springer. https://doi.org/10.1007/978-981-10-1703-2

Bateman, A., and Danby, S. (2013). Recovering from the earthquake: early childhood teachers and children collaboratively telling stories about their experiences. *Disaster Management and Prevention Journal*, 22(5), 467–479. https://doi.org/10.1108/DPM-10–2013-0177

Bateman, A., Danby, S., and Howard, J. (2015). Using conversation analysis for understanding children's talk about traumatic events. In M. O'Reilly and J. Lester (eds.), *Handbook of Child Mental Health: Discourse and Conversation Studies* (pp. 402–421). New York, NY: Palgrave Macmillan. https://doi.org/10.1057/9781137428318

Blum-Kulka, S. (1990). You don't touch lettuce with your fingers: parental politeness in family discourse. *Journal of Pragmatics*, 14, 259–288. https://doi.org/10.1016/0378-2166(90)90083-P

Bruner, J. S. (1986). *Actual Minds, Possible Worlds*. Cambridge, MA: Harvard University Press.

Burdelski, M. (2019). Young children's multimodal participation in storytelling: analyzing talk and gesture in Japanese family interaction. In M. Burdelski and A-C. Evaldsson (eds.), *A Multimodal CA Perspective on Children's Collaborative Tellings of Events. Research on Children and Social Interaction, Special Issue*, 3(1–2), 1–5. https://doi.org/10.1558/rcsi.38982.

Burdelski, M., and Evaldsson, A-C. (eds.) (2019). *A Multimodal CA Perspective on Children's Collaborative Tellings of Events. Research on Children and Social Interaction, Special Issue*, 3(1–2), 1–5. https://doi.org/10.1558/rcsi.38982

Cekaite, A., and Björk-Willén, P. (2018). Enchantment in storytelling: co-operation and participation in children's aesthetic experience. *Linguistics and Education*, 48, 52–60. https://doi.org/org/10.1016/j.linged.2018.08.005

Engel, S. (1995). *The Stories Children Tell: Making Sense of the Narratives of Childhood*. New York, NY: W. H. Freeman.

Evaldsson, A-C., and Fernandes, O. A. (2019). Embodied performances and footings in a young child's spontaneous participation in bilingual Russian–Swedish storytelling. In M. Burdelski and A-C. Evaldsson (eds.), *A Multimodal CA Perspective on Children's Collaborative Tellings of Events. Research on Children and Social Interaction, Special Issue*, 3(1–2), 36–64. https://doi.org/10.1558/rcsi.37297

Farrant, K., and Reese, E. (2000). Maternal style and children's participation in reminiscing: stepping stones in children's autobiographical memory development. *Journal of Cognition and Development*, 1(2), 193–225.

Filipi, A. (2007). A toddler's treatment of mm and mm hm in talk with a parent. *Australian Review of Applied Linguistics*, 30(3), 1–17. https://doi.org/10.2104/ARAL0733

Filipi, A. (2009). *Toddler and Parent Interaction: The Organisation of Gaze, Pointing and Vocalization*. Amsterdam/Philadelphia: John Benjamins.

Filipi, A. (2017a). Exploring the recognisability of early story-telling through an interactional lens. *Research on Children and Social Interaction*, 1(2), 141–163. https://doi.org/10.1558/rcsi.31370

Filipi, A. (2017b). The emergence of early story-telling. In A. Bateman and A. Church (eds.), *Children's Knowledge-in-Interaction: Studies in Conversation Analysis* (pp. 279–295). Singapore: Springer. https://doi.org/10.1007/978-981-10-1703-2

Filipi, A. (2018a). Making teacher talk comprehensible through language alternation practices. In A. Filipi and N. Markee (eds.), *Conversation Analysis and Language Alternation: Capturing Transitions in the Classroom* (pp. 183–204). Amsterdam/Philadelphia: John Benjamins. https://doi.org/10.1075/pbns.295

Filipi, A. (2018b). Using language alternation to establish epistemic status in an Italian as a second language lesson. In P. Seedhouse, O. Sert, and U. Balaman (eds.), *Conversation Analytic Studies on Teaching and Learning Practices: International Perspectives. Hacettepe University Journal of Education, Special Issue*, 33, 36–53. https://doi.org/10.16986/HUJE.2018038795

Filipi, A. (2019). Snapshots of how story-telling is triggered in interactions with children aged two, three and three and a half. In M. Burdelski and A-C. Evaldsson (eds.), *A Multimodal CA Perspective on Children's Collaborative Tellings of Events. Research on Children and Social Interaction, Special Issue*, 3(1–2), 219–143. https://doi.org/10.1558/rcsi.37285

Filipi, A. (2022). The shape of child-initiated in pretend play in interactions with a parent at ages 15 months and 3. In A. Filipi, B. T. Ta, and M. Theobald (eds.), *Storytelling Practices in Home and Educational Contexts: Perspectives from Conversation Analysis*. Cham: Springer.

Goodwin, M. H., and Kyratzis, A. (2011). Peer language socialization. In A. Duranti, E. Ochs, and B. B. Schiefflein (eds.), *The Handbook of Language Socialization (pp. 365–390)*. Malden, NJ: Blackwell. https://doi.org/10.1002/9781444342901.ch16

Heath, S. B. (1983). *Ways with Words: Language, Life and Work in Communities and Classrooms*. New York, NY: Cambridge University Press.

Heller, V. (2019). Embodied displacements in young German children's storytelling: layering of spaces, voices and bodies. In M. Burdelski and A-C. Evaldsson (eds.), *A Multimodal CA Perspective on Children's Collaborative Tellings of Events. Research on Children and Social Interaction, Special Issue*, 3(1–2), 168–195. https://doi.org/10.1558/rcsi.37311

Heritage, J. (2012). The epistemic engine: sequence organization and territories of knowledge. *Research on Language and Social Interaction*, 45(1), 30–52. https://doi.org/10.1080/08351813.2012.646685

Heritage, J., and Sorjonen, M-L. (1994). Constituting and maintaining activities across sequences: and-prefacing as a feature of question design. *Language in Society*, 23(1), 1–29. https://doi.org/10.1017/S0047404500017656

Horsdal, M. (2012). *Telling Lives: Exploring Dimensions of Narratives*. New York, NY: Routledge.

Hutchby, I., and Wooffitt, R. (2008). *Conversation Analysis* (2nd ed.). Cambridge: Polity Press.

Labov, W., and Waletzky, J. (1967). Narrative analysis: oral versions of personal experience. In J. Helm (ed.), *Essays on the Verbal and Visual Arts* (pp. 12–34). Seattle, WA: University of Washington Press.

Lerner, G. (1992). Assisted storytelling: deploying shared knowledge as a practical matter. *Qualitative Sociology*, 15(3), 247–271. https://doi.org/10.1007/BF00990328

Mandelbaum, J. (2012). Story-telling in conversation. In J. Sidnell and T. Stivers (eds.), *The Handbook of Conversation Analysis* (pp. 492–508). Chichester: Wiley-Blackwell. https://doi.org/10.1002/9781118325001.ch24

Martin, B. Jr. (1994). *Brown Bear*. New York, NY: Henry Holt & Company Inc.

McCabe, A., and Peterson, C. (1991). Getting the story: a longitudinal study of parental styles in eliciting narratives and developing narrative skill. In A. McCabe and C. Peterson (eds.), *Developing Narrative Structure* (pp. 217–253). Hillsdale, NJ: Erlbaum.

Mehan, H. (1979). *Learning Lessons: Social Organization in the Classroom*. Boston, MA: Harvard University Press. https://doi.org/10.4159/harvard.9780674420106

Morita, E. (2019). Japanese two-year-olds' spontaneous participation in storytelling activities as social interaction. In M. Burdelski and A-C. Evaldsson (eds.), *A Multimodal CA Perspective on Children's Collaborative Tellings of Events. Research on Children and Social Interaction, Special Issue*, 3(1–2), 65–91. https://doi.org/10.1558/rcsi.37312

Nelson, K. (1996). *Language in Cognitive Development*. New York, NY: Cambridge University Press.

Nevile, M. (2006). Making sequentiality salient: and-prefacing in the talk of airline pilots. *Discourse Studies*, 8(2), 279–302. https://doi.org//10.1177/1461445606061797

Nicolopoulou, A. (2016). Young children's pretend play and storytelling as modes of narrative activity. In S. Douglas and L. Stirling (eds.), *Children's Play, Pretense, and Story: Studies in Culture, Context, and Autism Spectrum Disorder* (pp. 6–27). New York/London: Routledge.

Peterson, C., and Jesso, B. (2008). Parent/caregiver: narrative development (37–48 months). In L. Phillips (ed.), *Handbook of Language and Literacy Development: A Roadmap from 0–60 Months* (pp. 1–10). London, ON: Canadian Language and Literacy Research Network.

Peterson, C., & McCabe, A. (1983). *Developmental Psycholinguistics: Three Ways of Looking at a Child's Narrative*. New York, NY: Plenum.

Radford, J., and Mahon, M. (2010). Multi-modal participation in storybook sharing. In H. Gardner and M. Forrester (eds.), *Analysing Interactions in Childhood: Insights from Conversation Analysis (pp. 209–226)*. West Sussex: John Wiley. https://doi.org/10.1111/j.1460–6984.2011.00098.x

Reese, E. (1995). Predicting children's literacy from mother-child conversations. *Cognitive Development*, 10(3), 381–405. https://doi.org/10.1016/0885–2014(95)90003-9

Reese, E., and Brown, N. (2000). Reminiscing and recounting in the preschool years. *Applied Cognitive Psychology*, 14(1), 1–17 https://doi.org/10.1002/(SICI)1099-0720(200001)14:1<::AID-ACP625>3.0.CO;2-G

Reese, E., Haden, C. A., and Fivush, R. (1993). Mother–child conversations about the past: relationships of style and memory over time. *Cognitive Development*, 8, 403–430. https://doi.org/10.1016/S0885-2014(05)80002-4

Rome-Flanders, T., Cronk, C., and Gourde, C. (1995). Maternal scaffolding in mother-infant games and its relationship to language development: a longitudinal study. *First Language*, 15(3), 339–355. https://doi.org/10.1177/014272379501504505

Sacks, H. (1992). Long sequences. In G. Jefferson (ed.), *Lectures on Conversation* (vol. 2, pp. 354–359). Oxford: Blackwell.

Schegloff, E. A. (1988). Presequences and indirection. Applying speech act theory to ordinary conversation. *Journal of Pragmatics*, 12, 55–62. https://doi.org/10.1016/0378-2166(88)90019-7

Schegloff, E. A. (1991). Reflections on talk and social structure. In D. Boden and D. H. Zimmerman (eds.), *Talk and Social Structure* (pp. 44–70). Cambridge: Polity Press.

Schegloff, E. A. (2007). *Sequence Organization in Interaction: A Primer in Conversation Analysis*. Cambridge: Cambridge University Press.

Schick, A., and Melzi, G. (2010). The development of children's oral narratives across contexts. *Early Education and Development*, 21(3), 293–317. https://doi.org/10.1080/10409281003680578

Searles, D. K. (2019). Positioning updates as relevant: an analysis of child-initiated updating in American and Canadian families. In M. Burdelski and A-C. Evaldsson (eds.), *A Multimodal CA Perspective on Children's Collaborative Tellings of Events. Special Issue, Research on Children and Social Interaction*, 3(1–2), 144–167. https://doi.org/10.1558/rcsi.37286

Shaw, R., and Kitzinger, C. (2007). Memory in interaction: an analysis of repeat calls to a home birth helpline. *Research on Language & Social Interaction*, 40(1), 117–144. https://doi.org/10.1080/08351810701331307

Sidnell, J. (2010). *Conversation Analysis*. West Sussex: Wiley-Blackwell.

Snow, C. E., Tabors, P. O., and Dickinson, D. K. (2001). Language development in the preschool years. In D. K. Dickinson and P. O. Tabors (eds.), *Beginning Literacy with Language: Young Children Learning at Home and School* (pp. 1–25). Baltimore, MD: P. H. Brookes Publishing.

Stokoe, E., and Edwards, D. (2006). Story formulations in talk-in-interaction. *Narrative Inquiry*, 16(1), 56–65. https://doi.org/10.1075/ni.16.1.09sto

Takada, A., and Kawashima, M. (2019). Caregivers' strategies for eliciting storytelling from toddlers in Japanese caregiver–child picture book reading activities. In M. Burdelski and A-C. Evaldsson (eds.), *A Multimodal CA Perspective on Children's Collaborative Tellings of Events. Research on Children and Social Interaction, Special Issue*, 3(1–2), 196–223. https://doi.org/10.1558/rcsi.37287

Takagi, T. (2019). Referring to past actions in caregiver–child interaction in Japanese. In M. Burdelski and A-C. Evaldsson (eds.), *A Multimodal CA Perspective on Children's Collaborative Tellings of Events. Research on Children and Social Interaction, Special Issue*, 3(1–2), 92–118. https://doi.org/10.1558/rcsi.37384

Theobald, M. (2016). Achieving competence: the interactional features of children's storytelling. *Childhood*, 23(10), 87–104. https://doi.org/10.1177/0907568215571619

Theobald, M. (2019). Scaffolding storytelling and participation with a bilingual child in a culturally and linguistically diverse preschool in Australia. In M. Burdelski and A-C. Evaldsson (eds.), *A Multimodal CA Perspective on*

Children's Collaborative Tellings of Events. Research on Children and Social Interaction, Special Issue, 3(1–2), 224–247. https://doi.org/10.1558/rcsi.37294

Theobald, M., and Reynolds, E. (2015). In pursuit of some appreciation: assessment and group membership in children's second stories. *Text & Talk*, 35(3), 407–430. https://doi.org/10.1515/text-2015-0006

Vygotsky, L. S. (1962). *Thought and Language*. Cambridge, MA: MIT Press.

Wigglesworth, G., and Stavans, A. (2001). A cross-cultural investigation of parental interaction in narrative with children at a range of ages. In K. Nelson, A. Aksu-Koc, and C. Johnson (eds.), *Children's Language, Volume 10: Narrative and Discourse Development* (pp. 73–93). Mahwah, NJ: Lawrence Erlbaum Associates.

You, H-J. (2015). Reference to shared past events and memories. *Journal of Pragmatics*, 87, 238–250. https://doi.org/10.1016/j.pragma.2015.02.003

10 | Digital Technologies

SANDY HOUEN AND SUSAN DANBY

Introduction

In industrialized countries, children's lives are surrounded by digital technologies. The proliferation and seamless integration of digital technologies into children's home lives means that they are 'often taken for granted' (Danby et al., 2020, p. 1). Their uptake in early childhood education classrooms, however, can be more challenging. In this chapter, following Mantilla and Edwards (2019), we draw on Plowman's (2016) definition of digital technology, which is defined as 'digital devices (e.g., computers, tablets, games consoles) and the products of outputs (e.g., applications, Websites, games) viewed, played, read or created on these devices' (p. 96). Children use digital technologies in their everyday lives to access knowledge; to communicate with others; to document memories, ideas, and thoughts; and to navigate digital platforms to seek new knowledge (Danby et al., 2020).

Conflicting views on the impact of digital technologies on children's lives creates tension for those making decisions about young children's use of specific technologies, including in early childhood classrooms. The two most differentiated positions are the health and education perspectives (Straker et al., 2018). From a health perspective, the appropriateness of digital technologies for young children's health, development, and wellbeing has been questioned, with accompanying guidelines establishing caution. Generally, health authorities recommend young children's use of digital technology should be minimal, if at all (AAP Council on Communications and Media, 2016).

Often, health claims point to digital technologies contributing to adverse developmental outcomes for children, including poor posture (Howie et al., 2017), sleep problems such as delayed onset and shortened duration (Kahn et al., 2020; Vijakkhana et al., 2015), and increased externalizing behaviour (Vijakkhana et al., 2015) when exposed to violent media or media not

The authors thank the Australian Research Council for the following funded projects that supported the research discussed in this chapter: (1) Investigating Mobile Technologies in Young Children's Everyday Worlds (ARC Future Fellow FT120100731, Susan Danby); (2) Interacting with Knowledge, Interacting with People: Web Searching in Early Childhood (ARC Discovery DP110104227; Susan Danby, Karen Thorpe, Christina Davidson).

in line with age recommendations (Vijakkhana et al., 2015). On the other hand, digital technology has been valued in supporting young children's development for their sleep and social/emotional development (Garrison & Christakis, 2012), such as the use of relaxation and guided meditation applications. The caveat for differing benefits relates to children's healthy media use, underpinned by adults selecting age-appropriate content and interacting with children during engagement with digital technology.

Educational perspectives, on the other hand, value digital technologies for their potential to transform education. The inclusion of digital technology in curriculum and learning frameworks set an expectation that they will be incorporated into classrooms, including in early childhood contexts. For example, in Australia, the national early learning framework, *Belonging, Being, & Becoming* (Department of Education and Training, 2009), states that 'children benefit from opportunities to explore their world using technologies and to develop confidence in using digital media' (p. 38). How best to harness the potential of digital technology and align its use with theories about how young children learn is the focus of educators and the early childhood education and care (ECEC) sector worldwide.

Although early childhood educators can look to Early Childhood Australia's (ECA) *Statement on young children and digital technologies* (Early Childhood Australia, 2018) to inform decision-making about using digital technologies with young children, there is limited evidence to guide ECEC practices (Mantilla & Edwards, 2019). What is known is that, while many young children demonstrate competence and confidence to use digital technology, the importance of interactions with knowledgeable others for children's engagement is increasingly recognized (Danby et al., 2016; Danby & Davidson, 2019; Davidson, 2010; Davidson et al., 2018, 2020; Houen et al., 2017; Hurwitz & Schmitt, 2020; Livingstone et al., 2015; Spink et al., 2010). For example, an early study by Spink and colleagues (2010) found that children aged between five and six years could create Web queries, browse, formulate, and re-formulate search queries, make relevance judgements about the information they retrieve, and manage search results. This study also noted that children, particularly those with emerging literacy skills, relied on teachers to support them to enter the search query, read, and engage with the search results. Advice relating to young children's digital technology use, from both health and educational perspectives, points to the importance of adults in supporting young children's engagement with digital technology.

It can be a challenge to effectively integrate digital technologies into early childhood education programmes (Edwards, 2016; Edwards et al., 2020; Garvis & Lemon, 2016; Marsh et al., 2005; Vidal-Hall et al., 2020;

Yelland, 2008, 2011). Barriers that influence the uptake of digital technologies include a lack of empirical advice about digital technologies, limited professional development to guide digital technology use by and with children (Mantilla & Edwards, 2019; Thorpe et al., 2015), and inadequate time and space for critical reflection of their use (Vidal-Hall et al., 2020). Their slow uptake may be attributed to viewpoints that digital technologies do not align with play- and inquiry-based approaches esteemed in early childhood education (Danby et al., 2016; Edwards, 2016; Garvis & Lemon, 2016). Yet, a further challenge is that children are increasingly being involved in digital technologies at home and school, and these practices are being implemented within curriculum and pedagogic documents.

Beliefs associated with digital technologies can be shifted through a range of strategies, including critical reflection, opportunities to observe children engaging with digital technologies, and utilizing pedagogical practices already in use in other areas of the classroom (Vidal-Hall et al., 2020). For example, a recent classroom-based intervention enabled time and space for practitioner reflection, fostered collegial discussion about digital technologies and their integration with early childhood pedagogy, and encouraged the teacher to experiment with integrating digital technologies within a child-led curriculum. This study challenged teacher-held views that digital technologies did not align with child-centred philosophies (Vidal-Hall et al., 2020). During the intervention, teacher-led reflections highlighted possibilities for engagement with digital technologies in ways that aligned with child-led practices. The teacher interacted with children as they explored digital games, followed the child's lead, situated digital experiences as a joint activity, and positioned children as experts by asking them to explain how to use digital media. Rarely, however, do teachers have opportunities to conduct deep dives into current practices, nor do they have many opportunities to observe how other teachers integrate digital technologies into early childhood classrooms. This chapter provides two examples of practice – searching the Web and sending an email – allowing others to 'see' interactional practices that shape children's engagement with digital technology.

Using Digital Technologies in Early Childhood Classrooms

In the following sections, we present examples of digital technology use in early childhood settings in Australia. We draw on studies that apply conversation analysis to explicate how children's engagement with digital technologies is achieved by and through social interaction involving teachers and children, to highlight how digital technologies can support inquiry-based learning, problem solving, and conceptual engagement. Teacher-planned activities are not the focus. Instead, the focus is on how spontaneous digital experiences are seamlessly integrated into everyday activities and suggested by either children or offered by educators in response to children's ongoing ideas, inquiries, and projects.

Web Searching to Access New Knowledge

In early childhood classrooms, Web searches can be conducted in response to children's interests, such as wanting to find out about a butterfly found in the garden, or to extend children's current ideas, such as a child wanting to find images of an army tank in order to construct a model out of collage materials. Web searches usually progress through relatively predictable phases (Davidson et al., 2018; Houen, 2012), including: (1) identifying a search topic; (2) entering the search topic into the search engine; (3) assessing the search options; and (4) engaging with the search results (Houen, 2012). In this process, there are several opportunities to support children's learning about and with digital technologies.

We show an extended sequence of classroom interaction involving a teacher (pseudonym: SUSIE) and two children (pseudonyms: ETHAN and HARRY) aged between 5 and 6 years, who are co-located at a desktop computer in a preschool classroom. The teacher and children co-constructed and successfully accomplished a search about what tadpoles eat (Houen, 2012, 2017). We present four extracts that correspond to the four phases of Web searching to show the teacher's pedagogical strategies that promoted opportunities for children's inquiry-based learning, problem-solving, and engagement with digital technology concepts such as digital literacy skills and critical literacy.

Extract 10.1 Phase 1 – Finding a search topic

(Houen et al., 2017, p. 62)

```
SUS: Exactly. that was endangered, now¿ what are we going
     to sea:rch no:w what did you deci:de you wanted to
     look for?
```

```
610          (1.4)
611 ETH:  Um (.) what eats a crocodile¿
612          (0.8)
.
.            ((talk about their prior search occurs))
.
631 HAR:  [Susie I'd like] to find out what would um what eats
632          what do tadpoles eat (cause I don't really know)
633 SUS:  What do tadpoles eat (.) good questio:n=
634 ETH:  tadpoles we don't know
635 SUS:  Well do you want to do a search for tadpoles (food)
636 ETH:  Oh what(.) if we sear:ch what do blue whales eat=
.
.            ((talk about text entered for previous search))
.
642 SUS:  Which one are we going to go:: with
643          (0.6)
644 HAR:  Tadpoles I'm wanna do tadpoles (Ethan (.))
645 ETH:  What (.) do (0.4) >what do< puppies eat
646 SUS:  Puppies
647 HAR:  (um no puppies don't)=
648 SUS:  =Smelly socks, (0.4) slippers,(.) all so::rts of
64           things okay
650 HAR:  Harry you sta::rt
```

As Houen and colleagues (2017) point out, the teacher orients to inquiry-based learning by first consulting children about their search topic preference. Here, the teacher poses a question to find out the children's interests (line 607–609). She affords time and space for the children to proffer their ideas (line 610). When the children suggest different search topics, including what crocodiles/blue whales/ puppies/ tadpoles eat (lines 611, 631, 636, 645), the teacher navigates these differing suggestions. She defers the decision-making to the children by consulting them about which topic they will select (line 642). When it seems that the children do not reach consensus, the teacher provides an answer to Ethan's preferred search about what puppies eat (line 648–649). In this way, she has not discounted Ethan's question, but as she has provided an answer to his question, the search for this topic is rendered unnecessary. She then directs Harry to start (line 650). Susie's directive can be seen to prompt action that has not yet happened. Directives can be responded to by complying or rejecting them through next actions (Goodwin, 2006). Susie's position as teacher, however, places her in a position of authority, and it is less likely that a rejection will be forthcoming from the child. This directive also indicates that it is Harry's search topic that will be entered into the search engine.

In summary, this example has shown us that when teachers consult children about their search topics, the children are positioned as competent decision-makers who have knowledge about Web searches and who can decide about search subjects. The teacher positions their role as one able to extend and stretch children's learning by following a child's lead.

The second phase, below, involves keying the search topic into the search engine. Harry is supported by the teacher to do this entry, and the extract shows the opportunities for problem-solving and engagement with digital technology concepts presented by the teacher when children are charged with entering the topic.

Extract 10.2 Phase 2 – Entering the search topic

(Houen, 2012, pp. 69–72)

SUS: O:ka::y (.) so (sort it out) >what shall we do<=
HAR: =We can move the cursor forward=
SUS: =Okay (look for) the arrow,
ETH: No (.) I know=
SUS: =>see here<
(2.6)
ETH: I know
SUS: And we wanted to keep the 'what' and the 'do'
(1.0)
SUS: Yep
HAR: *What [do] ((reads from screen))*
SUS: [Har]ry it's a bit like when you're doing your
writing with a finger spa:ce, (.) you need to use
the space ba:r, (2.0)
HAR: ((Harry presses space bar))
SUS: tadpo:les
(2.6)
SUS: wo::::
(1.8)
SUS: what do you reckon
ETH: tee::::

724 SUS: (.) Ye:::::::S
725 HAR: Ay
726 SUS: Ye::::S (0.4)tad
727 HAR: Dee
728 SUS: Ye:as
729 (1.0)
730 HAR: (tad:::) (0.8) °puh° puh
731 (8.0)
732 SUS: Can he find it (.) ca:::n he fi:nd the 'p'?
733 (1.0)
734 SUS: do [you think he can]((touched Ethan's arm))
735 ETH: [I know where it is]((points to 'p' key)))
736 HAR: [(there)]
737 SUS: [ye:p]
.
.
.
753 SUS: "What do tadpo::::↑les"
754 (0.4)
755 HAR: Eat
756 (2.0)
757 SUS: >where's the bit< Where's the bit that says eat,
758 (4.0)
759 HAR: i:↑:
760 (4.0)
761 HAR: E:at oh ((Harry looks at SUSIE))
762 SUS: ((nods yes))
763 (1.0)
764 HAR: (i:::tee)
765 (0.8)
766 HAR: Oh tee tee (?)
767 SUS: (Righto)
768 ETH: (?)
769 SUS: Now what's the next step Ethan?
770 (2.0)
771 HAR: What do tadpoles eat
772 SUS: Well we've typed it i:n what's the next step
773 HAR: ((pointing at screen)) Click tha:t
774 (1.4)
775 ETH: Tha:t ((presses the enter button))
776 HAR: (yeah ?)

When Harry is directed by the teacher to start the search (line 650), they face their first problem. The search bar is already populated with a previous search term. The teacher shifts the responsibility of 'sorting it out' (line 703), from Harry alone to a shared responsibility by using the pronoun 'we'. She asks about what they will do (line 703). The teacher demonstrates that she is attuned to the children's possible skill levels and provides an opportunity for Harry to display what he knows. Future interactions can be responsive and based on contingencies to children's previous turns (Bateman, 2013; Lee, 2007). Harry proffers his idea to move the cursor forward (line 704). Accepted by Susie, she seamlessly embeds digital technology terms into her turns at talk and directs him to look for the arrow (line 705). After the teacher issues the directive, there is silence for 2.6 seconds (line 708). This silence is a pedagogical strategy that allows Harry time to action the directive and, at the same time, sets up an interactional space for the teacher's next action to be based on contingency (e.g. if Harry cannot locate the arrow on the keyboard, the teacher can scaffold his attempt). Ethan recycles his assertion that he knows (line 709). Susie informs them that they keep the words 'what' and 'do', which are already entered as part of the prior search (line 710). Harry reads aloud, 'what' and 'do', indicating he has located the words they will keep (line 713).

In lines 714–716, Susie connects traditional literacy concepts with digital literacy concepts. She makes this connection by explaining that using a space bar between words when typing is like leaving 'finger' spaces between words when writing (line 714–716). This connection is a pedagogical strategy that aligns with early childhood curriculum pedagogy to connect new learning with children's prior knowledge (Department of Education and Training, 2009). After pressing the space bar (line 717), Susie says 'tadpoles' (line 718), adding emphasis to the onset of the word. She then asks, 'what do you reckon?' (line 722) calling for the children's thoughts about the sounds that were emphasized. The interaction now follows a familiar pattern that targets children's phonological awareness. The children proffer the letter and then Harry locates and presses the corresponding button on the keyboard (lines 722–737) to spell/type the word 'tadpole'. The strategy of segmenting words into onset and rimes is used often to support beginning readers and spellers during traditional writing activities (Australian Curriculum Assessment and Reporting Authority, n.d.; Wohlwend, 2010). Here we see the same strategies being used by the teacher during a learning experience that follows children's interests and in the context of digital technology.

After keying in the word 'tadpoles', Susie reads the words entered, 'what do tadpoles' (note that the word 'eat' is missing at present). She elongates the final syllable of the word 'tadpole' and finishes with rising intonation (line 753). Rising intonation can be a response-mobilizing strategy (Stivers & Rossano, 2010). This strategy, coupled with an incomplete utterance, is a pedagogical strategy for eliciting children's knowledge (Koshik, 2002). In education terms, this strategy is called an *oral cloze* (Queensland Curriculum and Assessment Authority, 2010). Harry treats Susie's turn as a call for him to respond by saying, 'eat' (line 755). After a lengthy pause (line 756), the teacher asks about the word 'eat' (line 757). Without explicitly assessing Harry, an interactional space is made available for him to self-repair (line 760) (Theobald, 2019). Repair – fixing an error or misunderstanding in conversation – is a common feature in interaction that can be initiated by the individual who made the mistake or by other members of the interaction (Hutchby & Wooffitt, 2008). How repair is initiated in teacher-child interaction, however, can influence a child's continued participation (Theobald, 2019). In line 761, Harry orients to the word 'eats', and follows with 'oh' (line 761). 'Oh' is a change of state token (Heritage, 1984) that reveals a change in a person's 'knowledge, information, orientation or awareness' (p. 209). Harry signifies his awareness of the missing word 'eat', and instead of activating the search, he now attends to amending his mistake (lines 763–767).

When teachers use literacy strategies such as oral cloze, and connect digital technologies with prior knowledge such as when to leave spaces between words, they promote opportunities for new learning in new contexts at times that are meaningful to the child. When children are provided with space and time to explore their own ideas and solutions to digital technological problems, their problem-solving skills are enhanced.

The third phase involves the teacher and children assessing the result options that were returned after the search was activated.

Extract 10.3 Phase 3 – Considering the result options

(Houen, 2012, p. 75)

777 SUS: Harry Ye::s Harry look what we've got (for choices)
778 (0.4)
779 *how to raise tadpoles,* (.) *what kind of ca:re do*
780 *tadpoles need* a:nd *what do they eat* and this one
781 [says]
782 HAR: [↑What] do they eat?
783 SUS: Ye::s but look at this one Harry, (.) *tadpo:les for*
784 *children inclu:ding how to ca:re for tadpoles* (1.0)

and he:re's another one that sa:ys (.) *what do*
tadpoles eat, which(.) which one do you wa:nt to try.
ETH: This o:ne ((Ethan points at screen to indicate his
choice))
SUS: ↑Alright, ((Harry clicks on Ethan's choice))
(6.4)((waiting for selected results page to load))

The teacher embeds an experience that involves critical literacy. Critical literacy is particularly relevant in the digital age due to the plethora of information available on all topics. Discerning between factual and fictional information, and the specific information sought, is a necessary skill for users. (See Theobald et. al., (2020) for advice on using the Connect-Contest-Create questioning framework to provide opportunities for children to learn critical literacy skills).

In this extract, Susie points out that they need to consider their choices (line 777), highlighting the importance of reflecting on the search results so that the selection aligns with the information they require. Orienting to Ethan and Harry's emerging literacy, she reads their choices aloud (lines 779–781). Harry locates one result option that aligned with their search topic when he says, 'what do they eat?' (line 782). The teacher acknowledges Harry's turn and locates an option that is specifically designed for children (line 783–785) before asking them to decide which result they want to try (line 786). Ethan points to the screen to select and his selection is accepted verbally by Susie (line 789) and then physically by Harry who clicks on Ethan's selection (line 790).

The teacher's role is in reading aloud the search options, including highlighting the result that was written specifically for children, enabling time for children to consider and discuss the possible options, and choose which option provided opportunities for children to develop and extend their critical literacy skills.

The information from the selected result that is displayed on the screen becomes the focus of the interaction. After a short sequence of talk that orients to having the children nominate where the teacher should start reading from, the teacher reads from the screen.

Extract 10.4 Phase 4 – Engaging with the selected result

(Houen, 2012, pp. 84–85)

SUS: It says keep tadpoles as well as frogs eggs in wa:ter
all the ti:me=
ETH: =(Oh I [wanna] see that)
SUS: [Cha:n]ge

```
HAR: (>↑Yeah but I'm looking [for] what tadpoles eat<)=
SUS:                                [>Harry<]
SUS: =it tells us there so just (hang o:n) cha- I I'll
     rea:d the rest (.) change ha:lf the water no more
     than once a week" o::h "the best di:et and diet is
     another name for f:: food source (.) the be:st
     foo::d is probably baby cere:↑al, (0.6) fresh gree::n
     leafy veggies and a bit of egg yo:lk (0.4) from and
     it sa::ys provide a rock islands when the legs of the
     tadpo:les appear, what do you think that means? What
     are rock islands?
HAR: (I've done that)
ETH: I kno::w (0.6) put put put some ro:ck and make an
     island in some water) on top
SUS: Putting rocks on each other
ETH: Yes to make a island
SUS: Will the island have to be under the water or above
     the water
HAR: Under
ETH: Under
HAR: (I've already done that)
ETH: Under
SUS: No::: no: it's not under,
ETH: Up
SUS: Mmm
ETH: Oh (?)
SUS: Do you know why the rock has to be out of the top
     once (.)because once the tadpo:les got le::gs (.)
     starting to develop le:gs it's going to need
     somewhere where it can get ou::t of the water,
     (2.0)
HAR: I've got tadpoles at my house (?)
SUS: You know I've I've kept tadpoles before too and I've
     never given them baby cereal, you know what I've
     given the:m?
HAR: What
SUS: Boiled lettuce (0.6) but I have to tell you boiled
     lettuce looks really awful and it's very sli:my but
     tadpoles just think it's gorgeous.
```

Factual knowledge can be transferred from one person (e.g. expert) to another (e.g. novice) via a range of strategies, such as telling someone something they do not know. Conversation analysts call these strategies *informings* (Gardner & Mushin, 2013). Teachers in early childhood classrooms often are more knowledgeable than the children they teach and could utilize informings frequently to impart knowledge to children. An early childhood education philosophy, however, values children's participation in the process rather than merely the end-product. The process of conducting a Web search can provide opportunities for children to develop 'problem-solving, inquiry, experimentation, hypothesizing, researching and investigating' skills (Department of Education and Training, 2009, p. 3). In this interaction, it is likely that the teacher already knew the answer to the information they sought (i.e. what tadpoles eat). The motivation to conduct the search was likely driven by the opportunities for children to engage with the process of Web searching. The computer in this regard is treated as the holder of knowledge and therefore used to provide the 'informing'. It is the teacher, however, who selects the passage to read. The selected passage is likely to be an intentional decision; contingent on the information the children originally sought melded with the information available on the Web page.

Susie supports Harry's and Ethan's engagement with their inquiry by reading the information to them (lines 838–839). When Susie's turn appears that it might have come to an end, Ethan squeezes in a shift in his agenda indicated by a change of state token ('oh'), followed by his assertion about wanting to see something on the screen (line 840). Harry flags that he is interested in finding out what tadpoles eat (line 842) and not the information that she has read so far. Susie names Harry and tells him to 'hang on' and she'll read the rest (line 844) indicating to Harry that the information he seeks may be forthcoming (line 844). Susie continues reading and uses informings (Gardner & Mushin, 2013) to offer explanations of words that may be more difficult to comprehend (lines 844–852).

While the information provided in the read-aloud activity does provide advice about what to feed tadpoles, Susie continues reading and initiates a question about providing a rock island when the legs of the tadpoles appear. At this point, Harry informs them that he has done 'that' (line 853), although we cannot be sure what he means by 'that'. The information about tadpole diets provided in lines 847–849 does not become the focus. Instead, the conversation focuses on the question initiated by Susie in line 852: 'What are rock islands?'. Harry, Ethan, and Susie discuss what rock islands are, and how and why they should be placed out of the top of the water (line 854–867). The sequence closes after Susie informs the children that the rock needs to be out of the top (of the water) so that the tadpole can get out of the water once it has legs (line 868–871). Harry talks about having tadpoles at home (line 873). Susie offers a second story (for more on second stories, see Filipi, Chapter 9, this volume). Second stories typically work to display and encourage shared understandings through the production of similar stories (Bateman et al., 2013). In this instance, the teacher offers her own story about keeping tadpoles (line 874) at home and the food she gave them (line 878), and reverts the focus back to the original search topic: the food that tadpoles eat. She connects the information previously read about baby cereal being the best food for tadpoles with her own experiences, saying that she has never given baby cereal, but she has given boiled lettuce (line 874–878). At this point, Susie describes the boiled lettuce as slimy and provides an assessment that tadpoles think it is gorgeous (line 878–879). She then directs Harry and Ethan's attention to the hyperlinks, not associated with tadpoles, listed on the right. At this point, the Web search about what tadpoles eat ends.

Reflecting on the role of the teacher, her interactions were fundamental in following the children's agendas. The question, 'what are rock islands?' (line 852), though, potentially hijacks (Peters & Davis, 2011) the children's agenda by diverting the focus away from the initial search topic, which was to find out what tadpoles eat. Instead of facilitating a sustained shared conversation about the information read concerning tadpole food, the discussion shifted to focus on rock islands. As the interaction unfolds, however, the teacher skilfully returns to what tadpoles eat by orienting to Harry who talks about having tadpoles at home and her second story about her own experiences linking personal experiences and shared stories to the original search topic. In so doing, the children are informed about what tadpoles eat.

Using Email to Communicate and Support Relationships

Our second example, reproduced from Danby and colleagues (2016), illuminates the pedagogical strategies that one teacher used during a whole-class activity when composing an email to a past staff member. The reason for sending the email emerged during outside play, when a child noticed that the preschool's hen had laid its first egg. When outside the teacher suggested that they take a photograph of the egg and she consulted the children about how they could share this news with the staff member who had recently left the centre (named here with the pseudonym 'Protection Bay South'). It was decided that they would email the former staff member to tell her the news.

This example shows how the teacher orients to digital technology concepts during the whole-class experience. The teacher initiates opportunities for the children to explore and display their knowledge about the generic structure of an email (i.e. greeting, body of the email, and closure), as we see in the following extracts.

Extract 10.5 'Where do we start?'

(Danby et al., 2016, p. 8)

```
188   TEA:   ↑what↓ are we going to say to miss sue.
189          =how ↑do ↓we start.=
190          =how will ↑we↓ start.=
191          =how do we start a letter.
192   C18:   ↑eh↓we miss you¿
193   TEA:   we miss you¿
194          but h-how sh-
195   C19:   =we love you¿
196   TEA:   we love you,
197   C19:   em em_ (0.7)
198          we got th- we got some eggs.
199          (0.7)
200   TEA:   I would start with ()
201   C20:   [(someone get the mail.)]
202   C21:   [they laid.             ]
203   TEA:   from protection bay south (),
204   C22:   they l:aid.
205   TEA:   the chickens hav-
206          =↑I↓ would start off with dear miss s:ue.
207          can you¿ (0.7)
208          do you think that's a good idea?
209          Dear
210   C23:   [love (0.2)love kindergarten protection bay.
211   TEA:   [and ↑you↓ watch the letters come up.
212          watch the letters come up as we type.
213   C24:   ((inaudible))
214          (0.7)
215   TEA:   <dear miss sue>.
```

After navigating the login procedures and opening the email programme, the class is ready to commence the activity. The teacher first asks what they would like to say to Miss Sue (line 188), the staff member who recently left the preschool. Without waiting for children's responses, the teacher quickly follows with a different question, 'how do we start?' (line 189–190). This second question narrows the focus of the interaction and targets the greeting section of the email. The children, however, follow with a range of suggestions that orient to the teacher's first question (lines 192, 195, 197–198), including, 'we love you' (line 192), 'we miss you' (line 195), and 'we got some eggs' (line 198). The teacher displays to the children that their suggestions are heard by repeating their responses (lines 193, 196), although she does not action them by keying them at this stage. The teacher reveals her focus when she commences an informing (Gardner & Mushin, 2013) about how she would start (line 200), before stopping when other children initiate turns at talk that focus on what they would like to say (line 201–204). The teacher reiterates how she would start the email (line 206) and instructs them to watch as the letters appear on the screen (line 211–212).

The teacher used questions to prompt children's displays of knowledge about the opening of an email. When the children did not provide an answer that aligned with this question, the teacher informed them of how she would start. Using an informing strategy (Gardner & Mushin, 2013), the teacher shaped the trajectory of the interaction to focus on the greeting of the email, the first part of the generic structure. At the same time, when the children proffered their ideas about what they will say to Miss Sue, the teacher did not explicitly assess the children's suggestions as incorrect, but instead she deferred discussing their ideas until relevant within the email structure. The delayed responses became relevant in the flow of the activity, and provide an example of guided participation (Rogoff et al., 1993). Guided participation is highly valued in early childhood education as it prioritizes 'involvement of individuals with others, as they communicate and engage in shared endeavours' (Rogoff et al., 1993, p. 6). The teacher fostered this shared endeavour by consulting children about what to write and subsequently utilized children's ideas at fitting times and according to the generic structure of the email to progress the writing.

Once the greeting was entered, the teacher next focused on the body of the email. As the interaction unfolds, we see how the teacher incorporates the children's earlier suggestions:

Extract 10.6 The body of the email

(Danby et al., 2016, p. 8)

```
216  TEA:  okay.
217        (0.8)
218  TEA:  who said we miss you.
```

(1.2)
TEA: anna wants to write we miss you?
C24: and we love you?
TEA: okay,
C25: and the chickens hatched.
C26: and (.) and the chickens hatched some eggs,
C27: and chickens
TEA: ok so_
C28: [and the chickens]
C29: [((inaudible))]
C30: [and chickens hatched em eggs.]
TEA: we love you they said¿
C27: and ((inaudible))
Em
(0.5)
C27: love and we love to (catch some eggs)¿
TEA: yes,
C31: <and (0.2) the em the and the chickens em we can make
some stuff with the chicken eggs.>
C32: what about my word?
(1.0)
TEA: okay=
a::nd okay so_
C33: =and we miss her.
TEA: yeh.
C34: from protection bay south.
TEA: from protection bay south?
okay.
=now that probably would be good at the end.
okay?
so hold on to that Ross,
Colin now you can go and sit ↑right↓ at Miss Larne's
feet so she can help you listen.
we miss you,
we love you.
you know what I would say?
(.)
<something exciting happened at kindy.>
what do you reckon,
C35: YEP,
C36: YEH,

The teacher revisits the children's earlier suggestions and asks who suggested 'we miss you?' (line 218) before naming the child and repeating the suggestion (line 220). Several other suggestions are provided (lines 221, 223–225, 227–229) that are minimally acknowledged before the teacher returns to the earlier suggestion, 'we love you' (line 230). Others contributed suggestions that are inaudible and sometimes in overlap with each other (lines 231, 234, 236–237, 238), which made it difficult for suggestions to be heard and oriented to. One idea that is addressed by the teacher orients to the final component of an email, that of closing (or signing off) the email. The child tells the teacher that they need to include, 'from Protection Bay South' (line 244) (a pseudonym for the name of the school). The teacher renders this contribution as important by repeating it (line 245), accepting it ('okay') (line 246), and informing the children that this contribution would be good at the end (line 247) and instructing the child to 'hold onto that Ross' (line 249). As the teacher's spoken words are keyed into the email, she repeats the earlier responses (lines 252, 253) before telling the children that she would say, 'something exciting happened at kindy' (line 256). In so doing, the teacher renders the information in the email correspondence as newsworthy, implying to the children the importance of newsworthy information as a feature of correspondence. She seeks confirmation from the children (line 257) to include her suggestion.

As shown by Danby and colleagues (2016), the teacher's interactional strategies included repeating children's earlier ideas to show these ideas as relevant at points in time when they are relevant. In addition, the teacher made suggestions that highlighted the generic structure of an email (e.g. that would go at the end), and email as a communication tool. While this experience shows how digital technology can be used to promote literacy skills, the activity also highlights the potential of digital technologies to support children's emotional wellbeing by maintaining contact with people they care about. Children's emotional wellbeing is an important part of early learning and this example illustrates how digital technologies can support this aspect of learning (Department of Education and Training, 2009).

Recommendations for Practice

How digital technology is used in early childhood classrooms is dependent on educators' philosophical views, confidence, and the support concerning use and availability of digital technologies. Educators sometimes feel competing agendas as they juggle addressing children's health as part of the curriculum with educational learning involving digital technologies. In recent years, these competing discourses have come to the fore through policy and curriculum. In this chapter, we presented examples to support teacher practices where teacher beliefs of child-focused agency and learning coexist with child and teacher engagement with digital technologies. In reality, these examples of reading texts and composing texts are usual practices in an early childhood classroom.

When children are able to access digital technologies in the classroom, educator beliefs are the strongest influencer of technology use (Blackwell et al., 2014; Thorpe et al., 2015), followed by teacher confidence and support to use digital technology. Professional development should continue to enhance teacher confidence and focus on the effective integration of digital technology in ECEC classrooms, such as Web searching in classrooms (Thorpe et al., 2015). These priorities support alignment between the expectations outlined in curriculum documents and actual classroom practices in relation to digital technologies. Until recently, there are few empirical studies to inform about appropriate digital technology use 'by and with' young children (Mantilla & Edwards, 2019). Teacher beliefs are identified as a major issue for the utilization of digital technologies in early childhood classrooms, but beliefs can shift (Vidal-Hall et al., 2020). Educator opportunities to reflect on everyday practices is an important strategy to support the evolution of pedagogies associated with digital technology integration.

The real-life classroom interactions described in this chapter offer opportunities to 'see', 'hear', and reflect on how teachers integrated digital technologies into their classrooms. Conversation analysis applied to these examples enabled the identification of pedagogical and interactional strategies that support children's inquiry-based learning, problem solving, and conceptual engagement when using digital technologies.

The following pedagogical strategies encourage children's inquiry-based learning, problem solving, and conceptual engagement when engaging with digital technologies:

- Follow the child's lead – consulting children about next steps.
- Afford time for exploration of children's ideas.
- Offer suggestions rather than mandating what children should do next.
- Position children as possessing knowledge rather than void of knowledge and adjusting responses to children's talk accordingly (e.g. 'What shall we do?').

- Consult children about identifying the problems faced when engaging in Web searches.
- Elicit (and follow) children's ideas to solve problems involving digital technologies.
- Make relevant digital literacy skills (e.g. learning about the generic structure of emails) meaningful to the children's everyday learning experiences.
- Conduct Web searches that respond to children's interests and critically reflect on the choices found using Theobald et al.'s (2020) Connect-Contest-Create: 3C Questioning Framework for relational information literacy.
- Connect prior knowledge to possible new learning.
- Use digital technology terms (e.g. cursor) integrated into conversations and classroom experiences rather than create pre-planned activities.

This chapter illustrates the importance of social interaction for children's engagement with digital technologies aligned with early childhood pedagogy. By describing in detail the everyday learning interactions, educators may notice that the pedagogical strategies explained in this chapter have synergy with teaching strategies employed in other early childhood classroom contexts. When digital technology is viewed as a classroom resource, rather than as a separate entity, it can be used at opportune times to support children's inquiry-learning, problem solving, and conceptual engagement in authentic learning experiences.

References

AAP Council on Communications and Media. (2016). Media and Young Minds. *Pediatrics*, 138(5). https://doi.org/10.1542/peds.2016-2591

Australian Curriculum Assessment and Reporting Authority. (n.d.). *Reading and viewing | The Australian Curriculum*. Available from: www.australiancurriculum.edu.au/resources/national-literacy-and-numeracy-learning-progressions/national-literacy-learning-progression/reading-and-viewing/?subElementId=50892&searchTerm=onset#dimension-content [last accessed 15 December 2021].

Bateman, A. (2013). Responding to children's answers: questions embedded in the social context of early childhood education. *Early Years*, 33(3), 275–288. https://doi.org/10.1080/09575146.2013.800844

Bateman, A., Danby, S., and Howard, J. (2013). Everyday preschool talk about Christchurch earthquakes. *Australian Journal of Communication*, 40(1), 103–122. https://search.informit.com.au/fullText

Blackwell, C. K., Lauricella, A. R., and Wartella, E. (2014). Factors influencing digital technology use in early childhood education. *Computers & Education*, 77, 82–90. https://doi.org/10.1016/j.compedu.2014.04.013

Danby, S., and Davidson, C. (2019). Webs of relationships: young children's engagement with Web searching. In R. Flewitt and O. Erstad (eds.), *Routledge Handbook of Digital Literacies*. Abingdon: Routledge.

Danby, S., Davidson, C., Given, L., and Thorpe, K. (2016). Composing an email: social interaction in a preschool classroom. In S. Garvis and N. Lemon (eds.), *Understanding Digital Technologies and Young Children: An International Perspective* (pp. 5–18). Abingdon: Routledge (Taylor & Francis Group).

Danby, S., Fleer, M., Davidson, C., and Hatzigianni, M. (2020). Digital childhoods across contexts and countries. In S. Danby, M. Fleer, C. Davidson, and M. Hatzigianni (eds.), *Digital Childhoods: Technologies and Children's Everyday Lives* (pp. 1–14). London: Springer. https://doi.org/10.4135/9781529714388.n230

Davidson, C. (2010). 'Click on the big red car': the social accomplishment of playing a wiggles computer game. *Convergence*, 16(4), 375–394. https://doi.org/10.1177/1354856510375526

Davidson, C., Danby, S., Ekberg, S., and Thorpe, K. (2020). The interactional achievement of reading aloud by young children and parents during digital technology use. *Journal of Early Childhood Literacy* (online). https://doi.org/10.1177/1468798419896040

Davidson, C., Danby, S., Given, L. M., and Thorpe, K. (2018). Producing contexts for young children's digital technology use: Web searching during adult-child interactions at home and preschool. In S. Danby, M. Fleer, C. Davidson, and M. Hatzigianni (eds.), *Digital Childhood* (vol. 22, pp. 65–82). London: Springer. https://doi.org/10.1007/978-981-10-6484-5_5

Department of Education and Training. (2009). *Belonging, Being and Becoming – The Early Years Learning Framework for Australia*. Commonwealth of Australia. http://nla.gov.au/nla.arc-109966

Early Childhood Australia. (2018). *Statement on young children and digital technologies*. Available from: www.earlychildhoodaustralia.org.au/wp-content/uploads/2018/10/Digital-policy-statement.pdf [last accessed 15 December 2021].

Edwards, S. (2016). New concepts of play and the problem of technology, digital media and popular-culture integration with play-based learning in early childhood education. *Technology, Pedagogy and Education*, 25(4), 513–532. https://doi.org/10.1080/1475939X.2015.1108929

Edwards, S., Mantilla, A., Grieshaber, S., Nuttall, J., and Wood, E. (2020). Converged play characteristics for early childhood education: multi-modal, global-local, and traditional-digital. *Oxford Review of Education*, 46(5), 637–660. https://doi.org/10.1080/03054985.2020.1750358

Gardner, R., and Mushin, I. (2013). Teachers telling: informings in an Early Years classroom. *Australian Journal of Communication*, 40(2), 63–82. http://austjourcomm.org/index.php/ajc/article/view/6

Garrison, M. M., and Christakis, D. A. (2012). The impact of a healthy media use intervention on sleep in preschool children. *Pediatrics*, 130(3), 492–499. https://doi.org/10.1542/peds.2011-3153

Garvis, S., and Lemon, N. (2016). Introduction. In S. Garvis and N. Lemon (eds.), *Understanding Digital Technologies and Young Children: An International Perspective* (pp. 1–5). Abingdon: Routledge.

Goodwin, M. (2006). Participation, affect, and trajectory in family directive/response sequences. *Text & Talk*, 26(4–5), 515–543.

Heritage, J. (1984). A change-of-state token and aspects of its sequential placement. In J. Atkinson and J. Heritage (eds.), *Structures of Social Action* (pp. 299–345). Cambridge: Cambridge University Press.

Houen, S. (2012). *Talk and Web searching in an Early Years classroom*. Masters Dissertation, Queenland University of Technology. http://eprints.qut.edu.au/54617/

Houen, S., Danby, S., Farrell, A., and Thorpe, K. (2017). Web searching as a context to build on young children's displayed knowledge. In A. Bateman and A. Church (eds.), *Children's Knowledge-in-Interaction: Studies in Conversation Analysis* (pp. 57–72). London: Springer. https://doi.org/10.1007/978–981-10–1703-2_4

Howie, E. K., Coenen, P., Campbell, A. C., Ranelli, S., and Straker, L. M. (2017). Head, trunk and arm posture amplitude and variation, muscle activity, sedentariness and physical activity of 3- to 5-year-old children during tablet computer use compared to television watching and toy play. *Applied Ergonomics*, 65, 41–50. https://doi.org/10.1016/j.apergo.2017.05.011

Hurwitz, L. B., and Schmitt, K. L. (2020). Can children benefit from early Internet exposure? Short- and long-term links between Internet use, digital skill, and academic performance. *Computers & Education*, 146, 103750. https//doi.org/10.1016/j.compedu.2019.103750

Hutchby, I., and Wooffitt, R. (2008). *Conversation Analysis* (2nd ed.). Cambridge: Polity Press.

Kahn, M., Schnabel, O., Gradisar, M., Rozen, G. S., Slone, M., et al. (2020). Sleep, screen time and behaviour problems in preschool children: an actigraphy study. *European Child & Adolescent Psychiatry*, 30(11), 1793–1802. https://doi.org/10.1007/s00787-020-01654-w

Koshik, I. (2002). Designedly incomplete utterances: a pedagogical practice for eliciting knowledge displays in error correction sequences. *Research on Language and Social Interaction*, 35(3), 277–309. https://doi.org/10.1207/S15327973RLSI3503

Lee, Y. (2007). Third turn position in teacher talk: contingency and the work of teaching. *Journal of Pragmatics*, 39(1), 1204–1230. https://doi.org/10.1016/j.pragma.2006.11.003

Livingstone, S., Mascheroni, G., and Staksrud, E. (2015). *Developing a Framework for Researching Children' s Online Risks and Opportunities in Europe*. London: EU Kids Online.

Mantilla, A., and Edwards, S. (2019). Digital technology use by and with young children: a systematic review for the Statement on Young Children and Digital Technologies. *Australasian Journal of Early Childhood*, 44(2), 182–195. https://doi.org/10.1177/1836939119832744

Marsh, J., Brooks, G., Hughes, J., Ritchie, L., Roberts, S., & Wright, K. (2005). *Digital Beginnings: Young Children's Use of Popular Culture, Media and New Technologies*. London: Routledge. https://doi.org/10.4324/9780203420324

Peters, S., and Davis, K. (2011). Fostering children's working theories: pedagogic issues and dilemmas in New Zealand. *Early Years*, 31(1), 5–17. https://doi.org/10.1080/09575146.2010.549107

Plowman, L. (2016). Learning technology at home and preschool. In N. Rushby and D. Surry (eds.), *The Wiley Handbook of Learning Technology* (pp. 96–112). Chichester: John Wiley.

Queensland Curriculum and Assessment Authority. (2010). *Teaching reading and viewing: Comprehension strategies and activities for Years 1–9*.

Rogoff, B., Mistry, J., Goncu, A., and Mosier, C. (1993). Guided participation in cultural activity by toddlers and caregivers. *Monographs of the Society for Research in Child Development*, 58(7), 1–174.

Spink, A., Danby, S., Mallan, K., and Butler, C. (2010). Exploring young children's web searching and technoliteracy. *Journal of Documentation*, 66(2), 91–206. https://doi.org/10.1108/00220411011023616

Stivers, T., and Rossano, F. (2010). Mobilizing response. *Research on Language & Social Interaction*, 43(1), 3–31. https://doi.org/10.1080/08351810903471258

Straker, L., Zabatiero, J., Danby, S., Thorpe, K., and Edwards, S. (2018). Conflicting guidelines on young children's screen time and use of digital technology create policy and practice dilemmas. *The Journal of Pediatrics*, 202, 300–303. https://doi.org/10.1016/j.jpeds.2018.07.019

Theobald, M. (2019). Scaffolding storytelling and participation with a bilingual child in a culturally and linguistically diverse preschool in Australia. *Research on Children and Social Interaction*, 3(1–2), 224–247. https://doi.org/10.1558/rcsi.37294

Theobald, M., McFadden, A., Lunn, J., et al. (2020). *Digital play in early childhood education: Connect-Contest-Create: 3C questioning framework for relational information literacy*. https://eprints.qut.edu.au/202505/

Thorpe, K., Hansen, J., Danby, S., et al. (2015). Digital access to knowledge in the preschool classroom: reports from Australia. *Early Childhood Research Quarterly*, 32, 174–182. https://doi.org/10.1016/j.ecresq.2015.04.001

Vidal-Hall, C., Flewitt, R., and Wyse, D. (2020). Early childhood practitioner beliefs about digital media: integrating technology into a child-centred classroom environment. *European Early Childhood Education Research Journal*, 28(1), 1–15. https://doi.org/10.1080/1350293X.2020.1735727

Vijakkhana, N., Wilaisakditipakorn, T., Ruedeekhajorn, K., Pruksananonda, C., and Chonchaiya, W. (2015). Evening media exposure reduces night-time sleep. *Acta Paediatrica*, 104(3), 306–312. https://doi.org/10.1111/apa.12904

Wohlwend, K. E. (2010). A is for avatar: young children in literacy 2.0 worlds and literacy 1.0 schools. *Language Arts*, 88(2), 144–152.

Yelland, N. (2008). New times, new learning, new pedagogies: ICT and education in the 21st Century. *Rethinking Education with ICT* (online). https://vuir.vu.edu.au/id/eprint/6166

Yelland, N. (2011). Reconceptualising play and learning in the lives of young children. *Australasian Journal of Early Childhood*, 36(2), 4–12.

11 | Mathematics

CAROLINE COHRSSEN

Introduction

The characteristics of 'high quality' early childhood education have been under the spotlight for many years. Two core components of quality are generally recognized: structural quality and process quality (Howes et al., 2008; Peisner-Feinberg et al., 2001). Structural quality includes teacher qualifications, centre resourcing, and staff-child ratios. These tend to be easy to observe. Process quality includes the enactment of purposefully planned opportunities for children to consolidate and extend their thinking. These learning opportunities are influenced by teachers' planned and responsive interactions with children. In order for such interactions to promote learning and development, effective teachers are attuned to the diverse – and sometimes unexpected – ways in which children reveal their knowledge and ideas in the context of a play-based, informal curriculum. In this chapter, we focus on the importance of promoting children's mathematical thinking as one aspect of high-quality early childhood education.

Mathematics in Early Childhood Education

Early mathematical skills predict later academic capabilities and thus lifelong trajectories (Duncan et al., 2007). People use mathematical thinking all the time: when judging how many objects will fit into a shopping bag, allocating different items to different shopping bags so that the weight is balanced when we walk home, ensuring that there is enough petrol in the car to last a week or enough money on the public transport card – each of these everyday activities requires the ability to apply mathematical thinking to solve problems. We use mathematical thinking in more creative ways too – when arranging furniture in a room or deciding how much colour to add to white paint to obtain the exact hue.

From very early in life, children compare quantities and orient towards shapes and size. Nonetheless, early childhood educators may feel more comfortable encouraging children to 'use their words' when responding to sharing resources or resolving peer disputes (Church et al., 2018), than encouraging children to use mathematical language. In addition, parents may be reluctant for their child to be 'taught mathematics' in early childhood, having visions of worksheets and formal education.

More than ten years ago, nine misconceptions about teaching mathematics in early childhood were identified (Lee & Ginsburg, 2009). Indeed, we still need to address broader misconceptions by reframing the understanding of the general public, which includes children's parents and caregivers (Nichols et al., 2019). Drawing on data collected from 7,709 people in the United States, Nichols and colleagues framed challenges that may arise from differing perspectives of early childhood mathematics. Some of these challenges are addressed below.

- The general public may think that mathematical thinking is limited to basic numeracy – counting, and naming shapes. However, as teachers know, early mathematics learning also includes problem-solving and critical thinking. For example, young children use mathematical thinking during block construction play to solve problems like, 'If all the rectangular blocks have been used, I could put two triangular blocks together to make the shape I need!'
- The general public may see mathematics as a separate discipline area. However, early childhood educators know that play, underpinned by mathematical thinking, also supports other developing capabilities such as self-regulation and turn-taking (Cohrssen et al., 2014a, 2014b). Children demonstrate mathematical thinking using their words as well as their bodies as they draw, gesture, and dance – often in ways that are difficult for adults to predict (Deans & Cohrssen, 2015; Hedge & Cohrssen, 2019; Pollitt et al., 2015) – and as they negotiate their environments, lowering their bodies enough to wiggle under furniture to retrieve a ball (Franzén, 2015).
- People may see children's language learning as important, without prioritizing *mathematical* language. Parents ask less demanding mathematics-related questions of their children than literacy-related questions (Uscianowski et al., 2020), yet exposure to maths talk has an important influence on child outcomes (Klibanoff et al., 2006; Levine et al., 2010). Advanced language for one child may be learning one new word, such as when a toddler reaches up to an adult, and the adult says, 'Up?'. Advanced language for another child may be putting two words together to form a sentence, such as 'big apple'. 'Up' is a word that indicates direction. 'Big' is a word that indicates size (and perhaps, comparison). Both are examples of mathematical language. Encouraging the use of such

language should occur in everyday contexts – not just in a designated mathematics activity. Early childhood specialists understand the importance of children being exposed to maths talk from birth, so that they acquire the language that equips them to communicate their thinking.

- People may believe that children should learn mathematics when they start school. Early childhood specialists recognize that children are learning from birth and that *all* children should have opportunities to engage in learning experiences that support mathematical thinking (Cohrssen & Page, 2016). This sets children up to see themselves as competent mathematicians. If children are encouraged to explore mathematical concepts and to acquire and rehearse mathematical language for the first time at the age of 5 or 6 years when they start school, their mathematical skills may be behind their peers who have had such opportunities from birth. This causes inequity and a gap that may never be closed without targeted intervention.

Reframing the concept of mathematics in early childhood education requires early childhood educators to emphasize that mathematical thinking is not an add-on activity but rather deeply embedded in children's play and the way in which young children understand and negotiate their worlds. Early childhood educators have a professional responsibility to respond to children's innate curiosity about the world and to support them acquiring the skills and language that emerge from birth. Early childhood educators recognize mathematical thinking when it is demonstrated – this positions the child as leading learning.

Spatial Thinking

This chapter focuses on spatial thinking (sometimes referred to as spatial reasoning or spatial intelligence) as one critical strand of mathematical thinking. Spatial thinking includes spatial orientation and spatial visualization (Clements & Sarama, 2021). Clements and Sarama (2021) explain spatial orientation as knowing where you are in relation to other objects, and the ability to move through space. They explain spatial visualization as having mental images of shapes and objects and the ability to manipulate them in your mind. Spatial thinking is important for understanding number and quantity, for recognizing the structure of patterns, and for understanding units of measurement. Yet, early childhood educators frequently overlook including opportunities for spatial thinking in their planning, perhaps due to a belief that spatial thinking ability is set at birth, like the colour of one's eyes. How often does one hear, 'Oh, I'm so bad at reading a map' or, 'I have no sense of direction'!

Research suggests that spatial thinking develops with rehearsal (Newcombe & Frick, 2010), highlighting the importance of children participating in activities that provide them with rehearsal opportunities. Play offers endless opportunities for children to rehearse spatial concepts and, with adult support, to acquire the conceptual language. This includes words that describe shapes (such as tall, short, round, curved, straight, edge, flat, solid) as well as the names of shapes (such as square, circle, triangle, semi-circle). Additional language that describes location and direction is learned (such as over, under, between, behind, on top, beside). However, many early childhood educators may be unsure how to do this without taking a teacher-directed approach which requires children to follow instructions, rather than to learn through play.

In the section that follows, examples of authentic, play-based teacher-child interactions will be put under the spotlight to show how spatial thinking can be supported in the context of an informal early childhood curriculum.

Revealing the 'How' of Supporting Spatial Thinking

In the context of early childhood education, teaching and learning go hand in hand. Indeed, in high-quality, play-based early childhood classrooms, educators move iteratively in and out of play, frequently taking on roles allocated to them by the child. There are multiple indicators of high-quality early childhood practice, and multiple lenses we can use to observe and document these practices. Conversation analysis is used to explore the data in this chapter, but within the framework of the Classroom Assessment Scoring System (CLASS; Pianta et al., 2008).

The CLASS measure is curriculum-neutral and focuses on interactions as the vehicle for child learning and making process quality visible. CLASS identifies three broad domains of classroom-level interactional quality: emotional support, classroom organization, and instructional support (Pianta et al., 2008). Research has found consistent associations between CLASS measures of interactional quality and child outcomes; however, in many countries around the world, the quality of instructional support is in the low range (Egert et al., 2020). Raising the quality of instructional support is thus a priority and to achieve this, it is necessary to focus more purposefully on the characteristics of instructional support within the context of a play-based curriculum.

Within the CLASS domain of instructional support are three dimensions: 'concept development', 'quality of feedback', and 'language modelling' (Pianta et al., 2008). Teachers who enact high quality concept development support children's analysis and reasoning and encourage children to think creatively. When introducing new ideas, teachers integrate them with a child's existing knowledge and skills, making explicit connections to the child's lived experience. Turning to the dimension called 'quality of feedback', the focus is on the process of learning, rather than children answering questions correctly. To achieve this, teachers provide hints and assistance to scaffold the child's learning or to clarify misunderstandings. Further, teachers encourage children to persist, facilitating sustained engagement and attention, and thus increasing opportunities for learning. Engaging in sustained shared thinking (Siraj & Asani, 2015) is important: it encourages attention, perseverance and the rehearsal of new concepts and skills. The third dimension of instructional support focuses on the teacher's use of language to encourage the child to learn new vocabulary and to support opportunities to rehearse language through frequent conversations. Strategies to achieve this include asking open ended questions that encourage the child to reply with answers that use more than one word, repeating and extending comments a child makes, and narrating their own or the child's actions with language. Indeed, the contingency and contiguity of talk – the way in which early childhood educators facilitate sequences of back-and-forth conversations deepens thinking (Cohrssen & Church, 2017) – and encourages sustained engagement. Asking children to explain or justify their thinking encourages higher order thinking yet given the low levels of instructional support that characterize many early childhood programmes, is seldom observed (Egert et al., 2020). When conversations of this type are consistently observed, we have evidence of high-quality interactions that support mathematical thinking.

Using Conversation Analysis to Illuminate Instructional Support

Applying a conversation analytic approach shines the spotlight on talk-in-interaction to demonstrate the way in which high quality instructional support (Pianta et al., 2008) is operationalized. Conversation analysis (CA) examines very closely how people use language in social interactions (Sacks et al., 1974; Sidnell & Stivers, 2013; ten Have, 2007). When applying a CA approach, the researcher examines each participant's turn in detail to understand its contribution to the conversation, paying attention to pauses within one speaker's turn and between speakers, to the rise and fall of intonation, to the words on which the speaker places emphasis, and to how the second turn (as turns may be verbal or non-verbal) responds to the content of the first turn. This is particularly relevant to a focus on spatial thinking, as research has established the important contribution made by adults' gesture to child learning (Ehrlich et al., 2006) and children may demonstrate spatial thinking in non-verbal ways (Deans & Cohrssen, 2015; Hedge & Cohrssen, 2019). Indeed, research has shown that from the age of 2 or 3 years, children understand that gesture contains meaning from which they can gain information (Hurst et al., 2019; see also Kern, Chapter 4, and Kidwell, Chapter 2, this volume).

Starting School: A Seemingly Non-Mathematical Topic

This chapter draws on a body of video-recorded interactions between teachers and a class of 19 children aged from 4 years, 2 months to 5 years, 10 months in a kindergarten classroom, towards the end of the year prior to starting school (Cohrssen et al., 2017). A six-week project on 'Starting School' was the vehicle for a focus on spatial thinking, presenting multimodal and responsive opportunities for children to engage with shapes, spatial orientation and spatial visualization, and to rehearse spatial language. The videos were transcribed and the extracts presented here illustrate children's abilities in spatial thinking and where teachers can extend and scaffold this learning.

The children were the enthusiastic experts in this project, as all children were transitioning from kindergarten to school. Each week, different core learning experiences were presented. Each related to the transition to school such as drawing maps of their new schools, building their new schools with blocks, and mapping the route from home to school (Cohrssen & Pearn, 2019). Learning objectives for each learning experience responded to observations of children's existing knowledge.

In Extract 11.1, the teacher has joined three children who built a block construction of their new school. This activity afforded opportunities to discuss the transition process, as well as to rehearse locational and directional language while they negotiated the building of their school. The teacher takes on the role of a furniture delivery person. This was a planned role, purposefully designed in order to support play-based assessment: the teacher has prepared small cards showing images of objects to be placed in particular locations in the building. Correct placement of the objects will provide evidence of conceptual understanding of locational and directional language as one element of spatial thinking. Two simultaneous conversations are under way and so the interactions between the teacher and Humphrey only have been provided.

Extract 11.1 Between a red and yellow window

9	TEA:	computer, well done, now this computer,
10		[needs ta go::,] on top of the::: red no=in
11		between a red an yellow window, please.
12		*passes card to Humphrey*
13	HUM:	*raises his right hand to represent*
14		*speaking on a telephone]* *then lowers hand*
15		*and takes the card* (okay,) *walks around*
16		*the table to a position opposite the*
17		*teacher*
...		
20	TEA:	in=between, a red an yellow window. (4.0)
...		
24	HUM:	*walks around the table, looking at the sides*
25		*of the block construction of a school*
26		*building*
...		
31	HUM:	red=an-yellow window (3.0) *walks back around*
32		*the table then places card on top of red and*
33		*yellow windows*
...	TEA:	[hello?
38	HUM:	*removes card and slides it between the red*
39		*and yellow translucent centred blocks*
...		
42	HUM:	*card slips out and he slides it back*
43		*between the red and yellow blocks*

The teacher asks Humphrey to place a computer 'between a red and yellow window' (line 11). 'Between' is an example of language that draws on spatial reasoning and one that is conceptually complex. In order for an object to be between two objects, the position of the two other objects must be noted, along with the position of the third object in relation to both, simultaneously. This is conceptually different from 'beside' which requires a person to be mindful of the location of one other object only. Accurate use of the word 'between' is thus an example of advanced language.

In this extract, Humphrey and his friends Gary and Christian are co-conspirators in a sustained interaction characterized by high spirits that may have caused a less confident educator to abandon the activity (lines 13–30)! Indeed, the furniture delivery man (i.e. the teacher) has already been told that the person he asked to speak to on the telephone is unavailable and Gary and Christian are more concerned with the location of a snake picture than where the computer is going (lines 18–30).

In this example, many turns are non-verbal (italicized text). We observe from Humphrey's actions that he remains on task over a sustained period of time. However, the teacher repeats the location word with emphasis – 'between' (line 19) – and provides a purposeful pause that provides thinking time (Cohrssen et al., 2014a, 2014b). This serves to support Humphrey's attention to the task at hand as evidenced by his self-talk at line 31, which again is followed by a sustained pause before the teacher takes the next turn. This is a small group learning experience and so the teacher continues, sustaining the playful approach by speaking into his 'telephone' (lines 34–36) by attracting the attention of Gary (lines 34–41) who answers his telephone using a playful sing-song voice (line 40), after which the activity continues.

Importantly, while the teacher is attracting Gary's attention, Humphrey self-corrects the placement of the computer (lines 38–39). This deliberate re-placement of the computer is evident as he picks up the object when it slips out and reinserts it between the red and yellow window (lines 42–43). Humphrey *shows*, rather than speaks, understanding.

In this brief extract from a longer, playful interaction between the teacher and three children, we observe the teacher's dual purpose: setting up opportunities to assess the children's understanding of language of direction and location (in this instance, 'between') as well as making connections within the broader programme, as the word 'between' was being explored in other learning experiences (Cohrssen et al., 2017). By using the block construction of the children's new school as the context for the purposeful interaction, objects of interest to the children (computers and snakes) and social actors with whom children were likely to be familiar (a delivery person), the teacher situated the task within the children's lived experience. We observe the child achieving success in the context of a small-group assessment activity – without sacrificing the playful quality of this interaction.

In Extract 11.2, we see again the focus on the concept of 'between'. The children and their teachers are looking at a map of their kindergarten's outdoor play area and discussing the location of a rock pit.

The children are seated in a circle with the map positioned facing Bella. Some of the children have their backs to the video camera and speakers are

Figure 11.1 Looking at the map.

thus not always identifiable. We join the conversation while Bella is looking for the rock pit on the map.

Extract 11.2 The rock pit

10	TEA:	*watching Bella who is looking at the map* (8.4)
11		now re↑member ↑Bella:,
12	CH:	I [↑see::]
13	TEA:	[the ↑r]ock pit (.) >is it< ↑i:n (.) the
14		↑middle of the yard or is it on the edge,
15	CHN:	the ↑e:dge
16	BEL:	°the e- e:dge,°
17	TEA:	the edge (0.4) okay (0.4) ↑so:,. (0.4) what ↑I'd
18		like you to do is go round the ↑e:dge,
19		(.)*running finger down the left hand side of the*
20		*map* with your ↑finger and when you ↑think
21		↑you've ↑seen ↑someth- (.) ↑seen something will
22		don't point to ↑i:t, (0.4) when you ↑think
23		you've seen something that looks like, (0.4) the
24		↑rock pi:t, (0.6) °big ↑shout ou:t°
25	CH:	↑shou::t?
26	TEA:	↑yeah,
27	CH:	↑I: see something (?)
28	BEL:	*running finger down the left hand side of the*

29		*map and then along the bottom*
30	TEA:	>so she's< going round [the ↑edge,]
31	TEA2:	[°↓o::::::h°] (tracing
32		the ↑e:dge::) (6.0) >so Bella ↑is< the< rock pit
33		closer to the sa:nd ↑pit or is it closer to the
34		blue ↓shed (0.6) what do you think
35	CH:	°↑closer to the::,°
36	BEL:	*begins to run finger back along the bottom of*
37		*the map*
38	TEA2:	↑a:h look the finger is ↑sli:ding ↑back ↑now,
39		(0.6) ↑u:h ↓u::h
40	TEA:	see the trees (0.4) *points to objects on the map*
41		*at the bottom* round he:re (0.6) ↑now do you
42		reckon that you could go::, (0.4) >I'm gonna<
43		send you on a ↑mission (0.6) can ↑you head on
44		out↑si::de, (0.8) °there are teachers out there
45		↑right?°
46	TEA2:	↑yeah

Rather than telling children what the marks on the map represent, we observe the teacher encouraging the child(ren) to solve this problem themselves. The teacher says, 'Now remember, Bella, the rock pit, is it in the middle of the yard or is it on the edge?' (lines 11–14). Bella is very familiar with the rock pit in the outdoor area at the kindergarten and so the teacher persists, using feedback loops and at the same time, making an explicit connection between the map in front of Bella and her real-world knowledge of the rock pit.

The teacher continues, '… go around the edge with your finger, and when you've seen something that looks like the rock pit … shout out' (lines 18–24). The provision of feedback in the form of hints and assistance – encouraging Bella to trace the edge of the map which will lead her to the position of the rock pit – encourages Bella's continued participation in the task. Demonstrating parallel talk, the teacher maps Bella's actions with words supporting the acquisition of vocabulary such as 'edge' (line 30). The second teacher interjects to reinforce this before asking, 'is the rock pit closer to the sand pit or is it closer to the blue shed?' (lines 32–34), further drawing on the child's expert knowledge of the outdoor environment and providing an additional hint that scaffolds Bella's ability to complete the task.

To provide an additional opportunity for Bella to pay attention to environmental landmarks in the outdoor area, and to assist her recognition of their symbolic representation on the two-dimensional map, the first teacher sends Bella and a friend to check where the rock pit is and where the big trees are. Here, the teacher models the *process* of learning by showing the children in the group how to find information in the form of environmental landmarks to solve the problem.

Extract 11.3 It's between two trees

104	TEA:	Bella can you ↑figure out where the rock ↑pit is
105		on the ↑map?
106	BEL:	*looking at the map*
107	CH:	(?) she's gonna kno:w,
108	NIC:	*looks up, [smiling]*
109	CH:	[↑it's ↑↑so ↑↑ha:rd ↑it's [(?)]
110	TEA:	[Nicola] if you had to descri:be it
111		without ↑↑pointing to tha ↓ma:p (0.4) how would
112		you use your ↑wo:rds to descri:be, (0.4) ↑whe:re
113		the rock pit ↑i:s in relation to other thi:ngs
114	CH:	↑I kno::w
115	TEA:	so, (0.4) ↑Nicola's gonna look at the ↑map,
116		(0.4) she's gonna figure out a way to: (0.4)
117		↑say it to Bella
118		[without pointing to it,]
119	BEL:	*looks at Nicola, smiling, then looks back at the*
120		*map*
121	CH:	[<I ↑ca::n't ↑see::::>]
122	CH:	↑I:
123	TEA:	↑just say ex↑cuse ↑me (Edgar)°
124	(1.8)	
125	NIC:	it's be↑↑twee::n
126	TEA2:	↑oo:::h
127	TEA:	O:::H that's a ↑great [clue:] did everyone >hear
128		↑that<=
129	TEA2:	[°ye:s°]
130	BEL:	[I=

131	TEA:	[=can you say that ↑once more bit lou↑de:r,
132	NIC:	i:t's (.) be↑↑twee::n ↑two trees
133	TEA:	<°it's bet↑wee:n (.) two trees°>
134	BEL:	yep (.) an I rem↑ember because it's ↑facing (.)
135		.hh the ↑eco (.) cubby *looks briefly at the*
136		*teacher then looks at the map*
137	TEA:	it's [facing the eco cubby,]

On the girls' return, the teacher scaffolds Bella's thinking again by asking Nicola, who had accompanied Bella, to use her words to describe where it is 'in relation to other things' (lines 110–113). This is an example of the way in which teachers can use a variety of words that map onto known concepts (i.e. language modelling). Nicola's response demonstrates her ability to map the correct word onto the positional concept: 'It's between two trees' (lines 125 and 132). This peer scaffolding prompts Bella to state, 'I remember because it's facing the eco cubby' – using another spatial term: 'facing' (line 134).

Felix adds a further clue at line 139 in Extract 11.4 by raising four fingers to emphasize the number four. One teacher praises Felix (line 142); the lead teacher specifically praises his provision of a clue (line 143). By using the word 'clue', the teacher again models advanced language by labelling Felix's provision of additional information instead of the answer.

Extract 11.4 Four little bushes

139	FEL:	[>and you also ↑have, (.)] ↑fou:r bushes *raises*
140		*four fingers on right hand and holds right hand*
141		*with left hand* four [bushes]
142	TEA2:	[well d]one (?) [(↑good) (?)]
143	TEA:	[oh ↑goo:d] ↑clue Fe↑::lix
144		it's [got] ↑fou::r little bushes on ↑it
145	FEL:	↑yep (.) ↑fou::r [little ones]
146	TEA:	[and it's be]↑tween two trees,
147	CH:	ye:p

The teacher persists by asking a follow-up question at line 148: 'So where are those big trees, Bella?' Bella points to the trees on the map, moving her finger quickly from one to the next (line 151) and the teacher provides a further hint (line 152). When Bella achieves success at line 156, there is an outburst of 'Yes!' and clapping from Bella's peers and the teachers to celebrate her success. The scaffolding provided by the teacher and her peers throughout this learning experience enabled Bella to solve the problem herself.

Extract 11.5 Yes!!!

148	TEA:	so: ↑where are those ↑big trees [↑Bella?]
149	CH:	[it has]
150		(something around)
151	BEL:	*points at three points on the map*
152	TEA:	↑the:re? (.) ↑so: it's be↑tween (.) two of
153		↑↑those ↑trees *exaggerated excited face to*
154		*children opposite Bella, shows forefinger and*
155		*thumb held close together mouthing* like that
156	BEL:	°↑↑the:re? ° *points to an object on the map*
157	CH:	↑ye:s
158	CHN:	[↑yea:::::::::h] (multiple children) *applauding*

The Impact of Gesture on Learning Interactions

People do not always use spoken words to communicate and particularly when communicating spatial concepts, may use gesture to augment their communication, such as pointing when saying, 'It's over there.'

One of the challenges for early childhood teachers is to assess what a child already knows (or is thinking) to respond appropriately. Care must be taken to distinguish between lacking conceptual knowledge of mathematical concepts and not yet having the language to describe them (Mushin et al., 2013). Sensitivity to a child's use of gesture to communicate thinking when they do not have the words to use, and the teacher's use of gesture to support understanding, both play an important role. Indeed, research suggests that gesture supports conceptual understanding (Elia et al., 2014).

In Figure 11.2, we see the teacher tracing the edge of the map with one finger, using gesture to augment the conceptual meaning of the word, 'edge'.

In Extract 11.6 below, we see how both the child and the teacher use gesture as they discuss Emma's drawing of the route from home to her new school. The teacher uses gesture to demonstrate what he means by a pointy roof (lines 10–14). Emma confirms that some houses in her map have pointy roofs using gesture and repeating the teacher's word 'pointy' but then distinguishes between pointed roofs and flat roofs by saying

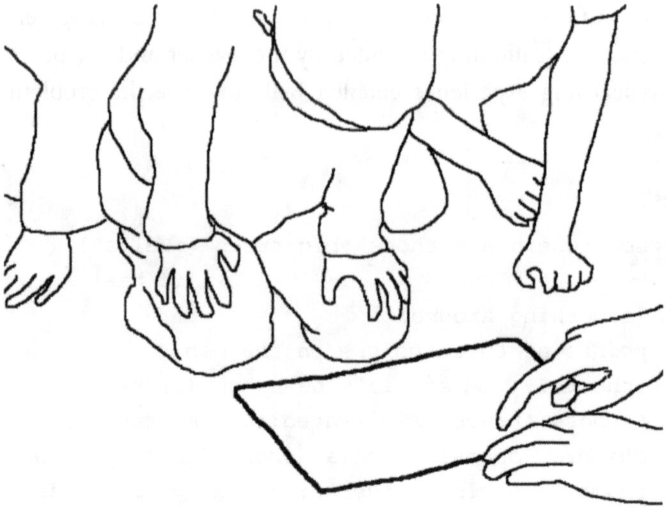

Figure 11.2 Teacher uses gesture to demonstrate the meaning of the word, 'edge.'

'and some are like that one', using gesture to demonstrate a flat roof (lines 15–19). The teacher imitates Emma's pointy-roofed house at line 20 and begins to respond at line 21 but is interrupted by Emma at line 22 who explains that their neighbour's roof resembles the roof of her own house: it is also flat.

Extract 11.6 Some are like pointy

EMM: I can see houthes? lots of houth[(es,)]
TEA: [lots of]
houses? (0.9)
TEA: >would you like to< draw those? (1.2) cos then
we'll know that we're on the right way. (0.9)
what shape are your houses? (0.9)
EMM: u::m,
TEA: >aretheyth'sameas< yours?(0.4)
EMM: no (it's)
TEA: cs you said that you di'nt'ave a r-
TEA: (1.0) you di'nt a [ve a °pointy roof°] *uses*
both hands with fingertips touching to show
flat roof then raises touching fingertips to
show pointed roof
EMM: [and some are like-] some

16 *uses both hands with fingertips touching to*
17 *show pointed roof* are like pointy and some are
18 like dat o [ne.] *uses both hands with*
fingertips
19 *touching to show flat roof*
20 TEA: *imitates Emma's pointy shape*
21 TEA: [okay.] (0.5) cn you draw s-
22 EMM: and our nexdoor neighbours a'got the same *uses*
23 *both hands with fingertips touching to show*
24 *flat roof then keeping hands parallel to the*
25 *floor, widens arms* one as me.
26 TEA: oh. well if your neighbour's house is the same
27 as yours cn you draw another, (1.0) house,
28 (2.3) f'your neighbour's house,

Three important points are illustrated by this back-and-forth exchange. First, the teacher clearly values Emma's expertise. This is evident by his acknowledgement that she is familiar with landmarks along the route from home to school (lines 1–9). Second, whilst Emma did not have the vocabulary to distinguish between the pitched roofs on her street, she had observed the differing attributes of the roof shapes and classified those that were alike (the roof of her house and that of her neighbour's house – lines 22–25). Third, the teacher's uses of the word 'pointy' supported by gesture (lines 11–14) was correctly repeated by Emma (Figure 11.3a; lines 15–17) demonstrating that she was learning the association between the word and the concept, and was able to distinguish between that concept and the concept of a flat roof for which

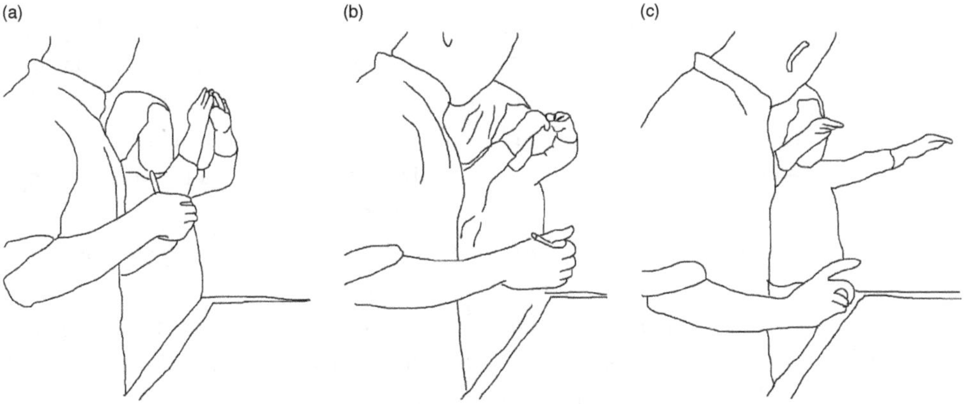

Figure 11.3 Emma uses gesture to demonstrate (a) pointy, (b) flat, and (c) matching.

she did not use a spoken word but rather the gesture of flat hands (Figure 11.3b) followed by an opening of her arms whilst maintaining the flat-hand position (Figure 11.3c; lines 22–25).

Conclusions

Research suggests that spatial thinking is seldom deliberately supported in play-based curricula, yet the ability to navigate one's environment is arguably a life skill. In these extracts, the teacher demonstrates high expectations of children, adjusting the learning experiences in response to the children's affect and learning needs. In the first extract, we see the teacher joining in with the play, talking on the 'telephone' with the children. Despite two children sustaining a parallel conversation, the teacher recognized that they were still benefiting from the intended opportunity to rehearse location and directional language and so the teacher persevered with the learning experience.

Bella's learning needs differed from those of her peers and in this instance, rather than telling Bella the answer, the teacher modelled the learning process – demonstrating to the group that when one does not have an answer to a problem, it is important to problem-solve and find ways to reach a solution. In both instances, we observe developmentally appropriate, play-based learning (and assessment). The teacher's sustained shared attention is not disrupted by high jinks and giggles, or by the need to provide multiple hints to support Bella's learning. Having a clear sense of the objective of each task, the teacher is able to demonstrate flexibility to respond to the children's level of excitement in one instance, and to provide additional time for learning in the second.

We observed Emma use gesture to demonstrate her knowledge of the shapes of the roofs on her street. Whilst her ability to use spoken language to describe these shapes was emerging with support, her conceptual understanding was well established, highlighting the importance of joint attention – both teacher and child focusing on the same activity simultaneously – and of the teacher recognizing the distinction between concept knowledge and vocabulary skills. We observed Felix using gesture to emphasize the word 'four'. We observed multiple instances of the teacher's use of gesture in the context of accompanying self-talk.

These examples remind us of the importance of gesture in teaching and learning – particularly in the context of emerging spatial thinking – and provide evidence to inform our practice.

Recommendations for Practice

- Learning needs to be relevant to the child. In this project, the children were deeply vested in the process of transitioning to school. At the same time, mathematics is all around us: we live in a three-dimensional world that comprises images and objects that have edges and curves. They are positioned in relation to other objects and to ourselves. Exploring spatial concepts whilst following children's interest in their new schools meant that mathematical concept development – specifically, spatial thinking – was closely connected to children's real-world experience. In addition, this approach positioned the children as the experts in the learning and the teacher as facilitating the learning by responding to children's expertise and extending it.
- Asking children questions that encourage them to find answers with the teacher's support shifts the focus from learning as a *product*, to learning as a *process*. Learning how to learn is a transferable skill that once acquired, can be applied in other contexts. Grappling with new ideas and achieving success encourages intrinsic motivation and a sense of agency, both of which are cornerstones of positive learning dispositions throughout life.
- It is challenging for teachers to be constantly attuned to what individual children are interested in, what each child knows already, and what they are ready to learn next. However, joint attention requires both participants in an interaction to be attentive. At times, children communicate using words and at other times, teachers need to wait and watch to observe what is communicated by the child non-verbally.
- Using gesture to support understanding of spatial concepts is very effective. In the same way that showing three fingers whilst saying the word, 'three' supports number value acquisition, using gesture to support concepts such as straight, edge, curve, between, and above also supports concept development and models advanced language.

Whilst much is known about the relationship between early childhood education quality and child outcomes, the fine-grained analysis afforded by a conversation-analytic approach enables teachers to see how quality interactions are enacted in practice. Laying bare the detail of high-quality interactions may support teachers replicating these interactions in their own classrooms, thus contributing to increasing access to high quality early learning for every child.

References

Church, A., Mashford-Scott, A., and Cohrssen, C. (2018). Supporting children to resolve disputes. *Journal of Early Childhood Research*, 16(1), 92–103. https://doi.org/10.1177/147671818X171770055414

Clements, D., and Sarama, J. (2021). *Learning and Teaching Early Math: The Learning Trajectories Approach* (3.ed). New York: Routledge.

Cohrssen, C., and Church, A. (2017). Mathematics knowledge in early childhood: intentional teaching in the third turn. In A. Bateman and A. Church (eds.), *Children's Knowledge-in-Interaction*. Singapore: Springer. https://doi.org/10.1007/978-981-10-1703-2_5

Cohrssen, C., Church, A., and Tayler, C. (2014a). Pausing for learning: responsive engagement in mathematics activities in early childhood settings. *Australasian Journal of Early Childhood*, 39(4), 95–102.

Cohrssen, C., Church, A., and Tayler, C. (2014b). Purposeful pauses: teacher talk during early childhood mathematics activities. *International Journal of Early Years Education*, 22(2), 169–183. https://doi.org/10.1080/09669760.2014.900476

Cohrssen, C., de Quadros Wander, B., Page, J., and Klarin, S. (2017). Between the big trees: a project-based approach to investigating shape and spatial thinking in a kindergarten program. *Australasian Journal of Early Childhood*, 42(1), 94–104. https://doi.org/10.23965/AJEC.42.1.011

Cohrssen, C., and Page, J. (2016). Articulating a rights-based argument for mathematics teaching and learning in early childhood education. *Australasian Journal of Early Childhood*, 41(3), 104–108.

Cohrssen, C., and Pearn, C. (2019). Assessing preschool children's maps against the first four levels of the primary curriculum: lessons to learn. *Mathematics Education Research Journal*, 33, 43–60. https://doi.org/10.1007/s13394-019-00298-7

Deans, J., and Cohrssen, C. (2015). Young children dancing mathematical thinking. *Australasian Journal of Early Childhood*, 40(3), 61–67.

Duncan, G. J., Claessens, A., Huston, A., et al. (2007). School readiness and later achievement. *Developmental Psychology*, 43(6), 1428–1446.

Egert, F., Dederer, V., and Fukkink, R. G. (2020). The impact of in-service professional development on the quality of teacher-child interactions in early childhood education and care: a meta-analysis. *Educational Research Review*, 29(1), 100309. https://doi.org/10.1016/j.edurev.2019.100309

Ehrlich, S. B., Levine, C., and Goldin-Meadow, S. (2006). The importance of gesture in children's spatial reasoning. *Developmental Psychology*, 42(6), 1259–1268.

Elia, I., Gagatsis, A., and van den Heuvel-Panhuizen, M. (2014). The role of gestures in making connections between space and shape aspects and their verbal representations in the early years: findings from a case study. *Mathematics Education Research Journal*, 26(4), 735–761.

Franzén, K. (2015). Under threes' mathematical learning. *European Early Childhood Education Research Journal*, 23(1), 43–54. https://doi.org/10.1080/1350293X.2014.970855

Hedge, K., and Cohrssen, C. (2019). Between the red and yellow windows: a fine-grained focus on supporting children's spatial thinking during play. *SAGE Open* (online). https://doi.org/10.1177/2158244019809551

Howes, C., Burchinal, M., Pianta, R., Bryant, D., Early, D., & Clifford, R. (2008). Ready to learn? Children's pre-academic achievement in pre-kindergarten programs. *Early Childhood Research Quarterly*, 23, 27–50. https://doi.org/10.1016/j.ecresq.2007.05.002

Klibanoff, R., Levine, S., Huttenlocher, J., Vasilyeva, M., and Hedges, L. (2006). Preschool children's mathematical knowledge: the effect of teacher 'math talk'. *Developmental Psychology*, 42(1), 59–69.

Lee, J. S., and Ginsburg, H. P. (2009). Early childhood teachers' misconceptions about mathematics education for young children in the United States. *Australasian Journal of Early Childhood*, 34(4), 37–45.

Levine, S., Whealton Suriyakham, L., Rowe, K., Huttenlocher, J., and Gunderson, E. (2010). What counts in the development of young children's number knowledge? *Developmental Psychology*, 46(5), 1309–1319.

Mushin, I., Gardner, R., and Munro, J. (2013). Language matters in demonstrations of understanding in early years maths assessment. *Mathematics Education Research Journal*, 25(2), 415–433. https://doi.org/DOI 10.1007/s13394-013-0077-4

Newcombe, N. S., and Frick, A. (2010). Early education for spatial intelligence: why, what and how. *Mind, Brain and Education*, 4(3), 102–111.

Nichols, J., Levay, K., O'Neil, M., and Volmert, A. (2019). Reframing early math learning. Available from: https://www.frameworksinstitute.org/publication/reframing-early-math-learning/ [last accessed 5 January 2022].

Peisner-Feinberg, E. S., Burchinal, M. R., Clifford, R. M., Culkin, M. L., Howes, C., Kagan, S. L., and Yazejian, N. (2001). The relation of preschool child-care quality to children's cognitive and social developmental trajectories through second grade. *Child Development*, 72(5), 1534–1553. https://doi.org/10.1111/1467-8624.00364

Pianta, R., La Paro, K., and Hamre, B. K. (2008). *Classroom Assessment Scoring System (CLASS) Manual, pre-K.* Baltimore, MD: Paul H. Brookes Publishing Co.

Pollitt, R., Cohrssen, C., Church, A., and Wright, S. (2015). Thirty-one is a lot! Assessing four-year-old children's number knowledge during an open-ended activity. *Australasian Journal of Early Childhood*, 40(1), 13–22.

Sacks, H., Schegloff, E. A., and Jefferson, G. (1974). A simplest systematics for the organization of turn-taking for conversation. *Language*, 50(4), 696–735. http://www.jstor.org/stable/412243

Sidnell, J., and Stivers, T. (eds.). (2013). *The Handbook of Conversation Analysis*. Chichester: John Wiley.

Siraj, I., and Asani, R. (2015). The role of sustained shared thinking, play and metacognition in children's learning. In S. Robson and S. Quinn (eds.), *Routledge International Handbook of Young Children's Thinking* (pp. 403–415). Abingdon: Routledge.

ten Have, P. (2007). *Doing Conversation Analysis: A Practical Guide* (2nd ed.). London: Sage Publications.

Uscianowski, C., Almeda, M. V., and Ginsburg, H. P. (2020). Differences in the complexity of math and literacy questions parents pose during storybook reading. *Early Childhood Research Quarterly*, 50, 40–50. https://doi.org/10.1016/j.ecresq.2018.07.003

12 | Creativity

CHRISTINE LEE

Introduction

Creativity can have multiple meanings, with definitions varying across different disciplines, theories, and fields. Consequently, this can make formulating a single and concise understanding of creativity difficult (Newton, 2013; Prentice, 2000). On a larger level, creativity is visible in producing products (e.g. art, music, publications, discoveries, inventions, etc.), where the emphasis is placed on creating a product with original and meaningful contributions to society (Rhodes, 1961). Research on this larger level of creativity thus assesses products to capture the game-changing ideas that impact our world (Kaufman & Beghetto, 2009). However, research on early childhood education often draws from personal or personally meaningful frameworks of creativity to understand children's creative sensemaking and learning that unfolds every day (Burnett & Smith, 2019).

Children's creativity often manifests in childhood activities like play, and it is through these playful activities where curiosities and questions are explored in imaginative and innovative ways (Lindqvist, 2003; Nicolopoulou et al., 2009; Sicart, 2017; Vygotsky, 1990). While the larger level frameworks of creativity focus on examining a product's societal impacts, they may not be as relevant in early childhood classrooms. In contrast to these larger views of creativity, this chapter will focus on personal levels of creativity. Personal creativity includes the everyday moments of learning and doing. Instead of measuring creativity through end products, the creative *process* of learning and exploring in these personally meaningful moments are examined (Cropley, 1990; Runco & Cayirdag, 2012). Creativity in early childhood activities is most visible at this personal level where the everyday moments of sensemaking takes place (Alkuş & Olgan, 2014). To understand creativity in early childhood education, this chapter blends perspectives that highlight creativity as *part of* children's sensemaking – which focuses our attention towards the process and meaningful experience of engaging in creative work in everyday early childhood classrooms. The aim of this chapter is to examine (1) how children creatively engage in learning and (2) how educators can design and support learning through creative, imaginative, and playful inquiry.

Creativity in Early Childhood Education

Across the literature, scholars consistently position creativity as a valuable part of learning that needs to be fostered in early childhood years (Craft, 2002; Kemple & Nissenberg, 2000; Leggett, 2017; May, 2009). It can greatly shape children's socio-emotional development, social skills, and confidence in doing future creative learning activities (Ahmadi & Besançon, 2017; Galton, 2010; Harrington, Block, & Block, 1983; Wright & Diener, 2012). Globally, creativity in education has been frequently pitched as an important need for the future workforce, highlighting the importance of innovative thinking for future society (Mishra & Mehta, 2017; Wagner, 2014). This is especially relevant in our technology-driven world, where creative skills are valued and needed (Ata-Akturk & Sevimli-Celik, 2020). Early childhood is a significant time for cultivating children's creativity and is where we can lay the foundations for future creative skills as children develop.

In early childhood education, researchers often turn to personal levels of creativity that emerge in children's everyday activities. The focus on the personal levels of creativity captures the creative process children engage in while discovering and learning new things; whether those discoveries are new and impactful to society is not relevant (Kaufman & Beghetto, 2009). Kaufman & Beghetto (2009) further described the personal level as *mini-c*, where creativity can emerge in shorter timescales within moments of learning and interacting in early childhood settings and the early years of primary school. In contrast to product-driven creativity standards, personal creativity (or mini-c) is meaningful to the child as they explore and learn new things. For example, when children play with clay for the first time, they might learn how to manipulate, shape, and form the clay with their hands. By engaging in this playful and explorative activity, creative work becomes visible when children discover and form new and interesting shapes with the clay. At this personal level of creativity, children learn from birth, where the ways in which they engage with new learning experiences can be made visible through their creative practices (Beghetto, et al., 2012; Runco & Cayirdag, 2012).

By adopting these perspectives, we attend to the creative exploration and process of learning, instead of focusing on end-products to evaluate and determine children's creativity. These creative moments are child-led interactions that are open-ended, improvised, playful, and imaginative (Sawyer, 2015). Children are already playing, experimenting, exploring, and discovering the world around them; and recognizing and supporting the learning moments afforded in these activities are important so that children can engage in creative discovery, thinking, and learning (Eshach & Fried,

2005; Fromberg & Bergen, 2006; McCaslin, 2006; Vygotsky, 1990). This repositions children as competent and capable learners who have agency, freedom, and ownership of their learning (Cremin et al., 2006). It also furthers the importance of personal and everyday creativity in early childhood classrooms because it positions creativity as a space for children to have the freedom to explore and understand learning in their own inventive and meaningful ways.

Supporting Creativity in Early Childhood Classrooms

Despite the wealth of research documenting the importance of creativity in early childhood, there are also dichotomous views that position creativity as an activity outside of the classroom or as a supplement to learning (Beghetto, 2008; Thomson & Sefton-Green, 2011). This can often stem from the misconception that the arts are exclusively synonymous with creative work, where educators mistakenly associate creativity narrowly and exclusively with children's art (Diakidoy & Kanari, 1999). However, this perspective limits who gets to be creative and creates a barrier between creativity and learning, where creative interactions are not considered relevant in children's education and are not 'serious' learning activities that belong in classrooms (Glăveanu, 2014; Paek & Sumners, 2017).

To develop a classroom culture of creativity, it is important to consider how early childhood teachers support the emergent and creative work children engage in. Children need to have agency and ownership of their ideas in these creative spaces (Davies et al., 2013; Saracho, 2002). Therefore, early childhood teachers should guide and react to children's creative work by being open-minded, humorous, supportive, spontaneous, and playful (Hotaman, 2010; Sawyer, 2004). This can give opportunities for children to invent solutions, generate ideas, take risks, be curious, explore problems, or come up with alternative ways of using materials (Burnett & Smith, 2019; Cremin, 2006). The importance of these practices is that creativity is supported and encouraged through openness and respect for children's spontaneous, imaginative, and unusual ideas (Sawyer, 2015).

Designing a Play-Based Curriculum

The data presented in this chapter is from a multi-age classroom of 6–8-year-olds at a progressive elementary school in a large western city in the United States. The children from this classroom were in a dual language programme, where instruction was both in English and Spanish. Following the school's philosophy, the teacher (Lily) practises inquiry-based teaching pedagogies, cognitive guided instruction, and engages in child-centred activities like play. As a result, Lily's classroom was a fusion of spaces equally dedicated to structured instruction and imaginative activities. In addition to having groups of tables, chairs, and a rug space for whole-class discussions, Lily also dedicated parts of the room with blocks, art supplies, and miscellaneous materials for child-centred activities. The children in the class regularly played in these spaces, and she often joined in to document the children's ideas and questions that arose during these activities to inspire reflective sensemaking and discussions.

Data in this chapter is from a larger design-based research project (Design Based Research Collective, 2003) where teachers and researchers co-constructed a play-based curriculum on the interdependent relationships in marine ecosystems. Children learned through play by taking on the roles of various marine creatures that lived within the kelp forest and dramatically performed how each character lived, interacted, and relied on one another for survival. As part of the curriculum, children spent several weeks researching their respective marine roles, created costumes that represented their marine creatures, and dramatically played and explored how they would interact with others within the kelp forest. For example, one of the play lessons in the study was on the food chain, where children playing as sea urchins pretended to 'eat' kelp and children playing as fish tried to swim away from their friends who played as larger predators.

The data presented in this chapter is from one play-based lesson that took place at the end of the curriculum. In the extracts, conversation analysis (CA) is used to capture the creative work children engage in when teachers purposively provide child-centred spaces for play and imagination to thrive. Due to the playful, dramatic, and joyful nature of the play lessons, the spaces that Lily usually dedicated to play and art transformed into the official 'changing area' for the children. Before and after every play lesson, children would put on their costumes in these areas to engage in inquiry. The first three extracts occurred moments *before* Lily began her play lesson; six children spontaneously began to play as marine creatures in the changing area. The fine-grain analysis of these extracts reveals how children's dramatic and playful enactments of the marine ecosystem led to creative reflections, argumentations, and scientific conclusions. The second set of extracts were from the end of the same play lesson and examines how Lily utilized children's creativity during a discussion to make scientific conclusions. In these extracts, we see how Lily balances children's agency, imagination, joy, and playful dispositions with larger instructional goals.

Creative Science Discourse

While learning about the kelp forest food web, children grew increasingly interested in how humans impacted the marine ecosystem. Children regularly approached Lily with questions on how plastic pollution impacted our oceans and how society can reduce the negative impacts on our planet. Following children's curiosities, this play lesson was designed to discuss, explore, and address questions on plastic pollution. As a result, this play lesson was a chance for children to embody various characters to perform and discuss how humans impact the kelp forest. The children were given opportunities to play as several roles: littering humans, reporters, scientists, or to continue playing as the marine creatures of the kelp forest. The children playing as Littering Humans gathered plastic bottles from home and brought them to school. As Littering Humans, children pretended to litter and pollute the kelp forest with these plastic bottles. Children playing as Reporters and Scientists grabbed iPads and clipboards to report the news and document what would happen to the marine creatures when Littering Humans polluted the ocean.

We follow six children who played as Phytoplankton, Kelp, Fish, Shark, Sea Cucumber, and Sea Urchin. Except for Lily (the teacher), children are identified in the transcripts by their marine role. The interactions occurred just after the children finished putting on their kelp forest costumes in the changing area. During this time, Lily was occupied with another group of children at the other end of the classroom. While waiting for Lily to begin the play lesson, the six children spontaneously engaged in their own dramatic and playful interactions. The extract begins with a child playing as Phytoplankton. Like the other five children in the group, she just finished putting on her costume and gets up to dramatically and joyfully engage her peers.

Extract 12.1

```
Phytoplankton:  I gotta warn all my friends so that
                ((Phytoplankton stands up))
Phytoplankton:  [ACCORDING TO ALL MY PHYTOPLANKTON FRIENDS!]
Kelp:           [Five ( ) can hide behind me]
```

```
05 Phytoplankton:   ((Phytoplankton paces back and forth))
06                  ACCORDING TO ALL MY PHYTOPLANKTON FRIENDS
07                  WE'RE ALL GONNA DIE
```

The extract begins when Phytoplankton stands up after putting on her costume. She turns her attention to the other five children and dramatically exclaims that they (as marine creatures) were all going to die (lines 6–7). What is interesting about the beginning of this interaction is that once she finishes putting on her costume, Phytoplankton immediately begins to play while being in character. Instead of stating that humans would cause marine creatures to die, she states that 'I' (line 1) must warn her friends because 'WE'RE' (line 7) all going to die. This is significant because Phytoplankton initiates a creative performance of a scientific problem. As we later see in Extract 12.2, the problem is that when humans litter, marine animals die. By adopting and embodying the role of being phytoplankton, we see how her display of stance (Du Bois, 2007) invites the other children to align and join her creative and dramatic work. When a speaker displays stance, they reveal and communicate their positions and views within the conversation (Biber et al., 1999; Du Bois, 2007; Jaffe, 2007). With a raised volume, Phytoplankton displays an affective stance of concern (lines 6–7). The affective stance shows Phytoplankton's affective position or view on how humans impact marine life (Maynard, 1993; Ochs 1996). What is most important about these first few lines is how Phytoplankton creatively used her knowledge and perspective of being a member of the kelp forest ecosystem to inform her stance.

We also saw that the changing area transformed into a small stage for children to continuously and dramatically embody their marine characters. As one can imagine, the audio of this interaction was loud with overlapping talk because children were excitedly getting ready to play and perform how humans impact the kelp forest. Lily did not once request children to stop talking or playing in the classroom. Thus, the absence of a teacher did not mean that children stopped thinking about science, or stopped playing as marine creatures. Since Lily established and made room for these creative spaces, Phytoplankton had the agency and creative license to begin her own dramatic performance. This first extract is important in demonstrating how children initiated and engaged in their own scientific play of the marine ecosystem. It also supports and further argues that teachers need to establish and value physical space in the classroom where creative child-led activities can spontaneously occur (Cremin et al., 2006; Davies et al., 2013; Saracho, 2002; Sawyer, 2015).

In Extract 12.2, we follow the six children in the changing area as Phytoplankton continues to dramatically and playfully engage the other children on the dire future of the kelp forest. Interestingly, in this next extract, we see a transformation in the conversation as the other children engage with Phytoplankton. While the first extract illustrated how children take up opportunities to engage in agentic and creative activities, the second extract details how children align and monitor scientific conversation while collaboratively engaging in dramatic interactions.

Extract 12.2

```
08 Phytoplankton: A::::HH ((walks to the other side of the
09                changing area))
10 Kelp:          You're microscopic they~won't ((gestures to
11                Phytoplankton while looking at her))
12                PHYTOPLANKTON you're microscopic they won't
13                hurt you
14 Phytoplankton: Oh right!
15 Fish:          Well I can eat you[nam~nam~nam~nam~nam]
16 Phytoplankton:                   [No! They are gonna eat me.]
17                Cuz ((points to Zooplankton)) Zooplankton
18                eats me.
19 Fish:          Nam nam nam na:m ((while pretending to eat
20                Phytoplankton))
21 Phytoplankton: And he ((touching Fish on the chest)) eats me
22                and then they ( ) so
23                I'm~inside~of~his~belly and I'm dea::::d
24 Fish:          Nam~[nam~nam~nam~nam~nam~nam~nam]
25 Phytoplankton:     [A:::::h] ((Phytoplankton walks back to
26                the other side of the changing area)) A::::h
27                Ba:::h Ba:h
```

In this extract, we see stancetaking as a central part of arguing and discussing science as Phytoplankton changes her stance multiple times throughout the interaction. As Phytoplankton strongly states in Extract 12.1, her original stance on humans ('WE'RE ALL GONNA DIE') also became an invitation for the other children to join the playful and dramatic doom of the upcoming play lesson where humans come to litter the kelp forest. Phytoplankton's stance is then corrected by Kelp, who loudly reminds her in lines 10–13 that she is microscopic, and if she is microscopic, humans cannot harm her with plastic rubbish. Here, we see a multimodal display of Kelp's stance as he uses a combination of verbal and physical cues to strongly communicate his perspective to Phytoplankton (Kendon, 2004;

Sidnell, 2006; Streeck, 2009). In lines 10–11, Kelp turns to look at Phytoplankton while gesturing towards her to grab her attention. Then, with a raised volume, '**PHYTOPLANKTON**', he reminds Phytoplankton in lines 12–13 that she cannot be harmed.

Creative work is collaborative (Kupers et al., 2019), and through these interactions, we see how children engage in playful sensemaking experiences as they negotiate and argue concepts using their science knowledge. Kelp and Phytoplankton's creative work lies in how they make sense of the science concepts by playfully and dramatically making scientific arguments while remaining in character to inform their stance. When Kelp reminds Phytoplankton of the marine character she embodies and uses the imaginative role to argue the point that humans cannot harm microscopic marine life, Phytoplankton revises her original stance and aligns with Kelp, 'Oh right!' (line 14). This shift in stance is one of the most significant turns in this extract because Kelp engages with Phytoplankton by assessing and challenging her stance through scientific reasoning. Kelp does not refute Phytoplankton's claim that humans would harm the ecosystem, just that they won't be able to directly harm *her*. This is an important distinction to make, because while Kelp and Phytoplankton are dramatically role playing as marine creatures, they are also creatively engaged in science by considering the real-life structures and features of the marine animals in the kelp forest to inform their conversation and shifts in stance.

The creative work behind the changes in stance continued to rely on science knowledge as Fish joined the interactions between Kelp and Phytoplankton. In line 15, Fish enters the interaction by disagreeing with Kelp and Phytoplankton, emphasizing that he can '**eat**' Phytoplankton. This leads to Phytoplankton shifting back to her original stance, no longer aligning with Kelp. In line 16, Phytoplankton immediately responds and begins her turn with a raised volume '**No!**' to clearly communicate her opposition (Goodwin, 1990, 1995; Goodwin et al., 2002) to Kelp's argument from lines 10–13. This is because Phytoplankton is a primary producer and is the foundation of the marine food web. In lines 16–18 and 21–23, Phytoplankton remembers this about herself, and reconsiders her stance as she gestures to both Zooplankton (line 17) and Fish (line 21) because they both rely on her for survival (Zooplankton eats Phytoplankton, and Fish eats Zooplankton). Therefore, it does not matter if she was microscopic or not, because even if the plastic does not harm her, the argument that she would die continues to hold.

The significance of Extract 12.2 is that it illustrates how creativity lies in children's conversations while playing and performing with roles and ideas rooted in scientific arguments. Children in play are actively negotiating, arguing, imagining, and reflecting on the world around them, and it is through these interactions we see how play is a form of learning and creativity (Fisher et al., 2011; Hirsh-Pasek et al., 2009; Lindqvist, 2003; Varelas et al., 2010; Vygotsky, 1990). The original and unique way children used their knowledge of the kelp forest ecosystem to argue or negotiate with Phytoplankton is where the creative process of learning is most visible. Not only did children take into consideration the structure and function of their role (like being microscopic), but they also used their knowledge of the complex marine food web to inform their stance. This further supports the literature on creativity in early childhood education by illustrating the creative and intellectual power behind collaborative sensemaking activities like play (Kupers, et al., 2019; Sawyer, 2004; Wright & Diener, 2012).

In the following extract, we continue to see how children creatively use their kelp forest knowledge during play. The focus of this extract is how Kelp positions himself amongst the group of children to creatively come up with a solution to the pollution problem the marine animals will face.

Extract 12.3

```
Kelp:            Everybody FIGHT THE HUMANS
                 ((points to the "Littering Humans"))
                 [AND HIDE BEHIND ME!]((points behind him))
Phytoplankton:   [Wait! Wait! Wait!] ((touches Kelp's arm)) We
                 gotta we gotta warn all our friends
                 ACCORDING TO MY RESEARCH PHYTOPLANKTON FRIENDS
                 ((touches her temple)) (0.1) humans are coming
                 we're all gonna die::
Sea Cucumber:    No we're not
Kelp:            Okay everybody
Sea Cucumber:    Not everyone
Kelp:            So TWO OF YOU GUYS
Sea Urchin:      CALM down ((raises her arms above her head))
Shark:           There's only five humans calm down
Kelp:            Two~peo- two (0.1) two animals hide behind me
Fish:            [ME! Me me!]
Shark:           [Me~me~me~me~me~me]
```

The importance of being in character is further illustrated in this extract when we see Kelp in line 42 self-initiate a self-repair from 'two-peo-' to 'two animals' (Hutchby & Wooffitt, 1998; Schegloff et al., 1977). The repair from 'two-peo-' (Kelp aborts his original call for two *people*) to animals solidifies the importance of being, imagining, and acting in character, at least important enough for him to repair his own talk as he addressed his peers. Therefore, a defining feature of creativity in this data is the process of how children adopt and work to maintain their marine roles in order to drive both their play and science discourse.

We also continue to see the rich knowledge of the kelp forest creatively surface in imaginative ways as Kelp comes up with a solution to the pollution problem (lines 28–30 and 42). At first, the other children do not immediately take up his directive because Phytoplankton is still loudly declaring her stance of the upcoming situation; that everyone will die (lines 31–35). We also start to see the other children interjecting across several turns by disagreeing with Phytoplankton's stance on the coming problem (lines 36, 38, 40, and 41). At the start of this extract, Kelp issues what Tulbert & Goodwin (2011) call a *conjoined directive* – where 'physical and verbal actions work together to create a sense of force' (Tulbert & Goodwin, 2011, pp. 83). In line 28, Kelp loudly states, 'Everybody FIGHT THE HUMANS' with a pointing gesture at the children playing as Littering Humans. He then issues another directive in a raised volume to his marine friends 'AND HIDE BEHIND ME!' (line 30). Again, he pairs and aligns his verbal directive with a pointing gesture behind him, indicating to his peers that they needed to hide in order to escape the effects of the Littering Humans.

While the conjoined directive helped Kelp display a sense of force and urgency (Tulbert & Goodwin, 2011), it also placed Kelp in the powerful role as protector. Like Extract 12.2, we must consider the intellectual work that supports Kelp's role and ideas. Kelp is a very tall and large algae seaweed that grows densely in underwater forests. It plays an important role in our oceans, sustaining biodiverse marine life, providing habitats and food for smaller creatures, and sheltering smaller creatures from large prey. Kelp intelligently uses his knowledge of the science (specifically the structure and function of kelp in marine ecosystems) to develop an imaginative, inventive, and creative solution. For this reason, Kelp had the power to declare and playfully organize a solution for his classmates. Thus, the creative process of solving the problem of Littering Humans was evident in Kelp's conjoined directive, which was dramatically and creatively based on his knowledge of science.

Enabling Creative Discussions for Learning Science

After playing as Reporters, Scientists, marine creatures, and Littering Humans, Lily (teacher) began a discussion to bring together children's concluding ideas on how plastic pollution can impact the ecosystem. During the play lesson, Littering Humans left plastic bottles in the ocean, Scientists recorded and documented the collapse of the kelp forest on their clipboards, and Reporters video-recorded the events with their iPads. The extracts in this section occurred at the end of the same play lesson and details how Lily guides discussion as she works to align and maintain children's creative and playful interactions. Extract 12.4 begins just after the children finished playing and performing the collapse of the kelp forest.

Extract 12.4

Lily:	**Reporters** (0.1) I'm noticing that all~of~a
	sudden this **room** is really (0.1) really (0.1)
	°quiet°
Phytoplankton:	((raises her hand))
Lily:	Phytoplankton ((calling on her))
Phytoplankton:	((moves in front of Reporters and Scientists
	to speak while marine creatures are still
	playing dead))

Due to the plastic pollution, children playing as marine creatures in the kelp forest were lying on the floor, pretending to be dead. This observation is shared in lines 45–47 when Lily calls to children by their roles, '**Reporters**', to share her noticing that the room was quiet. The importance of this turn is not only that Lily invited children into discussion with an observation, but that she addressed the children according to their roles with an open-ended prompt (Bateman, 2017). This is unlike traditional patterns of classroom talk, where teachers often ask questions with known answers to evaluate children's knowledge (Cazden, 2001; Mehan, 1979). Instead, Lily preserves children's creative work by maintaining children's agency and ownership of the learning experience with an open-ended prompt to participate in discussion while remaining in character. We see evidence of this successfully being taken up by Phytoplankton in line 48, as she quickly raises her hand after hearing her teacher's observation.

Lily also aligned with children's creative work when she used a combination of repeating words, a soft tone, and pauses to dramatize her observation that the room was 'really (0.1) really (0.1) °quiet°' (lines 46–47). Lily repeats the word 'really' twice in her turn, and says 'quiet' with a soft tone, emphasizing that due to the death of the marine creatures, the kelp forest was very quiet. Lily also pauses for brief moments after each time that she says 'really' (line 46). Previous research documents the importance of teacher pauses as ways to guide and give opportunities for children to contribute ideas during instruction (Bateman, 2017; Cohrssen et al., 2014). In this case, Lily's pauses also added a dramatic and playful effect on the observation that the marine animals had died. The pauses in Lily's turn further maintained the dramatic and creative flow of activity (Csikszentmihalyi, 1997). The concept of flow, or flow state, is when a person is fully concentrated and immersed in an activity (Csikszentmihalyi, 1997; Spencer, 2016). Throughout this chapter, children's discourse continuously illustrated the importance of immersing in character (as evident in Extracts 12.2 and 12.3). Therefore, the combination of dramatic pauses, repeated words, and softer tones with Lily's decision to call children 'Reporters', sustained, oriented, and aligned with the flow of children's play.

Following lines 50–52 (from Extract 12.4), Phytoplankton moved to the centre of the room to explain why she thought plastic pollution impacted all living things (including smaller and microscopic creatures). In the final excerpt, we examine children's talk to further illustrate how Lily maintained the flow of creative and playful science discourse.

Extract 12.5

53	Reporters:	((Reporters are recording Phytoplankton's talk
54		with iPads at the centre of the room))
55	Phytoplankton:	So you know how there's thousands of
56		phytoplankton and zooplankton? Even **US** die
57		because glass and plastic tiny glass and
58		plastic that's microscopic like as big as **us**
59		**STICK inside** of us and then kill even me
60		phytoplankton and zooplankton. So if you think
61		you're still alive animals like~like umm kelp
62		bass and phytoplankton and zooplankton you
63	Kelp:	((Kelp sits up from being dead))
64	Phytoplankton:	aren't because plastics °tiny° ( )((makes a
65		gesture with fingers to show how tiny plastics
66		are)) sticks inside and aww::: ((lies down to
67		show she died))
68	Lily:	So **Phytoplank[ton]**
69	Kelp:	[WELL] a~**and**
70	Lily:	Go ahead **Kelp**
71	Kelp:	This is also going to affect **you** humans
72		((pointing to Reporters & Scientists)) because
73	Lily:	Oh:: **why**?

Literature on creativity emphasizes the importance of teachers remaining spontaneous and open to children's unusual and inventive sensemaking experiences (Burnett & Smith, 2019; Cremin, 2006; Sawyer, 2004, 2015). Throughout this extract, Lily does not move to rearrange or disrupt the

Figure 12.1 Reporter video-records destroyed marine life.

creative flow of children's play and discussion. For example, in Figure 12.1 we see a Reporter walk into the play space to video-record Phytoplankton's talk (lines 53–54) while the other kelp forest creatures remained on the ground to show that they were still dead. In lines 55–62 and lines 64–67, Phytoplankton describes how plastic pollution can endanger microscopic life (such as herself) while remaining in character (she refers to '**us**' dying, and that 'you aren't' alive). Interestingly, Kelp adds to Phytoplankton's conclusions by sitting up from being dead on the ground to describe how plastic pollution would also impact human beings (lines 69 and 71–72). Like Extract 12.2, Kelp used a multimodal display of verbal and physical gestures by pointing to both Reporters and Scientists as he states that 'you' humans would also be impacted (lines 71–72). Therefore, the creative flow of being immersed in play (Csikszentmihalyi, 2014) was not only important enough for children to engage in discussion while remaining in character, but for Lily to align with children to sustain it (as we also saw in Extract 12.4). As a result, it shows how Lily's willingness to be open to children's creative learning process led to children sharing reflections and conclusions on how humans impact our planet.

Recommendations for Practice

The findings in this chapter illustrate how children engage in inquiry learning through dramatic and creative performances of marine ecosystems. The creative ways of engaging in scientific argumentations, conjectures, and discussions were rooted in how the teacher made physical and conversational space for children's play and creativity. Across Extracts 12.1–12.3, we see how these implications were important for children to have the agency and freedom to express and make sense of science in their own creative and meaningful ways. Therefore, some key implications for inspiring and cultivating creativity in early childhood classrooms are:

- Establishing classroom space for children to creatively engage in child-led interactions and activities (i.e. play, art, etc.). Additionally, it is important that instructors position the interactions and activities that take place in this space as a valuable form of participating in the classroom.
- Encourage children to have the agency to imagine, transform, and utilize the space in their own ways (similar to how children in the study transformed the play space into a 'changing area' for marine creatures).

The in-depth analysis of children's conversations made clear that creativity lies within the process and experience of being marine creatures during play. As we saw in Extracts 12.2–12.3, children used their roles to dramatically and thoughtfully engage in scientific inquiry practices and discourse. Thus, it is important to consider creativity through perspectives that position child-driven activities like play as an important and essential part of learning.

- Creativity can often be in the messy *process* of discovering and sensemaking new concepts (Wilson, 2018). It can spontaneously emerge 'in the moment', where children's imaginative and playful interactions became rich and meaningful ways of engaging in learning. It is important to be supportive of these improvised sensemaking experiences as they emerge in the classroom.
- Children engage in creative ways because they are curious, excited, and wondrous. Therefore, it is important to create learning environments that are inviting and potentiating (Claxton & Carr, 2004), where children have the agency to ask questions, invent solutions, collaborate with peers, and develop ideas in their own dramatic and playful ways (Burnett & Smith, 2019).

Finally, it is also important to summarize how teachers can sustain and bring children's creativity into classroom interactions and conversations. In Extracts 12.4–12.5 Lily implemented conversational moves that not only placed value on the dramatic ways of sensemaking, but also maintained the creative flow of play and science discourse.

- There is breadth in creative learning – what children learn and do in creative activities (like play) are applicable to other domains and activities (Claxton & Carr, 2004). For example, creative learning can be a platform for children to engage in skills like scientific argumentation and observation.
- How teachers affirm children's creative work has the power to shape and support learning. By accepting and aligning with children's creative work (i.e. encouraging and sustaining flow), activities like play can transform into a powerful platform for inquiry and learning.
- Creativity is affective; it can be dramatic, playful, joyful, and even frustrating. To support children's creative work is not only to listen and guide talk, but to also join the affective experiences in children's learning.

References

Ahmadi, N., and Besançon, M. (2017). Creativity as a stepping stone towards developing other competencies in classrooms. *Education Research International.* 2017(2). https://doi.org/10.1155/2017/1357456.

Alkuş, A., and Olgan, R. (2014). Pre-service and in-service preschool teachers' views regarding creativity in early childhood education. *Early Child Development and Care*, 184(12), 1902–1919. https://doi.org/10.1080/03004430.2014.893236.

Ata-Akturk, A., and Sevimli-Celik, S. (2020). Creativity in early childhood teacher education: beliefs and practices. *International Journal of Early Years Education* (online). https://doi.org/10.1080/09669760.2020.1754174.

Bateman, A. (2017). Hearing children's voices through a conversation analysis approach. *International Journal of Early Years Education*, 25(3), 241–256. https://doi.org/10.1080/09669760.2017.1344624.

Beghetto, R. A. (2008). Prospective teachers' beliefs about imaginative thinking in K–12 schooling. *Thinking Skills and Creativity*, 3(2), 134–142. https://doi.org/10.1016/j.tsc.2008.06.001.

Beghetto, R. A., Kaufman, J. A., Hegarty, B., Hammond, H. L., and Wilcox-Herzog, A. (2012). Cultivating creativity in early childhood education: a 4 C perspective. In. O. Saracho (ed.), *Contemporary Perspectives on Research in Creativity in Early Childhood Education* (pp. 251–270).Charlotte, NC: IAP-Information Age Publishing.

Biber, D., Johansson, S., Leech, G., Conrad, S., and Finegan, E. (1999). *Longman Grammar of Spoken and Written English.*Essex: Pearson Education.

Burnett, C., and Smith, S. (2019). Reaching for the star: a model for integrating creativity in education. In C. A. Mullen (ed.), *Creativity Under Duress in Education?* (pp. 179–199). Cham, Switzerland: Springer.

Cazden, C. (2001). *Classroom Discourse: The Language of Teaching and Learning*. Portsmouth: Heinemann.

Claxton, G., and Carr, M. (2004). A framework for teaching learning: the dynamics of disposition. *Early Years*, 24(1), 87–97. https://doi.org/10.1080/0957514032 0001790898.

Cohrssen, C., Church, A., and Tayler, C. (2014). Purposeful pauses: teacher talk during early childhood mathematics activities. *International Journal of Early Years Education*, 22(2), 169–183. http://dx.doi.org/10.1080/09669760.2014.900476.

Craft, A. (2002). *Creativity and Early Years Education: A Lifewide Foundation*. London: Bookcraft.

Cremin, T. (2006). Creativity, uncertainty and discomfort: teachers as writers. *Cambridge Journal of Education*, 36(3), 415–433. https://doi .org/10.1080/03057640600866023.

Cremin, T., Burnard, P., and Craft, A. (2006). Pedagogy and possibility thinking in the early years. *Thinking Skills & Creativity*, 1(2), 108–119. https://doi .org/10.1016/j.tsc.2006.07.001

Cropley, A. J. (1990). Creativity and mental health in everyday life. *Creativity Research Journal*, 3(3), 167–178. https://doi.org/10.1080/10400419009534351

Csikszentmihalyi, M. (1997). *Finding Flow: The Psychology of Engagement with Everyday Life*. New York, NY: Basic Books.

Csikszentmihalyi, M. (2014). *Flow and the Foundations of Positive Psychology: The Collected Works of Mihaly Csikszentmihalyi*. Dordrecht: Springer.

Davies, D., Jindal-Snape, D., Collier, C., Digby, R., Hay, P., and Howe, A. (2013). Creative learning environments in education: a systematic literature review. *Thinking Skills and Creativity*, 8, 80–91. https://doi.org/10.1016/j .tsc.2012.07.004.

Design-Based Research Collective. (2003). Design-based research: an emerging paradigm for educational inquiry. *Educational Researcher*, 32(1), 5–8.

Diakidoy, I. A. N., and Kanari, E. (1999). Student teachers' beliefs about creativity. *British Educational Research Journal*, 25(2), 225–243. https://doi .org/10.1080/0141192990250206.

Du Bois, J. W. (2007). The stance triangle. In R. Englebretson (ed.), *Stancetaking in Discourse: Subjectivity, Evaluation, Interaction* (pp. 139–182). Amsterdam/ New York: John Benjamins.

Eshach, H., and Fried, M. (2005). Should science be taught in early childhood? *Journal of Science Education and Technology*, 14(3), 315–336. http://dx.doi .org/10.1007/s10956-005-7198-9.

Fisher, K., Hirsh-Pasek, K., Golinkoff, R. M., Singer, D. G., and Berk, L. (2011). Playing around in school: implications for learning and educational policy. In A. D. Pellegrini (ed.), *The Oxford Handbook of the Development of Play* (pp. 341–360). Oxford: Oxford University Press.

Fromberg, D. P., and Bergen, D. (2006), Introduction. In D. P. Fromberg and D. Bergen (eds.), *Play from Birth to Twelve: Contexts, Perspectives and Meanings*. Abingdon: Routledge.

Galton, M. (2010). Going with the flow or back to normal? The impact of creative practitioners in schools and classrooms. *Research Papers in Education*, 25(4), 355–375. https://doi.org/10.1080/02671520903082429.

Glăveanu, V. P. (2014). Revisiting the 'art bias' in lay conceptions of creativity. *Creativity Research Journal*, 26(1), 11–20. https://doi.org/10.1080/10400419.2014.873656.

Goodwin, M. H. (1990). *He-Said-She-Said: Talk as Social Organization among Black Children*. Bloomington, IN: Indiana University Press.

Goodwin, M. H. (1995). Co-construction in girls' hopscotch. *Research on Language and Social Interaction*, 28(3), 261–281. https://doi.org/10.1207/s15327973rlsi2803_5.

Goodwin, M. H., Goodwin, C., and Yaeger-Dror, M. (2002). Multi-modality in girls' game disputes. *Journal of Pragmatics*, 34, 1621–1649.

Harrington, D. M., Block, J., and Block, J. H. (1983). Predicting creativity in preadolescence from divergent thinking in early childhood. *Journal of Personality and Social Psychology*, 45(3), 609–623. https://doi.org/10.1037/0022-3514.45.3.609

Hirsh-Pasek, K., Golinkoff, R. M., Berk, L. E., and Singer, D. G. (2009). *A Mandate for Playful Learning in School: Presenting the Evidence*. Oxford: Oxford University Press.

Hotaman, D. (2010). The teaching profession: knowledge of subject matter, teaching skills and personality traits. *Procedia – Social and Behavioral Sciences*, 2(2), 1416–1420.

Hutchby, I., and Wooffitt, R. (1998). *Conversation Analysis: Principles, Practices, and Applications*. Cambridge: Polity Press.

Jaffe, A. (2007). Codeswitching and stance: issues in interpretation. *Journal of Language, Identity & Education*, 6(1), 53–77. https://doi.org/10.1080/15348450701341006.

Kaufman J. C., and Beghetto R. A. (2009). Beyond big and little: the four C model of creativity. *Review of General Psychology*, 13(1), 1–12. https://doi.org/10.1037/a0013688.

Kemple, K. M., and Nissenberg, S. A. (2000). Nurturing creativity in early childhood education: families are part of it. *Early Childhood Education Journal*, 28(1), 67–71. https://doi.org/10.1023/A:1009555805909.

Kendon, A. (2004). *Gesture: Visible Action as Utterance*. Cambridge: Cambridge University Press.

Kupers, E., Lehmann-Wermser, A., McPherson, G., and van Geert, P. (2019). Children's creativity: a theoretical framework and systematic review. *Review of Educational Research*, 89(1), 93–124. https://doi.org/10.3102/0034654318815707.

Leggett, N. (2017). Early childhood creativity: challenging educators in their role to intentionally develop creative thinking in children. *Early Childhood Education Journal*, 45(6), 845–853. https://doi.org/10.1007/s10643-016-0836-4.

Lindqvist, G. (2003). Vygotsky's theory of creativity. *Creativity Research Journal*, 15(2–3), 245–251. https://doi.org/10.1080/10400419.2003.9651416.

May, P. (2009) *Creative Development in the Early Years Foundation Stage*. Abingdon: Routledge.

Maynard, S. K. (1993). *Discourse Modality: Subjectivity, Emotion, and Voice in the Japanese Language*. Amsterdam/New York: John Benjamins.

McCaslin, N. (2006). *Creative Drama in the Classroom and Beyond*. Boston, MA: Allyn & Bacon.

Mehan, H. (1979). *Learning Lessons: Social Organization in the Classroom*. Cambridge, MA: Harvard University Press.

Mishra, P., and Mehta, R. (2017). What we educators get wrong about 21st-century learning: results of a survey. *Journal of Digital Learning in Teacher Education*, 33(1), 6–19. https://doi.org/10.1080/21532974.2016.1242392.

Newton, D. P. (2013). Moods, emotions and creative thinking: a framework for teaching. *Thinking Skills and Creativity*, 8, 34–44. https://doi.org/10.1016/j.tsc.2012.05.006.

Nicolopoulou, A., Barbosa de Sá, A., Ilgaz, H., and Brockmeyer, C. (2009). Using the transformative power of play to educate hearts and minds: from Vygotsky to Vivian Paley and beyond. *Mind, Culture, and Activity*, 17(1), 42–58. https://doi.org/10.1080/10749030903312512.

Ochs, E. (1996). Linguistic resources for socializing humanity. In J. J. Gumperz and S. C. Levinson (eds.), *Rethinking Linguistic Relativity* (pp. 407–437). Cambridge: Cambridge University Press.

Paek, S. H., and Sumners, S. E. (2017). The indirect effect of teachers' creative mindsets on teaching creativity. *Journal of Creative Behavior*, 53(3), 298–311. https://doi.org/10.1002/jocb.180.

Prentice, R. (2000). Creativity: a reaffirmation of its place in early. *childhood education. Curriculum Journal*, 11(2), 145–158. https://doi.org/10.1080/09585170050045173.

Rhodes, M. (1961). An analysis of creativity. *The Phi Delta Kappan*, 42(7), 305–310.

Runco, M. A., and Cayirdag, N. (2012). The theory of personal creativity and implications for the fulfillment of children's potentials. In. O. Saracho (ed.), *Contemporary Perspectives on Research in Creativity in Early Childhood Education* (pp. 31–44). Charlotte, NC: IAP-Information Age Publishing.

Saracho, O. (2002). Young children's creativity and pretend play. *Early Child Development and Care*, 172(5), 431–438. https://doi.org/10.1080/03004430214553.

Sawyer, K. (2004). Creative teaching: collaborative discussion as disciplined improvisation. *Educational Researcher*, 33(2), 12–20. https://doi.org/10.3102/0013189X033002012.

Sawyer, K. (2015). A call to action: the challenges of creative teaching and learning. *Teachers College Record*, 117(20), 1–34.

Schegloff, E. A., Jefferson, G., and Sacks, H. (1977). The preference for self-correction in the organization of repair in conversation. *Language*, 53(2), 361–382. https://doi.org/10.2307/413107.

Sicart, M. (2017). *Play Matters*. Cambridge, MA: MIT Press.

Sidnell, J. (2006). Coordinating gesture, talk and gaze in re-enactments. *Research on Language and Social Interaction*, 39(4), 377–409. https://doi.org/10.1207/s15327973rlsi3904_2.

Spencer, J. (2016). *Making Learning Flow*. Bloomington, IN: Solution Tree Publishing.

Streeck, J. (2009). *Gesturecraft: The Manufacture of Meaning*. Amsterdam/New York: John Benjamins.

Thomson, P., and Sefton-Green, J. (2011). Introduction. In P. Thomson and J. Sefton-Green (eds.), *Researching Creative Learning Methods and Issues* (pp. 1–14). Abingdon: Routledge.

Tulbert, E., and Goodwin, M. H. (2011). Choreographies of attention: multimodality in a routine family activity. In J. Streeck, C. Goodwin, and C. LeBaron (eds.), *Embodied Interaction: Language and Body in the Material World* (pp. 79–92). Cambridge: Cambridge University Press.

Varelas, M., Pappas, C. C., Tucker-Raymond, E., et al. (2010). Drama activities as ideational resources for primary-grade children in urban science classrooms. *Journal of Research in Science Teaching*, 47(3), 302–325. https://doi.org/10.1002/tea.20336.

Vygotsky, L. S. (1990). Imagination and creativity in childhood. *Soviet Psychology*, 28(1), 84–96. https://doi.org/10.2753/RPO1061-0405280184.

Wagner, T. (2014). *The Global Achievement Gap: Why Even Our Best Schools Don't Teach the New Survival Skills Our Children Need and What We Can Do About It*. New York: Basic Books.

Wilson, R. (2018). *Nature and Young Children: Encouraging Creative Play and Learning in Natural Environments* (3rd ed.). Abingdon: Routledge.

Wright, C., and Diener, M. L. (2012). Play, creativity, and socioemotional development. In. O. Saracho (eds.), *Contemporary Perspectives on Research in Creativity in Early Childhood Education* (pp. 31–44). Charlott, NC: IAP-Information Age Publishing.

13 | Multilingualism

JAKOB CROMDAL AND KIRSTEN STOEWER

Introduction

Most children the world over grow up speaking more than one language (Romaine, 1989; Tucker, 1998). For many, growing up bi- or multilingual means speaking or being exposed to one or more languages at home and learning yet another one in school. Educators in Western countries where there is only one official language often wonder about the best way to work with children who speak or are learning more than one language. Multilingualism is often viewed as something unusual or problematic – something that might get in the way of or complicate the learning process or communication between teacher and student (Auer, 2007; Baker, 2011). At the societal level, the minority language may be associated with problems, i.e. viewed as the 'cause of social, economic, educational problems, rather than an effect of such problems' (Baker, 2011, p. 369). This chapter offers a critical discussion of some of the underlying reasons behind the idea that multilingualism in children is in some way exceptional or even detrimental to their development. We begin by tracing some of the roots underlying the misconception back to the early days of linguistic theory before moving on to show how the monolingual bias (e.g. Auer, 2007; Cromdal, 2000; Grosjean, 1982) carries implications for teachers today.

Through the empirical analysis in this chapter that follows, we will argue that paying closer attention to children's multilingual repertoires as they are displayed *in practice* in educational settings might help create a better understanding of the ways that interaction in more than one language – far from being a sign of some kind of deficit – is one of many resources available to participants as they strive towards mutual understanding in various Early Childhood Education (ECE) settings. Through this understanding, teachers will be better equipped to reflect on their own practices and the ways they can support children's multilingual development. Although some of the examples we analyse in the chapter are taken from primary school (language) classrooms, we believe the actions they highlight will be recognizable and relevant to ECE teachers who frequently encounter children from a variety of different linguistic backgrounds.

Linguistics and Monolingualism

To understand how multilingualism came to be viewed as something out of the ordinary or even potentially problematic, it is helpful to briefly turn our gaze back to the historical origins of linguistics, a scientific field that derives its understanding of what constitutes a language from a strict, monolingual perspective. The most widespread definition of language can be traced back to Ferdinand de Saussure (1916/1977) and the European structuralists, according to whom language is an abstract, arbitrary system of signs, governed by rules. The structuralist conception of language as a unified system and the subsequent establishment of linguistics as a discipline came into being at a time when (mainly) European nation-state ideology sought to create standardized versions of languages that would symbolically reflect national unity (Auer, 2007). A fundamental component of this enterprise was the construction of a 'natural' order of language identity and national belonging. Multilingualism, in this view, is seen as a deviance from the goal of achieving one standard language across nations – the result of some problem of unnatural language contact (Auer & Li, 2009). Within this framework, bilingualism could only be considered an anomaly (Auer, 2007). In other words, 'what we perceive as the problems surrounding multilingualism today are to a large degree a consequence of the monolingualism demanded, fostered and cherished by the nation states in Europe and their knock-offs around the world' (Auer & Li, 2009, p. 3; see also Baker, 2011, on the notion of bilingualism and bilingual education as a threat to national unity). The idea that bi-/multilingualism or bi-/multilingual education is detrimental to a person's cognitive and emotional development can therefore be traced back to this ideology (Auer & Li, 2009; Baker, 2011).

Another important factor contributing to how language and multilingualism is often perceived has to do with how we view children's innate capacity for language development. Linguistic theory has long been dominated by the idea that language exists within each individual as a unified, formal, rule-bound system, and that the human brain is hard-wired to allow for the rules of a language to settle during the first years of life. Accordingly, linguistic inquiry into child language traditionally involved mapping the order of the child's acquisition of language rules. Because successful acquisition of the rules depended on the child's access to language input, it was assumed that exposing young children to several languages would confuse the mental processes by which the rules are laid down, resulting in flawed language development. As a result, an idealized, monolingual 'native speaker' has been foregrounded as the model against which all language learning has been held up (cf. Cromdal, 2020; Musk & Cromdal, 2018).

This idea that humans are mentally pre-programmed to naturally acquire one language – or *linguistic nativism* (Chomsky, 1965) – has led researchers to ask how it is possible for people to learn new languages at all. The research field dedicated to this question is known as Second Language Acquisition (SLA). Just like linguistic theory, research in SLA has been dominated by a *cognitivist* perspective, which views language acquisition strictly as a mental process (Atkinson, 2011). This has raised serious methodological problems, since mental structures cannot readily be observed. One popular solution was to focus the inquiry on the errors made by language learners, as this was believed to yield insight into their evolving competence in the new language. As Gardner and Wagner (2004) point out, 'Such research [SLA] has focused [...] more on examining occurrences of language form rather than on exploring the interactional behaviours of second language learners, with a consequent tendency among some to see such learner performance from the perspective of inadequacy or deficiency' (p. vii). This error-focus disregards the reality of language learners and overlooks the bi-/multilingual competence on display in the language learning process (Cook, 1999; Hellerman & Lee, 2014; Ortega, 2005). Indeed, the preoccupation with language errors results in a notion of bi-/multilingual competence as inherently problematic.

A Monolingually Biased, Deficit View of Bi- and Multilingualism in Education Settings

A fundamental consequence of viewing language acquisition as something individual and mental has been that monolingualism has been used as the benchmark against which second language learning is measured (Block, 1996; Cromdal, 2000; Cromdal & Evaldsson, 2003; Firth & Wagner, 1997; Jørgensen & Holmen, 1997; May, 2015; Ortega, 2005). This has resulted in a deficit view of multilingualism, insofar as (second) language learners have been conceptualized as less-than-complete holders of language, striving towards an unattainable norm of (dual) monolingual proficiency (Grosjean, 1982; Jørgensen & Holmen, 1997) which holds that a bilingual speaker 'should ideally be the equivalent of two monolingual native speakers rolled into one' (Musk, 2006, p. 42). Outdated views of striving towards 'balanced' bilingualism as well as the idea that the ideal bilingual child would be on their way to 'developing equal proficiency in both languages' (Martin-Jones

& Romaine, 1985, p. 32) are fundamentally flawed and lie behind policies of strict language separation common in language classrooms and bilingual educational settings. As Grosjean (2002) explains: 'Bilingualism is the use of two (or more) languages in one's everyday life and *not* knowing two or more languages equally well (as most laypersons think)' (p. 2).

In the past two decades or so, research on bilingualism as well as studies in second language acquisition have witnessed a social turn (Block, 2003; Firth & Wagner, 2007; see Cromdal, 2013, for a review), as well as more recent calls for a multilingual turn (e.g. Hellerman & Lee, 2014; May, 2015) resulting in a theoretically as well as empirically grounded critique of cognitivist perspectives on language learning along with the monolingual bias that they bring to the table. While not seeking to argue against the relevance of cognitive processes involved in language acquisition, scholars of social interaction insisted on broadening the scope of inquiry to include the study of the social use of language practices in bi- and multilingual settings, treating language learning and other 'inner states' as context-bound, socially distributed, and embodied (e.g. Firth & Wagner, 1997; Eskildsen & Majlesi, 2018; see Cromdal, 2013; Filipi & Markee, 2018; and Musk & Cromdal, 2018, for reviews). Moreover, while much of the research on second language acquisition as well as bilingualism has given priority to issues of language proficiency, the interest in children's social use of language turns the analytic focus to highlight participants' actions-in-interaction.

Although this turn has sparked some effort to explore the practices of ECE in bilingual contexts (see e.g. Björk-Willén, 2007, 2008; Cekaite & Björk-Willén, 2013; Karrebaek, 2008; Stoewer, 2018, for examples from Scandinavian contexts), showing how the availability of two or more languages may be embraced and exploited to enhance instructional activities, the monolingually informed perspective of bilingualism has continued to inform ECE practitioners and still exerts significant influence over teacher education. As stated above, idealized notions of 'native' (monolingual) language proficiency and the resulting deficit view of bi- or multilingual talk lurk beneath explicit as well as implicit policies of strict language separation. In the case of young children, the use of more than one language – or 'language mixing' – has been taken to indicate problems in their language development. Although several decades' worth of research in speech communities across the globe has demonstrated the usefulness of bilingual communicative practices such as code-switching and language alternation, in the context of education the issue of young children's bilingualism has continued to cause significant concern to teachers as well as to parents.

Before we move on, let us briefly address terminology: for the purposes of this chapter, we use the terms code-switching and language alternation interchangeably to refer to the act of alternating between more than one language during a conversation or stretch of talk (Musk & Cromdal, 2018). Another term that has become increasingly popular, particularly in the literature on education, is translanguaging. Translanguaging is often used as an umbrella term covering a wide array of multilingual discursive practices (García & Kleifgen, 2010; Gort & Sembiante, 2015; Palmer, Martínez, Mateus, & Henderson, 2014; see also Li Wei, 2011). Our analytical framework of conversation analysis and its meticulous attention to demonstrating participants' own understandings of what is relevant for them in any given communicative context calls for a higher degree of conceptual precision. Our choice of the terms language alternation or code-switching in this chapter is therefore motivated by the need for analytical clarity.

Opening Up the Multilingual Early Childhood Education Classroom

In this chapter, we seek to open up the multilingual ECE classroom by drawing on a few samples of ECE practice in different language settings. Deliberately painting in broad strokes, we use this small sample of examples to illustrate a variety of routine bilingual practices through which teaching and learning of different subject matter is routinely accomplished by teachers and students. By showing how such work is done in the classroom, this chapter offers a critical, empirically grounded account aimed to counter the ongoing fossilization of the deficit view of bi-/multilingual and second or additional language learning in children in ECE and elsewhere. It may need stressing that we do not suggest that there are no challenges – linguistic or other – involved in teaching young children in multilingual classrooms, only that such problems need to be dealt with by the participants in the context in which they occur and leaving aside pre-conceived notions that use of more than one language in the classroom is something to be remedied.

We begin the analysis by examining one such exchange that took place in a mixed-age English heritage language (HL)[1] classroom for 6- to 9-year-olds in Sweden. The extract below focuses on an exchange between the HL teacher (T) and 9-year-old Jens. Jens, who had been absent from the previous lesson,

[1] Heritage language lessons are referred to as mother tongue instruction (MTI) in Swedish policy documents.

had arrived early to this lesson and the teacher had given him a task from the previous week to complete while she finished up with an older student and they were waiting for the remaining students in Jens's group to arrive. Being an after-hours lesson, it was located in a classroom usually used for teaching other students in the school. Jens had just picked up a (lead) pencil from a desk belonging to some other student, and the teacher asks him to use one of the (coloured) pencils she has given him instead.

Extract 13.1 Pencil

[Teacher (T), Jens (Je; 9 years). English in regular type, Swedish in italics. Adapted from Stoewer, 2018.]

```
01   T:    Can you use these pencils? and not- (.) the
02         things that are here?
03   T:    Cuz thee- because these are- these are- (0.4)
04         things of the kids that are sitting here=
05   Je:   =Is (0.9) Do you have [(0.3) blyerts°penna.°=
                                        lead pencil
                                 [((smiles, gazes up))
06   T:    =Uh: what's a blyertspenna in English.
                         lead pencil
07   Je:   I don't
08   T:    A PENCIL. (0.8) Do I have a pencil?=
09   T:    =Uh:::m ((searching in her own bag)
10         (0.9)
11   T:    You need to bring your own pen-case. I keep
12         telling you.
```

It seems that for the task at hand, Jens is not well served just by any type of pencil. What he needs is a lead pencil, but as the cut-off, restart, and hesitation pauses (line 5) indicate, he is struggling to ask for it in English. He therefore switches into Swedish, asking for a '*blyertspenna*'. While producing the target word in Swedish, he looks up at the teacher, smiling.

Through this turn design – particularly the initial hesitation and his smiling while producing the Swedish word – Jens displays his awareness that he is breaking the implicit English-only rule in place in this classroom. Indeed, the teacher makes use of this spontaneous teaching opportunity and, rather than supplying the correct term, explicitly asks Jens to translate '*blyertspenna*' into English (line 6). Stoewer (2018) demonstrated how such counter questions, by which students are asked to translate words and phrases back into English, are common teacher responses to the students' use of Swedish during these HL lessons. When Jens begins to explain that he does not know the English term, the teacher loudly articulates it for him ('A PENCIL'), perhaps suggesting this is a word she expects him to know. She continues by enacting his earlier request – thereby showing what it normatively would have sounded like – then by searching her bag and verbalizing the embodied response through a delay-token 'uh:::m' (lines 8–9), which informs Jens that she is trying to find a pen for him.

While shared knowledge of Swedish is clearly a resource for participants in that it drives the interaction forward, its use is nonetheless treated by both participants as an infraction of the local order, and may call for repair. That is, Jens anticipates that using the Swedish word will not be acceptable (evident in his smile and looking towards the teacher as he says '*blyertspenna*'), which turns out to be the case as the teacher asks him for the English word.

It is worth noting that this exchange takes place in a language classroom, where the objective is to develop students' (presumed) first language, which the student in question speaks quite well. In contrast to other types of multilingual contexts, in the language classroom, the target language (in this case English) is both the vehicle and object of instruction (Seedhouse, 2004). What we show in this extract is how Jens's use of Swedish is productive in several respects: it allows Jens to make his need known to the teacher, and at the same time, his failure to find the correct word in English creates a learning opportunity that the teacher exploits by initiating a translation sequence (Stoewer, 2018).

The next example is drawn from the same group of HL students, only here two students are present: Thomas (6 years) and Jens (9 years) as well as the teacher. The students have been given a worksheet that shows a drawing of a human-like bear with lines next to different parts of the bear's body. As such, the activity requires identifying the correct body part and then writing the name of the part on the lines provided.

Extract 13.2 Knee

[Teacher (T), Jens (Je; 9 years), Thomas (Th; 6 years). English in regular type, Swedish in italics.]

```
01    Th:    =#is this leg¿
      fig    #fig. 13.1
```

Figure 13.1

```
02   T:    NO:¿ (.) the next one, (.) the next one they're
03         showing in the front=next one they're showing
04         this. #((taps knee 4 times))
    fig          #fig. 13.2
```

Figure 13.2

```
05   T:    KNÄ
           Knee
06   Je:   knä=
           Knee
```

```
07   T:    =↑what's ↑KNÄ:: in english¿=
08   Je:   =KN[EE
09   Th:      [ö:hn
10         (0.9)
11   Je:   KNEE!
12   T:    knee, but how do you ↑spell knee?
```

Having completed writing the previous target word, Thomas points to the worksheet and asks the teacher to clarify that he has correctly identified the next item (Figure 13.1), 'leg'. The teacher rejects the candidate item, explaining that the body part in focus is specifically on the front side of the leg. She then produces a verbal instruction 'next one they're showing is this' (lines 3–4), embodying the deictic referent ('this') by bending forward and tapping her right knee (Figure 13.2). She follows her embodied clue with a verbal one, given in Swedish: 'KNÄ' (knee, line 5), which Jens quietly repeats.

Unlike in the previous example, this time it is the teacher who makes use of Swedish as an additional resource to elicit the word she is looking for from the students. Yet her translation request in line 7 reveals that what is called for here is a word in English. Moreover, by keeping her gaze on Thomas (the younger student), to whom she was responding, she attempts to give him the opportunity to respond, but he is beaten to the punch by Jens (line 8). At the same time, Thomas looks back and forth between the teacher and his worksheet and produces a sound to indicate he is thinking (line 9), after which Jens loudly repeats his answer ('KNEE!', line 11). It is only then that the teacher acknowledges Jens's correct answer by repeating it and nodding but she immediately ups the ante, asking how knee is spelled, while turning towards the whiteboard. In this way, she attends to the fact that, in order to complete the task, the word not only needs to be identified (in the correct language) but also written down on the worksheet. Given that the word 'knee' begins with a silent letter, this is not a simple task. Although both of these students receive their ordinary schooling in Swedish, we might also assume that their experience of spelling in English differs, given their age difference.

The two examples demonstrate different ways bilingual resources – in the shape of alternation into Swedish – are mobilized to verbalize singular concepts momentarily unavailable to the speaker in English. The availability of two languages thus preserves the coherent flow of the interaction. We suggest that the problems encountered here are not to do with intelligibility of the talk, but with the shared expectations concerning participants' language choice: the monolingual use of English which comprises the *medium of instruction*, is also the preferred choice for interacting during English heritage language sessions. It is what Bonacina & Gafaranga (2011) termed the *medium of classroom interaction*. So how can we explain the teacher's apparent breach of the classroom norm in line 5? Bearing in mind that her tapping the knee did not bring it home for Thomas, alternating to Swedish affords her another means of helping the student identify the body part in focus, while seeking to elicit the English term ('knee') from him. In other words, the teacher code-switches into Swedish to elicit English from the students (cf. Üstünel & Seedhouse, 2005). As the strategy backfires with Jens simply repeating the Swedish word (line 6), she resorts to the same type of translation request that we saw her use in Extract 13.1. Through these requests the students are afforded ample opportunity to engage in routine translation – an inherently bilingual practice.

The next example was recorded in a third-grade classroom for eight- and nine-year-olds in Bangladesh, where according to the school's policy, all school subjects, with the exception of Bengali, are to be taught in English. The interaction took place during an English lesson dedicated to the reading, reciting, and analysing of a poem ('Waters' by Edith H. Newlin) that uses colourful verse to describe the lively behaviour of a creek flowing through the land. Part of the work with the poem involved unpacking and elaborating on the meaning and connotation of some of the words. As we enter the interaction the teacher is focusing the class on the next target word: twinkling.

Extract 13.3 Twinkling Tiny Brook

[Teacher (T), Su (Su), Rafiq (Ra). Age span 8–8.5 years. English in regular type, Bangla in italics. Adapted from Huq et al., 2017]

```
01   T:    ↑twinkling ↑tiny brook
02         (0.8)
03   T:    twinkling mane ki?
                     meaning what?
04         (0.5)
05   T:    tomra oi: <kobita ta ki> porecho♪♪
             have you read that poem?
06         twin[::kle↓ twin::kl:e↓ [li:ttl:e:: &sta:r::]♪♪
               [((rotates index finger rythmically))
07   Su:       [ little es:tar    ]
08   Ra:   =↑TWINkl:e [↑↑TWIN:::kl::e::                ]
```

09 T: [<what is the meaning> (.) of the word]
10 Ra: [≈litt::::le]
11 T: [what do you say?]
12 Ra: =es::sta::::r] °how:: I°≈
13 T: =*jhik mik] kora, jwal jwal kora.*
something glittering something shimmering
14 Su: jhik- ↑*tara jwal jwal kore setake jhik mik bole*
stars spark which is called glittering
15 T: exactly *setai.*
that's it

Having read a new line of the poem (line 1), the teacher looks up and, facing the class, repeats the word 'twinkling' embedded in a question in Bengali about its meaning (line 3). In sequential terms, the repetition followed by a meaning-query highlights the word as the new target of exploration. As Huq et al. (2017) demonstrated, the teacher systematically uses these bilingual queries to focus the talk on the poem's vocabulary and to elicit translation of select words into Bengali.

In the absence of student bids for the floor, the teacher continues by asking the class if they are familiar with the nursery rhyme, then in a singing voice produces the first verse of 'Twinkle, twinkle little star', moving his index finger to the beat of the words (lines 5–6). This invites two of the students to chime in with their versions of the song (lines 7–12). The teacher's attempt to return to the task of analysing the meaning in the poem, now produced in English (lines 9 and 11) is overlapped with and appears outvoiced by Rafiq's singing. Clearly, introducing the nursery rhyme proved detrimental to the teacher's agenda, as it took the students' focus off the vocabulary activity. In line 13, the teacher interruptedly produces two Bengali alternatives for the target word ('glittering' and 'shimmering'), thereby himself performing the actions that he asked of the students in line 3. This successfully refocuses student attention on the meaning of 'twinkling' and we find Sumon suggesting a new concept ('to spark'), embedding it in a sentence in Bengali that combines the astral theme of the nursery rhyme with the teacher's translation: 'stars spark which is called glittering' (line 14). The teacher's positive bilingual assessment in line 15 brings the translation sequence to an end, after which he moves on to the next stanza.

The extract offers a glimpse of how language alternation can facilitate understanding of difficult vocabulary when reading a poem in an L2 classroom. The loosening of the school's English-only language policy not only engages the students, it allows all participants to produce several translation alternatives, thereby negotiating the meaning of the poem. These observations hint at the diversity of organized instructional practice in bilingual classrooms across the world.

In our final example, we turn to consider how local educational norms and practices are embraced and acted upon in the mundane activities of the peer group. The example is drafted from a corpus of data recorded at a multilingual preschool in Sweden, where instruction was offered to all children in English and Spanish, alongside Swedish. Although no specific language policy was promoted by the preschool or its teachers, language-focused group sessions were part of the weekly routine. Accordingly, during the activities of the Spanish group the teacher would predominantly address the children in Spanish, while in the English group the teacher would predominantly speak English. Being the *lingua franca*, Swedish was the default choice in most activities outside the language-focused groups.

The extract below shows the beginning of a 'free play' episode during which a group of girls (aged 4.5 years to 5.5 years) perform self-introduction routines in Spanish. The activity is modelled on an exercise that they had been doing during Spanish group with their teacher on the day before. It involves sitting in a circle on the floor with their legs stretched out and spread wide apart, so that the floor space forms a star-shaped play area in which they pass a ball to one another (Figure 13.3). The player currently holding the ball will introduce herself by name, then roll the ball to the next player of choice, asking for their name, according to the following formula: '*yo me llamo X*/my name is X' – pass ball – '*como te llamas tú*/what is your name?' The transcript begins as Elsa passes the ball to Sally.

Figure 13.3

Extract 13.4 *Como te llamas* – doing Spanish group

[Elsa (El), Ktarina (Ka), Lisa (Li), Olivia (Ol) and Sally (Sa). Age span 4.5–5.5 years. Swedish in regular type, Spanish in italics. Adapted from Björk-Willén & Cromdal, 2009]

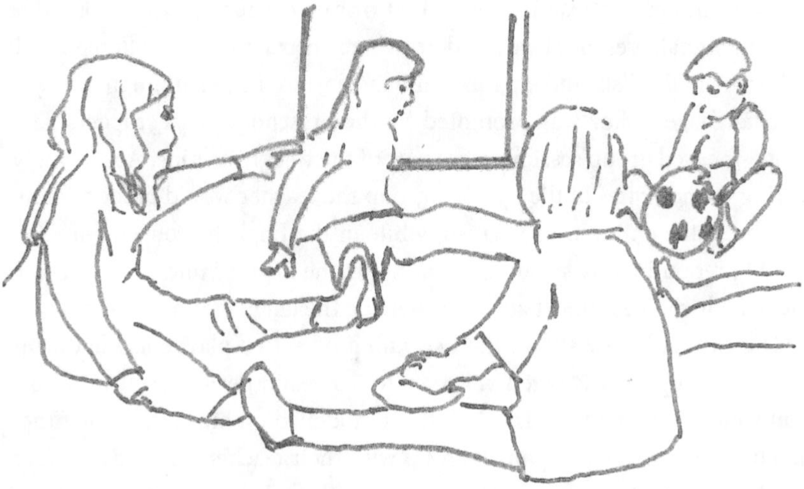

Figure 13.4

```
01  El:  =como te ll[amas tú?
         what is your name?
02                   [((passes the ball to Sally))
03  Sa:  ä::ja heter sall↑y::
         eh my name is sally
04  Ka:  >co#mo te lla[ma<s::
         >what's your name<
    Fig     #13.4
05  Li:                [Sally du kan inte
                        Sally you can´t
06       hålla så >då måste [alla< försöka=
         hold like that then everyone has to try
07                          [((bouncing gesture))
08       =studsa [ö::ver dina fötter↓
         bouncing over your feet
09  Sa:          [((stretches out legs, rolls ball to Lisa))
10  Li:  ((receives the ball)
11               [yo# me  (.)  <lla#mo Lisa>
                  my            name is Lisa
    fig            #13.5         #13.6
```

12 [((points at herself with both hands,
13 *como te llama* (.) [#s*tú?!*=NEJ!
what's your name?=NO!
14 [((rolls the ball to Elsa))
fig #13.7

Figure 13.5

Figure 13.6

Figure 13.7

15 £jahh£ (.) skicka f↓e::l
£ I £ (.) passed it wrong

Sally receives the ball, looking up at the other players. After some initial hesitation she introduces herself in Swedish (line 3). However, before she reaches the second part of the routine, Katarina raises her arm pointing at Sally (Figure 13.4) and interruptedly supplies the next part in Spanish 'como te llamas' (line 4). Katarina thereby orients to Sally's move as locally inappropriate, and as we shall see below, her move initiates language repair. At the same time, Lisa overlaps Katarina's turn, complaining (in Swedish) about Sally's sitting position – knees raised and spread to the side (Figure 13.4) – explaining that it forces the others to make bouncing passes. The pragmatic force of the complaint is enhanced by combining the talk with a gestural enactment of a bouncing trajectory of the ball across the play field (line 7). In response, Sally stretches out her legs on the floor and rolls the ball over to Lisa without completing the verbal routine.

It is evident that our data show a strictly organized play activity, where the re-enactment of the self-introductions is fuelled by the children's joint experience from the teacher-led Spanish group session the previous day. As we have seen, successful participation requires a degree of competence, as the performance of the moves is being monitored by the other players. Specifically, two errors were identified and sanctioned in Sally's move: one concerning the embodied aspects of passing the ball around by rolling, the other to do with her failure to produce the introduction in Spanish.

In the interaction that follows, in lines 11 through 14, Lisa delivers a corrective illustration. Receiving the ball from Sally, she carefully articulates the first part of the routine ('yo me llamo Lisa', line 11), coordinating her speech with the movement of her arms, first upwards then down towards her own chest, resulting in an overly amplified pointing gesture to herself (Figures 13.5 and 13.6). She then produces the second part of the routine (erroneously parsing its words as 'como te llama (.) stu' in line 13), and passes the ball (Figure 13.7) to Elsa on reaching the last syllable.

This carefully executed performance of the routine can be seen as a retrospectively oriented correction of Sally's false move. Prospectively, it also serves as a pedagogic illustration by which Lisa shows the other players how to perform the moves correctly (save for the fact that she sent the ball off to the wrong next player, which immediately becomes a source of conflict).

The corrective actions in this example reveal to us the players' normative expectations on how to participate in playing Spanish group. Clearly, the in-play verbal moves comprising the introduction routine need to be produced in Spanish, while the out-of-play corrections of sitting arrangements need not. From this we learn that the order of this peer group activity is strictly informed by the formal, teacher-led proceedings of the Spanish group, and that the children monitor one another's moves as well as sanction any infractions of this order. This then is another piece of evidence that matters of language choice in bilingual ECE settings are not simply a teacher's concern. On the contrary, the example shows that the bilingual practices of the peer group also reveal students' orientations to different aspects of the local interactional order.

Recommendations for Practice

In this chapter, we have reviewed some of the central sources of the widespread monolingual bias that continues to permeate educational policy and practice in multilingual settings and have offered a handful of empirical samples to demonstrate what the educational practice of early childhood as well as early school years may look like in settings where more than one language is available to the participants. We have shown that participants use bilingual resources productively – moving the interaction forward, producing relevant responsive actions, and enhancing student participation or understanding, all in the local flow of talk-in-interaction. These actions are all managed while simultaneously displaying their sensitivity to the institutional orders in which the exchanges take place, and are thereby reflexively implementing the wider educational goals underpinning each context.

It is important to emphasize that no claim has been made that children's bilingualism does not raise challenges for ECE and educators. To the contrary, our data show ample instances of teachers as well as students orienting to language-related problems. But that is just the point: they are *participants'* problems to be handled in the course of their interactions. There is a promising source of insight. Examining just how participants go about their joint activities of bi-/multilingualism in early years settings, we may learn about the relationship between pedagogy and interaction where one of the affordances relevant to the participants is the presence of two or more languages. Importantly, the use of more than one language is one among many verbal and embodied communicative resources available to children and teachers – a resource that can potentially support engagement and learning if it is encouraged.

Although the examples we have shown involve situations where the teacher and children share two languages, we suggest that taking on the perspective of language alternation as an asset rather than deficit and allowing for 'flexible bilingualism and flexible pedagogy' (Creese & Blackledge, 2010, p. 112; see also Palmer et al., 2014) can be a valuable approach for educators in classrooms where the children's first language is unknown to the teacher. For example, Bonacina-Pugh (2013) has shown how 'multilingual label quests' have successfully been used in induction classrooms in France where the students (aged 6–11) speak a number of different languages not shared by the teacher. Importantly, the study shows how drawing upon students' multilingual repertoires to support learning of new words in French boosted participation and helped students learn new words in the majority language (Bonacina-Pugh, 2013).

We realize, in closing, that ECE teachers and other practitioners act within a professional landscape that is often fuelled by lay conceptions of childhood bilingualism as a challenge in successful developmental, educational, or social outcomes. The promise of resisting such a perspective is nothing less than a glimpse of bilingualism from within – that is, as it appears to those who act in, and produce bilingual settings. This strikes us as a fertile ground for multilingual learning in early childhood education.

On the basis of our analyses, we highlight the following key implications for teachers working with children who are, or are on their way to becoming, multilingual:

- Recognize that language alternation is *always* present in multilingual contexts and that it is one of many resources available to multilingual children and adults to communicate their thoughts and needs.

- Focus on situated practice, i.e. what the child is *actually* doing at any given moment when resorting to another language, instead of rigidly adhering to one-language-only or one-language-at-a-time policies (cf. Li Wei & Wu, 2009).
- Language alternation is a productive resource that has the potential to facilitate, rather than undermine, learning – regardless of whether the goal is language skills or subject matter.
- Using language alternation to handle interactional trouble is commonplace and not a problem for learning. Even though children may momentarily struggle to find the right expression in the target language, this provides opportunities for educators to respond to individual learning needs (e.g. translation requests).

References

Atkinson, D. (2011). Introduction. Cognitivism and second language acquisition. In D. Atkinson (ed.), *Alternative Approaches to Second Language Acquisition* (pp. 1–23). London: Routledge.

Auer, P. (2007). The monolingual bias in bilingualism research, or: why bilingual talk is (still) a challenge for linguistics. In M. Heller (ed.), *Bilingualism: A Social Approach* (pp. 319–339). New York: Palgrave Macmillan.

Auer, P., and Li Wei (2009). Introduction: multilingualism as a problem? Monolingualism as a problem? In P. Auer and Li Wei (eds.), *Handbook of Multilingualism and Multilingual Communication* (pp. 1–12). Berlin: Mouton de Gruyter.

Baker, C. (2011). *Foundations of Bilingual Education and Bilingualism* (5th ed.) Bristol: Multilingual Matters.

Block, D. (1996). Not so fast: some thoughts on theory culling, relativism, accepted findings and the heart and soul of SLA. *Applied Linguistics*, 17, 63–83.

Block, D. (2003). *The Social Turn in Second Language Acquisition*. Edinburgh: Edinburgh University Press.

Bonacina, F., and Gafaranga, J. (2011). 'Medium of instruction' vs. 'medium of classroom interaction': language choice in a French complementary school classroom in Scotland. *International Journal of Bilingual Education and Bilingualism*, 14, 319–334.

Bonacina-Pugh, F. (2013). Multilingual label quests: a practice for the 'asymmetrical' multilingual classroom. *Linguistics and Education*, 24(2), 142–164.

Björk-Willén, P. (2007). Participation in multilingual preschool play: shadowing and crossing as interactional resources. *Journal of Pragmatics*, 39(12), 2133–2215.

Björk-Willén, P. (2008). Routine trouble: how preschool children participate in multilingual instruction. *Applied Linguistics*, 29(4), 555–577.

Björk-Willén,P. and Cromdal, J. (2009). When education seeps into 'free play': how preschool children accomplish multilingual education. *Journal of Pragmatics*, 41, 1493–1518.

Cekaite, A., and Björk-Willén, P. (2013). Peer group interactions in multilingual educational settings: co-constructing social order and norms for language use. *The International Journal of Bilingualism*, 17(2), 174–188.

Chomsky, N. (1965). *Aspects of the Theory of Syntax*. Cambridge, MA: MIT Press.

Cook, V. (1999). Going beyond the native speaker in language teaching. *TESOL Quarterly*, 33(2), 185–209. https://doi.org/10.2307/3587717

Creese, A., and Blackledge, A. (2010). Translanguaging in the bilingual classroom: a pedagogy for learning and teaching? *The Modern Language Journal*, 94(1), 103–115.

Cromdal, J. (2000). *Code-switching for all practical purposes: Bilingual organization of children's play*. Dissertation. Linköping: Linköping University.

Cromdal, J. (2013). Bilingual and second language interactions: views from Scandinavia. *International Journal of Bilingualism*, 17, 121–131.

Cromdal, J. (2020). Bilingualism and multilingualism. In: D. T. Cook (ed.), *The SAGE Encyclopedia of Children and Childhood Studies* (pp. 120–121). Thousand Oaks, CA: Sage Publications.

Cromdal, J., and Evaldsson, A.-C. (2003). Flerspråkighet till vardags – en introduktion [Multilingualism day-to-day – an introduction]. In J. Cromdal and A.-C. Evaldsson (eds.), *Ett vardagsliv med flera språk* [Everyday life with several languages]. Stockholm: Liber.

Eskildsen, S. W., and Majlesi, A. R. (2018). Learnables and teachables in second language talk: advancing a social reconceptualization of central SLA tenets. Introduction to the special issue. *The Modern Language Journal*, 102, 3–10.

Filipi, A., and Markee, N. (2018). Transitions in the language classroom as important sites for language alternation. In: A. Filipi and N. Markee (eds.), *Conversation Analysis and Language Alternation*. Amsterdam: John Benjamins.

Firth, A., and Wagner, J. (1997). On discourse, communication, and (some) fundamental concepts in SLA research. *Modern Language Journal*, 81, 285–300.

Firth, A., and Wagner, J. (2007). Second/foreign language learning as a social accomplishment: elaborations on a reconceptualized SLA. *Modern Language Journal*, 91, 800–819.

Garcìa, O., and Kleifgen, J. A. (2010). *Educating emergent bilinguals: policies, programs, and practices for English language learners*. New York, NY: Teachers College Press.

Gardner, R., and Wagner, J. (2004). Introduction. In R. Gardner and J. Wagner (eds.), *Second Language Conversations* (pp. 1–17). New York, NY: Continuum.

Gort, M., and Sembiante, S. F. (2015). Navigating hybridized language learning spaces through translanguaging pedagogy: dual language preschool teachers' languaging practices in support of emergent bilingual children's performance of academic discourse. *International Multilingual Research Journal*, 9(1), 7–25.

Grosjean, F. (1982). *Life with Two Languages: An Introduction to Bilingualism*. Cambridge, MA: Harvard University Press.

Grosjean, F. (2002). *An interview of François Grosjean on bilingualism*. By J. Navracsics (14 April 2006). Available from: https://www.francoisgrosjean.ch/interview_en.html [last accessed 5 January 2022].

Hellerman, J., and Lee, Y. A. (2014). Members and their competencies: contributions of ethnomethodological conversation analysis to a multilingual turn in second language acquisition. *System*, 44, 54–65.

Huq, R., Eriksson Barajas, K. and Cromdal, J. (2017). Sparkling, wrinkling, softly tinkling: on poetry and word meaning in a bilingual primary classroom. In A. Bateman and A. Church (eds.), *Children's Knowledge-in-Interaction* (pp. 189–209). Springer: Singapore.

Jørgensen J., and Holmen, A. (1997). The development of successive bilingualism in school-age children. *Copenhagen Studies in Bilingualism*, 27, Aarhus: Aarhus University Press.

Karrebaek, M. S. (2008). *Att blive ett bornehavebarn. En minoritetsdrengssprog, interaktion og deltagelse i bornefalleskaepet*. Ph.D. dissertation, Copenhagen University.

Li Wei (2011). Moment analysis and translanguaging space: discursive construction of identities by multilingual Chinese youth in Britain. *Journal of Pragmatics*, 43(5), 1222–1235.

Li Wei, and Wu, C.-J. (2009). Polite Chinese children revisited: creativity and the use of codeswitching in the Chinese complementary school classroom. *International Journal of Bilingual Education and Bilingualism*, 12(2), 193–211.

Martin-Jones. M., and Romaine, S. (1985). Semilingualism: a half-baked theory of communicative competence. *Applied Linguistics*, 6, 105–17.

May, S. (2015). Disciplinary divides, knowledge construction and the multilingual turn. In S. May (ed.), *The Multilingual Turn: Implications for SLA, TESOL and Bilingual Education*. London: Routledge.

Musk, N. (2006). *Performing bilingualism in Wales with the spotlight on Welsh: a study of language policy and the language practices of young people in bilingual education*. Ph.D. dissertation. Linköping: Linköping University.

Musk, N., and Cromdal, J. (2018). Analysing bilingual talk: conversation analysis and language alternation. In: A. Filippi and N. Markee (eds.), *Conversation Analysis and Language Alternation* (pp. 15–34). Amsterdam: John Benjamins.

Ortega, L. (2005). Methodology, epistemology, and ethics in instructed SLA research: an introduction. *The Modern Language Journal*, 89, 317–327.

Palmer, D. K., Martínez, R. A., Mateus, S. G., and Henderson, K. (2014). Reframing the debate on language separation: toward a vision for translanguaging pedagogies in the dual language classroom. *The Modern Language Journal*, 98(3), 757–772. https://doi.org/10.1111/ modl.121121

Romaine, S. (1989). *Bilingualism*. Oxford: Blackwell.

De Saussure, F. (1916). *Cours de linguistique générale*, edited by C. Bally and A. Sechehaye, with the collaboration of A. Riedlinger. Lausanne and Paris: Payot. Trans. W. Baskin, Course in General Linguistics, Glasgow: Fontana/ Collins, 1977.

Seedhouse, P. (2004). *The Interactional Architecture of the Language Classroom: A Conversation Analysis Perspective*: Malden, MA: Blackwell.

Skutnabb-Kangas, T. (1981). *Tvåspråkighet* [Bilingualism]. Lund: Liber.

Stoewer, K. (2018). What is it in Swedish? Translation requests as a resource for vocabulary explanation in English mother tongue instruction. In: A. Filippi and N. Markee (eds.), *Conversation Analysis and Language Alternation* (pp. 83–106). Amsterdam: John Benjamins.

Tucker R. (1998). A global perspective on multilingualism and multilingual education. In J. Cenoz and F. Genesee (eds.), *Beyond Bilingualism: Multilingualism and Multilingual Education* (pp. 3–15). Bristol: Multilingual Matters.

Üstünel, E., and Seedhouse, P. (2005). Why that, in that language, right now? Code-switching and pedagogical focus. *International Journal of Applied Linguistics*, 15(3), 302–325.

14 | Belonging

POLLY BJÖRK-WILLÉN

Introduction

For children entering preschool, belonging is essential for wellbeing, development, and learning. Belonging is about emotional attachment and feeling 'at home' and safe (Yuval-Davis, 2006). Belonging can be understood at different levels, where one can be related to close relationships, i.e. belonging to a family or a group of peers for example at preschool (Gordon, O´Toole & Whitman, 2008). Belonging can also be viewed in a wider perspective that deals with being a part of society and its culture and language(s). This *emotional meaning* of the concept is often known as a 'sense of belonging'. The term 'politics of belonging' on the other hand comprises specific *political projects* aimed at constructing belonging in the society in particular ways. Politics of belonging also refers to how different groups continuously negotiate, produce, and reproduce their membership (Nagel, 2011; Stratigos, Bradley, & Sumsion, 2014), like preschoolers' everyday negotiation in the peer group. Yuval-Davis (2011) points out that:

People can 'belong' in many different ways and to many different objects of attachment. These can vary from a particular person to the whole of humanity, in a concrete or abstract way, by self or other identification, in a stable, contested or transient way. Even in its most stable 'primordial' forms, however, belonging is always a dynamic process, not a reified fixity (p. 12).

From Yuval-Davis' point of view, belonging is always a dynamic process that has no permanence, since belonging is a constantly ongoing construction of individual and collective identities (Yuval-Davis, 2006).

Many preschool curricula emphasize the importance of belonging. However, in various practices different facets of the concept are highlighted. In Australia this is stressed through the title 'Belonging, Being and Becoming: The Early Years Learning Framework for Australia' (Department of Education and Training (2009/2019), where belonging is defined as follows:

Experiencing belonging – knowing where and with whom you belong – is integral to human existence. Children belong first to a family, a cultural group, a neighbourhood and a wider community. Belonging acknowledges children's interdependence with others and the basis of relationships in defining identities. In early childhood, and throughout life, relationships are crucial to a sense of belonging. Belonging is central to being and becoming in that it shapes who children are and who they can become (p. 7).

Belonging as described here can be seen as a *pre-requisite* for the child's further development. In New Zealand's curriculum, *Te Whāriki*, belonging means that every child is accepted for *who they are* and emphasizes the importance to give every child a sense of connection to others and the environment (Ministry of Education, 2017). In the Swedish curriculum, belonging relates to the child's development of responsibility and solidarity, as a part of the socialization in *civics and democracy*. The curriculum points out that the teachers should 'show respect for the individual and help in creating a democratic climate in the preschool, where children have the opportunity to feel a sense of *belonging* and to develop responsibility and solidarity' (Swedish National Agency for Education, 2018, p. 14, emphasis added). This wording relates to the politics of belonging and to a wider national democratic project, though it has its origin in the sense of belonging, which means that the child's needs and rights are being recognized and met, respected and included (Woodhead & Brooker, 2008).

In this chapter, belonging is foremost defined in terms of sense of belonging and the individual child's inclusion in a group, and how the preschool environment enables the child to attach to peers and adults. The aim of the chapter is to show how belonging can be accomplished in everyday practice in preschool through activities and embodied talk that reinforce each child's sense of identity and the elements of a welcoming environment.

Belonging in Curricula and as a Pedagogical Task

Cultural Practices

In addition to fostering democracy, the Swedish curriculum also suggests that the preschool should contribute to 'transferring and developing a cultural heritage – values, traditions and history, language and knowledge – from one generation to the next' (Swedish National Agency for Education, 2018, p. 9), and also make for children's intercultural awareness. Puskás (2016) discusses this challenging duality in relation to the practice and children's sense of belonging. She studied a young immigrant boy's introduction to a preschool where few of the children and teachers belonged to the national majority. Puskás provides a detailed example of the children rehearsing songs for the traditional Swedish festival of Santa Lucia. This activity could not be described as culturally responsive, as the primary focus was on transmitting a national tradition, but Puskás emphasizes that the activity also managed to be linguistically responsive and *inclusive*. Even though the children sang the Lucia songs in Swedish, they were encouraged to discuss their costumes (dressing up as Lucia, 'Star boy', or 'ginger bread' etc.) with each other in the language of their choice. The performance of Lucia also gave the children 'access to cultural and social resources that allowed the children from diverse backgrounds to share and perform a tradition that was a part of being a preschool child in Sweden' (p. 34). Puskás (2016) questions if the immigrant children's participation in a national tradition automatically leads to cultural inclusion, but as a local practice, children were supported to participate in the group identity. How belonging can be supported through early childhood education, especially when very different cultural beliefs require negotiation, is a current question in many countries since immigration is increasing.

Transition Practices

A transition from home to preschool can be a cultural challenge for a child. When children encounter new situations and settings, like beginning at preschool, they initially may struggle to feel that they belong (Woodhead & Brooker, 2008). This is especially demanding for children who have a home language other than the majority, who's talk when entering the preschool setting has to undergo a transformation from their mother tongue(s) into the majority language. In a study about everyday talk and social interaction between immigrant families and Swedish-speaking teachers, the everyday talk in the entrance hall of a Swedish preschool was investigated (Björk-Willén, 2016). The analysis shows how the educators, in an effort to support the children's bilingual development, promoted the parents to use their mother tongue when talking to their children. As a result, the entrance hall often sounded of different languages, where the parent's language alternation (the alternating use of two recognizable grammatical systems – two 'languages') and code-switching (changing from one language to another within turns at talk) balanced the need of communicating in Swedish with supporting the children's language acquisition of their mother tongue. Hence, the teachers' language policy also facilitated the children's language transition from mother tongue to Swedish and promoted the children's sense of belonging. Transition of language and cultural belonging can however be accomplished in different ways depending on the context.

In a case study from a refugee family centre in New Zealand, Mitchell and Bateman (2018) investigated how belonging can be supported through early childhood education. They show how the teachers in their study made a conscious effort to greet children and their families in a multimodal way and that a welcoming attitude and embodied greetings promoted children's belonging. Here multimodal means that the teachers, who were bilingual, greeted and welcomed each child and their family using both English and the family's home language, where the use of the family's home language comprises both verbal and non-verbal ways of greeting. The study shows in meticulous detail that belonging can be supported in a systematic and intentional way, and also as a collaborative project where the teachers interact with the children in a cultural and nuanced manner.

The arrival at preschool is a significant part of the child's experience of being a member of the group (Løkken, 2004). The responsibility to promote children's sense of belonging rests on the teacher's way of responding to children's needs and behaviour, which is pointed out in a Finnish research project (Salonen, Laakso, & Sevón, 2016). The study investigated the children's transition from home to preschool with focus on the processes related to young children's belonging during arrival at a day-and-night care, which is available for children in families working nonstandard hours. In contrast to ordinary preschools, the children's arrival time here varies a lot, hence making the transition more challenging for the children to get access to already established peer relations and play. The analysis shows that the teachers sensitively recognized the children's interactional initiative and provided physical closeness and assistance, verbalizing the situation and offering choices that supported the interaction between the child and familiar peers. These responses encouraged the child's social membership as it helped the child to join the ongoing activities and to experience a sense of belonging (Salonen, Laakso, & Sevón, 2016).

Children's Mental Health

Children's sense of belonging can also be related to children's mental health (Krause, 2011). Haraldsson, Isaksson, and Eriksson (2017) have carried out an action research study on how to promote children's mental health at preschool in relation to children's sense of belonging. Their results show that the teachers, based on the wellbeing of the children, promoted group belonging through creating different activities, changing the environment, and sometimes dividing the children into smaller groups. The teachers improved their way of observing what was happening in the child groups, and if necessary, they gave children a helping hand to access a group. The teachers also provided a structure for the children's free play, further involved parents in the practice of the preschool, and informed both parents and children about various things that soon would happen. This information was of special importance for families with non-Swedish backgrounds. According to the teachers, this change of organization and pedagogical approach promoted the children's wellbeing, as the children demonstrated more security, curiosity, joy, and satisfaction, and there were fewer conflicts between them. Furthermore, they liked being at the preschool (Haraldsson et al., 2017).

From every individual child's perspective, a sense of belonging is essential for their wellbeing (Haraldsson et al., 2017), as well as for their development and learning at preschool (Peers & Fleer, 2014). A great deal of children's sense of belonging at preschool deals with play and peer relations. From an early age, a child is aware of other children and makes spontaneous initiatives to interact with peers (Engdahl, 2012). However, to get access to a peer group and to be a ratified 'belonger' can sometimes be hard. This darker side of belonging is closely connected to questions of inclusion and exclusion (Yuval-Davis, 2011).

Peer Inclusion and Exclusion

Peer group activities contribute to children's socialization, development, and (language) learning, and this underlines the importance of peer group and peer cultures in children's everyday experiences (Cekaite, Blum-Kulka, Groever, & Teubal, 2014). With increasing age, relationships with peers and belonging to a peer group becomes of greater importance for most children. However, as mentioned above, it can sometimes be hard for a child to get access to a peer group, especially in a preschool setting, because other children tend to protect objects, shared space, and ongoing play from the entry of others (Corsaro, 2018). According to Corsaro (2018), the protection of interactive space is related to the fragility of peer interaction and the possibilities of disruption in most preschool settings. Holm Kvist (2018) shows that most disputes among young children at preschool are caused when children claim their possession of a toy or space while playing together. Materiality does play a crucial role in children's negotiation of belonging, where certain types of toys could serve as a key to enter the play, or lack of toys could appear as a reason for exclusion (Bateman & Church,

2017; Boldermo, 2020; Juutinen, Puroila, & Johansson, 2018). Notable is the importance of such entrance behaviours for children at a very young age, when it comes to negotiations of belonging and togetherness in diverse peer groups (Boldermo, 2020).

Observing children's play in detail can be a source of knowledge for teachers to understand how children adopt and transform the social order of preschool into their own play activities, because in the course of 'free play' children enact previous experiences from preschool practice into their play and peer relations (Björk-Willén & Cromdal, 2009). Boldermo (2020). for example, demonstrates that very young children's negotiation of belonging, including shared emotional connection and membership, was an ongoing child-initiated activity that occurred in *parallel* within the institutional practices. In a study of Icelandic children's play Ólafsdóttir, Danby, Einarsdóttir, and Theobald (2017) show that the children knew the rules, the social order of the preschool, and did what was expected of them. However, they also made their own rules for the purpose of the play activity; that means they resisted the educators' rules without breaking them (see also Löfdahl, 2010). Similarly, Björk-Willén (2018) shows how children were mirroring the social and moral order of the apology practices at preschool and used it for their own purposes in their play, e.g. avoiding 'tattling' or 'telling on others' or making the ongoing play sustainable.

As Corsaro (2018) has pointed out, belonging to a peer group at preschool can be fragile. The language or lack of language can make accessibility to peer play even more difficult. Karrebæk (2010) points out that language use and socialization processes among preschool children are complex negotiations of membership and shared emotional connection in peer groups. This phenomenon of children's access problem is also highlighted by Blum-Kulka and Garbott (2014) who have studied immigrant children's difficulties to belong in a preschool setting in Israel. They point out that immigrant children need to have rudimentary communication skills to be conversant with their language-majority peers. The exclusion of newcomers is also noticed by Rydland, Grøver, and Lawrence (2014) when studying second language learners in Norway. They highlight the importance of teaching assistants to help the newcomers to gain access to other children's play. Scaffolding a child's access to other children's play can be approached in many ways. For example, introducing a new play activity that involves the target child and others often attracts new children to take part (see also Theobald, Chapter 18, this volume). Teachers might also take on the role of a playmate, where the teacher has a crucial role to introduce central words in the play, which can help the language novice child to learn key words for upcoming play with peers.

In summary, the research above highlights the importance of teachers' awareness of children's culture, and also an awareness that a child sometimes needs to be scaffolded by an adult to gain access to play and other peer activities (see Extract 14.4). In this way, belonging is achieved by avoiding exclusion and creating inclusion.

Earlier research displays a range of different examples related to children's belonging at preschool. However, there are only a few studies that detail *how* belonging is interactionally achieved. The accomplishment of a child's sense of belonging is not always obvious and visible. What can be made visible is the social interaction and multimodal interchange between teachers and children and between children. In the next section I aim to show, in more detail, how teachers and children are 'doing belonging' using some examples from Swedish preschools, investigating and analysing how belonging can be accomplished in situ, and through everyday talk-in-interaction.

Belonging as a Joint Accomplishment: Some Empirical Examples from Swedish Preschool Practices

Method

The data below are drawn from two different projects. The first two examples derive from a project that studies the daily talk and interaction between parents and teachers in Swedish preschools. In this project, most families have a language background other than Swedish, while most teachers are monolingual Swedish speakers.[1] The second set of examples derive from a larger video ethnography on the moral and emotional socialization of children in preschool and in families in Sweden.[2] The participants' talk and social interaction has been video-recorded and transcribed using conversation analytic methods. The theoretical framework of the study is influenced by theories on language socialization and by ethnomethodological work on social actions; focusing on the participants' methods of accomplishing and making sense of social activities (Burdelski, Chapter 6, this volume; Garfinkel, 1967; Goodwin, 2000; Sacks, 1992).

[1] *Ethnicity in preschool: social interaction and institutional practice.* Financial support from the Swedish Research Council, Grant 4843–201700, Pl Polly Björk-Willén.

[2] *Communicating morality, embodying emotions.* Financial support from the Swedish Research Council, Grant 742–2013-7626, PL Asta Cekaite.

Greetings

Greetings display involvement and connectedness to the other, and the recipient is obligated to show that the message has been received and appreciated (Goffman, 1971). In a Swedish preschool context, the preschool hall is the place where most of the cooperation between family and institution takes place and where the family is welcomed and greeted. This form of cooperation between home and preschool, when parents drop off and pick up their children, occurs every day, everywhere in Sweden, and it is the most important place for information exchange between parents and educators. Leaving a small child in another person's care is not always easy for a parent, and therefore the daily contact and the way the exchange takes place are of great importance. It is also a key to making both parents and children feel secure, and to give children (and the parents) a sense of *belonging*. Björk-Willén (2013) shows how the ritual for drop off entailed taking off outdoor clothes, putting the dummy on the shelf, kissing and hugging, saying 'bye-bye', and finally waving through the window or door. Rituals build on repeated actions and recognizability, in turn giving the child (and the parents) a sense of security and belonging.

The two first extracts presented below derive from a Swedish preschool and a toddler classroom where the smallest children (aged 1 to 3 years) are cared for. The preschool is located in a residential area where most families have a migrant background and only few families have Swedish as their first language (see Björk-Willén, 2013). The first extract illustrates how greeting can be a collaborative business. It is in the morning and time for the children to arrive at preschool. The arriving families are met by the educators in the entrance hall. Helmi and his father have just arrived, and they are welcomed by a teacher and Jenny, another two-year-old child. The teacher has encouraged Jenny to help her do the welcoming. Enlisting the help of a child in greeting peers in the morning is a way to facilitate the transition between parent and preschool for the arriving child, and to give her/him an initial sense of belonging.

Extract 14.1 Participants: preschool teacher, Ahmed (father), Helmi (his son), Jenny (child)

1 Teacher: Ska vi ta emot Helmi du och jag Jenny
Should we welcome Helmi you and I Jenny.
2 ((walking hand in hand with Jenny to the
3 entrance hall))
4 (2) ((Ahmed and Helmi come through the
5 door))

6	Ahmed:	Hej
		Hello!
7		((looks at the teacher and Jenny - puts
8		Helmi on a low bench and begins to take
9		off Helmi's outer clothes))
10	Teacher:	[he:j↑ Helmi he:[j Helmi
		Hello Helmi Hello Helmi!
11		((high-pitched voice))
12	Jenny:	[dä Helmi [dä Helmi
		There's Helmi there's Helmi
13	Ahmed:	he↑j hej
		Hello hello!
14	Teacher:	kommer Jenny också och möter dig (.) ja::↑
		Jenny also welcomes you yea.
15		((high-pitched voice))

When the teacher includes Jenny in the morning welcome ritual (line 1), she gives Jenny an equal and important role. Jenny takes up this important role, demonstrated as she responds immediately, in an overlap with the teacher's greetings of Helmi, and repeats 'tha Helmi' (there's Helmi) (line 12). Helmi looks at them quietly, and his father responds with a greeting on Helmi's behalf (line 13). The teacher's and Jane's collaborative welcoming is highlighted when the teacher adds 'Jenny also welcomes you yeah' (line 14), addressing Helmi. The analysis shows how the teacher displays a welcoming attitude to Helmi, but also makes *the welcoming a joint accomplishment* involving Jenny. Jenny's greeting is produced simultaneously with the teacher's, underlining their collaboration. In this short sequence, the teacher intentionally includes both of the children – Jenny who is welcoming and Helmi who is welcomed – into the social framework of the preschool.

The next example, which is taken from the research project *Ethnicity in preschool*, shows how the welcoming ritual can be further embodied and how the welcoming and greeting ritual is initiated by the arriving child. This data was collected during the Swedish winter and it is icy cold outdoors. A couple of parents and their children are entering the preschool for drop off. Jane (aged 2 years) arrives first with her mother and older siblings. Jane was born in Sweden, but her parents have an immigrant background where their mother tongue is Arabic.

Extract 14.2 Participants: Jane (2 years), Jane's mother and two older siblings, Sofie (2 years), her mother and one older sibling, Ruben (2 years), and the preschool teacher.

```
1    Teacher:  kommer [Jane
               Jane is coming.
2              ((calling from the inside room))
3    Jane:           [HE:J hej hej
                      Hallo hallo hallo!
4              ((stops within the door followed by her
5              mother and two siblings))
6    Teacher:  Gomorron hej ha ha ha
               Good morning hallo ha ha ha
7              ((enters the hall))
8              Hej  Jane  hej x hej
               Hallo Jane hallo hallo!
9              ((squats close to the door and opens her
10             arms))
11   Jane:     ((walks into teacher´s arms and they hug
12             each other))
13   Teacher:  [oh oh va kall du [va
               Oh oh how cold you are.
14             oh va kall du va
               Oh how cold you are.
15             [((Sofia carried by her mother enters
16             together with her sibling))
17   Jane:                      [hej hej
                                 Hallo hallo!
18   Ruben:    ((Ruben appears from the classroom [touches
19             and then pinches Jane´s cheeks))
20   Teacher:                                    [Oh oh
21             oh ((smiley voice - takes away Ruben´s
22             hands)) ha ha ha
23   Adults:   ((mutual laughter))
24   Mother:   Xx
25             ((Sofie's mother puts Sofie down on the
26             floor))
27   Sofie:    ((runs into the teacher's (still squatting)
28             arms for a hug))
```

29	Teacher:	hej oh oj: va kalla kramar de blev [oh va
		Hallo oh oh what cold hugs it was
30		kall du är
		oh how cold you are.
31	Jane:	[HEJ HEJ
		Hallo hallo!
32	Adults:	((mutual laughter))
33	Teacher:	va kalla ni är ja ska ni komma in i värmen
		How cold you are yes you should come into
34		ah ska ni komma in i värmen
		the warmth you should come into the warmth.

Jane stops at the doorway repeatedly calling 'hallo' with a happy and high-pitched voice (lines 3–5). The teacher responds to Jane's loud greetings with a 'Good morning' and laughter (line 8) as Jane's happiness is contagious. The teacher squats and opens her arms, and Jane walks straight into her outstretched arms and they hug each other. The teacher looks at Jane and points out that she is cold. When kneeling the teacher puts herself at the same level as Jane, which gives them natural eye contact (Goodwin, 2000). This physical position also signals that the child has been placed at the centre of the teacher's attention.

At the same time the next family is entering preschool. Lina, also two years old, is carried by her mother (lines 15–16). Jane now bursts out in another 'hallo hallo' directed towards Lina. Løkken (2004) shows that toddlers have their own greeting rituals that sometimes can be prolonged, including repeated naming, hugging, and embracing. This is evident in Jane's actions in response to Lina's arrival, repeating her hallo several times, and with more hallos later. Ruben, two years old, enters the hall from the classroom and goes straight to Jane and touches her cheeks. Perhaps he has heard the teacher talking about Jane being cold and wants to feel it, or it could be his way to greet her (Løkken, 2004). However, his touch seems to be kind of harsh, because the teacher immediately takes away his hands with an 'Oh oh oh' in a smiley voice (lines 20–22). This is followed by a mutual laughter from the teacher and Jane's mother. Jane doesn't seem to react from Ruben's harsh touch, perhaps because of the teacher's quick interference, and the adult's laughter, signalling no danger. The teacher is still kneeling and Lina, who now has been put down on the floor, comes running straight into her arms at high speed, almost turning the teacher over (lines 27–28). They hug each other, and the teacher observes that Lina also is cold, and that today she is the recipient of cold hugs (lines 29–30). Jane simultaneously greets Lina, again with a loud 'hallo hallo' (line 31), followed by more laughter from the adults. The teacher again highlights that the children are cold and that they should come into the warmth, and this comment sets up the invitation for the children to move into the preschool classroom.

The extract displays a welcoming atmosphere, where the teacher, when kneeling, meets the children on their own physical level, and with her arms open she invites them into a welcoming hug. Hugs generally provide a mutually organized activity that constitute close social relationships (Goffman, 1971). However, in hugs between non-intimate persons, like in the extract, the haptic contact is shorter than between for example family members. Further, the hugging between the teacher and the children in the extract, is *mutually monitored* and carried out on the initiative of the children (Goodwin & Cekaite, 2018). This in turn shows a respectful attitude towards the child and supports the child's confidence and sense of belonging to the social framework of the preschool.

In summary, the two extracts above have stressed how a welcoming attitude and *embodied greetings* (Mitchell & Bateman, 2018) that configure different modalities (holding hands, kneeling, hugging, naming, and gazing) (Goodwin, 2000) promote the toddlers belonging to the preschool practice and its social framework. The respectful and inclusive treatment of the children and their families shown in the extracts is especially important as the target children have to transfer, not only between home and preschool, but also between languages and cultures.

Belonging to Preschool and to a Peer Group

Sometimes a child's investment in belonging with an adult or a peer is not reciprocated. Woodhead and Brooker (2008) claim that a child's needs and rights must be recognized and met, respected, and included. A basic condition to reach this is to take notice of the individual child. In preschool practice, teachers often have to manage groups with a lot of children, which of course reduces opportunities to spend quality time with each child. Dividing children into smaller groups, if possible, can be an alternative (Haraldsson et al., 2017) but is not always feasible. However, to find a balance between the individual child and the group is a pedagogical challenge for educators, though it can be accomplished in many ways, depending on the situation.

The following extracts derive from two preschools located in middle-class areas where the majority of the families have Swedish as their home language. The preschools were attended by one- to five-year-old children, divided into two age-separate groups (1–3 and 4–5 years old). The first extract, taken from the project *Communicating morality, embodying emotions*, aims to exemplify how each child in a small group of three-year-old children can be made visible. It is 'fruit time' at the preschool. There are six children sitting in a circle on the floor together with a teacher eating fruit, when a second teacher (Teacher 2) arrives and takes place in the circle. She greets the children, facing each of them. This individual attention can be discussed in terms of promoting each child's sense of identity and belonging to the preschool group.

Extract 14.3 Participants: six children (3 years old) and two teachers

1	Teacher 2:	x ser vi varandra gomorron
		Now we see each other good morning.
2		(laughter))
3	Clara:	Hej Lena
		Hallo Lena!
4		((Lena is the name of Teacher 2[3]))
5	Teacher 2:	((turns to the child on her right side
6		facing her closely))
7		är du här idag↑
		Are you here today?
8		((high-pitched voice - laughter))
9	Bea:	((smiles with her mouth full of fruit))
10	Teacher 2:	((smiles and faces Jane on the left side
11		bending closely towards her))
12		är du här idag jaa:
		Are you here today yes!
13	Jane:	((nods))
14	Teacher 2:	((puts her hand on the back of Sue next
15		to her bending her own head and getting
16		eye contact with the child))
17		och du
		And you!
18	Sue:	((nods))

[3] In Sweden children address their teachers with their first name.

```
19   Teacher 2:   ((moving her gaze between the children
20                sitting in front of her))
21                och Noel och Inge och Lisa och jag
                  And Noel and Inge and Lisa and I.
```

The second teacher (Lena) joins the group of children who are sitting in a circle together with another teacher eating fruits. She sits down between Bea and Sue, and Clara next to Bea, immediately welcomes her (line 3). The teacher then begins to greet the children one by one, turning her body against each child and using a 'lighthouse' gaze (Cekaite & Björk-Willén, 2018), i.e. her gaze moves from child to child, like the scanning of a lighthouse light, in order to make sustained, intentional eye contact with each member of the group. She initially greets the first two children, Bea and Jane, with a question 'Are you here today?' (lines 7 and 12) and the third child, Sue, with the confirming comment 'and you' (line 17), touching her back. The question 'are *you* here today?' underlines the importance of the individual child being at preschool. When she finally greets the last three children, sitting opposite to her, she calls them by name, ending with herself: 'and I' (line 21). Naming someone also emphasizes that every individual is important. The extract shows how the teacher uses both verbal and embodied methods to secure the children's attention during her greeting performance, as she configures bodily movement and gazes with verbal comments (Goodwin, 2000). Her embodied greeting has an inclusive agenda, in which she makes *every child visible*. The children also respond with greeting, smiling, laughter, nodding, and eye contact. Their responses display a spirit of togetherness that can be related to the teacher's actions and to the inclusion and belonging that her pedagogy promotes.

The last extract shows how a preschool teacher rearranges the initial play situation, where a child begins to cry when being excluded from a 'bus play'. Without making anyone accountable for their peer's crying the teacher scaffolds the children's peer interaction (Holm Kvist & Cekaite, 2020).

Extract 14.4 Participants: Neah, Naomi, Stina, all 2;5 years old, and Josephine (3 years) and the preschool teacher

```
1    Neah:        ((moves closer to the 'bus'))
2    Josephine:   nä du får inte va med Neah
                  No you can't join Neah.
3    Neah:        ((takes up a sock and sits down in the
4                 'bus'))
```

5	Josephine:	du får inte vara med Neah du får inte
		You can't join Neah you can't
6		vara med
		join.
7		((pushes Neah))
8	Neah:	((sits down at the floor and begins to
9		cry))
10		Uä::::Ä::
11	Naomi:	((looks at Neah))
12	Josephine:	Neah får inte va med
		Neah can't join
13	Stina:	det är min strumpa
		That's my sock.
14		((takes the sock from Neah))
15	Neah:	Eh::::
16		((walks towards the teacher))
17	Teacher:	((approaches the children))
18	Josephine:	men Neah får inte vara med (.) för vi kör
		But Neah can't join because we're driving
19		fort
		fast.
20		((looks at the teacher))
21	Teacher:	men hon kan också åka jättefort (.) men
		But she can also go very fast but
22		om jag är med kan nog Neah också vara med
		if I join Neah can join as well.
23		((takes Neah's hand and joins the 'bus'))

Naomi, Stina, and Josephine are playing 'bus driving' when Neah approaches. Immediately Josephine tells Neah that she is not welcome to participate (line 2), clearly protecting her and the other peer's interactive space (Corsaro, 2018). When Neah still steps on the bus, Josephine repeats her message and pushes Neah, who leaves the bus and begins to cry in a loud voice (lines 8–10), walking towards the nearby teacher. When the teacher approaches the bus play together with Neah, Josephine looks at the teacher and again repeats that Neah can't join the play, but now she makes an account for why, telling the teacher that they are driving too fast (lines 18–19). However, the teacher claims that Neah certainly dares to go fast and adds, taking Neah's hand, 'but if I join Neah can join as well' (lines 21–22). At this point Josephine accepts the teacher's argument and Neah together with the teacher get access to the bus play.

In a tangible way the teacher supports Neah's participation by also taking part in the play. She smoothly enacts an example of a preferred way of how to respond to a peer's distress, and she does so in a way that respects the children's initial play framework (Corsaro, 2003). To scaffold children's peer relations in play and at the same time *keep respect for their play framework* is a demanding assignment for preschool teachers. However, one way to find pedagogical strategies is to learn more about the children's own practice and culture.

Recommendations for Practice

It is difficult to know if a child has achieved a sense of belonging, yet this has important implications for curriculum implementation where Belonging is a central principle. What can be shown is the way the child responds to the adult and peers' attempts to support a sense of belonging, through displays of wellbeing, happiness, and playfulness at preschool. When making detailed analyses, interactional patterns can however be made visible, patterns that preschool teachers do not always recognize in their daily practice (Ólafsdóttir et al., 2017). It is often small, barely noticeable interactional moments that build the foundations for a child's sense of belonging. With the examples above I have aimed to show different ways and different levels of 'doing belonging', and below I highlight some of the findings that can promote the everyday educational practice of belonging.

- *Welcoming as a joint accomplishment* – In the first extract, the teacher gave a child an equal and important role to welcome another child/peer who just arrived at the preschool (Björk-Willén, 2013, 2016; Løkken, 2004). Inviting children to join in the welcoming shows that they are competent and capable, and so empowers them in the collaborative welcoming, promoting peer relations and giving them a sense of belonging to those who welcome others to the centre/school.
- *Embodied greetings* – In the second extract, embodied greetings were displayed, showing how the teacher has configured different modalities in her salutations (Björk-Willén, 2013; Mitchell & Bateman, 2018). To do this, the teacher bent down to meet the children on their physical level when they arrived in the preschool hallway in the morning. With her arms open, the teacher was also prepared for a hug, though respectfully awaiting the children's initiative, showing confidence in the child's agency. These embodied greetings transcend language barriers and demonstrate to the children and family that they are welcome and that they belong.

- *Being visible* – In the third extract, a teacher's greetings to a group of children at fruit time were analysed. The teacher displays an embodied greeting procedure where she acknowledges every single child using modalities like bodily movement, touching, commenting, naming and gazing toward each child, and making eye contact. In that way she promotes each child's sense of identity as being a valued member who belongs within the preschool group.
- *Respecting children's play framework* – Earlier research points out that children sometimes engage in conflict in the social order of the preschool, contributing to an excluding practice where some children do not get access to peer play. The fourth extract shows how a preschool teacher manages the inclusion of the rejected child into the children's play while acknowledging the children's established rules of the play (Holm Kvist & Cekaite, 2020). Hence, she opens up an alternative way of including the child without disruption of the continued play, using herself as a play mate and bringing in the excluded child. The teacher's respect of the children's play framework balances children's own access rules, and the preschool's moral order of inclusion. This pedagogy requires a *present* adult, who has a sensitive and listening attitude to children's argument and creative ways of ensuring that every child has the support to belong within their chosen play framework of peers.

As has been shown in this chapter, a crucial point for a child's sense of belonging at preschool is the educators' attitude and view of the child and her/his agency. It is the teachers that set the framework for a successful accomplishment of a child's belonging at preschool, which starts as soon as the child begins preschool and includes the whole family, as a child's belonging is strongly linked to the sense of belonging the family experiences. Belonging, according to Yuval-Davis (2011), is always a dynamic process and not fixed – consequently belonging has to be accomplished on an everyday basis and has no ending. This chapter has demonstrated some ways in which belonging can be accomplished in temporal everyday interactions, with a focus on what early childhood teachers can do to help children and families feel they belong.

References

Bateman, A., and Church, A. (2017) Children's use of objects in an Early Years playground. *European Early Childhood Education Research Journal*, 25(1), 55–71.

Björk-Willén, P. (2013). Samtal i förskolans tambur – på skilda villkor. (Talk in the preschool entrance hall – on different terms). In P. Björk-Willén, S. Gruber, and T. Puskás. *Nationell förskola med mångkulturellt uppdrag* (pp. 91–115). Stockholm: Liber.

Björk-Willén, P. (2016). The preschool entrance hall: a bilingual transit zone for preschoolers, In A. Bateman and A. Church (eds.), *Children's Knowledge-in-Interaction. Studies in Conversation Analysis* (pp.169–187). Singapore: Springer.

Björk-Willén, P. (2018). Learning to apologise – moral socialisation as an interactional practice in preschool. *Research on Children and Social Interaction*, 2(2), 177–194.

Björk-Willén, P., and Cromdal, J. (2009). When education seeps into 'free play': how preschool children accomplish multilingual education. *Journal of Pragmatics*, 41, 1493–1518.

Blum-Kulka, S., and Gorbatt, N. (2014). 'Say princess'; the challenges and affordances of young Hebrew L2 novices' interaction with their peers. In A. Cekaite, S. Blum-Kulka, V. Grøver, and E. Teubal (eds.), *Children's Peer Talk: Learning from Each Other* (pp. 169–193). Cambridge: Cambridge University Press.

Boldermo, S. (2020). Fleeting moments: young children's negotiations of belonging and togetherness, *International Journal of Early Years Education*, 28(2), 136–150.

Cekaite, A., and Björk-Willén, P. (2018). Enchantment in storytelling: co-operation and participation in children's aesthetic experience. *Linguistics and Education*, 48, 52–60.

Cekaite, A., Blum-Kulka, S., Grøver, V., and Teubal, E. (eds.). (2014). *Children's Peer Talk: Learning from Each Other*. Cambridge: Cambridge University Press.

Corsaro, W. A. (2003). *We're Friends, Right? Inside Kids' Cultures*. Washington, DC: Joseph Henry Press.

Corsaro, W. A. (2018). *The Sociology of Childhood* (5th ed.). London: Sage Publications.

Department of Education and Training. (2009/2019). *Belonging, Being & Becoming – The Early Years Learning Framework for Australia*. Department of Education, Employment, and Workplace Relations, Council of Australian Governments.

Engdahl, I. (2012). Doing friendship during the second year of life in a Swedish preschool. *European Early Childhood Education Research Journal*, 20, 83–98.

Garfinkel, H. (1967). *Studies in Ethnomethodology*. New Jersey, NJ: Prentice-Hall Inc.

Goffman, E. (1971). *Relation in Public: Microstudies of the Public Order*. New York, NY: Harper & Row.

Goodwin, C. (2000). Action and embodiment within situated human interaction. *Journal of Pragmatics*, 32, 1489–1522.

Goodwin, M. H., and Cekaite, A. (2018). *Embodied Family Choreography. Practices of Control, Care and Mundane Creativity*. London/New York: Routledge.

Gordon, J., O'Toole, L., and Whitman, C. (2008). A sense of belonging as part of children's wellbeing. *Early Childhood Matters*, 111, 7–12.

Haraldsson,K., Isaksson, P., and Eriksson, M. (2017). 'Happy when they arrive, happy when they go home' – focusing on promoting children's mental health creates a sense of trust at preschools. *Early Years*, 37(4), 386–399. https://doi.org/10.1080/09575146.2016.1191442

Holm Kvist, M. (2018). Children's crying in play conflicts: a locus for moral and emotional socialization. *Research on Children and Social Interaction*, 2(2). https://doi.org/10.1558/rcsi.37386

Holm Kvist, M., and Cekaite, A. (2020). Emotion socialization-compassion or non-engagement in young children's responses to peer distress. *Language, Culture and Social Interaction*, 28, 100462.

Juutinen, J., Puroila, A-M., and Johansson, E. (2018). 'There is no room for you!' The politics of belonging in children's play situation. In E. Johansson, A. Emilson, and A.-M. Puroila (eds.), *Values Education in Early Childhood Settings, Concepts, Approaches and Practices* (pp. 249–264). New York: Springer.

Karrebæk, M. S. 2010. 'I can be with!' a novice kindergartner's successes and challenges in play participation and the development of communicative skills. *Pragmatics & Language Learning*, 12, 325–358.

Krause, K. (2011). Developing sense of coherence in educational contexts: making progress in promoting mental health in children. *International Review of Psychiatry*, 23(6), 525–532.

Løkken, G. (2004). Greetings and welcomes among toddler peers in a Norwegian barnehage. *International Journal of Early Childhood*, 36(2), 43–58.

Löfdahl, A. (2010). Who gets to play? Peer groups, power and play in early childhood settings. In L. Brooker and S. Edwards (eds.), *Engaging Play* (pp. 122–135). Milton Keynes: Open University Press.

Ministry of Education. (2017). *Te Whāriki. He Whāriki mātauranga mō ngā mokopuna o Aotearoa: Early Childhood Curriculum*. Wellington, New Zealand: Ministry of Education.

Mitchell, L., and Bateman, A. (2018). Belonging and culturally nuanced communication in a refugee early childhood centre in Aotearoa New Zealand. *Early Childhood*, 19(4), 379–391.

Nagel, C. (2011). Belonging. In V. J. Del Casino Jr, M. E. Thomas, P. Cloke, and R. Panelli (eds.), *A Companion to Social Geography* (pp. 108–124). Chichester: Wiley-Blackwell.

Ólafsdóttir, S. M., Danby, S., Einarsdóttir, J., and Theobald, M. (2017). 'You need to own cats to be a part of the play': Icelandic preschool children challenge adult-initiated rules in play. *European Early Childhood Education Research Journal*, 25 (6), 824–837.

Peers, C., and Fleer, M. (2014). The theory of 'belonging': defining concepts used within belonging, being and becoming—The Australian Early Years Learning Framework. *Educational Philosophy and Theory*, 46(8), 914–928. https://doi.org/10.1080/00131857.2013.781495

Puskás, T. (2016). Doing 'belonging' in a Swedish preschool. *Early Childhood Folio*, 20 (1), 30–34.

Rydland, V., Grøver, V., and Lawrence, J. (2014). The potentials and challenges of learning words from peers in preschool: a longitudinal study of second language learners in Norway. In A. Cekaite, S. Blum-Kulka, V. Grøver, and E. Teubal (eds.), *Children's Peer Talk: Learning from Each Other* (pp. 214–234). Cambridge: Cambridge University Press.

Sacks, H. (1992). *Lectures on Conversation* (vol. 2). Oxford: Blackwell.

Salonen, E., Laakso, M.-L., and Sevón, E. (2016). Young children in day and night care: negotiating and constructing belonging during daily arrivals. *Early Child Development and Care*, 186 (12), 2022–2033. https://doi.org/10.1080/03004430.2016.1146717

Stratigos, T., Bradley, B., and Sumsion, J. (2014). Infants, family day care and the politics of belonging. *International Journal of Early Childhood*, 46, 171–186. https://doi.org/10.1007/s13158-014-0110-0

Swedish National Agency for Education. (2018). *Curriculum for the Preschool, Lpfö,18*. Stockholm: Fritzes.

Woodhead, M., and Brooker, L. (2008). A sense of belonging. *Early Childhood Matters* (111), 3–6.

Yuval-Davis, N. (2006). Belonging and the politics of belonging. *Patterns of Prejudice*, 40(3), 197–214.

Yuval-Davis, N. (2011). *The Politics of Belonging: Intersectional Contestations*. London: Sage Publications.

PART III

Interaction and Inclusion

15 | Play

ANNUKKA PURSI

Introduction

Play is central to young children's learning and the focus of much research in early childhood education (e.g. Bruce, Hakkarainen, & Bredikyte, 2017; Cheng & Johnson, 2010; Hännikäinen, Singer, & van Oers, 2013; Pramling Samuelsson, & Fleer, 2008; Pyle, DeLuca, & Daniels, 2017). Play has been examined as an individual phenomenon (e.g. Eddowes, 1991), a social phenomenon between children (e.g. Corsaro, 1979), and as a pedagogical phenomenon that children and adults construct together (e.g. Vygotsky, 1967). The adult role in relation to children's play has been examined from a range of perspectives, such as formulating various role classifications (Kontos, 1999), describing pedagogical practices (Fleer, 2015; Lobman, 2006), and analysing the construction of play situations turn by turn (Bateman, 2015; Pursi, 2019b).

In this chapter, conversation analysis is used to examine the construction of playful encounters in a particular group of Finnish toddlers. The data extracts and analysis detail what adults orient towards and what they actually do when they participate in constructing and maintaining multi-party playful encounters with children under the age of three. These playful encounters show face-to-face interaction in which the participants are oriented towards one another and are showing each other a playful stance using various interactional resources, such as gestures, facial expressions, gaze, touch, movement, speech, and the objects in the material environment. Multi-party playful encounters mean interactions where at least three participants reach a shared understanding that 'this is play' (Bateson, 1976).

Investigating multi-party playful encounters in groups is important, because early childhood education in a day-care centre is in principle a group activity (Dalli, White, Rockel, Duhn, et al., 2011; Degotardi & Pearson,

[1] wish to thank all the children, parents, and ECEC practitioners who participated in the study. Many of the ideas for the analyses in this paper originated in data sessions: I am grateful to Anssi Peräkylä and other members of the Emotion team as well as Asta Cekaite and her research group for sharing their views and ideas. This work was supported by the Emil Aaltonen Foundation (200185 NV).

2009). Interaction is rarely realized in dyadic relations between an adult and a child in isolation. Interaction studies have shown that creating and maintaining dyadic encounters is relatively straightforward (especially in western cultures), while creating and maintaining multi-party interactions requires some kind of specific interactional work (De León, 2012; Ford & Stickle, 2012; Molinari, Cigala, Corsano, & Venturelli, 2017; Mondada, 2013; Rogoff, 2003). Multi-party interactions invoke interactional challenges such as negotiation about participants' roles (Goodwin, 2007; Kalliala, 2014; Karrebæk, 2011), or maintaining and repairing interactions (Kidwell, 2013; Mehus, 2011). Investigating the talk-in-interaction of multi-party playful encounters is essential to understand the participation frameworks of child-adult interaction in early childhood education (see Bateman, Chapter 3, this volume).

The data in this chapter highlights pedagogical practices within multi-party playful encounters between adults and young children. Even though young children are able to structure their activities appropriately in different social group situations and adapt their communication, taking into account what they and the other participants are doing (Kidwell & Zimmerman, 2006; Løkken, 2000a, 2000b), they are still developing the pragmatic competencies of adults and older children (Mehus, 2011; Stivers, Sidnell, & Bergen, 2018; Trevarthen, 2011). As this Handbook is for early childhood educators, particular attention is given here to the role of the adult in creating and maintaining long-lasting multi-party playful encounters. This chapter begins with an overview of the research literature on adult participation in play, then provides detailed examples of playful interaction between adults and toddlers, and finally, reflects on the importance of play in the interaction between adults and young children, providing some recommendations for play-based pedagogy.

Adult Participation in Children's Play

Interaction analyses of the construction of playful encounters in early childhood education have mainly focused on peer interaction between children over the age of three (Björk-Willén, 2007; Björk-Willén & Cromdahl, 2009; Butler & Weatherall, 2006; Cobb-Moore, 2012; Danby & Baker, 2000; Farver, 1992; Kyratzis, 2007; Sawyer, 1993; Sidnell, 2011; Stivers & Sidnell, 2016; Tykkyläinen & Laakso, 2010; Whalen, 1995). The organization of playful encounters with toddlers, however, has been very little researched to date (Bateman, 2015; Hännikäinen & Munter, 2018; Løkken,

2000b). *Multi-party* playful encounters between adults and young children are a virtually unexplored area (Pursi, 2019b). One possible reason for this may be the developmental psychology perspective that has prevailed for some time in research with very young children, focusing on dyadic interactions (e.g. the interaction between parent and child). This preoccupation with adult-child dyads has also strongly influenced research-based understanding of the interaction between children under the age of three and adults in early childhood education.

Adult physical and emotional availability and playful, supportive, and enriching participation has been found to significantly influence young children's commitment to play and in particular the sustainability and complexity of play in toddler groups (Bateman, 2015; Jung, 2013; Kalliala, 2014; Lobman, 2006; Singer et al., 2014). Existing research shows us that constructing and maintaining playful encounters as complex social activities requires adults to take concrete pedagogical action, such as the following:

(1) During the playful encounters, adults act on the basis of their observations, alternating between observing the play from the sidelines, joining the play as a partner, verbalizing play, and leading play (Jung, 2013; Kalliala, 2014; Lobman, 2006; Trawick-Smith & Dziurgot, 2011; White, Ellis, O'Malley, Rockel, Stover, & Toso, 2009).
(2) Embodied interaction plays a key role in the adult's actions. Exchanging gaze, touch, and reaching out to the other play an important role for enabling a young child to experience that 'we are playing' (Bateman, 2015; Pursi, 2019b).
(3) The adult invites the child to playful encounters by sitting down on the floor at the child's level, focusing 100 per cent on observing the child's play (Kalliala, 2014; Singer et al., 2014).
(4) Through their facial expressions, gestures, body movements, and tone of voice, the adult involved in play displays vibrancy and warmth, building heightened emotive involvement in the child's play activities (Kalliala, 2014; Pursi, Lipponen, & Sajaniemi, 2018).
(5) While playing, the adult turns their attention to extremely small things – such as a tiny grain of sand or stone collection – which a young child finds interesting and worth sharing (Bateman, 2015; Kalliala, 2014).

To detail what participation in play looks like, Lobman (2006) provides concrete examples of what an adult does in toddler groups to construct, sustain, and extend playful encounters. In order to maintain playful encounters, the adult responds to the child's play initiatives with 'yes and' responses. In other words, the adult accepts a child's play initiatives ('yes' to create a shared understanding of the playful encounter) and takes them further ('and' to encourage continuation of the playful encounter). Siraj-Blatchford (2009) shows that adult participation in constructing and maintaining playful encounters can be realized cumulatively, so that the adult returns to the same playful themes and content with the children at the day-care centre over and over again; during the same day or over a number of days. However, in toddler research, there are very few depictions of pedagogical practices designed for cumulative interactions (Pursi, 2019b).

Jung (2011, 2013) has looked at how adults participate in play with children starting day care. Jung (2011) shows that, in the role of co-player, an adult can support toddlers to face the emotionally distressing situations of daily separations. For example, when the children are coming into the day-care centre, the adult's playfulness can build emotional transitions from the child's expressions of separation anxiety to playful encounter (see also Pursi, 2019b). Jung's (2013) research also shows that adults typically move from observing and verbalizing play to more active participative roles in building their relationship with the newest children in toddler groups. When the relationship is strengthened by dyadic interactions between the adult and the child, the adult can begin to focus on creating multi-party playful encounters. At this stage the lamination of the adult's roles in play become more clearly visible and rapid transitions from one role to another are increasingly common. The results of Jung's (2011, 2013) research, based on a four-month observation period in childcare centres in New York city, field notes, and interviews with adults, deepen our understanding of the dynamism of the adult role, but leave open the question of *how* an adult creates role transitions and role lamination in interaction. For this type of analysis, we need study designs based on video observation.

Bateman's (2015) micro-interaction analyses based on a video observational study deepen our understanding of the role transitions and role lamination related to constructing and maintaining playful encounters. The results show that in constructing and maintaining playful encounters, the adult is oriented towards creating a shared understanding between the participants. The adult verbalizes playful encounters, play roles and the child's embodied play turns to build a shared understanding and to connect the new participants in the playful encounter. By participating in play, an adult can also strengthen the interaction between children. In order to maintain interactions, the adult seeks to repeat and introduce their own prompts, if the child does not initiate play ideas for continuing the interaction (see also Dalhgren, 2017; Pursi et al., 2018).

In their work, Lobman (2006), Jung (2013), and Bateman (2015) all confirm that embodied interaction plays a key role in constructing and maintaining playful encounters between adults and very young children. Research on toddlers' play in early childhood education should include observations of embodied interactions, for example using drawings or screenshots of video recordings (Cekaite & Kvist Holm, 2017; Kidwell, 2012). Describing embodied interaction and investigating it turn by turn are important (research) practices through which we can more profoundly understand both young children's playful experiences and adults' orientation towards children's experiences and emotions. Such research deepens our understanding of how everyday playful encounters are constructed and of the role of the adult, and responds to the growing interest in the social organization of embodied interaction (Nevile, 2015).

Play as a Platform for Emotional Education in Toddler Groups

In this section, empirical evidence provides details of practices for engaging in multi-party play; screenshots and transcriptions from video data show what kind of things teachers of young children are paying attention to when participating in play. The examples are drawn from the data collected for the doctoral thesis, entitled *Intersubjectivity in adult-child play interaction. Institutional multi-party interaction and pedagogical practice in a toddler classroom* (Pursi, 2019a). The data (150h) was collected in 2016 from one toddler group in a Finnish municipal day-care setting. The day-care centre was located in an outer suburb of Helsinki, a southern city of Finland. At the time of the research project, the group had one qualified kindergarten teacher, two qualified nursery nurses, and one personal assistant to a child with special needs. There were thirteen children in the group, and they were all under the age of three (15–33 months). All the practitioners and children who participated in the study were native Finns and their mother tongue was Finnish.

In Finland, documents guiding and regulating early childhood education have begun to approach the importance of play in the interaction between adults and children in a new way (Paananen & Rainio, 2019). The national core curriculum for early childhood education (Finnish National Agency for Education, 2018) defines the adult's role as follows:

(1) It is necessary for the staff to understand the intrinsic value of play for the children as well as the pedagogical significance of play in children's holistic learning, growth, and wellbeing.

(2) The task of staff is to secure the conditions of play, to guide play in an appropriate manner, and to ensure that every child has the opportunity to be involved in play according to their own skills and capabilities.
(3) Staff must systematically and purposefully support the development of children's play and guide it from the outside or by being personally involved in play.

In early childhood education and care (ECEC), defining the role of adults in play is important. However, we need a substantive professional discussion of what we actually mean by appropriate or suitable methods and practices for guiding play and supporting children's holistic learning, growth, and wellbeing. To explore these issues, I have selected extracts from the data in which multi-party playful encounters between adults and children serve as a platform for emotional education when children are starting day care. With the notion of play as a platform for emotional education I mean interactional situations in which participants explore personal reflections of the emotionally heightened real-life experiences in a shared imaginary play frame (Bateman et al., 2013; see also *feelings-talk*, Hutchby, 2005). Interaction studies have suggested that through play, children can navigate and accommodate a variety of emotionally distressing situations together with adults and peers (Bateman et al., 2013; Jung, 2011; Pursi, 2019b; Pursi et al., 2018). This research-based understanding aligns with what is stated in the Finnish national core curriculum for early childhood education: 'Through play, children can process experiences that they found difficult' (Finnish National Agency for Education, 2018).

For many young children, starting day care is the first experience of separation from their parents or guardians and is accompanied by strong emotions, such as separation anxiety, sadness, and longing (e.g. Ahnert et al., 2004; Datler et al., 2012; Jung, 2011). From the child's point of view, the first separations are often emotionally distressing incidents. Without adult support, few young children can find the words and meanings of sadness, anxiety, and missing someone. Extracts 15.1–15.3 show how an adult can deal with situations and emotions related to separation through playful encounters with children in an imaginary play context. Playful encounters offer interactional resources for an adult to organize emotionally distressing situations with children in a sensitive way that respects children's perspective and supports their participation. With imaginary play I mean a form of activity that involves transformation of ordinary objects, persons, and situations into characters in a fictional world (Garvey & Berndt, 1975).

Multi-Party Playful Encounter after Separation from Parents

Extracts 15.1 and 15.2 occurred in the early morning, the time when Venla (V; 16 months) separates from her father (Figure 15.1) and encounters the teacher (T) and group of children (Figure 15.2). In lines 1–8, the teacher's speech is directed at Venla, who is showing signs of separation anxiety by crying. It is noteworthy that Venla's crying calms down in line 9, just when the teacher starts a playful encounter by making an imaginary call to Venla's father, who has already left the room.

Extract 15.1 Making an imaginary call to daddy

Figures 15.1. and 15.2 Separation anxiety in interaction.

01 T: katotaan et mihin me mennään tekemään hommat
let's see where do we go to do things
02 T: kyllä (.) {helistellään puhelimella isille mitä:
yes let's make a call to daddy huh
03 {*((puts Venla down and straightens her shirt))* Fig 15.3
04 T: {otetaan puhelimet ja helistellään vähän
let's take the phone and let's make a call
05 {*((lifts a toy phone from the floor))*
06 T: {sanotaan et *((picks up the receiver))*
let's say that
07 V: {*((orients to T, still crying))*
08 T: {.Hh missä se isi viipottaa joko sinä ehdit autoon
.Hh where's daddy going did you make it to the car already
09 V: {*((stops crying, mutual gaze with T))* Fig.15.4

First, the teacher puts the crying and struggling Venla down on the floor (Figure 15.3). Then she lifts a toy phone from the floor to make an imagined call to Venla's father, who has just left (Figure 15.4). At the same time as the teacher puts the receiver to her ear (line 6) and initiates a call by taking a deep breath (line 8), Venla calms down and stops crying (line 9).

In her play turn (line 8) the teacher uses amazement ('.Hh') and wondering ('where's daddy going') as an interactive resource to direct Venla's attention to the playful encounter of 'making a call to daddy'. The first part of the teacher's in-frame talk (i.e. being inside the play frame/being personally involved in play, Finnish National Agency for Education, 2018) is addressed to Venla (an inquiry about the daddy's location, '.Hh where's daddy going') and the latter part to the imagined daddy ('did you make it to the car already'). Given this dual addressing, the teacher's play turn performs two tasks: apart from attracting Venla's undivided attention, the teacher also creates a multi-party encounter between herself, Venla, and Venla's daddy in a shared imaginary play frame. Venla's response indicates firm alignment (line 9, Figure 15.4, a mutual gaze and bodily orientation) and minimal affiliation on the level of emotions (Figures 15.3 → 15.4, an emotional stance shift from escalated crying towards a more neutral stance).

As a result, Extract 15.1 shows us how the teacher engages Venla in a shift to a playful stance to accommodate her experience of distress. Here

Figures 15.3 and 15.4 From a dyadic encounter towards a triadic encounter.

play works as a resource to acknowledge and soothe Venla's emotional distress. From an emotional education perspective (e.g. Finnish National Agency for Education, 2018), it is essential that the teacher's play turn enables Venla to process the situation behind her emotional distress, that is, her father's departure. The teacher does not direct attention away from Venla's emotional distress, but adds a new perspective to the separation through an imaginary play frame. A remote connection to Venla's father is created by the imagined call. From Venla's perspective, reality (longing for her father) and the imaginary play frame (being in contact with her father) are interconnected in a meaningful way in a playful encounter with the teacher.

Another interesting perspective for this particular playful encounter is how it is extended beyond the dyad, and moves to include other children. First, Figure 15.4 reveals that another child, Lily, is aligning with the playful encounter as she positions as an onlooker by actively shifting her bodily orientation between the teacher and Venla. Second, if we go back to Figure 15.2, we find that throughout the episode, the overhearing children's attention is directed to the encounter between Venla and the teacher. On the video recording, it is possible to detect children frowning, opening their mouths, and raising their eyebrows. These embodied signals indicate that Venla's crying is not only her own emotion, but a phenomenon created in interaction (Peräkylä & Sorjonen, 2012). The entire group of children is aware of and attentive to Venla's separation anxiety and the subsequent shift to a play frame.

Extract 15.2, which is an almost direct continuation of the previous extract, confirms our description of the group's attention. As the encounter progresses, the imagined call created by Venla and the teacher expands into a multi-party playful encounter. With the teacher's help, Sofia (S, 27 months) and Lily (L, 33 months) take turns to call the 'calming down service'. Also Matias (M, 16 months) is included in the shared play frame.

Extract 15.2 Opening up the imaginary play to multiple participants

16 T: se:lvä↓(0.5) joo ja kaikki hyvin$_{Fig.15.5}$
ok yes and everything is all right
17 T: .hh no ↑venlakin täällä hiljeni kuuntelemaan
(0.4) hm-m (0.4)
.hh well here venla also quieted down to listen
hm-m
18 T: [joo-o matiaskin hiljeni] kuuntelemaan=
yes matias also quieted down to listen
19 S: [MINÄKIN OLEN]
I am too
20 S: =MINÄKIN$_{Fig.15.6}$
me too
21 T: v- hh ↑no Sofiakin=haluatko Sofia jutella jotain
v- hh well sofia as well do you want to say
something sofia
22 T: ((offers the receiver to S)) $_{Fig.15.7}$
((The conversation continues between T and S $_{Fig.15.8}$, lines 23-33 omitted))

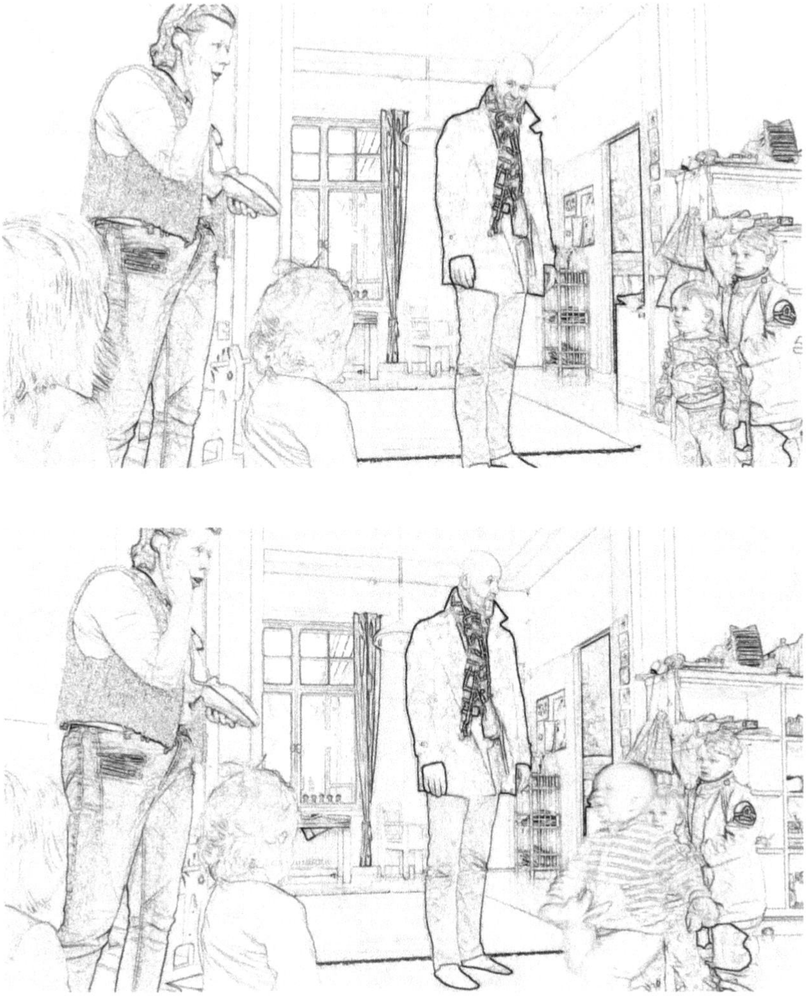

Figures 15.5 and 15.6 Multi-party playful encounter.

34 L: vauvakin haluaa jutella
baby wants to talk as well
35 T: on on >tuu< joo katotaan otetaan uus puhelu
yes yes come yes let's see let's take another call
36 T: sanotaan että *((lifts the receiver on her ear))*=
let's say that
37 T: =onko rauhottumispalvelu=
it is the calming down service
38 T: =*((offers the receiver to L))*

Figures 15.7 and 15.8 Sustained multi-party playful encounter.

At the beginning of the extract, in line 16, the teacher is about to end the telephone conversation. At the same time, however, her gaze shifts from Venla to other children in the group and she detects that the attention of several children is directed to the telephone conversation (Figure 15.5). Instead of deciding to end the imaginary call, the teacher continues the conversation (line 17) and begins to bring the other children in the group into the playful encounter (Figures 15.6–15.8, lines 18, 21–22, 35–38). Rather than focusing exclusively on an individual child, the teacher gives the whole group the opportunity to participate. Some of the children enthusiastically respond to the invitation by expressing the wish to participate in the imaginary telephone conversation (Figures 15.6–15.8, lines 19–20 and 34).

Multi-party play becomes possible when the teacher shifts her attention from Venla to the group of children and decides to continue the imagined call. The teacher's stance is not to limit playful encounters to one child at a time, but to identify and collaboratively build contexts in which the interaction can be expanded to involve more participants. In terms of emotional education, it is noteworthy that the teacher creates a playful encounter from Venla's situation and to the generalized experience of separation. In this way the teacher enables other children in the group to participate in processing and verbalizing the emotionally distressing situation, which has become the centre of their attention. Separation anxiety is processed by making imagined calls to the 'calming down service'. Everyone who wants to is provided with the opportunity to talk on the phone, and the teacher makes time for starting and ending phone calls, e.g. with Sofia and Lily.

To conclude, if we return to the beginning of the episode and look at the change in Venla's emotional stance in the screenshots, we can see that the initial distress caused by separation anxiety (Figures 15.1–15.3) transitions through calm (Figure 15.4) to enjoyment (Figure 15.8). The teacher's playful stance and construction of a sustained multi-party playful encounter serves as a pedagogical practice for dealing with emotional distress caused by separation among the children in the group (see also Jung, 2011). The extracts show us how children's emotional experiences and subsequent soothing and self-regulation can be achieved moment-by-moment, in everyday interaction, through playful encounters between adults and children. Turn by turn the participants co-produce the context of supportive environment. Cultures of care (Osgood, 2010), tenderness (Brennan, 2007), and compassion (Lipponen, 2018) are evident in the situation and facilitated by the teacher in skilful ways.

Multi-Party Playful Encounter during Whole-Group Circle Time

Continuing on the theme of managing emotional states, Extract 15.3 illustrates how a teacher can work with situations and emotions related to separation through playful encounters with the children during whole-group circle time. A playful encounter dealing with separation, sadness, and missing someone begins when one of the children, Lily (L, 33 months) aligns to the toy sheep in the teacher's hand and produces a play turn in which she imagines the sheep feeling sad (line 1).

Extract 15.3 Feeling sad and longing for someone in a playful encounter

Figures 15.9 and 15.10 Playful encounter during whole-group circle time.

```
01  L:  HEI_Fig.15.9 sil on paha mie:li:=
        hey it's feeling sad
02  T:  =tälläkö paha mie:li (.) no millä me se
        lohdutellaan
        is this one feeling sad huh well how should we
        comfort it
03  L:  se haluu äitiä
        it wants its mummy
04  T:  [no niin haluais se huutaa et äi:ti: missä
        ole:t_Fig.15.10
        well yes it does it's shouting mummy where are you
```

05 [((Lily and other children are coordinating
06 their gaze between the adult and the sheep figure
07 some of the children are making sad faces by
frowning))
08 T: minä kurkkaan tänne
I'll check over here ((peeks inside the barn))
09 T: tiedättekö mitä (.) hyh (.) nyt meidän täytyy sitä
lohdutella
you know what uh now we have to comfort it
10 lisää kato ku sen äiti on lähteny töihin
even more because its mom has gone to work
11 ei näy koko navetassa
she's not in the barn ((shakes her head))
12 T: joutuu sanomaan sille että he:i:: täällä hoidetaan
hyvin
***we have to say to it that hey you'll be treated
well here***
13 äidit tulee iltapäivällä
mothers will come back in the afternoon
14 T: mitähän se siitä tykkää
what is it gonna think about that
15 E: äiti lammasta
mom sheep
16 T: no niinpä
well yes exactly
17 L: se itkee: kun äiti tulee
it'll cry when mom comes back

Lily's play turn in line 1 (Figure 15.9) contains a strong emotional message; empathy and sorrow that the sheep is feeling sad (e.g. the stretched vowels in sympathetic tone). While Lily is talking, the teacher affirms her emotional stance with gaze and facial expressions: the teacher directs her gaze towards Lily, cranes her neck to move closer, and pouts her lips. After Lily's play turn, the teacher aligns her own play response with Lily's playful and emotional stance (line 2, the stretched vowels in sympathetic tone). In substance, the teacher responds to Lily's idea for play, as if saying 'yes, and' (Lobman, 2006), i.e. she adopts the child's idea for play ('is this one feeling sad huh') and develops it ('well how should we comfort it'). When in line 3 Lily does not take up the teacher's idea for comforting the sheep, the teacher aligns her stance to the child's turn and creates an opportunity for reflecting on the sadness and longing more deeply.

By saying 'it wants its mommy' Lily expands the imagined emotional stance of the sheep by adding new emotional nuances of longing to the initial feeling of sadness. The teacher's play response in line 4 and especially the in-frame talk ('mummy where are you'), which richly expresses sadness and longing (extended vowels and empathetic tone of voice) animates the sheep character's feelings. Besides sadness and longing, the teacher sends comforting and compassionate signals by physically stroking the toy sheep (Figure 15.10). It is evident in the situation that the teacher is engaging in active listening of a child's feelings-talk (Hutchby, 2005). However, this emotionally heightened playful encounter and feelings-talk is not just between an adult and one child, but a multi-party playful encounter. In lines 5–7 (Figure 15.10) we can see empathetic expressions which animate the play content (sadness and longing) on more and more of the children's faces (e.g. frowns, raised eyebrows, open mouths, gaze directed towards the toy sheep and the teacher). As the interaction unfolds further, Lily will expand the talk about emotions with the teacher. Also, Ella (E, 26 months) will find a way to contribute verbally.

In line 8, a new playful and emotional element emerges in the imaginary play as the teacher cannot find the mom sheep. As a consequence, the most evident way to find comfort to the feelings of longing and sadness is not available. The teacher needs to spontaneously invent her next play turn in order to secure the progression of the playful encounter. In lines 9–13, the teacher brings young children's real-life trajectories and experiences to the play ('mom has gone to work'). This kind of orientation explicates the idea that the sheep figure's feelings and ongoing imaginary play could be some sort of representation of the children's real emotional lifeworld. Line 14 closes the teacher's play turn as she provides an open-ended question for the group. Lines 15–17 reveal that the teacher's open-ended question actually works to facilitate the children's verbal participation (line 16) and feelings-talk (line 17). In line 17 Lily demonstrates her willingness to take a deeper look to the feelings of longing and sadness as she contributes to the play by verbalizing actions that describe the emotional stance of the sheep ('It'll cry'). Interestingly, she ties the crying to the reunion ('when mom comes back').

Overall, Extract 15.3 confirms that in early childhood education, emotional education can be implemented in everyday interaction, through playful encounters between adults and children. Sustained multi-party play creates possibilities for adults and children to explore personal reflections of emotionally heightened real-life experiences in a shared imaginary play frame (Bateman et al., 2013). The teacher's participation in play facilitates children's feelings-talk and allows space and time for the expression of emotions, both bodily and verbally.

Recommendations for Practice

Conversation analysis can be used to clarify, illustrate, and inspire the pedagogical practices of play, as well as to correct underlying assumptions about practices that are not based on everyday interaction (e.g. an emphasis on adult-child dyadic interaction in early childhood education for children under the age of three). In this chapter, findings from conversation analysis of the everyday organization of playful encounters have detailed actions to expand the repertoire of play-based pedagogical practices. The empirical evidence in this chapter shows us that multi-party playful encounters are an important form of play for toddler groups in early childhood education and adults play a key role in creating and maintaining these interactions. Extracts 15.1–15.3 deepen our understanding of the emotionally educative nature of playful encounters, and of how an adult can actually create, construct, and maintain emotionally educative playful encounters and facilitate children's feelings-talk. The key implications for teachers in talking with very young children about emotions and feelings during playful encounters are:

- Early childhood teachers and carers, as well as other professionals in the field, are encouraged to examine and define play not only as a fundamental right for children (UN Convention on the Rights of the Child, 1989), but also as an essential professional skill and one of the key forms of pedagogical interaction between adults and very young children.
- In early childhood education, playful encounters serve as a context for encountering, sharing, and processing emotionally heightened life experiences.
- In a toddler group, the adult constructs, maintains, and verbalizes playful encounters and the related emotional signals and feelings-talk.
- The adult's attuned communication and alignment with the group rather than the individual are pedagogical practices that expand playful encounters, making them multi-party interactions.
- When children are guided to play in multi-party groups as early as their toddler years and have the opportunity to practise joining and participating in play with the support of an adult, this can inform their peer relationships and expand repertoires of play.

- During sustained multi-party playful encounters, adults and children co-produce, turn by turn, the context of supportive environment in which cultures of care (Osgood, 2010), tenderness (Brennan, 2007) and compassion (Lipponen, 2018) are evident and facilitated by the teacher.

References

Ahnert, L., Gunnar, M. R. G., Lamb, M. E., and Barthel, M. (2004). Transition to childcare: associations with infant-mother attachment, infant negative emotion, and cortisol elevations. *Child Development*, 75, 639–650.

Bateman, A. (2015). *Conversation Analysis and Early Childhood Education: the co-production of knowledge and relationships* (pp. 41–66). London: Ashgate/Routledge.

Bateman, A., Danby, S., and Howard, J. (2013). Living in a broken world: how young children's well-being is supported through playing out their earthquake experiences. *International Journal of Play*, 2(3), 202–219.

Bateson, G. (1976). A theory of play and fantasy. In J. S. Bruner, A. Jolly, and K. Sylva (eds.), *Play – Its Role in Development and Evolution* (pp. 119–129). Harmondsworth: Penguin.

Björk-Willén, P. (2007). Participation in multilingual preschool play: shadowing and crossing as interactional resources. *Journal of Pragmatics*, 39, 2133–2158.

Björk-Willén, P., and Cromdal, J. (2009). When education seeps into 'free play': how preschool children accomplish multilingual education. *Journal of Pragmatics*, 41, 1493–1518.

Brennan, M. (2007). A culture of tenderness: teachers' socialisation practices in group care settings. *European Early Childhood Education Research Journal*, 15(1), 137–146.

Bruce, T., Hakkarainen, P., and Bredikyte, M. (eds.). (2017). *The Routledge International Handbook of Early Childhood Play*. New York, NY: Routledge.

Butler, C. W., and Weatherall, A. (2006). 'No we're not playing families': membership categorization in children's play. *Research on Language and Social Interaction*, 39(4), 441–470.

Cekaite, A., and Kvist Holm, M. (2017). The comforting touch: tactile intimacy and talk in managing children's distress. *Research on Language and Social Interaction*, 50(2), 109–127.

Cheng, M.-F., and Johnson, J. E. (2010). Research on children's play: analysis of developmental and early education journals from 2005 to 2007. *Early Childhood Education Journal*, 37(4), 249–259.

Cobb-Moore, C. (2012). 'Pretend I was mummy': children's production of authority and subordinance in their pretend play interaction during disputes. In S. Danby and M. Theobald (eds.), *Disputes in Everyday Life: Social and Moral Orders of Children and Young People* (pp. 85–118). Bradford: Emerald Insight.

Corsaro, W. A. (1979). 'We're friends, right?' Children's use of access rituals in a nursery school. *Language in Society*, 8, 315–336.

Dalgren, S. (2017). Questions and answers, a seesaw and embodied action: how children respond in informing sequences. In A. Bateman and A. Church (eds.) *Children's Knowledge-in-Interaction: Studies in Conversation Analysis* (pp. 37–56). Singapore: Springer.

Dalli, C., White, E. J., Rockel, J., et al. (2011). *Quality early childhood education for under-two-year-olds: What should it look like? A literature review*. Wellington, New Zealand: Ministry of Education.

Danby, S., and Baker, C. D. (2000). Unravelling the fabric of social order in block area. In S. Hester and D. Francis (eds.), *Local Educational Order: Ethnomethodological Studies of Knowledge in Action* (pp. 91–140). Amsterdam: John Benjamins.

Datler, W., Ereky-Stevens, K., Hover-Reisner, N., and Malmberg, L. E. (2012). Toddlers' transition to out-of-home day care: settling into a new care environment. *Infant Behavior and Development*, 35(3), 439–451.

Degotardi, S., and Pearson, E. (2009). Relationship theory in the nursery: attachment and beyond. *Contemporary Issues in Early Childhood*, 10, 144–155.

De León, L. (2012). Language socialization and multiparty participation frameworks. In A. Duranti, E. Ochs, and B. B. Schieffelin (eds.), *The Handbook of Language Socialization* (pp. 81–111). Malden, MA: Wiley-Blackwell.

Eddowes, E. A. (1991). Review of research: the benefits of solitary play. *Dimensions*, 20(1), 31–34.

Farver, J. A. M. (1992). Communicating shared meaning in social pretend play. *Early Childhood Research Quarterly*, 7, 501–516.

Finnish National Agency for Education. (2018). *National core curriculum for early childhood education and care 2018. Regulations and guidelines.*

Fleer, M. (2015). Pedagogical positioning in play – Teachers being inside and outside of children's imaginary play. *Early Child Development and Care*, 185, 1801–1814.

Ford, C. E., and Stickle, T. (2012). Securing recipiency in workplace meetings: multimodal practices. *Discourse Studies*, 14(1), 11–30.

Garvey, C., and Berndt, R. (1975). *The organization of pretend play*. Chicago: Paper presented at the Annual Meeting of the American Psychological Association.

Goodwin, M. H. (2007). Participation and embodied action in preadolescent girls' assessment activity. *Research on Language and Social Interaction*, 40(4), 353–375.

Hännikäinen, M., and Munter, H. (2018). Toddlers' play in early childhood education settings. In P. K. Smith and J. L. Roopnarine (eds.), *The Cambridge Handbook of Play: Developmental and Disciplinary Perspectives* (pp. 491–510). Cambridge: Cambridge University Press.

Hännikäinen, M., Singer, E., and van Oers, B. (2013). Promoting play for a better future. *Early Childhood Education Journal*, 21(2), 165–171.

Hutchby, I. (2005). 'Active listening': formulations and the elicitation of feelings-talk in child counselling. *Research on Language and Social Interaction*, 38(3), 303–329.

Jung, J. (2011). Caregivers' playfulness and infants' emotional stress during transitional time. *Early Child Development and Care*, 181(10), 1397–1407.

Jung, J. (2013). Teachers' roles in infants' play and its changing nature in a dynamic group care context. *Early Childhood Research Quarterly*, 28, 187–198.

Kalliala, M. (2014). Toddlers as both more and less competent social actors in Finnish day care centres. *Early Years*, 34(1), 4–17.

Karrebæk, M. S. (2011). It farts: the situated management of social organization in a kindergarten peer group. *Journal of Pragmatics*, 43, 2911–2931.

Kidwell, M. (2012). Interaction among children. In J. Sidnell and T. Stivers (eds.), *The Handbook of Conversation Analysis* (pp. 511–532). Chichester: Wiley-Blackwell.

Kidwell, M. (2013). Availability as a trouble source in directive-response sequences. In M. Hayashi, G. Raymond, and J. Sidnell (eds.), *Conversational Repair and Human Understanding* (pp. 234–260). Cambridge: Cambridge University Press.

Kidwell, M., and Zimmerman, D. (2006). 'Observability' in the interactions of very young children. *Communication Monographs*, 73, 1–28.

Klein, P. S., Kraft, R. R., and Shohet, C. (2010). Behaviour patterns in daily mother–child separations: possible opportunities for stress reduction. *Early Child Development and Care*, 180(3), 387–396.

Kontos, S. (1999). Preschool teachers' talk, roles and activity settings during free play. *Early Childhood Research Quarterly*, 14(3), 363–382.

Kyratzis, A. (2007). Using the social organizational affordances of pretend play in American preschool girls' interactions. *Research on Language and Social Interaction*, 40(4), 321–352.

Lipponen, L. (2018). Constituting cultures of compassion in early childhood educational settings. In S. Gravis and E. Eriksen Ødegaard (eds.), *Nordic Dialogues on Children and Families* (pp. 39–50). Abingdon: Routledge.

Lobman, C. L. (2006). Improvisation: an analytic tool for examining teacher-child interaction in the early childhood classroom. *Early Childhood Research Quarterly*, 21, 455–470.

Løkken, G. (2000a). Tracing the social style of toddler peers. *Scandinavian Journal of Educational Research*, 44, 163–177.

Løkken, G. (2000b). The playful quality of the toddling 'style'. *International Journal of Qualitative Studies in Education*, 13(5), 531–542.

Mehus, S. (2011). Creating contexts for actions: multimodal practices for managing children's conduct in the childcare classroom. In J. Streeck, C. Godwin, and C. LeBaron (eds.), *Embodied Interaction. Language and Body in the Material World* (pp. 123–136). New York, NY: Cambridge University Press.

Molinari, L., Cigala, A., Corsano, P., and Venturelli, E. (2017). Observing children's triadic play. In T. Bruce, P. Hakkarainen, and M. Bredikyte (eds.), *The*

Routledge International Handbook of Early Childhood Play (pp. 216–229). New York, NY: Routledge.

Mondada, L. (2013). Embodied and spatial resources for turn-taking in institutional multi-party interactions: participatory democracy debates. *Journal of Pragmatics*, 46(1), 39–68.

Nevile, M. (2015). The embodied turn in research on language and social interaction. *Research on Language and Social Interaction*, 48(2), 121–151.

Osgood, J. (2010). Reconstructing professionalism in ECEC: the case for the 'critically reflective emotional professional'. *Early Years*, 30(2), 119–133.

Paananen, M., and Rainio, A. P. (2019). Micro-policies of adult-child joint play in the context of the Finnish ECEC system. In S. Alcock and N. Stobbs, *Rethinking Play as Pedagogy*. New York, NY: Routledge.

Peräkylä, A., and Sorjonen, M.-J. (eds.). (2012). *Emotion in Interaction*. London: Yale University Press.

Pramling Samuelsson, I., and Fleer, M. (eds.). (2008). *Play and learning in early childhood settings: international perspectives*. New York, NY: Springer.

Pursi, A. (2019a). *Intersubjectivity in adult-child play interaction. Institutional multi-party interaction and pedagogical practice in a toddler classroom*. Ph.D. thesis, University of Helsinki. Helsinki: Unigrafia.

Pursi, A. (2019b). Play in adult-child interaction: institutional multi-party interaction and pedagogical practice in a toddler classroom. *Learning, Culture and Social Interaction*, 21, 136–150.

Pursi, A., Lipponen, L., and Sajaniemi, N. (2018). Emotional and playful stance taking in joint play between adults and very young children. *Learning, Culture and Social Interaction*, 18, 28–45.

Pyle, A., DeLuca, C., and Danniels, E. (2017). A scoping review of research on play-based pedagogies in kindergarten education. *The Review of Education*, 5(3), 311–351.

Rogoff, B. (2003). *The Cultural Nature of Human Development*. New York, NY: Oxford University Press.

Sawyer, K. (1993). The pragmatics of play: interactional strategies during children's pretend play. *Pragmatics*, 3(3), 259–282.

Sidnell, J. (2011). The epistemics of make-believe. In T. Stivers, L. Mondada, and J. Steensig (eds.), *The Morality of Knowledge in Conversation* (pp. 131–155). Cambridge: Cambridge University Press.

Singer, E., Nederend, M., Penninx, L., Tajik, M., and Boom, J. (2014). The teacher's role in supporting young children's level of play engagement. *Early Child Development and Care*, 184(8), 1233–1249.

Siraj-Blatchford, I. (2009). Conceptualising progression in the pedagogy of play and sustained shared thinking in early childhood education: a Vygotskian perspective. *Educational & Child Psychology*, 26(2), 77–89.

Stivers, T., and Sidnell, J. (2016). Proposals for activity collaboration. *Research on Language and Social Interaction*, 49(2), 148–166.

Stivers, T., Sidnell, J., and Bergen, C. (2018). Children's responses to questions in peer interaction: a window into the ontogenesis of interactional competence. *Journal of Pragmatics*, 124, 14–30.

Trawick-Smith, J., and Dziurgot, T. (2011). 'Good-fit' teacher–child play interactions and the subsequent autonomous play of preschool children. *Early Childhood Research Quarterly*, 26, 110–123.

Trevarthen, C. (2011). What young children give to their learning, making education work to sustain a community and its culture. *European Early Childhood Education Research Journal*, 19, 173–193.

Tykkyläinen, T., and Laakso, M. (2010). Five-year-old girls negotiating pretend play: proposals with the Finnish particle *jooko*. *Journal of Pragmatics*, 42, 242–256.

Vygotsky, L. S. (1967). Play and its role in the mental development of the child. *Soviet Psychology*, 5(3), 6–18.

Whalen, M. R. (1995). Working toward play: complexity in children's fantasy activities. *Language in Society*, 24, 315–347.

White, J., Ellis, F., O'Malley, A., Rockel, J., Stover, S., and Toso, M. (2009). Play and learning in Aotearoa/New Zealand early childhood education. In I. Pramling Samuelsson and M. Fleer (eds.), *Play and Learning in Early Childhood Settings: International Perspectives* (pp. 19–49). New York, NY: Springer.

16 | Mental Health and Wellbeing

MICHELLE O'REILLY AND JESSICA NINA LESTER

Introduction

Child mental health is attracting greater global attention, with prevention, promotion, early identification, and intervention considered crucial. As children spend significant amounts of time in educational settings, educators have been positioned as playing an important role in promoting children's positive mental health and wellbeing, as well as reducing or attending to mental health need (Adams et al., 2019). In England, for example, the Department for Education has advocated that education settings take a graduated response to assess, plan, review, and meet the mental health and wellbeing needs of the children they work with. In other words, educators are increasingly expected to assess mental health needs in the educational context, plan education to meet a range of mental health needs, implement adjustments to teaching approaches, and where required, refer to more specialist help. It can, however, be challenging for educators to accurately distinguish between emotions children experience as part of their normal development and lives, and emotions and behaviours that may raise concern, especially as younger children may find it challenging to articulate their emotions to others (Adams et al., 2019). This is compounded further by the complexity and difficulties of communicating about mental health with children.

In this chapter, we promote cross-disciplinary learning and the translation of knowledge to practice. In so doing, we highlight some of the work that has been conducted in terms of communicating with children across the age spectrum *about* mental health, emotional regulation, and wellbeing, and with those children *diagnosed* with clinical mental health need. We argue that mental health practitioners who work with children with diagnosed mental health conditions have the skills and practices to engage children effectively. Thus, by spotlighting mental health practitioners *doing* their job as they assess children to determine mental health need, best practices in communication can be translated and transformed for other settings like education. To do this, we draw upon our research focused on mental health assessments, where we specifically examined how the design of questions for children is crucial for engagement. During this project, we found that asking children about their emotions, feelings, and wellbeing is a complex endeavour. In our discussion, therefore, we illustrate *how* this takes place in real-world clinical settings to provide a clear communication 'toolkit' for educators that can be used to talk to children about emotions, wellbeing, and mental health in early educational settings (e.g. schools, pre-schools, nurseries and the like). We also account for the importance of educators' own wellbeing and mental health, and consider the pressures of attending to child mental health.

Contextualizing Core Concepts

To foreground our discussion, we first critically contextualize some of the taken-for-granted concepts we employ. Notions of 'the child', of 'mental health', 'resilience', 'wellbeing', and 'mental health condition' may seem obvious, but there is an enlightening literature that highlights how these meanings came to be and critically questions some of the common assumptions associated with them.

Conceptualizing Children and Childhood

Over the years, understandings of children and childhood has changed and has been conceptualized by two major fields, which present different perspectives: developmental psychology and sociology. First, is developmental theory, which grouped children by their chronological age and outlined differences across categories in terms of intellectual, cognitive, moral, social, emotional, and physical stages of development. The introduction of formal education for children in the United States and United Kingdom is relatively recent (late nineteenth century), meaning children became more visible as a distinct group and the focus of more formal study (Karim, 2015). This was part of a movement that conceptualized childhood as a distinct period in one's lifespan and contributed to the emergence of developmental psychology and child psychiatry as separate branches of their respective fields (O'Reilly & Lester, 2017).

Alternative ideas about children grew from the 'sociology of childhood' that positioned childhood as a social construct rather than a natural one, and has influenced our understanding of children as culturally, politically, and historically situated (Prout & James, 2015). This kind of philosophical shift in thinking has therefore helped us to see children as competent and capable, moving us away from perspectives that have previously focused on deficit. These different ideas about children and childhood are important when we think about children's mental health and wellbeing, as our perspectives have implications for what can be considered 'normal' behaviour.

Conceptualizing 'Normal Development' and Mental Health

Historically, conceptualizing the 'normal' child and by contrast the child with mental health need relied predominantly on the disciplines of psychology and psychiatry. Practitioners from these fields have relied on standardized measures of behaviour and development. Such perspectives have been validated by medical ideas about illness of the mind. Thus, it is common that children with mental health need are described with medical language, with many practitioners inside and outside of medicine using words like 'symptoms', 'illness', 'treatment', 'patient', and 'cure'. This kind of language is consistent with the classification systems, such as the *Diagnostic and Statistical Manual of Mental Disorders* (DSM-5), that practitioners use to determine who and who does not fall within the category of a 'disorder' (American Psychiatric Association [APA], 2013).

While this medical language is commonly used to understand the mental health needs of children, the language itself is problematic. This is because such an approach is seen as deficit-focused and socially constructed (Frances, 2013), positioning children as ultimately needing to be 'fixed' (O'Reilly & Lester, 2017). It has been argued that these kind of naturalized prescriptions of the child are misguided (Burman, 2008) and it is not entirely appropriate to benchmark children's functioning across childhood (Brownlow & Lamont-Mills, 2015). In other words, 'normal' behaviour and 'normal' emotions are measured and then, using statistics, society is provided with an 'average' or a 'norm' (Davis, 1995); yet no child ever truly lies at this baseline (Burman, 2008). Alternatively, it is arguably beneficial to consider the sociological arguments of childhood and children's behaviour and development. These views claim that any understanding of the child is *created* via professional practices rather than revealed by them (Burman, 2008).

The reason why we point out these critical arguments is twofold. First, language always matters. Language plays a central role in communication, but also in our understanding of mental health and wellbeing, and its meaning to children and families (see O'Reilly et al., 2020). Second, the methodology we utilize in identifying good communication practices is conversation analysis (discussed later), which takes a position that mental health need is socially constructed. This does not deny the reality of mental health conditions or people's experiences of them; rather, it recognizes the ways that certain kinds of scientific knowledge have been privileged (Thomas et al., 2018), and emphasizes the importance of attending to language, social interaction, and communication. For example, the term 'depressed' is frequently co-opted into lay language to reflect a general feeling of unhappiness that is a very normal response to certain life events and in this way can give a good indication of how a child is feeling. However, clinically, depression is a diagnosable condition with a more profound emotional state for a sustained period that impacts on quality of life and functioning (APA, 2013).

The very notion 'mental health' is frequently confused and misrepresented. Speakers often use the term 'mental health' when meaning 'mental health condition' (or 'mental illness' in medical terms), so clarification of these core concepts is necessary. Probably, the most often cited definition of mental health was provided by the World Health Organization (2014), as:

> … a state of well-being in which every individual realizes his or her own potential, can cope with the normal stresses of life, can work productively and fruitfully, and is able to make a contribution to her or his community.

Thus, being mentally healthy is not simply the absence of disease but is a more overall positive state of wellbeing with an ability to cope with life's events. By contrast, mental illness, a term we resist because of its highly medicalized overtone, is when an individual has a cluster of symptoms for a sustained time, impacting on life, and consistent with criteria in diagnostic manuals (APA, 2013).

In education settings, the concept of mental health is often juxtaposed with other related concepts, that of resilience and wellbeing. It can be argued that these terms are grounded in developmentalist, individualized notions of childhood and normality. Typically, when we read about a resilient child, it rests on the modern ideology that resilience is dispositional to the child and something that can be built. Like other concepts, resilience has also received some critical attention for being overly simplistic due to the range of systems in which the child operates. More critical perspectives have argued that resilience is not located within the child, but in the mutual networks, groups, and social structures around them (Theron, 2016). Because of this emphasis on social ecologies of resilience, it is important to emphasize the interactions between children and others and their environment (Ungar, 2012). Definitions of wellbeing have typically focused on individuals too, defining the individual as being physically healthy and happy, such as the original World Health Organization (WHO) definition, but have been criticized for failing to account for the intersection between the biopsychosocial (i.e. the combination of biological, psychological, and social factors) and spiritual wellness of the child (Larson, 1996). In other words, resilience, wellbeing, and positive mental health need a much broader conceptualization that accounts for both the individual and systemic circumstances of each child.

We argue therefore that educators need to remain reflective and critically mindful of different perspectives about children and mental health and wellbeing. Taking a language-focused approach to examining communication with children helps to emphasize a paradigm that is competence focused, which we suggest is a more positive way forward. In such a framework, we can find evidence of how children manage and employ resources in competent ways, such as engaging in social interaction that is meaningful (Hutchby & Moran-Ellis, 1998). Children display their competencies as they interact with one another and adults. Thus, their competence is achieved within an interaction itself and in a range of contexts. Importantly, this competence is not an adult-imposed assessment of capability, but rather authentically arising from the children themselves (O'Reilly et al., 2019; Theobald, 2016). We suggest that it is useful for educators to employ evidence-based communication strategies that serve to acknowledge and expand the ways in which children display their competencies, especially in the early years.

Mental Health, Wellbeing, and the Role of Educational Settings

Increasingly, educational settings are finding that they need to be responsive to issues related to mental health and wellbeing. Globally, there has been an increase in the number of children diagnosed with mental health conditions (Bor et al., 2014) and those with milder emotional health needs who do not necessarily meet the threshold for diagnosis. It has therefore become imperative that educators have the skills to recognize when children in their classes are experiencing challenges to their mental health. More particularly, educators need to be adequately trained to build skills and have the confidence not only to recognize the signs of a mental health concern, but also in to communicate with children about their emotions, feelings, and behaviours. Globally, early childhood education curricula have emphasized the relevance and importance of focusing on the social-emotional skills and the growth of children. Yet, in practice, research shows that mental health is an area that teachers often feel the least confident about (Rothi et al., 2008) and typically have limited training or skills in managing mental-health-related concerns (Reinke et al., 2011). Many countries are beginning to respond to this need however, with some governments developing strategies and policies to support educators. We offer a simple outline of signs or indicators for the two most common emotional health conditions, anxiety and mood disorders, in Table 16.1, as adapted from the information available from the UK National Health Service.

Table 16.1 Signs and indicators of emotional conditions

	Anxiety	Depression
Signs and indicators to look for in young children	• The child may find concentrating on their work or play activities difficult. • The child may have reduced appetite or complain of stomach-ache or sickness. • The child may anger quickly or display irritability. They may display inappropriate outbursts of behaviour. • It may become evident that the child is worrying or fearful in certain situations. • The child may tense up physically, be fidgety or engage in frequent requests to visit the toilet. • The child may express negative thoughts. • The child may be clingy and require a lot of educator attention and reassurance. • The child may frequently cry.	• The child displays a frequent sadness and low mood that fails to dissipate. • The child may come across as irritable and grumpy most days. • When an educator tries to engage the child in things they used to enjoy, they no longer display pleasure or excitement with them. • The child may be yawning during activity and complain of feeling tired. • The child may have trouble concentrating on the tasks set. • There may be challenges with peer relations and the child interacts less or is less interested in peers. • The child might seem to have limited confidence. • There is often a change in appetite, either with excessive eating or insufficient eating. • The child may have trouble relaxing. • The child may report feeling sad or numb. • There is a risk of self-harm, even in very young children, and there are often physical indicators (burns and cuts).

While upskilling educators is valuable, there is a misguided assumption that quality training in mental health is easily provided and immediately translates at a practical level (O'Reilly et al., 2018). While educators are expected to implement curricula with a focus on positive mental health and wellbeing, in everyday practice this can be far more challenging than policy expects, especially given some of the definitional challenges we outlined earlier. One area then that needs far more attention is communication. Talking with children, engaging them as co-participants in understanding their own experiences and understanding of wellbeing and health, and providing educators with communication skills that focus on emotional and mental health is one step in the right direction.

Talking with Children about Their Wellbeing

Communication is actually a highly complex process affected by an enormous range of factors (Karim et al., 2021). For communication to be effective, it is important that the educator has a good relationship with the child and can align with their perspective. Despite the value and central role of communication in education (and in health and social care for that matter), many trainees and practitioners rely on anecdotal evidence, training courses, and their own experiences to inform how they do so. For example, in textbooks designed for clinical trainees there is often an emphasis on asking open questions, but they rarely critically address what constitutes an open question or challenge the circumstances in which these might be less effective than closed questions. This is particularly problematic when working to engage children in educational settings, as children are not mini-adults and children with certain kinds of communication challenges (e.g. autism spectrum condition ['disorder' in medical terms], learning difficulties) may require modification when teaching them. Educators can take active steps to consult the children in their classroom in meaningful ways to help meet their needs. This is an important issue in the modern classroom with the advent of the United Nations Convention of the Rights of the Child (1989) that encourages child-centred communication and the child's right to be heard on matters that affect them.

We argue that the notion of child-centeredness is ambiguous and while many practitioners across different contexts believe they are child-centred, it is possibly the case that this is overestimated. The lack of consensus regarding the true meaning of child-centred practice hinders this further. We suggest that it is better to turn to research evidence that has language, communication, and social interaction at its core; evidence that takes note of what practitioners *actually* do in the real world, rather than asking them what they *think* they do. This kind of evidence does not rely on artificial situations or memories, but instead examines *what* practitioners are doing and *how* they do it. We illustrate the importance of communication with children and illuminate best practices that are translatable for education by turning our attention to data generated from our mental health assessment project.

The Mental Health Assessment Project

In many countries, when a child presents emotions or behaviours, or other characteristics that deviate from the usual developmental milestones that indicate 'normal development' (such as physical, language, social skills etc.), parents or other professionals involved with the family may raise concerns. When the child goes to nursery/preschool or school, and their behaviour stands out as different to other children (e.g. they are not speaking as many words as other children, they are crying all the time, they are not interacting with other children), then educators or parents might start to ask questions about whether the child needs some additional support. For children where there is concern about their development, parents may seek support from the educational setting and/or may raise concerns with their primary care doctor or paediatrician. Most children, where appropriate, will be referred to a specialist mental health service for the child to be assessed (in most western settings at least). This is not a straightforward endeavour, however, due to a lack of funding for mental health globally. Notably, research suggests that it can take an average of 3.1 years from initial concerns being raised to diagnosis of a condition (Shanley et al., 2008).

The mental health assessment itself is a crucial part of the overall process of determining the presence of a mental health condition. The initial mental health assessment is not usually a diagnosis – although the two can sometimes occur closely together – but is an initial screening appointment to identify need, ascertain risk, and to develop an initial formulation of what the presenting concern *might* be (Mash and Hunsley, 2005). Thus, the child and their family meet with mental health practitioner(s) to explore the story behind the referral and often seek additional information from other agencies like schools (Karim et al., 2021). The assessment of mental health is a necessary step toward diagnosis. It is through the assessment and the diagnosis processes that behaviour and emotions are defined as a mental health condition. The diagnosis of a condition is required for children and their families to access any kind of support in health and in education (APA, 2013).

While our work was focused on mental health practitioners, we have long seen the explicit connections that might be drawn to early childhood teachers. Specifically, although the practitioners in our study were focused on interacting with children across the age spectrum, this did include younger children (aged 6–11-years) and some of the features of question design were relevant and useful regardless of the child's age. Furthermore, how they interact can be studied to better understand the more effective ways by which to talk to young children about their mental health. Hence, in this chapter, we take data from United Kingdom mental health settings and we aim to tease out implications for early childhood educators across the globe.

Context of the Study

In the United Kingdom, children are referred to the Child and Adolescent Mental Health Service (CAMHS) for an assessment. Despite the importance of initial assessments in the process of identifying and supporting mental health need, there is limited research undertaken to examine such contexts. For our study, we collected data from one service whereby the team was multidisciplinary. Sampling included all consenting first appointments, although urgent cases were excluded for safeguarding and ethical reasons. We video-recorded the initial assessments of twenty-eight families who consented, and each assessment lasted approximately 90 minutes, with consultant, staff-grade and trainee child and adolescent psychiatrists, clinical and assistant psychologists, community psychiatric nurses, occupational therapists, and psychotherapists. The children were aged 6–17-years old and were always accompanied by one or both of their parents, and some were additionally accompanied by other family members and/or another professional. The sample consisted of 64 percent boys and 36 percent girls. Twelve children were referred into the service for formal diagnosis and treatment, eight were given a second assessment appointment for further investigation, and eight were discharged as not having mental health need. In this chapter, we draw from the whole dataset, but most examples are from children under the age of 11 years, due to their relevance.

Conversation Analysis

It is increasingly recognized that research focusing on language is especially useful for the field of mental health (O'Reilly & Lester, 2017). We therefore use conversation analysis (CA) to inform communication messages from the mental health assessment data to translate for the educational setting. CA is a qualitative approach that examines talk-in-interaction (for further introduction to CA see Chapter 1, this volume). Conversation analysts focus on what people actually say and do, rather than what they report they say and do (McCabe, 2006). CA is therefore useful for looking at how practitioners design their turns, including questions (Drew et al., 2001). Some conversation analysts focus on talk in institutional settings, such as classrooms, law courts, and medical consultations (Lester & O'Reilly, 2019). To accomplish this, they use naturally occurring data, i.e. recordings of events in the real world, as this can transparently show real-world practices without relying on retrospective reports (Kiyimba et al., 2019).

A Note on Ethics

In the United Kingdom, the National Health Service (NHS) has its own ethical process for research, and this service gave us formal approval to undertake the study. In practice this meant all practitioners, parents, and other adult members signed a consent form at the beginning and again at the end of the recording process, and children provided an assent form. All members received an information sheet with detailed information. Safeguarding issues were the responsibility of the clinic and were dealt with as part of the assessment procedures. To achieve a high-quality data set and analysis, we promoted a collaborative partnership with the clinic and the practitioners. This meant involving colleagues throughout the entire process and providing a workshop of findings to promote good practice.

The Importance of Question Design

Educators know that the way they ask a question influences the answer, with a great deal of research supporting this understanding (e.g. Walsh and Blewitt, 2006; Walsh and Hodge, 2018; Walsh, Sánchez, and Burnham, 2016). There are different ways to ask questions, and evidence suggests that these exist on an information-seeking continuum, ranging from questions designed to elicit factual information to questions designed to seek broader expression or elaboration from the recipient (Freed, 1994). Some questions have specific purposes that relate to an institutional agenda, and for educators many questions are designed to assess the child for educational purposes (e.g. '*what is 2+2?*') and follow a typical Initiation-Response-Feedback (IRE) structure (e.g. '*what is 2+2? – 'four' – 'that's right!'*). In the context of mental health, however, the *design* of the question is often quite complex and is especially important for eliciting more detailed and personal answers about emotions, wellbeing, and behaviour.

In our data, the mental health assessments included many questions, and across the twenty-eight families there were 9,086 asked in total (see O'Reilly et al., 2015). This was an average of one question roughly every 15 seconds. Of that total, 3,714 were directed toward a parent, 5,327 were directed toward the child, and the remainder did not select a recipient specifically. While the range of questions was diverse, we created a taxonomy of questions that were grouped in terms of their design, and we reproduce the table from O'Reilly et al. (2015) here to illustrate that (see Table 16.2).

For clarification, yes-no interrogatives are those questions that are designed to elicit a yes or no response (e.g. '*do you like the colour green?*'); wh-prefaced questions are those questions that start with a 'wh' word, like *what* and *where* (and also include how) (e.g. '*what sound does a cow make?*'); declarative questions are those that make a statement with a questioning tone (e.g. '*so you think the answer is six?*'); and tag questions are short question phrases tagged onto the end of a statement (e.g. '*you want the circle shape,* do you?'). When we paid closer attention to some of these questioning types, we found that some questions worked particularly well to encourage children to engage in talk about their wellbeing.

Encouraging Children to Engage

While there are developmental differences across children of different ages, the clinicians in our data used a range of question designs with children from as young as 6 years to as old as 17 years, using some of the same techniques

Table 16.2 Taxonomy of questions (from O'Reilly et al., 2015, p. 118)

	Yes-no interrogatives	*Wh*-prefaced questions	Declarative questions	Tag questions
PARENT	1,412	1,167	810	196
CHILD	2,226	1,920	683	371
BOTH	21	6	2	12
Total	**3659**	**3093**	**1495**	**579**

with the young children and with the older teenagers. Many of these questions were simple closed questions, designed to elicit simple descriptive but informative answers, and we give some examples of these from unpublished data:

Extract 16.1 Family 9 (child aged 8 years)

```
MHC       Do you have any friends at school?
Child     Yeah
```

Extract 16.2 Family 5 (child aged 6 years)

```
Doctor     You don't like the °↓hoover°?
Child      ((child shakes her head))
```

As well as seeking simple descriptive answers, sometimes the clinicians used closed questions to ask about feelings or behaviours, which provided them with some useful information to build upon later using more open techniques.

Extract 16.3 Family 4 (child aged 9 years)

```
Doctor     ↑Why do[n't yo]u like ↓Shane?
Child             [cos I-]
           because he hits ↓me
```

Extract 16.4 Family 11 (child aged 9 years)

```
Doctor    Do you do you get anxious if ↓cars are (0.31)
          goin' fast (0.62) on the r↑o:ad ↓or (0.73) um::
          (0.85) do you feel (0.40) you know somethin'
          ↑bad might ↑happen?
Child     Yeah
```

While these kinds of closed questions did elicit responses from children, they tended to be short answers. There were, therefore, many ways in which clinicians designed their questions in ways to encourage longer answers, some of which used this descriptive information in more detail later in the assessment. We focus on three types of question design that are especially useful with younger children and translate well to the educational context. These question designs are helpful if you are working with children with mental health need, communication or learning difficulties. We discuss in turn, (1) Subjective Units of Distress (SUDs); (2) three wishes; and (3) 'you said x' prefaced questions. Although a couple of our examples shown are with school-aged children, these designs can easily be utilized with children of all ages and were useful in encouraging all children to open up.

We begin with SUDs. This question technique was developed by Wolpe (1969) and is used with adults and children. Practitioners use them to gauge the person's level of distress (Matheson, 2014). SUDs are used commonly with young children and are often framed as '*on a scale of one-to-ten, how happy/sad/angry do you feel?*'. Our work showed that there are different ways of using SUDs with children to encourage them to engage in talking about feelings (Kiyimba & O'Reilly, 2020). In the mental health setting, using SUDs with younger children was often accompanied by a visual in the form of a drawing of a jug or teapot, and the child physically drew a line to show how 'full' the vessel would be with that emotion. See Figure 16.1.

We provide an example here of the ways in which those questions were asked of children.

Extract 16.5 (from Kiyimba & O'Reilly, 2020 p. 420 (child aged 11 years)

```
Clin-Psy    Imagine this teapot is, we're gonna put all
            your angry feelings in here, yeah?
            How angry you'd get?
Child       Yeah
Clin-Psy    If we were to take all the angry feelings out
            of you and pour 'em into this teapot how full
            would it be?
            (pause)
            you show me with your finger how full it
            would be?
            ((child indicates top of pot))
```

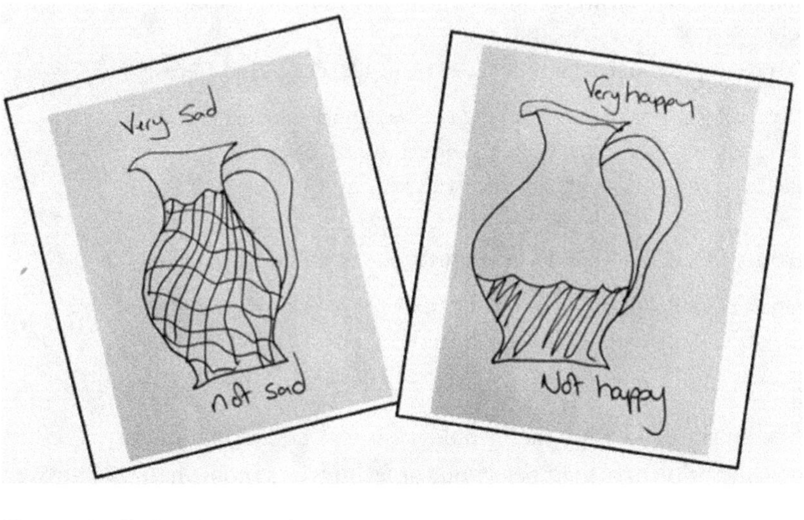

Figure 16.1 Feeling jug examples.

Perhaps, most importantly, we showed that it was important to only use a single emotion on the scale. In cases where the clinician used a dichotomous emotion, it caused confusion for the child or they opted for the middle rating which is arguably meaningless in a dichotomy. When referring to a dichotomous scale, we mean the following (from Kiyimba & O'Reilly, 2020, p. 422):

Extract 16.6

CPN One is feeling really really sad ten is feeling really really happy what number d'you think your mood has been in the last couple o' weeks?

What was especially useful when engaging children using SUDs was that practitioners could address the recency and longevity of feelings. In other words, they could ask the child to rate their emotions now and compare with previous timestamps and could find out how recent those emotions were for the child.

The second communication technique we discuss is 'three wishes', to ascertain a child's understanding of their feelings or behaviour. This is another common technique used with children and is something that sits within their domain of knowledge. Thus, when asking the child what they might use their three wishes for, it becomes a technique to see if emotions or behaviours are on their agenda and to start to benchmark the goals of the assessment (Kiyimba et al., 2018). For some children, this technique may highlight how challenging any mental health characteristics are to them, and for others they may not orient to the institutional business and give more child-like answers. Consider the two examples below.

Extract 16.7 (from Kiyimba et al., 2018, p. 423; child aged 13 years)

Clin Psy: ↑if you had three wishes (0.66) what ↓would you like to make happen

Adol: ↑my OCD'd ↓go (0.38) away

Extract 16.8 (from Kiyimba et al., 2018, p. 428; child aged 8 years)

Registrar: Okay you've got three wishes what would you wish to [see]

Child: [A million po]unds

Asking a child what they would wish for can help to identify whether the child prioritizes their behaviour or feelings as a problem. If they answer with 'money' or 'a superhero power' then this could indicate that wellbeing issues are not a high priority or a pressing concern for them.

Our final question design strategy is one that in our data showed to be successful in terms of eliciting longer and more elaborate answers from children in all cases of its use with all ages. By paying close attention to the way in which practitioners talked to children, we found that they often prefaced a question with 'you said x' and in those cases the children always answered the subsequent question in detail (Kiyimba & O'Reilly, 2018). Consider the example below from an older child and look at how much detail is given through the dialogue.

Extract 16.9 (from Kiyimba & O'Reilly, 2018, p. 151; child aged 13 years)

```
Prac     I'm ju↑st wo:↑ndering thou↓gh coz you (.) you
         said in the: (.) interview room that (.) it
         sta↑rted a couple of years ago [it FIRST]=
Child                                   [yeah its]
Prac     = ever >st[arted] a couple of years ago<=
Child              [yeah]
Prac:    = so why↑ do you think it it started the↓n?
Child    January it could be sorting out changing
         thi:ngs(0.70)I th↓ink it could be like (.)
         say↑ing me (.) is coz like (.) I dunno (0.63)
         chan↑ging schools an th↓at li↓ke
```

The key to this technique is that the adult develops a basis of shared knowledge with the child based on something that they have previously disclosed about when the behaviour first began. In this way, the child is actively encouraged to elaborate further by the question that follows it, and while our example only shows some in this interaction for brevity, it can be seen that this technique elicits a more elaborate and longer answer from the child. Importantly, the same technique also worked with younger children in eliciting more protracted answers to questions, even when the topic was sensitive and difficult in nature. See the example below.

Extract 16.10 (from Kiyimba & O'Reilly, 2018, p. 152; child aged 9 years)

```
Prac        So when you ↓said that you were going to take a
            ↓knife to yourself
      (0.99)
```

```
Prac         yeah?
      (1.15)
Prac         What were you ↓hoping would happen?
Child        erm (2.45) f::or me to ↓actually kill my↓self
```

This technique demonstrates its effectiveness here in a setting where there is the possibility that a child may be at risk of self-harming behaviour or suicidal ideation and is thus demonstrating significant mental health issues. By using the phrase 'you said' before the question about intention, the practitioner recognizes that the threat of 'taking a knife to yourself' was a disclosure by the child, and this is an important one for pursual. By using 'you said' here, the child does disclose suicidal intention. While the child did continue in elaborating her feelings, we simply illustrate here the value of the technique in encouraging elaboration and show how such phrases can be helpful even when talking about delicate matters like risk. In the context of education, this may also arise, and it is important that educators can ask children safeguarding questions that encourage talk about wellbeing.

Recommendations for Practice

Asking questions is a central practice for all educators. The central role of questions in the learning process has long been highlighted (e.g. Gall, 1970). What we offer here that is particularly unique is a focus on the place of questions for eliciting a better and deeper understanding of children's mental health and wellbeing. In so doing, we point to the importance of designing questions with care and being informed by the body of research that highlights what kinds of questions are most useful in eliciting meaningful information. Notably, how a question is designed shapes the degree to which one gains insight into a child's feelings and broader perspectives. As we noted, in our research we have found that subjective units of distress questions combined with visual elements/pictures, three wishes questions, and 'you said x' prefaced questions, are particularly useful for gaining a deeper understanding of a child's perspective of how they feel and experience their mental health. Doing so requires care in designing questions to assure that children offer responses – responses which are critical for determining whether additional supports can and should be secured for the child to support their mental health and wellbeing. Broadly, we aim to highlight here that there is useful evidence for how to design questions that can elicit important information about a child's mental health. Thus, using the question types we have offered here, we argue that educators can have useful tools for eliciting greater understanding about the mental health of the children they work with and for treating them as knowledgeable and competent to talk for themselves. Thus, we offer the following practitioner highlights as a toolkit for communication in this area.

- Use the communication evidence to help you. There is a growing literature in mental health communication, and much of this is created with practitioners in mind. Where possible engage with this literature, as it will provide insights regarding how to best communication with children about mental health.
- Record your own interactions with children (with appropriate permissions). Looking closely at your own interactions with children can be useful for you to identify areas where you are doing well and can help you see any areas of improvement.
- Techniques like the three wishes and Subjective Units of Distress (SUDs) are child-centred approaches that can encourage engagement.
- Shared knowledge can help a child. Using words previously said by the child and reflected to them in the form of 'you said x' before you ask a question can encourage a child to open up and share more relevant information.
- Acknowledge that feeling uncomfortable is possible, especially if you are engaging children in areas of mental health that may feel a bit riskier, like self-harm. Whether you are experienced or not in having these kinds of conversations with children, do not be afraid to seek out support from your colleagues and from other practitioners, such as mental health professionals.

Across many countries there is growing attention regarding what education settings might be able to do to address the growing mental health need of children. With prevalence rates rising, training teachers in mental health and resilience is seen as a central task (Public Health England, 2017). Although there is clearly a role for education settings in promoting positive mental health and wellbeing, teaching children strategies to cope with adversity, and reducing stigma, there are limits to this responsibility (O'Reilly et al., 2018). It is therefore important that educators work in partnership with specialist mental health services and the child's family in identifying and supporting need (Svirydzenka et al., 2016). We know that in many cases, educators have limited resources, support, and connections to mental health practitioners, and therefore feel overwhelmed. Research shows that those working in education feel that they have limited opportunities to debrief or process any emotional impact of responding to the mental health needs of the children and families with whom they work and lack the resources to manage issues with confidence (O'Reilly et al., 2018). This is concerning given that a survey from the United Kingdom conducted by the National Union of Teachers reported that nearly 50 per cent of teachers were considering leaving the profession and a core reason was their own mental wellbeing (The Guardian, 2017). It is evident, therefore, that educators need more support, need care for their own mental wellbeing, and need training and skills to communicate with children about mental health.

References

Adams, S., O'Reilly, M., and Karim, K. (2019). Why do teachers need to know about mental health? In C. Cardern (ed.), *Primary Teaching* (pp. 535–552). London: Sage Publications.

American Psychiatric Association. (2013). *Diagnostic and Statistical Manual of Mental Disorders* (5th ed.). Washington, DC: American Psychiatric Association.

Barrocas, A., Hankin, B., Young, J., and Abela, J. (2012). Rates of nonsuicidal self-injury in youth: age, sex, and behavioral methods in a community sample. *Pediatrics*, 130, 39–45.

Bor, W., Dean, A., and Najman, J. (2014). Are child and adolescent mental health problems increasing in the 21st century? A systematic review. *Australian and New Zealand Journal of Psychiatry*, 48(7), 606–616.

Brownlow, C., and Lamont-Mills, A. (2015). The production of the 'normal child': exploring co-constructions of parents, children and therapists. In M. O'Reilly and J. N. Lester (eds.), *The Palgrave Handbook of Child Mental Health: Discourse and Conversation Studies* (pp. 233–251). Basingstoke: Palgrave MacMillan.

Burman, E. (2008). *Deconstructing Developmental Psychology* (2nd ed.). London: Routledge.

Burns, I. M., Baylore, C., Dudgeon, B. J., Starks, H., and Yorkston, K. (2018). Health-care provider accommodations for patients with communication disorders. *Topics in Language Disorders*, 37(4), 311–333.

Chu, B., and Kendall, P. (2004). Positive associations of child involvement and treatment outcome within a manual-based cognitive behavioral treatment with anxiety. *Journal of Consulting and Clinical Psychology*, 72, 821–829.

Davis, L. (1995) *Enforcing Normalcy: Disability, Deafness, and the Body*. London: Verso.

Department for Education. (2018). Special educational needs and disability code of practice: 0 to 25 years. Available from: https://assets.publishing.service.gov.uk/government/uploads/system/uploads/attachment_data/file/398815/SEND_Code_of_Practice_January_2015.pdf [last accessed 16 December 2021].

Drew, P., Chatwin, J., and Collins, S. (2001). Conversation analysis: a method for research into interactions between patients and health-care practitioners. *Health Expectations*, 4(1), 58–70.

Frances, A. (2013). *Saving Normal: An Insider's Revolt against Out-of-Control Psychiatric Diagnosis, DSM-5, Big Pharma, and the Medicalisation of Ordinary Life*. New York, NY: HarperCollins.

Freed A. (1994). The form and function of questions in informal dyadic conversation. *Journal of Pragmatics*, 21, 621–644.

Gall, M. D. (1970). The use of questions in teaching. *Review of Educational Research*, 40(5), 707–721.

Hutchby, I., and Moran-Ellis, J. (1998). Situating children's competence. In I. Hutchby and J. Moran-Ellis (eds.), *Children and Social Competence: Arenas of Social Action* (pp. 7–26). London: The Falmer Press.

Karim, K. (2015). The value of conversation analysis: a child psychiatrist's perspective. In M. O'Reilly and J. N. Lester (eds.), *The Palgrave Handbook of Child Mental Health: Discourse and Conversation Studies* (pp. 25–41). Basingstoke: Palgrave MacMillan.

Karim, K., McSweeney, E., and O'Reilly, M. (in press). Communication in child mental health: improving engagement with families. In M. O'Reilly and J. Lester (eds.), *Improving Communication in Mental Health Settings: Evidence-Based Recommendations from Practitioner-Led Research*. London: Routledge.

Kiyimba, N., Lester, J., and O'Reilly, M. (2019). *Using Naturally Occurring Data in Health Research: A Practical Guide*. London: Springer.

Kiyimba, N., O'Reilly, M., and Lester, J. (2018). Agenda setting with children using the three wishes technique. *Journal of Child Health Care*, 22(3), 419–432.

Kiyimba, N., and O'Reilly, M. (2018). Reflecting on what 'you said' as a way of reintroducing difficult topics in child mental health assessments. *Child and Adolescent Mental Health*, 23(3), 148–154.

Kiyimba, N., and O'Reilly, M. (2020). The clinical use of Subjective Units of Distress scales (SUDs) in child mental health assessments: a thematic evaluation. *Journal of Mental Health*, 29(4), 418–423.

Larson, J. S. (1996). The World Health Organization's definition of health: social versus spiritual health. *Social Indicators Research*, 38, 181–192. https://doi.org/10.1007/BF00300458

Leiter, V. (2007). 'Nobody's just normal, you know': the social creation of developmental disability. *Social Science and Medicine*, 65(8), 1630–1641.

Lester, J., and O'Reilly, M. (2019). *Applied Conversation Analysis: Social Interaction in Institutional Settings*. Thousand Oaks, CA: Sage Publications.

Mash, E. J., and Hunsley, J. (2005). Special section: developing guidelines for the evidence-based assessment of child and adolescent disorders. *Journal of Child and Adolescent Psychology*, 34(3), 362–379.

Matheson, L. (2014). *Your Faithful Brain: Designed for So Much More!* Bloomington, IN: WestBow Press.

McCabe, R. (2006). Conversation analysis. In M. Slade and S. Priebe (eds.), *Choosing Methods in Mental Health Research: Mental Health Research from Theory to Practice* (pp. 24–46). Hove: Routledge.

O'Reilly, M., Adams, S., Whiteman, N., Hughes, J., Reilly, P., and Dogra, N. (2018). Whose responsibility is adolescent mental health in the UK? The perspectives of key stakeholders. *School Mental Health*, 10, 450–461.

O'Reilly, M., Hutchby, I., and Kiyimba, N. (2019). Children's competence in assessments. In J. Lamerichs, S. Danby, A. Bateman, and S. Ekberg (eds.), *Children's Social Competence in Mental Health Talk* (pp. 480–499). Basingstoke: Palgrave Macmillan.

O'Reilly, M., Karim, K., and Kiyimba, N. (2015). Question use in child mental health assessments and the challenges of listening to families. *British Journal of Psychiatry Open*, 1(2), 116–120.

O'Reilly, M., and Lester, J. (2017). *Examining Mental Health through Social Constructionism: The Language of Mental Health*. Basingstoke: Palgrave Macmillan.

O'Reilly M. Muskett, T., Karim, K., and Lester, J. (2020). Parents constructions of normality and pathology in child mental health assessments. *Sociology of Health and Illness*, 42(3), 544–564.

Persson, S., Hagquist, C., and Michelson, D. (2017). Young voices in mental health and care: exploring children's and adolescents' service experiences and preferences. *Clinical Child Psychology and Psychiatry*, 22(1), 140–151.

Prout, A., and James, A. (2015). A new paradigm for the sociology of childhood? Provenance, promise and problems. In A. James and A. Prout (eds.), *Constructing and Reconstructing Childhood: Contemporary Issues in the Sociological Study of Childhood* (Classic edition) (pp. 6–28). Abingdon: Routledge.

Public Health England. (2017). Secondary school staff get mental health 'first aid' training. Available from: www.gov.uk/government/news/secondary-school-staff-get-mental-health-first-aid-training [last accessed 16 December 2021].

Reinke, W. M., Stormont, M., Herman, K. C., Puri, R., and Goel, N. (2011). Supporting children's mental health in schools: teachers' perceptions of needs, roles and barriers. *School Psychology Quarterly*, 26(1), 1–13.

Rothi, D. M., Leavey, G., and Best, R. (2008). On the front-line: teachers as active observers of pupils' mental health. *Teaching and Teacher Education*, 24, 1217–1231.

Scott, D., Crossin, R., Ogeil, R., Smith, K., and Lubman, D. (2018). Exploring harms experienced by children aged 7 to 11 using ambulance attendance data: a

6-year comparison with adolescents aged 12–17. *International Journal of Environmental Research and Public Health*, 15, 1385–1398.

Shanley, D., Reid, G., and Evans, B. (2008) How parents seek help for children with mental health problems. *Administration and Policy in Mental Health*, 35, 135–146.

Svirydzenka, N., Aitken, J., and Dogra, N. (2016). Research and partnerships with schools. *Social Psychiatry and Psychiatric Epidemiology*, 51, 1203–1209.

The Guardian. (2017). *Demanding workload driving young teachers out of profession*. Available from: www.theguardian.com/education/2017/apr/15/demanding-workload-driving-young-teachers-out-of-profession [last accessed 16 December 2021].

Theobald, M. (2016). Achieving competence: the interactional features of children's storytelling. *Childhood*, 23(1), 87–104.

Theron, L. C. (2016). Toward a culturally and contextually sensitive understanding of resilience: privileging the voices of black, South African young people. *Journal of Adolescent Research*, 31, 635–670.

Thomas, F., Hansford, L., Ford, J., Wyatt, K., McCabe, R., and Byng, R. (2018). Moral narratives and mental health: rethinking understandings of distress and healthcare support in contexts of austerity and welfare reform. *Palgrave Communications*, 4(39).

Ungar, M. (2012). Researching and theorizing resilience across cultures and contexts. *Preventive Medicine*, 55(5), 387–389.

United Nations. (1989). *Conventions on the Rights of the Child*. New York, NY: United Nations.

Walsh, B. A., and Blewitt, P. (2006). The effect of questioning style during storybook reading on novel vocabulary acquisition of preschoolers. *Early Childhood Education Journal*, 33(4), 273–278.

Walsh, B. A., Sánchez, C., and Burnham, M. M. (2016). Shared storybook reading in head start: impact of questioning styles on the vocabulary of Hispanic dual language learners. *Early Childhood Education Journal*, 44(3), 263–273.

Walsh, R. L., and Hodge, K. A. (2018). Are we asking the right questions? An analysis of research on the effect of teachers' questioning on children's language during shared book reading with young children. *Journal of Early Childhood Literacy*, 18(2), 264–294.

Wolpe, J. (1969). *The Practice of Behavior Therapy*. New York, NY: Pergamon Press.

World Health Organization. (2014). *Mental health: A state of well-being*. Available from: www.who.int/features/factfiles/mental_health/en/ [last accessed 16 December 2021].

17 | Neurodiversity

LAURA STERPONI AND BETTY YU

Introduction

The inclusion of disabled[1] children in all aspects of education is acknowledged by the *United Nations Convention on the Rights of Persons with Disabilities* (United Nations, 2006) as a fundamental human right (Article 3). The United Nations Educational, Scientific, and Cultural Organization (UNESCO, 2003) has also identified inclusive education as an approach to address the learning needs of young children, particularly those who are vulnerable to marginalization. In the United States, the National Association for the Education of Young Children (NAEYC) and the Division of Early Childhood (DEC) of the Council for Exceptional Children affirm that 'early childhood inclusion embodies the values, policies, and practices that support the right of every infant and young child … to participate in a broad range of activities and contexts as full members of families, communities and society' (DEC/NAEYC, 2009).

Disability scholars argue that the practice of inclusive education, despite its robust rhetoric, often falls short of its promise because it tends to be conceived as simply positioning disabled children alongside non-disabled peers (Slee, 2011). For early childhood inclusive education to be truly transformative, a fundamental shift in the understanding of disability must occur (Acevedo & Nusbaum, 2020; Mackenzie, Cologon, & Fenech, 2016). Whereas disabilities are traditionally regarded as biopsychological deficits that require fixing, disability scholars and advocates have instead focused on dismantling the societal, institutional, attitudinal, and environmental barriers that prevent individuals from full participation (Burchardt, 2004; Tregaskis, 2004). They reframe disability as not only a biopsychological phenomenon but also a sociological and experiential one (World Health Organization, 2002). A shift towards a socially minded understanding of disability does not necessarily render individual interventions irrelevant, but foregrounds the removal of participatory barriers as the overarching goal.

[1] We adopt the terms *autistic, disabled*, or *on the autism spectrum*, consistent with the preferences of many disability and autistic advocates for identity-first language over person-first language (Brown, 2011).

Within the autistic community, the neurodiversity movement pushes for a similarly transformative understanding with regard to brain functioning and questions the very notions of normality and disability. Like biodiversity, which is seen as critical to the sustenance and health of ecosystems, neurodiversity asserts the value of neurological variation, promoting the recognition of different forms of brain wiring, which manifest in different ways of perceiving the world and others, none intrinsically defective or inferior (Brownlow & O'Dell, 2013; Silberman, 2015; Walker, 2012). All forms of neurological diversity are understood as natural states of variation. Differences are not posited as good or bad, especially not in reference to neurotypicality as the ideal. Conceptualizations of difference are offered that foreground lived experiences and embrace intersectionality and fluidity (Broderick & Ne'Eman, 2008; Brown, Ashkenazy, & Onaiwu, 2017; Milton, 2014a, 2014b). From this perspective, autism is regarded as both a difference and a disability, with disability being a function of the limitations caused by the lack of attention and accommodation to the needs of autistic persons (den Houting, 2018; Kapp, 2020).

The neurodiversity framework has brought about shifts in discourses and initiatives around autism that depart markedly from those of traditional clinical and educational practices. These include the endorsement of identity-first language (e.g. autistic person) over person-first terminology (e.g. person with autism) (Brown, 2011). Also include is the rejection of labels like 'high-functioning' versus 'low-functioning' autism because of the judgmental valences inherent in those labels and the ways in which they negate strengths and obscure challenges (Sequenzia, 2013). Neurodiversity advocates support educational and therapeutic programmes that affirm autistic identities and experiences and object to interventions designed to eliminate and mask autistic traits (Cage & Troxell-Whitman, 2019; Devita-Raeburn, 2016).

Although references to neurodiversity are rare in the early childhood education literature, there are natural alignments between the goals of inclusive education and the neurodiversity approach. Neurodiversity affirms the value of autism, promotes the achievement of self-directed goals, centers quality of life, and prioritizes the experiences and views of autistic individuals. Similarly, the Council for Exceptional Children's Division for Early Childhood (2018) identifies as essential inclusive practices: building on children's strengths, promoting interest-based learning within naturally occurring, meaningful routines, reducing barriers to participation and learning, and responding to families' priorities. These practices are promoted by the Early Childhood Technical Assistance Center as *authentic child assessments*

(2020a), *building on child strengths* (2020b) and *identifying child strengths* (2020c). Teachers usually rely on their own observations, as well as parent reports and developmental checklists as sources of information, but lack the tools and methods for systematically analysing and documenting displays of interests and strengths as they occur within naturally occurring interactions.

Contributions of Conversation Analysis to Inclusive and Neurodiversity-Affirming Education

The methods of conversation analysis (CA) contribute to the shared commitments of inclusive education and neurodiversity by: (1) surfacing dimensions of communicative competence in autistic children that were previously undocumented and largely unrecognized, and (2) identifying interactional processes that foster or constrain children's participation in communication exchanges. In this chapter, we demonstrate the ways in which CA methodology is uniquely suited for these aims and we review findings from CA studies illustrating this point. We will then offer examples of how early childhood educators might use insights from CA to identify autistic children's communicative competencies within everyday interactions, and to understand how interactions can be mediated to support their efforts of promoting inclusion and neurodiversity.

Surfacing Autistic Communicative Competence

Autism is defined diagnostically by difficulties in social interaction and communication, with a wide spectrum of linguistic competencies represented among autistic communicators, from non-verbal to highly verbal (American Psychological Association, 2013). While there is a growing body of studies examining strengths associated with autism across domains (Baron-Cohen, 2017; Remington & Fairnie, 2017; Van Hees, Moyson, & Roeyers, 2015), much of the current research and clinical literature about autistic interaction and communication reflects a deficit frame. The performance of autistic children is overwhelmingly measured against neurotypical norms and limited to clinical contexts; yet, the degree to which educators can understand autistic students through a strength-based lens is highly dependent on whether they are able to recognize the students' abilities in everyday contexts, especially when those abilities manifest in ways that are unconventional or unfamiliar (Vincent & Ralston, 2020).

Adopting a CA lens for observing autistic children's interaction and communication opens opportunities for discerning competencies that may be overlooked in traditional research and assessment methods. The observer/analyst, however, does not set out expressly to document moments of success. On the contrary, CA is a descriptive and not a prescriptive approach. In CA, what constitute moments of breakdown or progress are not determined by externally imposed concepts of 'inappropriate' or 'appropriate' behaviours, but are rather signalled by the participants themselves within the dynamics of the ongoing interaction. A breakdown, for example, might be made visible by a participant's initiation of a conversational repair (Geoffrey, Makoto, & Sidnell, 2013), where the speakers fix problems of (mis)understanding. Unconventional means of participation are not presumed to be problematic; nor are they ignored when they are referenced as sources of interactional trouble. By giving detailed attention to what autistic children actually do in interaction, CA studies can disrupt stereotypic understandings of autistic communication and suggest strategies for neurodiversity-affirming communication and teaching strategies.

Reframing Conversational Coherence

A common diagnostic trait and intervention target for autism is difficulties initiating and maintaining reciprocal interactions and conversations with others. These difficulties have been characterized in the clinical literature as difficulties staying on topic; difficulties providing novel, relevant information; perseveration; and decreased initiations and responses (Sng, Carter, & Stephenson, 2018). Correspondingly, most educational programmes targeting social and conversational skills have focused on lessening or eliminating these deficits in autistic students (Ke, Whalon, & Yun, 2017). One aspect that is rarely addressed in the intervention literature is how to facilitate change in the knowledge, perceptions, and attitudes of the teachers and other social partners so that they are better able to recognize and foster unique interactional competences that autistic children already display.

Ochs and Solomon (2005) observed that when conversational topics are difficult to understand, the autistic children in their study consistently remained engaged, but did so through expressions that were 'not quite in synch with the focal concern' yet still connected to the unfolding conversation (p. 158). One way the children accomplished this was by making a conversational contribution that was relevant in some way to the immediately prior turn, even if it did not fit the overarching scope of the larger conversation. Another strategy employed by some of the children for dealing with confusing personal statements shared by conversation partners was by invoking a piece of impersonal cultural knowledge that was topically related to the preceding personal statement. For example, one child responded to his mother's comment that it had been 'a long morning' by saying, 'In the summer, there's long days and short nights'. Whereas a traditional deficit-oriented perspective might have dismissed these types of utterances as incoherent, the authors showed that the children's contributions were proximally relevant and strategic. Though idiosyncratic from a neurotypical point of view, this conversation pattern reflects a capacity for details over the gestalt that autistic activist Phil Schawarz (2004) argues is intrinsically valuable.

In the excerpts below, we offer an example of repetitive language and delayed echolalia (also known as scripting), considered common symptoms of autism. The segments were extracted from video recordings of the everyday activities of an autistic child, Ben (pseudonym) and his family members (Sterponi's data corpus; more information can be found in Sterponi, deKirby, and Shankey, 2015). Diagnosed with autism at 3;6 years, Ben was 6;3 years old at the time of the video recording. His linguistic ability, as per the Mean Length of Utterance (MLU) measure (5.85), exceeded that of typically developing children of his age. The transcript was selected from bath time, a favourite moment of Ben's day. Throughout the duration of the bath, Ben was playing with his water toys and interacting with his mum, who was seated next to the bathtub.

Extract 17.1

1	Mum	Ben the water is cold.
2	(1.0)	
3	Mum	↑time to get out.
4	Ben	I'm not cold. I wanna stay in.
5	Mum	you'll get cold soon.
6	(3.0)	((mom gets up and looks for a towel under the sink))
7	Ben	winter is coming.

After approximately 15 minutes in the bath, Mum prompted Ben to get out of the bathtub (line 3), prefacing the directive with an account of the water getting cold (line 1). Albeit noncompliant, Ben's reply was highly resonant (Du Bois, Hobson, & Hobson, 2014) with Mum's preceding turn. He constructs his utterances ('I'm not cold. I wanna stay in') with parallel syntactic structure and repetition of words from her utterances ('the water is cold. time to get out'). Mum's next move (line 5) similarly mirrors Ben's turn in line 4. After a three-second pause, wherein both Ben and Mum seem to hold their respective preferred course of action – Ben extending the bath and Mum preparing for his exit from it – Ben utters the statement, 'winter is coming' (line 7). The utterance is consistent with what Ochs and Solomon (2005) referred to as *proximally relevant*. As discussed earlier, while this contribution is not on topic with the ongoing conversation in the conventional sense, the linkage of 'cold' and 'winter' demonstrates a sense of local coherence between conversational turns. Attention to this type of conversational composition enables us to notice how *parallelism and repetition across utterances and speakers* can be an alternate means of establishing conversational coherence and enabling speakers to make sense of one another.

Reframing Repetitive Speech

Extract 17.2 below is a continuation of the transcript (picking up from line 7) and illustrates the strategic and creative use of delayed echolalia, or scripted speech (the repetition of previously heard passages of talk, sometimes from movies and tv shows). Echolalia is another conversational feature that is widely cast as a pathological trait of autism in the clinical literature (Stiegler, 2015). Within autistic communities, however, echolalia is seen positively as a means of navigating conversational demands, conveying complex thoughts and emotions, communicating in times of stress, and providing comfort and pleasure (Arnold, 2019; Nolan & McBride, 2015; Yergeau, 2018). In the following excerpt, we highlight the ways in which *variation on repeated phrases* can be employed as an interactional resource.

Extract 17.2

7	Ben	winter is coming.
8	Mum	it is winter already Ben.
9	(1.0)	
10	Ben	winter is ↑comi::n':.
11	Mum	come on Ben. here's the towel.
12	Ben	you do not know cold.
13	Mum	are you thinking about game of thrones?
14	Ben	yeah ((giggling))

As discussed earlier, Ben's utterance in line 7 represents a proximally relevant contribution to the ongoing conversation and the utterance is taken up by Mum who engages by correcting the truth value of his statement (line 8). Ben then repeats his utterance with more emphasis placed on the last segment (line 10), with no indication that he intends to exit the bathtub. Mum delivers another prompt to end the bath, offering Ben a towel (line 11). Ben continues to stay put in the bath and utters another proximally relevant statement (line 12), 'you do not know cold'. At this point, Mum attributes the television show *Game of Thrones* as the potential source of Ben's scripted speech in the last few turns (line 13). In line 14, Ben both confirms and shows pleasure at her recognition.

The excerpt above demonstrates that echolalic speech should not be dismissed for being 'merely' repetitive. Repetitive speech at different points of an interactional flow can in fact serve as a means of creativity and renewal. Ben utters the quote 'winter is coming' from *Game of Thrones* twice (lines 7 and 10) but the second time in a perceivably different way. In this case, the persistent use of echolalic utterances as a response to Mum's command to get out of the bathtub functions as a strategic move to side-step noncompliance and direct conflict. Attention to utterance position and timing surfaces the ways in which scripted strips of speech can be creatively altered across turns and used strategically in interaction. These findings are consistent with Sterponi and Shankey's (2014) conclusions that far from being non-functional or arbitrary, echolalic speech can be a powerful and flexible resource to mark moment-by-moment affiliation or disaffiliation with other speakers.

The two examples offered highlight the importance of seeing children as competent communicators and understanding that competencies may not always manifest in ways that conform to neurotypical norms. Muskett (2017) suggested that adopting a CA frame of mind shifts the inquiry from '*Why do autistic children do X?*" to '*Why did* this *child just do X, and what did it mean* for them?' (p. 118). When competencies are redefined as an interactional accomplishment, shaped by what came before, and projecting what will follow, we create opportunities for children's efforts at communication to be recognized on their own terms.

Interactional Processes that Foster/Constrain Participation

Conversational analysis is built on the premise that interactions and conversations are co-constructed. Interactional outcomes are regarded as a shared responsibility and a collaborative phenomenon. Participants in an interaction actively and jointly construct and negotiate meaning as the conversation proceeds. This sense of shared effort at successful interaction is often missing from traditional special education programmes, where intervention goals specify only what new social skills the child is supposed to acquire, without accounting adequately for the contexts in which those skills are meant to be displayed, their interlocutor's contributions, or whether expectations for those skills are reasonable to begin with (Roberts, 2020). As a result, children's communicative performances are often judged as 'appropriate' or 'inappropriate' against normative standards and in the absence of context.

The problematic nature of decontextualized teaching was illustrated by Fasulo and Fiore (2007) in a CA study of therapist-child interactions in a social skills treatment centre. They found that therapists often insisted that their autistic students perform in ways deemed to be socially and linguistically appropriate even when those ways of interaction lacked fundamental characteristics of everyday conversational exchanges. For example, the children were expected to contribute to conversations around generic topics (e.g. 'What is a family?'), even though generic topics inherently lack *tellability*, or newsworthiness that would warrant conversation. The nature of the conversation prompt also signalled that the therapist was enacting a didactic interactional frame in which there were expected answers, thus raising the stakes of the conversation. Fasulo and Fiore described these dynamics as a violation of the trust that we all count on and offer each other in genuine conversations. The children in Fasulo and Fiore's study displayed frustration, resistance, and withdrawal in response to these demands.

Fasulo and Fiore's study is a reminder that while interlocutors can scaffold each other's interactions, they can also introduce obstacles and constraints (Goodwin & Heritage, 1990). Therefore, great caution is needed to avoid interpreting the quality of an interaction solely in terms of the child's perceived 'appropriate' or 'inappropriate' social skills without regard for the specific contingencies of interaction in which they are embedded (Gardner, 2009; Gardner & Forrester, 2010). To illustrate this point, we offer a CA analysis of a moment of breakdown in an interaction between a 6-year-old autistic child, Adam, and his parents.

The excerpt below was transcribed from a video recording taken originally as part of an initial assessment for speech and language therapy services offered by a local university in families' homes. At that time, Adam's parents described him as a mostly non-verbal communicator who made his needs known primarily through gestures, vocalization, body language, and some sign language. His speech was frequently echolalic. Adam's reliance on repetitive speech and non-verbal communication led his mother (Mummy) to characterize him as being 'able to speak, but not speaking'. In this recording, Adam and his parents were visiting a playground near their house that was part of Adam and his father's (Papi) weekday afternoon routine. In the moments prior, Adam was playing with an electronic flashcard reader while his parents watched.

Extract 17.3

1	Mommy	you wanna read [a book, [Adam? yes or no?
2	Adam	[((looks at mommy. Shakes head. Turns away forcefully.))
3	Papi	[it's ok
4	Mommy	no?
5	Papi	you don't want to read the book?
6	Adam	((points at Mommy and then in opposite direction))
7	Mommy	mommy go?
8	Adam	hhhh ((Grimace. Breathing hard. Palm open and up towards mom. Kicking.))
9	Mommy	say, mommy go
10	Adam	((Body relaxing)) mommy go=
11	Mommy	=ok ((Leaves table))

In line 1, Mommy asked Adam if he wanted to read a book, initiating a question that he answered decisively, albeit wordlessly, with a shaking of his head and a forceful turn away (line 2). The timing of his response occurred at a *transition-relevant place* (a point where one person could plausibly complete their turn), indicating that he not only understood her but could anticipate what she was asking him even before she finished her sentence. Papi's attempt to calm Adam (line 3) demonstrated a recognition of Adam's stance and affective intensity, even as Mommy pressed on with tags of 'Yes or no?' (line 1) and 'No?' (line 4). In line 5, Papi aligns with Mommy by elaborating on her question, 'You don't want to read the book?' Their continued request for clarification about Adam's stance, which he had already made quite clear, suggests that they were not actually in pursuit of information, but rather seeking a more satisfactory response (Keel, 2015). In line 6, in response to his parents' questions, Adam offered a repair. He elaborated on his initial response by using his finger to specify his mother as the subject, and then drawing a trajectory from her current position to a spot away from the table. As before, rather than responding to Adam's rather unambiguous nonverbal directive, Mommy continued her request for clarification (line 7). At this point, Adam became quite frustrated (line 8), which led Mommy to abandon her indirect prompts and to state explicitly, 'Say, mommy go' (line 9). Adam complied, relaxing visibly, and his mother reciprocated by leaving.

The excerpt above illustrates the contrast between 'talking correctly' and communicating successfully. Although Adam spoke little throughout the exchange, he showed himself to be a capable and collaborative interlocutor, employing timely turn-taking, contributing relevant and helpful responses, and offering clarifications and repairs. By contrast, in the context of this interaction, his parents were the ones violating pragmatic expectations. Whereas Adam was engaged in a good faith exchange about his preference for book reading, his parents were enacting a didactic exchange aimed at eliciting verbal utterances from him. The two objectives were at odds with each other, which ultimately resulted in a less than optimal interaction. These observations are consistent with Fasulo & Fiore's (2007) findings that adults' preoccupation with children's linguistic appropriateness often create barriers for the achievement of mutually enjoyable exchange and compromises interactional trust.

Focusing on Communicative Abilities

Whether as an analytic tool or simply as a way of seeing, CA has the potential to facilitate early childhood educators' engagement with neurodiversity-affirming and strength-based teaching. If verbal communication is understood as an accomplishment that is interactionally achieved, then efforts to support language development must focus on the interplay between the child, the people in their lives, and the environment in which they are all embedded. Rather than evaluating children's interactional, communication or language skills in isolation and as 'appropriate' or 'inappropriate', it is more informative to see whether there was a good *interactional fit* between the communicative partners, the environment, and the child. The educator can assist *both* the child and their partners in interaction and arrange a social and physical environment that is maximally supportive of communication. An example is in the area of peer relationships and inclusion. Whereas a child who has been identified with a disability is traditionally identified as the sole target of social skills intervention, educators can often make more of an impact by coaching neurotypical peers how to be a responsive friend and by bridging any interactional misalignments between peers. Peers can be taught, for example, to recognize and respond to less conventional means of expression, like 'stimming' or echolalia. This type of teaching approach affirms that successful interactions are not contingent upon children's ability to communicate in normative ways can be very effective in eliminating social and attitudinal barriers for children's participation.

In considering language as social action, teachers can offer children supportive interactions that align with their communicative intent, regardless of the form through which the intent is expressed. By attending to the contextual significance of children's vocalizations and actions within unfolding interactional sequences, teachers can become skilful in discerning the communicative functions of their students' contributions. By valuing function over form, teachers can convey that they prioritize what children are trying to share over how they do so. This opens the possibilities for more expanded interaction and joint attention. Autistic children who have more successful experiences with shared attention show the largest gains in both language and social development over time.

The notion of communication as more than spoken language directs educators' attention to the rich array of means through which children might make themselves known. It contrasts with the emphasis of most intervention programmes on the use of words and conventional written and picture symbols. Augmentative and alternative communication (AAC) has been found to be an effective support for many neurodivergent communicators. AAC refers to communication modalities that are used as an alternative to or as augmentation of an individual's speech (e.g. gestures, sign language, speech generation devices). A commonly expressed concern about AAC is that it would discourage learners from speaking. The research shows that children who experience success in communication as a result of having AAC supports tend to show an increase in both the amount and quality of speech they produce overall (Millar et al. 2006; Schlosser and Wendt, 2008). It is also important to emphasize that many speaking autistic people prefer to use AAC and advocate for the right to not speak (Donaldson, corbin, & McCoy, 2021).

Recommendations for Practice

In this chapter we have promoted a neurodiversity-affirming view of autism and leveraged insights from CA to unearth communicative resources and interactional dynamics that remain largely unacknowledged in most clinical studies. We have argued that CA complements the overlapping goals of early childhood special education and neurodiversity advocacy by offering an empirical method for examining naturally occurring interactions that is finely attuned to interactional phenomena that constitute communicative competence-in-interaction. Suggestions for how teachers can embed findings from this research into their practice include:

- Presume competence on part of the child and regard their actions as functional and meaningful. Explore the scope of young children's communicative attempts by paying attention to *when they happen*. Consider their contextual significance within interactional sequences.
- Support learners on the autism spectrum by observing, listening, and trying to understand their point of view. Listen beyond the words and consider their intent. For children who use many unconventional forms of communication, try to 'learn their language'. This may require talking with those close to the children to acquaint yourself with the unique meanings represented by the children's words and/or actions.
- Embrace and join in with students' unconventional forms of communication when you sense that they may be vehicles for connection. Often professionals are afraid to encourage 'problem behaviours' like echolalia or stimming, and as a consequence choose to ignore or actively extinguish them. By joining in, you may transform a solitary activity into an interactive one.
- Align the criteria for measuring students' progress with authentic and functional outcomes. A common measurement of progress in special education is for children to perform a social skill with 80 per cent accuracy. This implies there is an inherently correct way to display social competence irrespective of context, but that's not what happens in authentic interactions. Social communication is dynamic rather than mechanical and often better defined in qualitative rather than quantitative terms. Consider defining progress in terms of increased frequency and duration of successful participation in naturally occurring activities that are meaningful to the children and the people in their lives.

References

Acevedo, S., and Nusbaum, E. (2020). Autism, neurodiversity, and inclusive education. In *Oxford Research Encyclopedia of Education*. Oxford: Oxford University Press. https://doi.org/10.1093/acrefore/9780190264093.013.1260

American Psychological Association. (2013). *Diagnostic and Statistical Manual of Mental Disorders* (5th ed.). Arlington, VA: American Psychiatric Association.

Arnold, C. D. (2019). *Flipping the script: Prioritizing the autistic voice in the understanding of scripting as 'key to autistic identity'*. Ph.D. Dissertation. San

Francisco: University of San Francisco. Available from: https://repository.usfca.edu/diss/499 [last accessed 16 December 2021].

Baron-Cohen, S. (2017). Editorial perspective: neurodiversity – a revolutionary concept for autism and psychiatry. *Journal of Child Psychology and Psychiatry*, 58(6), 744–747. https://doi.org/10.1111/jcpp.12703

Broderick, A. A., and Ne'Eman, A. (2008). Autism as metaphor: narrative and counter-narrative. *International Journal of Inclusive Education*, 12(5–6), 459–476.

Brown, L. X. Z. (2011). *The significance of semantics: person-first language: why it matters*. Available from: www.autistichoya.com/2011/08/significance-of-semantics-person-first.html [last accesed 16 December 2021].

Brown, L. X. Z., Ashkenazy, E., and Onaiwu, M. (eds.). (2017). *All the Weight of Our Dreams: On Living Racialized Autism*: New York, NY: Dragon Bee Press.

Brownlow, C., and O'Dell, L. (2013). Autism as a form of biological citizenship. In J. Davidson and M. Orsini (eds.), *Worlds of Autism: Across the Spectrum of Neurological Difference* (pp. 97–114). Minnesota, MN: University of Minnesota Press.

Burchardt, T. (2004). Capabilities and disability: the capabilities framework and the social model of disability. *Disability & Society*, 19(7), 735–751. https://doi.org/10.1080/0968759042000284213

Cage, E., and Troxell-Whitman, Z. (2019). Understanding the reasons, contexts and costs of camouflaging for autistic adults. *Journal of Autism and Developmental Disorders*, 49(5), 1899–1911. https://doi.org/10.1007/s10803-018-03878-x

DEC/NAEYC. (2009). *Early childhood inclusion: a joint position statement of the Division for Early Childhood (DEC) and the National Association for the Education of Young Children (NAEYC)*. Chapel Hill: The University of North Carolina, FPG Child Development Institute.

den Houting, J. (2018). Neurodiversity: an insider's perspective. *Autism*, 23(2), 271–273. https://doi.org/10.1177/1362361318820762

Devita-Raeburn, E. (2016). The controversy over autism's most common therapy. *Spectrum*. Available from: www.spectrumnews.org/features/deep-dive/controversy-autisms-common-therapy/ [last accessed 16 December 2021].

Division for Early Childhood. (2018). *Division for Early Childhood Recommended Practices: A Quick Overview*. Available from: www.dec-sped.org/dec-recommended-practices [last accessed 16 December 2021].

Donaldson, A.L., corbin, e. and McCoy, J. (2021). "Everyone Deserves AAC": Preliminary Study of the Experiences of Speaking Autistic Adults Who Use Augmentative and Alternative Communication. *Perspectives*, 6(2), 315–326

Du Bois, J. W., Hobson, P. R., and Hobson, J. A. (2014). Dialogic resonance and intersubjective engagement in autism. *Cognitive Linguistics*, 25(3), 411–441.

Early Childhood Technical Assistance Center. (2020a). *Authentic child assessment*. Available from: https://ectacenter.org/~pdfs/decrp/PGP_ASM3_authentic_2018.pdf [last accessed 16 December 2021].

Early Childhood Technical Assistance Center. (2020b). *Building on child strengths*. Available from: https://ectacenter.org/~pdfs/decrp/PGP_ASM4_buildingstrengths_2018.pdf [last accessed 16 December 2021].

Early Childhood Technical Assistance Center. (2020c). *Identifying child strengths.* Available from: https://ectacenter.org/~pdfs/decrp/PGP_ASM5_identifying strengths_2018.pdf [last accessed 16 December 2021].

Fasulo, A., and Fiore, F. (2007). A valid person: non-competence as a conversational outcome. In A. Hepburn and S. Wiggins (eds.), *Discursive Research in Practice.* Cambridge: Cambridge University Press.

Gardner, H. (2009). Applying conversation analysis to interactions with atypically developing children. *Clinical Linguistics & Phonetics*, 23(8), 551–554.

Gardner, H., and Forrester, M. (2010). *Analysing Interactions in Childhood: Insights from Conversation Analysis.* Chichester: John Wiley.

Geoffrey, R., Makoto, H., and Sidnell, J. (eds.). (2013). *Conversational Repair and Human Understanding.* Cambridge: Cambridge University Press.

Goodwin, C., and Heritage, J. (1990). Conversation analysis. *Annual Review of Anthropology*, 19, 283–307.

Kapp, S. K. (ed.) (2020). *Autistic Community and the Neurodiversity Movement: Stories from the Frontline.* Singapore: Springer Nature.

Ke, F., Whalon, K., and Yun, J. (2017). Social skill interventions for youth and adults with autism spectrum disorder: a systematic review. *Review of Educational Research*, 88(1), 3–42. https://doi.org/10.3102/0034654317740334

Keel, S. (2015). Young children's embodied pursuits of a response to their initial assessments. *Journal of Pragmatics*, 75, 1–24. https://doi.org/10.1016/j.pragma.2014.10.005

Mackenzie, M., Cologon, K., and Fenech, M. (2016). 'Embracing everybody': approaching the inclusive early childhood education of a child labelled with autism from a social relational understanding of disability. *Australasian Journal of Early Childhood*, 41(2), 4–12. https://doi.org/10.1177/183693911604100202

Millar, D. C., Light, J. C., and Schlosser, R. W. (2006). The Impact of Augmentative and Alternative Communication Intervention on the Speech Production of Individuals With Developmental Disabilities: A Research Review. *Journal of Speech, Language & Hearing Research*, 49, 248-264. doi: doi:10.1044/1092-4388(2006/021)

Milton, D. (2014a). Autistic expertise: a critical reflection on the production of knowledge in autism studies. *Autism*, 18(7), 794–802.

Milton, D. (2014b). Embodied sociality and the conditioned relativism of dispositional diversity. *Autonomy, the Critical Journal of Interdisciplinary Autism Studies*, 1(3), 1–7.

Muskett, T. (2017). Using conversation analysis to assess the language and communication of people on the autism spectrum: a case-based tutorial. In M. O'Reilly, J. N. Lester, and T. Muskett (eds.), *A Practical Guide to Social Interaction Research in Autism Spectrum Disorders* (pp. 117–140). Basingstoke: Palgrave Macmillan.

Nolan, J., and McBride, M. (2015). Embodied semiosis: autistic 'stimming' as sensory praxis. In P. P. Trifonas (ed.), *International Handbook of Semiotics* (pp. 1069–1078). Dordrecht: Springer Netherlands.

Ochs, E., and Solomon, O. (2005). Practical logic and autism. In C. Casey and R. Edgerton (eds.), *A Companion to Psychological Anthropology: Modernity and Psychocultural Change* (pp. 140–167). Malden, MA: Wiley-Blackwell.

Remington, A., and Fairnie, J. (2017). A sound advantage: increased auditory capacity in autism. *Cognition*, 166, 459–465.

Roberts, J. (2020). *'Training' social skills is dehumanizing*. Available from: https://therapistndc.org/social-skills-training/ [last accessed 16 December 2021].

Schlosser, R. W., and Wendt, O. (2008). Effects of Augmentative and Alternative Communication Intervention on Speech Production in Children With Autism: A Systematic Review. *American Journal of Speech - Language Pathology*, 17, 212-230. doi:doi:10.1044/1058-0360(2008/021

Schwarz, P. (2004). Building alliances: community identity and the role of allies in autistic self-advocacy. In S. M. Shore (ed.), *Ask and Tell: Self-Advocacy and Disclosure for People on the Autism Spectrum* (pp. 143–176). Shawnee Mission: Autism/Asperger Network.

Sequenzia, A. (2013). *More problems with functioning labels*. Available from: https://ollibean.com/problems-functioning-labels/ [last accessed 16 December 2021].

Silberman, S. (2015). *Neurotribes: The Legacy of Autism and the Future of Neurodiversity*. New York, NY: Avery Press.

Slee, R. (2011). *The Irregular School: Exclusion, Schooling and Inclusive Education*. Abingdon: Taylor & Francis.

Sng, C. Y., Carter, M., and Stephenson, J. (2018). A systematic review of the comparative pragmatic differences in conversational skills of individuals with autism. *Autism & Developmental Language Impairments*, 3, 2396941518803806. https://doi.org/10.1177/2396941518803806

Sterponi, L., and Shankey, J. (2014). Rethinking echolalia: repetition as interactional resource in the communication of a child with autism. *Journal of Child Language*, 41(2), 275–304. http://dx.doi.org/10.1017/S0305000912000682

Sterponi, L., de Kirby, K., and Shankey, J. (2015). Rethinking language in autism. *Autism*, 19(5), 517–526. https://doi.org/10.1177/1362361314537125

Stiegler, L. N. (2015). Examining the echolalia literature: where do speech-language pathologists stand? *American Journal of Speech-Language Pathology*, 24(4), 750–762. https://doi.org/10.1044/2015_AJSLP-14-0166

Tregaskis, C. (2004). *Constructions of Disability*. London: Routledge.

UNESCO. (2003). *Overcoming exclusion through inclusive approaches in education: a challenge & a vision*. Available from: http://unesdoc.unesco.org/images/0013/001347/134785e.pdf [last accessed 16 December 2021].

United Nations. (2006). *Convention on the rights of persons with disabilities*. Available from: www.un.org/development/desa/disabilities/convention-on-the-rights-of-persons-with-disabilities.html [last accessed 16 December 2021].

Van Hees, V., Moyson, T., and Roeyers, H. (2015). Higher education experiences of students with autism spectrum disorder: challenges, benefits and support needs. *Journal of Autism and Developmental Disorders*, 45(6), 1673–1688.

Vincent, J., and Ralston, K. (2020). Trainee teachers' knowledge of autism: implications for understanding and inclusive practice. *Oxford Review of Education*, 46(2), 202–221. https://doi.org/10.1080/03054985.2019.1645651

Walker, N. (2012). Throw away the master's tools: liberating ourselves from the pathology paradigm. In J. Bascom (ed.), *Loud Hands: Autistic People, Speaking* (pp. 225–237). Washington, DC: The Autistic Press.

World Health Organization. (2002). *Towards a Common Language for Functioning, Disability, and Health: ICF*. Geneva: World Health Organization.

Yergeau, M. (2018). *Authoring Autism: On Rhetoric and Neurological Queerness*. Durham: Duke University Press.

18 | Friendships

MARYANNE THEOBALD

Introduction

Children seek to interact with peers, be included as part of a group and make friends. Making friends has a reflexive effect in that having friends increases the likelihood of making and keeping more friends. Friends offer support for children in times of uncertainty, such as starting at school (Danby, 2008; Dunn, 2004). These successful relationships in the early years lead to increased general knowledge and feelings of wellbeing, all necessary for successful life and work outcomes (Hartup, 2000; Laursen et al., 2007). Feelings of wellbeing can shield from loneliness and are important at any life stage.

Three characteristics differentiate friendships from other relationships. The first characteristic is that friendships are mutual, there is reciprocal connection. The second is that friendship is enduring, a relationship that is built and maintained over time. The third characteristic of friendship is that being a friend involves caring and feelings of closeness (Corsaro, 2003, 2017; Danby, 2008; Hartup, 2000; Theobald et al. 2020). These characteristics persist whether physically present or not.

Identifying friendship characteristics involves a consciousness of one's own emotions and understanding the effect of these on others (Björk-Willén, 2017; Corsaro, 2003). Although they may have varied capacities to express these emotions, even very young children have deep feelings of intimacy and long-lasting friendships (Corsaro, 2003; Theobald et al., 2020) and attend seriously to matters of participation and friendship. Children do have their own strategies for making and maintaining friends. Studies by both Danby et al. (2012) and Theobald et al. (2019) confirm a willingness by children to make connections with others. Their unique methods of interviewing children about making friends when starting a new school – and how they would make friends if they didn't share a common language – demonstrate the depth of children's competencies in making friends and the interactions involved. Playing with active toys and games such as play-dough, soccer or musical statues, making a group, or learning a common language, were identified by children as strategies that can support or hinder opportunities for others to participate and make friends. It is toward these intricate actions and child-coordinated activities that teachers should pay close attention.

The concept of friendship has been largely studied from a developmental focus that assumes an individual's social skills are the reason for a child being able to make friends or not. From this viewpoint, friendship is a theoretical notion that is generally thought of as a 'natural' *outcome* of childhood (Corsaro, 2017; Garcia-Sanchez, 2017). While providing useful observations about ways to improve an individual's strategies for making friends, this *outcome* view of friendship can overlook external elements such as the influences of the teachers' knowledge and understanding of children's relationships, how children's friendships are valued in the context and how children's agency in making friends is fostered (Carter & Nutbrown, 2016. Informed by sociology, a *process* approach to studying children's friendships (Corsaro, 2017), alternatively, identifies the interplay between an individual, the peer culture, and the social context.

A *process* approach emphasizes the criticality of the surrounding social context for children's opportunities to participate and make friends. Conversation analysis (Sacks, 1995; Sidnell & Stivers, 2012 in particular employs a process approach well suited to studying the interactional process of children's friendships. Conversation analysis closely examines the processes of interactions as they unfold and can be considered a micro analysis that highlights the fluidity of children's opportunities for making friends according to friendship. It is this approach that demonstrates how friendship is built and maintained within peer culture.

Responsive and respectful relationships are principal elements of early childhood curricula in many countries, with play the main context in and through which children make friends. Playing and 'doing things together' enable children to establish common interests, shared experiences, and opportunities for friendship (Corsaro, 2017, p. xii). The more children spend time with others the better equipped they are for making friends and the more friends they can make (Vaughn et al., 2000, 2001; Coelho et al., 2017). These factors have consequences for children's ongoing peer culture.

Play as a context in and through which friendships are constructed requires that children have a local understanding of what 'play' is in that setting, and how the 'play' gets done. This chapter presents play extracts collected in inner-city early childhood education centres and schools in Queensland, Australia. Analyses of these extracts highlight actual play processes of accessing play, using toys and objects, playing games, and joint projects to identify that being included and making friends is associated with the ongoing, inter-dependent actions of peers. Recommendations from the Process Approach to Building Friendships (PABF) Toolkit are presented to guide children's play with peers in early years settings so that friendships can develop.

Accessing Play

Joining play that is already established can be challenging. Teachers may encourage children to ask, 'Can I play?', as a way to enter play (Paley, 1993). This strategy, often offered by teachers, emphasizes a classroom moral order that focuses on including all children in play. Responding to what appears to be a simple question, 'Can I play?', is complex for children. And while underpinned by good intentions, 'no' is a legitimate response to this closed question, even though the question sets up an expectation of a positive response. Extract 18.1, from Theobald et al.'s (2017) study of children's friendships in a culturally and linguistically diverse preschool, highlights what can sometimes occur when an explicit request to play is used to gain play entry.

Extract 18.1 Requesting play access

01	SAM:	can I play with you:::?
02	RAJ:	(build) (the wa:ll)
03	TEA:	Um I think (.) u:m Samir was just asking you
04		Something
05		*pointing at Samir*
06	SAM:	can I play with you:::?
07	RAJ:	*shakes head*
08	RAJ:	but (.) you can play with [this]
09		[*points to blocks*]
10		(0.4)
11	SAM:	[ME::: (.) AND YOU:::,]
12		[*moves closely to Raj's face*]
13	RAJ:	[*gaze to teacher*]
14		[oka::y]
15	SAM:	*moves next to Raj*
16	TEA:	*leaves to get toy dinosaurs*
17	RAJ:	*walks away from Samir*

Samir's play entry here is marked by the teacher as she points out to Raj, 'I think Samir was just asking you something'. Samir asks, 'can I play with you', again in a creaky voice and with a foot shuffle that together display uncertainty. The teacher's attention to Samir's play request marks to Raj that his response here is under scrutiny. Raj avoids eye contact with Samir, and points to the blocks, shifting focus away from himself and to an inanimate object. By pointing to the blocks, Raj attempts to take away the responsibility of playing 'with' Samir, but still is technically agreeing for Samir to be involved in the play by using the relevant objects. The deflection is noticed by Samir who responds by moving very close to Raj and asks again, loudly. After gazing to the teacher, Raj responds, 'okay'. Raj's gaze highlights his awareness that the teacher is monitoring the interaction and brings to the fore the underpinning social expectation that he will play with Samir. The teacher asks about getting dinosaurs and leaves the block area.

In this interaction, the request to play was granted, however, the ongoing interaction was not sustained after the teacher left. The unfolding events above draws attention to the subsequent actions of teacher-imposed rather than peer-mediated sequences of play. Teachers can facilitate play entry in such ways, but these teacher-imposed approaches may not always be successful. An exception is Paley's (1993) classic study of a teacher who created a classroom rule, 'you can't say you can't play'. At first, the children rejected the rule, however, over time, a more inclusive social order of the classroom resulted. Rules, however, can create a division in the social order of the classroom, and children can ignore rules (McLeod et al., 2015). These studies illustrate how classroom expectation and rules have the potential to shift peer culture. By working *with* children to establish rules, teachers may have more success in their attempts to create harmonious relationships.

Critically, Extract 18.2 identifies an alternate technique for supporting children's access to play. This interaction, from the same study as Extract 18.1, takes place in the sand pit. Analysis identifies how teachers can facilitate play access and participation in a more seamless way using a pedagogy of 'notice, recognize, and respond' (Cowie & Bell, 1999). In this strategy, teachers notice children's input, recognize its significance, and respond in a way to reinforce a learning opportunity (Cowie & Bell, 1999). It is the responsivity of the teacher's turn that can create opportunities for friendship.

Extract 18.2 Seamless access to play

01 TEA: here comes Sa↑mi::r
02 DAN: come ↑o::n,
03 TEA: [[wait a minute Sami:r's coming with some
04 ↑↑mo:re
05 DAN: [[↑ba ↑ba ↑bao::w ↑ba ↑ba ↑ba:::
06 CHA: [[*points to hose, gaze to Samir*

```
07  MAN:  ↑there the:re ((gaze to Samir))
08  OWE:  he::re got some water
09  TEA:  yeah and [Sami:rs got some too:: ]
10                  [gaze to Samir]
11        that's container number ↑three:::, with Samir
12  SAM:  waits for a turn to pour water
13  TEA:  see if we've got any water coming out
14  SAM:  pours water into the hose
14  SAM:  >and another< (.) and another [another ]
15  TEA:                                [and some ]
16        ↑mo::re,
17        Looks to next child
```

Samir's entry into an existing play interaction is more seamless in this example. Samir is coming back from the tap with a bucket of water. Prior to the interaction presented here, Samir had been playing on the periphery of a group of children involved with pouring water from buckets into a long hose to see if they could fill up the hose.

The teacher paves the way for Samir's entry into the interaction by saying, 'Here comes Samir'. This simple comment, or 'noticing' by the teacher, brings Samir's possible involvement in the group's joint project to the group's attention. In response to the teacher's observation, Charles points and makes eye contact with Samir, facilitating Samir's inclusion in the activity. Manilla also directs Samir. A role is created in the play, as Samir is encouraged to be involved by bringing his bucket of water to their activity. The activity of pouring water into the hose and announcing, 'more water', marks Samir's membership in the game.

This extract contrasts with the interaction of Extract 18.1 in that there is no negotiation by Samir or the teacher to access the play. Neither is the play interrupted by the question, 'Can I play?', and Samir's participation into the activity is smooth. The teacher's noticing of Samir's aligned actions highlighted that Samir was engaged in an action that is recognizably relevant to the already established play. This noticing provided a critical transition point where Samir successfully transitioned to member of the play and contributed to the group's joint project. This seamless entry resulted in Samir's sustained participation as the play continued even when the teacher left the group. A consideration of the role of the teacher is important here, as it is part of a teacher's responsibility to facilitate play as this is critical for a sustained engagement that enables children to establish common interests and opportunities for making friends.

Objects

Objects, such as blocks, balls, or other play toys, can be useful in facilitating interaction. Objects can highlight similarities in world views and common interests, creating 'belonging' (Iqbal et al., 2017). Björk-Willén (2017) identified how the objects of alphabet wall charts became a focus of joint attention for four children in their study, who all had different language backgrounds. Working out the names of the pictures on the chart in their shared common language (Swedish) gave a shared focus that facilitated their interaction. Other studies (Kultti & Pramling, 2015) have identified that toy objects create ways for children to communicate with others even when they have developing verbal skills. These studies highlight how children strategically use objects to negotiate their participation and that of others, and how a teacher similarly use objects to enhance children's friendship opportunities in play.

Demonstrating the value of introducing new play objects in the next example, from Theobald et al. (2017), toy dinosaurs provided by the teacher facilitated interaction between Samir, Frank, Owen, and Raj, and assisted Samir to become part of the existing block play. Here, in this example, the teacher has just brought back a box of toy dinosaur figurines to the block corner where the children had been building a 'dinosaur city' with the blocks.

Extract 18.3 Introducing objects

SAM: *picks up a winged toy dinosaur from floor*
SAM: [↑doo::: ↑dee:::: .shhhh]
[flies dinosaur overhead]
j'dee:::: no::::::
wa:::a::::::::::::::::::::: (0.4) wa::::
wa:::::::: wa::::::::
RAJ: [woo::::]
[brings dinosaur to Owen]
wee:::::::::::
Owen's and Raj's dinosaurs fight
wo::::::::::::: (.) wa:::
[↑chop
[*bashes dinosaur on Owen's dinosaur]*
FRA: >look ↑at< (0.4) look at
my upside down one
↑↑wo:::::h ↑↑wa ↑↑wa ↑↑wa:::::::h
it's upside down
OWE: and this one can fly:: (0.4) and it can fly

```
19          upside down (0.4) mine can fly upside do::wn
20   SAM:   [woo::::::h woo:::::::h]
21          [gazes at Owen,Dan & Frank, inverts dinosaur]
22   RAJ:   [dama::: dama::::: ]
23          [bashes dinosaur near Samir]
24   OWE:   [ROA:::::::::::::R]
25          [dinosaur flying near Raj & Samir]
25   SAM:   a::::::::h
26          [gaze to Owen]
27   OWE:   okay (0.4) I can't kill you do::wn,
```

The introduction of plastic dinosaur toys shifts the focus for the children in this interaction from building the city to manipulating the objects. The objects offer Samir an opportunity to be involved as an active member of the play scenario. Gazing at Owen, Daniel, and Frank, Samir copies their actions, inverting his dinosaur in a similar way. Using an interactional strategy identified as 'shadowing' (Björk-Willén, 2007), Samir engages in similar activities that display to others he is a participating member of the 'dinosaur city' play and expresses his membership in multimodal ways. Samir's multimodal moves are responded to positively as Raj and Owen engage him in a dinosaur play fight.

Objects can be resources also for children to control others. Social or class divides, and competition can result, when objects are brought into play. For example, Bateman's study of children in a Welsh school found that children used physical objects of an apple or a playground hut to include or exclude others (Bateman, 2011; Bateman & Church, 2017). Possible negative consequences may emerge when including objects to facilitate play. Teachers need to be aware that these possible negative consequences, while unintended, may emerge.

Even imaginary objects become tools for children to manipulate the actions and involvement of peers. Children 'design' new uses for objects different to the object's original intention, resulting in objects becoming symbols of something else but relevant to the ongoing play (Kultti & Pramling Samuelsson, 2017). In Cobb-Moore et al.'s. (2010) study, an arch shape block became a locked door that only some children were able to 'unlock'. The children created elaborate strategies in the game to overcome the 'locked' door. This use of an imaginary object was also noted in Danby et al.'s. (2017) study of children playing a computer game, where a sound in the game became a pretend gun and children's success, or not, in the game governed whose turn was next. Typically, though, objects that can be transformed into different play objects provide children with more opportunities to co-create play, and thus establish common interests or shared goals.

Games

Being included in games provides children with opportunities to participate and organize their peer culture. Common interests can be found in all types of game play, including when children play games with rules, such as hide and seek, or spontaneous, made-up games. Games typically have 'a category set of players' with actions associated with these players (Sacks, 1995, p. 490). Being included in game play requires children to have a local understanding of the actions and roles within the game (Cromdal, 2009; Danby et al., 2017). For spontaneous, made-up games, these rules and roles are often created as the play evolves.

Children take on a particular role or position or are designated a role in games. Such positions are not fixed; rather members can be substituted with other children so that all necessary positions are filled (Butler 2008; Sacks, 1995). In games that follow a particular structure or rules, such as baseball, cricket, or tennis, there may be a limited number of places for members (Butler, 2008). When the correct number of children for a game are found, any children thereafter would be excluded. Ongoing participation in procedural games is contingent on holding a play position in the game, such as being the batter or the bowler in baseball or cricket or being a server and receiver in tennis.

Some game positions, or roles, offer more desirable social consequences than other positions. One example would be the children who are owners of the game or take on a position that instigates power or control. Butler et al. (2016) confirmed this criticality of game ownership, finding that recruiting members for a game divided peers into players and non-players. These strategies are effective in controlling the activities of others, and work to foster or impede participation and opportunities for friendship.

Common game interests are ways for children to build friendships. Having an idea for a game, and having support for that idea, has interactional collateral that steers the play. The next extract from Theobald's (2013) study of preschool children's participation and social order in the playground demonstrates the importance of 'surveying the scene' (Theobald et al., 2020) and forming alliances as a strategy for being part of the ongoing play. Two children, Paddy and Becky, are in dispute over whose idea for the game will be played. Paddy had an idea of a bowling game, and Becky claimed the items for a pretend school. As their dispute reaches a standoff, Jack enters the play setting, asking to have some of the game objects.

Extract 18.4 Ideas and game play

01	PAD:	w[ell you- ((*to Becky*))
02	JAC:	[*runs to take the two balls from cones*]
03		[can I have a-]
04	PAD:	((moves to cones))
05	JAC:	[can I have a tennis ball?
06	PAD:	[*takes the balls*
07		[naaa?-]
08	JAC:	[oh plea:se?]
09		*gaze to Paddy, fists clenched by side*
10	PAD:	*shakes head*
11	JAC:	[How about we get two ?]
12	PAD:	wh:y.
13		[*stands tapping balls together*]
14	JAC:	[*gaze to Paddy*]
15		[Paddy you're not allo:wed to-]
16	PAD:	[*hands Jack one ball*]
17		[but-but-bu- if you made (.)mine.]
18		it's a bowling? thing.
19	BEC:	[gazes at Jack and Paddy]
20		[*lifts and kicks tunnel*]
21		[well this is my school]
22		*moves away*
23	JAC:	no? how about-how about? we (.) do this.
24		*moves tunnel downstairs*
25		NATHAN I'VE GOT A GOOD IDEA
26		WHAT WE COULD DO WITH THE ROLLING BALL
27	PAD:	*moves close to Jack*
28	NAT:	*joins play space*
29		oh ye?::ah
30	PAD:	[*gaze to Jack*]
31		[ana-an-and=]
32	JAC:	[and it goes down there]
33		[*rolls ball through tunnel*]
34	PAD:	ye?::ah.
35	JAC:	yeah.
36	PAD:	[I got an idea AND I'VE GOT ANOTHER IDEA]
37		[*gaze to Jack & Nathan*]
38	JAC:	[what?]
39		[*gaze to Paddy*]
40	PAD:	I'll put these on the side so it won't fall off,

```
41          [places cones on either side of tunnel]
42          [ye:ah ]
43   BEC:   returns and places ball into tunnel
```

In this example, Jack enters the play to take two balls from the group of objects Paddy and Becky were using. Resisting Jack at first, Jack reminds Paddy of the playground rules, that he is not allowed to keep the shared objects to himself. Paddy releases two balls to Jack and proposes that Jack play his bowling game. Becky kicks the tunnel away, appearing to give up on her claim to the game idea. Jack takes that moment to propose a new idea for the objects, which is similar to Paddy's. As Jack recruits Nathan as a new member in the game, Paddy strategically aligns with Jack's idea for the game, perhaps seeing that this is gaining support, and that Becky has retreated. Although Paddy had to forgo his own idea for the game, aligning himself with Jack has now formed a majority within the group.

Children make alliances in their quest to achieve ownership of ideas and materials. Having an idea for a game, supported by others, can lead to winning a dispute and that game idea being used in the ongoing play and interaction. If others support another's game idea, children have more chance that their own game idea will be played. It is likely also that if their game idea is selected, they will be the owner of the game, and thus the one in charge of decisions and unfolding events (Theobald, 2013). If ownership is not possible, the preferred next option is to be a member of the majority. Aligning with the majority is strategic because 'at least one of them will be the leader' (Sacks, 1995, p. 170). It is being part of the majority that enables influence on the ongoing game events, an influence that ensures continued involvement in the play. While the teacher was not involved in this play interaction, identifying how children can be involved in an ongoing game is one way that teachers might assist children to find shared interests with peers, critical for enhancing friendships.

Joint Projects

Joint projects with shared goals are resources teachers can use to support children's interactions and opportunities to build friendships. In the next example, from Theobald et al. (2017), a group of preschool-aged children are playing in a sandpit. The children are pouring water from containers into a long hose. The teacher's question asks how many containers it takes before the water comes out of the hose. This question prompts a joint activity with a shared goal and was successful in encouraging participation among the group of children.

Extract 18.5 Joint water project

01	TEA:	Tony (.) did you ↑work out how much water you
02		needed to put in the hose before it came out
03		the other ↑end?
04	TON:	↑no,
06	TON:	*shrugs, gaze to Teacher*
07	TEA:	anyone worked out how many containers,
08		of water you had to ↑put ↑in?-
09	MAN:	↑u:::m,
10	TEA:	-to make it come ↑ou:t?
11	MAN:	[↑fi:ve,]
12	MAN:	[*holds up five fingers*]
13	CHA:	↑no::,
14	TEA:	anybody else ↑count them?
15	TON:	three?
16	TEA:	you had ↑three:::?
17	TON:	three at the end (0.6) okay.
18	TON:	CO:ME ON GU:::YS,
19	TON:	*points to the hose*
20	CHA:	[*pours in water*]
21	DAN:	[*brings another container of water*]
22	TEA:	[is that the first] container;or the second one?
23	TON:	[dum dum ↑dum ↑du:::n,] (0.4) ↑↑let's ↑↑get
24		↑↑water (0.4) ↑get ↑the ↑wate::r,
25		let's get the ↑↑wata::[:r]
27	TEA:	[so]↑now we're ↑putting in
28		number ↑↑two:::,

The extract commences with the teacher questioning Tony about how many containers were needed to fill the hoses. Tony shrugs and the teacher recycles the question to include the others by saying, 'anyone' (line 7). By using the indefinite pronoun, the teacher does not specify the recipient but instead opens up the question to *any* of the children. Manila replies holding up five fingers on her hand. When Charles disagrees with Manilla's answer, the teacher increases the specificity of her question, asking if anybody else (i.e. other than Manila, thereby expanding participation in the problem solving) had counted the containers. The teacher's continued interrogatives about the number of containers suggest there is a problem that needs solving.

Tony's directive, 'Come on Guys', is a call for participation. This turn and the children's next actions make explicit the joint project going forward.

The teacher's commentary about the number of containers used keeps the children's attention on the joint project and shared goal. Tony's high-pitched calls for water mark his excitement and alert the other children to the joint project. The teacher's continued questioning creates clear entry points for each child to participate, and a systematic turn-taking process is established. The focus on adding the water does not charge any one child with the responsibility of 'playing with' another, and the possible implications of what this might mean. The teacher's intervention results in an inclusive activity, in which *any* one can take part. Making explicit a common goal for the children to work towards helps children to feel aligned with each other and that they belong to the group.

Pretend Play

Pretend play offers children a way to make friends through exploring and creating roles and storylines that focus on joint interests. In make-believe games, certain roles, such as being a teacher or police officer, makes taking charge or making rules legitimate, expected activities. As such, children in these roles have more opportunity to direct others and the circumstances, and so manage their own participation and that of others (Theobald & Danby, 2019). While the link between pretend play and children's development is still not clear (Lilliard et al., 2013), we do know that children use pretend games also to build alliances with others and enforce their own social positions (Weisberg, 2015). The blurring of 'pretend' and 'real' in pretend play has implications for friendship as social orders are reassembled.

Intersubjectivity or shared understanding is a key part of pretend play (Göncü, 1993; Theobald, 2013). As children co-create an imaginary scene, they shift in, out, and between roles, displaying an intricate interplay between reality and pretence (Fleer, 2013). Children use explicit announcements and proposals about the possible next events in the pretend play scenario (Kyratzis, 2014). This creation of 'play scripts' can occur whilst children are in role, as their talk during the play scenario works to direct the play and require children to engage in meta-narratives (Danby et al., 2017; Kultti & Pramling Samuelsson, 2017, p. 12). These studies identify that while young children can competently achieve shared understanding in play, teachers might assist children by helping them to better identify the rules and roles associated with the play.

Friendships in Culturally and Linguistically Diverse Settings

Language and interactional resources become of particular importance in culturally and linguistically diverse settings. Barley's (2017) study in a culturally and linguistically diverse primary school highlighted how children used code-switching (switching between languages) to exclude or include peers. Björk-Willén's (2007) study of three children's interactions found that shadowing or copying the talk or actions of others was a more successful interactional tool than language-crossing or using the language of the other two. Attempts to use language-crossing were rejected, while shadowing indicated to the other two that she understood the play. In Cromdal's (2004) study, bilingual children, aged 6–8 years, used skills of code-switching (switching between languages) as a resource, ultimately hindering or enabling how others could play. Cekaite's (2006) study of bilingual children, aged 7–10 years, found that joking, body movements, and displays of emotion were effectively used by bilingual children to get along with others in class. Significantly these studies highlight how participation was constructed from the actions and reactions of each of the children involved, and the resources available to them, and not due to one child being more socially competent than the others.

A common language and a cultural identity have each been reported to be key elements for making friends. McDonnell's (2017) study of migrant children in Irish schools confirmed the pervasive influence that language has on making friends when they found that the school rule of 'English only' privileged friendship for those who were proficient in speaking English. Barley (2017) identified that for some children their first language became a proud symbol of identity, and that equally, other children shunned their minority language, as they did not feel it gave them any 'capital' in the school context, where English was the medium of instruction (p. 90). Iqbal et al.'s. (2017) study of friendships in schools characterized by diversity identified alternative strategies when children made friends across ethnicities and that material possessions were used to divide or align peers. Garcia-Sanchez's (2017) study of a group of Moroccan girls in a Spanish community showed how the girls of different ages became friends by playing each afternoon in the local park. Teaching each other new rules or offering different ways of playing games helped the girls achieve intersubjectivity, despite their differing skill levels. Having a shared understanding and goal meant that each girl's input was valued, resulting in trust and friendship. Interculturally aware teachers might focus on the similar interests of children in the group, rather than linguistic commonalities or ethnicities, in order to enhance cultural and linguistic crossings in children's belonging and friendships.

Peer Culture and Making Friends

The social and cultural values of the peer group and the social context has influence on children's friendships. Children draw on or resist accepted moral codes of the local context as they attend to their own social agendas (Evaldsson & Svahn, 2012). Children who display behaviours that fit in the rules and norms of the peer culture are typically more easily accepted (Rubin et al., 2006).

The next example, from Theobald et al. (2017), highlights that while Samir used a range of strategies to play, including being a 'best' friend, his attempts were rejected due to the current interests of the peer group.

Extract 18.6 Resisting play requests

SAM: Danie:::l (0.6) Danie:::l
DAN: ↑be careful Owen (0.4) my tai:l is
very spikey
SAM: Dani:::el, Dani:::el,
(0.6)
DAN: yeah,
gaze to blocks
SAM: I'm your best friend can you ↑play with me:
stilted staccato talk
DAN: no:::: I wanna play with Owen I don't wanna
play with you:
gaze to Samir then to blocks
SAM: what did you sa:::d?
DAN: I won't (.) play with you
walks away from Samir
SAM: [*follows Daniel, tailing him*]
SAM: [play with me:::,]
DAN: u::::m, (0.6) soon
SAM: are you buildi::ng?
DAN: *turns to gaze at Samir*
SAM: are you building?
DAN: u:::::m,(0.4) we::ll, I don't want to play with
You
I wanna play with OW::EN

```
25          bu:t, (.) play with [this]
26                              [points to blocks]
27   SAM:   walks over to blocks and plays
```

This extract begins as Samir approaches the block area where Daniel is involved in an established building project with Owen. Samir attempts to gain Daniel's attention by calling his name. His play request includes a justification, 'I'm your best friend', that draws on moral obligations established in the social context: best friends play with each other. Daniel rejects Samir's requests, the delicate nature of the exchange indicated by Daniel's avoidance of eye contact and movement away from Samir. Samir continues attempts to access play with a range of strategies including asking, 'are you building?' and 'tailing', following closely (Theobald et al., 2017, p. 187). Daniel mitigates his rejection by suggesting that he will play with Samir 'soon', and by offering Samir an object to play with, displays empathy to Samir.

This exchange highlights the fluidity of children's social interaction and the influence of the ongoing peer culture. While Daniel and Samir may be categorized as 'best' friends, according to Samir, being involved with the dominant play was a priority for Daniel at that time. Despite employing an array of interactional strategies to access play with Daniel, Samir was unsuccessful due to the social agenda at the time. By focusing on children 'reading' the immediately relevant rules and roles of the group members, teachers can reinforce that the peer culture is collaboratively and dynamically built. Teachers who help children to adopt an appropriate strategy to move into a game or ongoing play enhance children's interactions and their involvement in play.

Recommendations for Practice

Children's relationships are intertwined with adult expectations, societal rules, and the interests of the local peer culture. Teachers and children exercise social rules within play activities and this interplay gives fluidity and uncertainty to opportunities of friendship. This chapter has identified strategies such as using objects, playing games, doing joint projects and pretend play that teachers can use to support friendships in early childhood education settings. The extracts unveiled examples of the highly complex peer cultures that children must navigate as they go about making friends.

Teachers are continually faced with decisions that have consequences for children's friendships. This may involve dictating the social rules, leaving children to completely negotiate these relationships for themselves or supporting children to negotiate friendships. When teachers who adopt a 'pedagogy of friendship' that values friendships, respects children's agency (Carter & Nutbrown, 2016 p. 295) and builds their 'professional stock of knowledge' about friendships (Peräkylä & Vehvilfinen, 2003, p. 727), they can encourage children's respectful relationships. Teachers who scan and appraise the ongoing peer culture and the classroom context, develop responsiveness that is critical in establishing supportive environments where children have enhanced opportunities for friendships.

Teachers can create interactional situations and conditions that facilitate opportunities for friendships when they use tools from the Process Approach to Building Friendships (PABF) Toolkit:

- Guide play entry – using a pedagogy of 'notice, recognize, and respond' (Cowie & Bell, 1999) to focus on goal-orientated and seamless openings.
- Focus on joint projects with shared goals shifts the focus to being involved in activity itself from a focus on children's obligations to play *with* others.
- Facilitate opportunities for children to engage in pretend play. Pretend play enables children to take on a variety of roles.
- Encourage games or activities that are not dependent on language, to include all children regardless of their language capabilities.
- Provide materials and objects that can be transformed for different purposes, enabling children to have ongoing negotiations for shared understandings.
- Focus on activities in play scenarios rather than emphasizing obligations of 'playing with' others highlights access via a topic or activity, rather than drawing attention to access.
- Encourage children to 'scan' play interactions. This scanning involves identify the interests of the group, roles of members, and rules of games that are already established in order to correctly 'read' and negotiate play entry.
- Facilitate time and opportunities for participation. When children interact in informal or formal pairings during class activities, they become familiar with their peers and have opportunities to find peers with common interests.
- Encourage children to be 'friendly' with all peers, but not assuming that children will be friends. Just like adults, children will form close bonds with some peers over others, based on the mutuality of feelings, interests, and time spent together.

The processes for making and maintaining friends are serious matters for young children, at which they constantly work. Friendships require ongoing negotiations, interactional tactics, and have consequences for future participation. This chapter has identified how teachers can guide children to make friends in early childhood settings by implementing tools from the Process Approach to Building Friendships (PABF) Toolkit. A process approach, based on conversation analysis of the interaction of real children in real play contexts, identifies the criticality of the peer culture and social contexts and the actions of teachers to children's opportunities for participation and friendship.

References

Barley, R. (2017). Language identity and peer interaction at a linguistically diverse school. In M. Theobald (ed.), *Friendship and Peer Culture in Multilingual Settings* (pp. 89–112). Bingley: Emerald Publishing.

Bateman, A. (2011). Huts and heartache: the affordance of playground huts for legal debate in early childhood social organisation. *Journal of Pragmatics*, 43(13), 3111–3121.

Bateman, A., and Church, A. (2017). Children's use of objects in an early years playground. *European Early Childhood Education Research Journal*, 25(1), 55–71.

Björk-Willén, P. (2007). Participation in multilingual preschool play: shadowing and crossing as interactional resources. *Journal of Pragmatics*, 39, 2133–2158.

Björk-Willén, P. (2017). Peer collaboration in front of two alphabet charts: friendship and peer culture in multilingual settings. In M. Theobald (ed.), *Friendship and Peer Culture in Multilingual Settings* (pp. 143–169). Bingley: Emerald Publishing.

Butler, C. W. (2008). *Talk and Social Interaction in the Playground*. Aldershot: Ashgate.

Butler, C. W., Duncombe, R., Mason, C., and Sandford, R. (2016). Recruitments, engagements, and partitions: managing participation in play. *International Journal of Play*, 5(1), 47–63.

Carter, C., and Nutbrown, C. (2016). A pedagogy of friendship: young children's friendships and how schools can support them. *International Journal of Early Years Education*, 24(4), 395–413. https://doi.org/10.1080/09669760.2016.1189813

Cekaite, A. (2006). A child's development of interactional competence in a Swedish L2 classroom. *The Modern Language Journal*, 91(1), 45–62.

Cobb-Moore, C., Danby, S., and Farrell, A. (2010). Locking the unlockable: children's invocation of pretense to define and manage place. *Childhood*, 17(3), 376–395.

Coelho, L., Torres, N., Fernandes, C., and Santos, A. J. (2017). Quality of play, social acceptance and reciprocal friendship in preschool children. *European Early Childhood Education Research Journal*, 25(6), 812–823. https://doi.org/10.1080/1350293X.2017.1380879

Corsaro, W. A. (2003). *'We're Friends, Right?': Inside Kids' Culture*. Washington, DC: Joseph Henry Press.

Corsaro, W. A. (2017). Making and keeping friends in multilingual settings: what we know and where we are going (foreword). In M. Theobald (ed.). *Friendship and Peer Culture in Multilingual Settings* (pp. xi–xv). Bingley: Emerald Publishing.

Cowie, B., and Bell, B. (1999). A model of formative assessment in science education. *Assessment in Education: Principles, Policy & Practice*, 6(1),101–116. https://doi.org/10.1080/09695949993026

Cromdal, J. (2001). Overlap in bilingual play: some implications of code-switching for overlap resolution. *Research on Language and Social Interaction*, 34(4), 421–451. https://doi.org/10.1207/S15327973RLSI3404_02

Cromdal, J. (2004) 'Can I be with?': negotiating play entry in a bilingual school. *Journal of Pragmatics*, 33, 515–543.

Cromdal, J. (2009). Childhood and social interaction in everyday life: introduction to the special issue. *Journal of Pragmatics*, 41(8), 1473–1476.

Danby, S. J. (2008). The importance of friends; the value of friends; friendships within peer cultures. In L. Brooker and M. Woodhead (eds.), *Developing Positive Identities: Diversity and Young Children* (pp. 36–41). Milton Keynes: Open University Press.

Danby, S. J., Davidson, C., Theobald, M., Houen, S., and Thorpe, K. (2017). Pretend play and technology: young children making sense of their everyday worlds. In D. Pike, S. Lynch, and C. Beckett (eds.), *Multidisciplinary Perspectives on Play from Birth and Beyond* (pp. 231–246). London: Springer Nature.

Danby, S., Thompson, C., Theobald, M., and Thorpe, K. (2012). Children's strategies for making friends when starting school. *Australasian Journal of Early Childhood*, 37(2), 63–71.

Dunn, J. (2004). *Children's Friendships: The Beginnings of Intimacy*. Oxford: Blackwell.

Evaldsson, A.-C. (2007). Accounting for friendship: moral ordering and category membership in preadolescent girls' relational talk. *Research on Language and Social Interaction*, 40(4), 377–404.

Evaldsson, A.-C., and Svahn, J. (2012). School bullying and the micro-politics of girls' gossip disputes. In S. Danby and M. Theobald (eds.), *Disputes in Everyday Life* (pp. 297–323). Bingley: Emerald Publishing.

Fleer, M. (2013). Collective imagining in play. In I. Schousboe and D. Winther-Lindqvist (eds.), *Children's Play and Development: Cultural-Historical Perspectives* (pp. 73–79). London: Springer.

García Sánchez, I. M. (2017). Friendship, participation, and multimodality in Moroccan immigrant girls' peer groups. In M. Theobald (ed.), *Friendship and Peer Culture in Multilingual Settings* (pp. 1–32). Bingley: Emerald Publishing.

Göncü, A. (1993). Development of intersubjectivity in social pretend play. *Human Development*, 36(4), 185–198.

Hartup, W. W. (2000). The company they keep: friendships and their developmental significance. In W. Craig (ed.), *Childhood Social Development*. Oxford: Blackwell.

Iqbal, H., Neal, S., and Vincent, C. (2017). Children's friendships in super-diverse localities: encounters with social and ethnic difference. *Childhood*, 24(1), 128–142.

Kultti, A., and Pramling, N. (2015). Bring your own toy: socialisation of two-year-olds through tool-mediated activities in an Australian early childhood education context. *Early Childhood Education Journal*, 43(5), 367–376.

Kultti, A., and Pramling Samuelsson, I. (2017). Toys and the creation of cultural play scripts. In D. Pike, S. Lynch, and C. Beckett (eds.), *Multidisciplinary Perspectives on Play from Birth and Beyond* (pp. 217–230). London: Springer Nature.

Kyratzis, A. (2014). Peer interaction, framing, and literacy in preschool bilingual pretend play. In A. Cekaite, S. Blum-Kulka, V. Grøver, and E. Teubal (eds.), *Children's Peer Talk: Learning from Each Other* (pp. 129–148). Cambridge: Cambridge University Press.

Laursen, B., Bukowski, W. M., Aunola, K., and Nurmi, J. (2007). Friendship moderates prospective associations between social isolation and adjustment problems in young children. *Child Development*, 78(4), 1395–1404.

Lillard, A. S., Lerner, M. D., Hopkins, E. J., Dore, R. A., Smith, E. D., and Palmquist, C. M. (2013). The impact of pretend play on children's development: a review of the evidence. *Psychological Bulletin*, 139(1), 1–34. https://doi.org/10.1037/a0029321

McDonnell, S. (2017). Speaking distance: language, friendship and spaces of belonging in Irish primary schools. In M. Theobald (ed.), *Friendship and Peer Culture in Multilingual Settings* (pp. 33–54). Bingley: Emerald Publishing.

McLeod, S., Verdon, S., and Theobald, M. (2015). Becoming bilingual: children's insights about making friends in bilingual settings. *International Journal of Early Childhood*, 47(3), 385–402.

Paley, V. G. (1993). You can't say you can't play. Cambridge, MA: Harvard University Press.

Peräkylä, A., and Vehvil*f*inen, S. (2003). Conversation analysis and the professional stocks of interactional knowledge. *Discourse & Society*, 14(6), 727–750.

Rubin, K., Bukowski, W., and Parker, J. (2006). Peer interactions, relationships, and groups. In W. Damon, R. Lerner, and N, Eisenberg (eds.), *Handbook of Child Psychology: Vol. 3. Social, Emotional, and Personality Development* (6th ed., pp. 571–645). New York: Wiley.

Sacks, H. (1995). *Lectures on Conversation* (G. Jefferson, Trans. Vol. I and II). Oxford: Blackwell.

Sidnell, J., and Stivers, T. (eds.). (2012). *The Handbook of Conversation Analysis.* Oxford: Blackwell.

Theobald, M. (2013). Ideas as 'possessitives': claims and counter claims in a playground dispute. *Journal of Pragmatics*, 45(1), 1–12.

Theobald, M., Bateman, A., Busch, G., Laraghy, M., and Danby, S. J. (2017). 'I'm your best friend': peer interaction and friendship in a multilingual preschool. In M. Theobald (ed.), *Friendship and Peer Culture in Multilingual Settings* (pp. 171–196). Bingley: Emerald Publishing.

Theobald, M., Busch, G., and Laraghy, M. (2019). Children's views and strategies for making friends in linguistically diverse English medium instruction settings. In I. Liyanage and T. Walker (eds.), *Mulitlingual Education Yearbook 2019: Media of Instruction and Multilingual Settings* (pp. 151–174). London: Springer.

Theobald, M., and Danby, S. J. (2019). Children's competence and wellbeing in sensitive research: when video-stimulated accounts lead to dispute. In J. Lamerichs, S. J. Danby, A. Bateman, and S. Ekberg (eds.), *Children and Mental Health Talk: Perspectives on Social Competence* (pp. 137–166). Basingstoke: Palgrave Macmillan.

Theobald, M., Danby, S. J., Thompson, C., and Thorpe, K. (2020). Friendships. In S. Garvis and D. Pendergast (eds.), *Health and Wellbeing in Childhood* (3rd ed.) (pp. 235–256). Cambridge: Cambridge University Press.

Vaughn, B. E., Azria, M. R., Caya, L. R., Newell, W., Krysik, L., Bost, K.K., and Kazura, K. L. (2000). Friendship and social competence in a sample of preschool children attending Head Start. *Developmental Psychology*, 36(3), 326–338. https://doi.org/10.1037/0012-1649.36.3.326

Vaughn, B. E., Colvin, T. N., Azria, M. R., Caya, L. R., and Krysik, L. (2001). Dyadic analyses of friendship in a sample of preschool-age children attending head start: correspondence between measures and implications for social competence. *Child Development*, 72(3): 862–878. https://doi.org/10.1111/1467-8624.00320

Weisberg, D. S. (2015). Pretend play. *Wiley Interdisciplinary Reviews: Cognitive Science*, 6(3), 249–261.

19 | Conflict

AMELIA CHURCH AND EKATERINA MOORE

Introduction

Children argue. From a very young age, children attempt to assert their will on objects, outcomes, and status within relationships. Preverbal children are limited to vocalizations, gesture, and embodied demonstration of their displeasure (e.g. grabbing, pushing, or crying), but from around 3 years of age onwards, children have an increasing capacity to use a range of verbal strategies to persuade other people to do what they want. For the purposes of this chapter, disputes are considered as a productive site of social interaction (i.e. *not* including physical conflict), where children co-construct the argument and the dispute outcomes. This chapter will focus on one detailed example of being 'fair' in resolving a dispute, where the teacher elicits children's suggestions and scaffolds an equitable solution. This is one of only two in 102 observed teacher interventions in our data where the teacher invites children to propose solutions and then stays with the group to facilitate consensus and implementation of the solution. Before illustrating how teacher support can be done, the chapter provides a brief overview of research in children's conflict.

Children's Disputes

A dispute can be defined as mutual opposition which halts an ongoing activity (see Maynard, 1985). Disputes are sustained by repeated opposition, and resolved where both parties acquiesce (see Church, 2009b, for examples of dispute outcomes). Children tend to argue about ownership rights to objects (e.g. *'No, that's mine'*, Church & Hester, 2012, p. 247; Burdelski, 2020; Shantz, 1987), the organization of play (e.g. *'No, I am the mom'*,

Our thanks to Angie Mashford-Scott for her work in collecting the data in this chapter and her contribution to recommendations for teachers. Thanks also to Amanda Bateman and Frederieke Kern for their expert feedback on this chapter, and – as always – to the children and teachers who allowed us to film their everyday interactions.

Ahn, 2020; Björk-Willén, 2012), joining the play (e.g. *'Hey, you can't play'*, Corsaro, 1988, p. 8) and sanctions imposed by the rules of the centre (*'No fighting'*, Cobb-Moore, 2012, p. 103).

Disputes reveal children's concern with the principle of fairness, and infractions are punishable by exclusion from the activity (e.g. *'No, you can't join, Neah'*, Holm-Kvist & Cekaite, 2020, p. 9), withdrawing rights to future rewards (e.g. *'You can't come to my party'*, Church, 2009a, p. 138) or threatening to bring an end to the relationship (e. g. *'I'm not gonna be your friend'*, Church & Hester, 2012, p. 253). These threats are not in fact carried out, but nonetheless carry some weight depending on the existing relationship or perceived value of the withheld rights to an object or activity.

Studies have explored differences between boys' and girls' disputes (e.g. Danby and Baker, 1998; Gilligan, 1988; Sheldon, 1990), but we should be wary of gendered stereotypes, as girls, for example, can be aggressive (Goodwin, 2006; Kyratzis & Guo, 2001) and engage in disputes that have complex structures (Goodwin, 1990). Overall, similarities between how boys and girls engage in disputes outweigh any differences. For example, Goodwin and Goodwin (1987; also Goodwin, 1990, 2001) found that both genders structured their arguments in similar ways. Both boys and girls used opposition moves that reject the prior turn (e.g. *'No. I don't wanna wet it'*, p. 207) and format tying, where the opposition or objection recycles some part of the prior turn (e.g. one boy complains *'Why don't you get out my yard'* to which another boy responds, *'Why don't you make me get out the yard'*, p. 219).

As a social practice, arguing with peers is performed in ways that often reflect community cultural norms and values, and the local social order of children's peer culture. During disputes in a South Korean preschool, for example, children use honorifics (titles or words that mark respect) to perform politeness, authoritative and other socio-cultural meanings, as they negotiate local peer relationships (Ahn, 2020). Italian children participate in the genre of *discussione,* commonly seen among Italian adults, to actively negotiate social relationships and 'produce and extend peer culture' (Corsaro & Rizzo, 1988, p. 888). During episodes of conflict in Swedish preschools, children displayed or withheld empathy, which allowed them to engage in peer socialization and sustain peer-culture concerns (Holm Kvist & Cekaite, 2020). These research studies demonstrate a need to consider not only the ways in which broader cultural norms are reproduced in peer interactions, but also how the social worlds of the particular group of children are governed and monitored by the children themselves.

How Children Manage Disputes

Research from the 1930s onwards in developmental psychology has documented the types of strategies used by children in disputes, essentially categorizing speech acts or utterances as typified by Eisenberg & Garvey (1981): insistence, mitigation/aggravation, reasons, counter, conditional directive, compromise, requests for explanation, physical force, or ignoring (see also Boggs, 1978; Brenneis & Lein, 1977; Genishi & Di Paolo, 1982). This research documented the frequency of categories, and has considered the relationship between utterances insofar as how cycles of threats can escalate (Haslett, 1983), typical sequences of types of opposition moves (Boggs, 1978) and what strategies are most likely to bring about resolution (Vuchinich, 1990). Although this research identified what children do in disputes, it had less to say about the trajectories of conflict, and how each child's turn at talk responded to the prior complaints or opposition.

In the past thirty years, however, research in ethnomethodology and conversation analysis (EMCA) has shifted attention to the practice of disputes as sequences of collaborative and locally constructed actions, where the analyst studies how children orient to each subsequent turn, building and re-framing the ongoing dispute. Rather than seeing conflict as something to be avoided, EMCA research has shown how competent children are at challenging the underlying premise of another child's objections (Goodwin, Goodwin, & Yaeger-Dror, 2002), recruiting other children to align with their position in the dispute (Bateman, 2015), and pursuing agendas and social roles which give them (temporary) authority rights to objects or control over the direction of the play (Cobb-Moore, 2012).

In attuning and responding to each other's prior actions, children negotiate and construct their social worlds: they work on moral order (Danby & Theobald, 2012), navigate peer relationships (Bateman, 2012; Cobb-Moore, 2012; Cobb-Moore et al., 2008), and negotiate social norms and contracts (Burdelski, 2020; Church & Hester, 2012) that may take place in seeking a solution. Importantly, EMCA research has shown that children have agency in the co-construction of their social environment, capable of argument that responds to the concerns of others or benefits their own agenda (see Moore & Burdelski, 2020, for a concise summary). At times, however, disputes among young children can arrive at a stalemate, where neither party is prepared to compromise, and no legitimate proposals are made to satisfy all parties. When children reach this point – which can be escalation to the point of physically tussling over objects or play spaces, or a cycle of repeated opposition with no view to changing their position – the teacher may step in to disrupt the conflict.

The Role of the Teacher

A last resort strategy used by children – because it can affect one's status in the group (Newman, Murray, & Lussier, 2001) – is to complain to the teacher and ask them to intervene. The children's recruitment of teachers to resolve conflict is a testament of their growing understanding of the adult roles in the preschool as an institution, where teachers are often the enforcers of the rules (Chen et al., 2001). Children can threaten to '*tell the teacher*' (Theobald & Danby, 2017), but not necessarily follow through. When children do report the infringement or make a complaint about their peer(s) to the teacher, they are seeking an ally, often framing the other child/ren's behaviour as transgressive and worthy of reprimand (Evaldsson & Svahn, 2017).

Teachers' responses to requests to intervene vary in the degree to which they expect children to manage conflict by themselves. They may make suggestions and participate in the discussion (e.g. '*What do you think ....*' Church, Mashford-Scott, & Cohrssen, 2018, p. 98) or impose their own instructions to prohibit the conflict (e.g. '*This is not allowed,*' Moore, 2020). Teachers typically initiate intervention in children's disputes where there is shouting or some evidence of physical aggression (see Roseth et al., 2008). When their attention is drawn to 'anti-social' behaviour, teachers typically seek to stop the threat of harm (Theobald & Danby, 2012), establish what the infringement was (e.g. '*What happened?*' Cekaite, 2020) and propose some next steps (e.g. *[referring to a clock] 'When it reaches two, you can take turns again"* Burdelski, 2020; see also Burdelski, Chapter 6, this volume).

While the way conflict is conducted and resolved varies across cultures (e.g. Cohen, 2009; Moore & Burdelski, 2020), existing research shows us that teachers most commonly use cessation strategies, where the 'preferred teacher's role is one of stopping the dispute' even though the view of dispute as a dysfunctional activity is at 'odds with how the children themselves use conflict' (Danby & Baker, 2010, p. 344). There is scant evidence – whether intervention is sought by a child or initiated by the teacher – of how teachers can scaffold, rather than impose, children's resolution of disputes. The data in this chapter will show that where a teacher directs the children – i.e. telling them what they should do – the intervention is not effective. Where teachers encourage children to participate in the process of problem solving, however, the recommendations are more likely to resonate with children and result in the resumption of collaborative play – our definition of 'successful' or 'effective' resolution (Church, 2009b). In the data that follows, examples of teacher intervention will illustrate how children can be supported to resolve their own disputes.

Talking with Children to Resolve Conflict

This data was collected as part of a project investigating teacher's intervention in preschool conflict (see Church, Mashford-Scott, & Cohrssen, 2018). The project involved four different preschools in metropolitan Melbourne, with children aged 4–5 years, and their teachers, video-recording free play sessions for a total of 56 hours. Most often, in these recorded observations, teachers move quickly to shut down the conflict, and advise children what they should do next or how to resolve the disputes. For the purposes of this chapter, we will look at two examples of the same teacher intervening on different occasions in the same type of dispute over who gets to play with the marbles. In Extract 19.1, typical of direct instruction as intervention, the teacher offers the children her solution to their dispute (i.e. to share), questions Olivia's rights to all the marbles, and advises that the marbles belong to the early childhood centre (Kinder) rather than any one child.

Extract 19.1

```
1.  Teacher: Olivia (3.0) Olivia (1.0) could you share (2.0)
2.           the marbles.
3.  Olivia:  I've got all my marbles
4.           (0.2)
5.  Teacher: okay but do you think it's okay to have all the
6.           marbles?
7.           (1.0)
8.  Olivia:  Jackson gave me those.
9.  Teacher: okay, but they're not Jackson's marbles,
10.          they're Kinder's marbles.
             ((moving away from play area))
```

In Extract 19.1 the teacher has asked Olivia if she thinks it is fair (okay) to have all the marbles (note the inequality implied by the emphasizing '*all*' in line 3). Olivia defends her behaviour with a claim that she was gifted the collection of marbles by Jackson. The teacher rejects Jackson's authority to gift the marbles, because they belong to Kinder and therefore all children in the kindergarten theoretically have equal rights to the marbles. At this point the teacher moves away from the play area and the children continue to argue about access to the marbles. Proposing a solution and then leaving children to implement (or reject) the solution does not prove as effective as when the teacher remains with the children to scaffold the resolution of a dispute.

In the next, much longer extract, we will see how the teacher elicits the children's own solution to who gets to play with the marbles. Notably, the origin of the dispute is the same as in Extract 19.1 (i.e. arguing about access to the marbles), but is recorded on a different day and involves different children, but the same teacher. Extract 19.2 – analysed elsewhere to see how children's agency is supported by teachers (see Mashford-Scott & Church, 2011) – is used here to illustrate how educators can elicit children's own ideas for resolving disputes.

Creating a Space for Dispute Resolution

Joshua complains to the teacher that Rebecca and Sara have taken the marbles. The teacher approaches the play area and asks the five children who are playing with the marbles to join her sitting in a circle. She also asks the children to put all the marbles in the middle of the circle and explains to them that '*I want to have a discussion. What do you think we can do to make this fair?*', with some additional directions to collect all the marbles. The teacher devotes one minute to physically arranging children as participants in the discussion, asking each child to sit in a particular place so that the group can form 'a little circle' (see Figure 19.1). The children and the teacher are now each situated in a space that orients towards a centre occupied by the object of the discussion (the marbles) *and* allows visual attention to one another.

This embodied attention (Kendon, 2004; see also Kern, Chapter 4, this volume) creates a framework where active participation is made possible (see Bateman, Chapter 3, this volume); all are equally positioned members of a group established to resolve the problem of who will get to use the marbles. To shift the children's attention from the object (the marbles) to the process of resolution (having a discussion), the teacher ensures all marbles are collected on the floor in the middle of the circle rather than held by any one child ('*can everyone tip their marbles into the middle*'; '*we want to put [the marbles] all together*'). This organization of the group 'creates a public, shared focus of visual and cognitive attention' (Goodwin, 2007, p. 57), to each other and the marbles.

From the outset the teacher ratifies or acknowledges the children as co-participants in the search for a viable solution. In response to Joshua's request for intervention, rather than unilateral instruction – i.e. stating equal rights to the marbles as we saw in Extract 19.1 – the teacher proposes a multiparty discussion: '*let's go over and talk about it*'. The teacher states that the intent of gathering together as a group is to '*have a discussion*' with all parties contesting ownership of the marbles. The teacher opens the discussion

Figure 19.1 The teacher engages the children's attention.

by asking Joshua (the boy who sought the teacher out to intervene in the dispute) '*what do you think we can do to make this fair?*'. The teacher uses Joshua's name to call his attention as the primary recipient of the invitation to propose a 'fair' next action. As the interaction unfolds, however, the teacher makes the negotiation process open to all five children.

Soliciting Ideas from the Children

As the children are gathering the remaining marbles, the teacher re-solicits a possible equitable solution ('*what do you think we can do to make this fair with the marbles?*' lines, 51–52).

Extract 19.2a

```
50. Teacher:  what do you think?= ((pointing)) and those ones as
51.           well Sara. (.) what do you think we can do to make
52.           this fair, (.) with the marbles.
53.           (0.2)
54. Teacher:  wh- what's your sug:ges:tion (.) eve:ry:one?
55. Rebecca:  my: sug:gestion, is (.) like (.) we can each have
56.           a go, .hhh and we can have all of them instead (.)
57.           and then (.) there can be:: (0.2) we: can do (.)
58.           eeny miney mo (.) and then: (.) and then: (.) it-
59.           it- it chooses them. (0.2) then (.) they: get to take
60.           all the marbles? (.) and then another one? (.)and
```

61. another one (could).
62. Teacher: so? (.) [how many people are here?
63. Rebecca: [you can have-
64. (1.0)
65. Rebecca: ahh?=
66. Teacher: don't count me, *((to all children))* how many
67. children here?=
68. Children: five five (.) five five (.) five five
69. Teacher: ok:ay: (.) so Rose (.) er (.) Rebecca's saying (.)
70. ev::ery:body: could have a tu:rn of having all: the
71. marbles,
72. Rebecca: yes.=

Having explicitly named Joshua just prior to this extract as the recipient of the question '*what do you think we can do to make this fair?*', then repeating the question without selecting a next speaker (lines 51–52), the teacher opens the participation framework to explicitly include all members of the group in her next turn ('*what's your suggestion everyone?*' line 54). The teacher solicits possible solutions from the children, inviting '*everyone*' in the turn completion so that all five children are invited to self-select as next speaker (Sacks, Shegloff, & Jefferson, 1974). Rebecca makes the suggestion that each child have all the marbles one after the other (lines 55–61), which the teacher summarizes for the group: '*Rebecca's saying everybody could have a turn of having all the marbles*' (lines 69–70), a reformulation which is immediately confirmed by Rebecca ('*yes*', line 72). Note that the teacher does not evaluate Rebecca's prior turn; the 'Okay' (line 69) is used as a transition to the summary and the next speaker, rather than an evaluation of Rebecca's suggestion.

The teacher then moves immediately to invite alternate propositions from the group. As such, this discussion 'is jointly produced as various actors in the event take action in account of the actions of others, the variants chosen by the teacher have consequences for what the students will do and vice versa' (Erickson, 1982, p. 178).

Extract 19.2b

73. Teacher: =is there another way you could do it?=
74. =does anyone else have a su:ggestion:? *((holding all*
75. *marbles in her enclosed hands and gesturing towards*
76. *each child one by one around the circle))*
77. (1.5)
78. Rebecca: we can do (.) eeny miney mo [(.) and then it can
79. choose one (.) and then (.) if it chooses one (.)

80. then they: (.) have all the marbles? (.)
81. [[and then?
82. Teacher: [ye:ah?,
83. Teacher: [[o:kay, (.) let's count how many marbles
84. we've got?, *((pushes one marble away from pile on*
85. *the carpet))*
86. All ch.: one (0.2) two (.) three (.) four (.) five (.) six
87. (.) seven (.) eight (.) nine (.) ten?,
88. *((children chanting, as Teacher pushes a marble*
89. *aside with each number))*
90. Teacher: °o:kay. (0.2) now, (0.4) I ↑won:der if there's a
91. different way we could do it?
92. (.) what do you think.= *((to all children))*
93. Sara: =two each?
94. (0.2)

As no one proposes an alternative (see the pause in line 77), Rebecca reframes her suggestion – that each child will have a turn with all the marbles – by appealing to the collective '*we*' and the random selection afforded by '*eeney meeny miney mo*'. The teacher acknowledges – but, again, does not evaluate – Rebecca's suggestion. By withholding an evaluation of the prior turn the teacher effectively positions the children as the agents of possible solutions.

In order to guide children towards a solution (i.e. fair distribution of resources), the teacher asks the children to count how many marbles there are in total. She uses the inclusive '*let's*' and '*we*' (line 83–84), inviting all of the children to participate in an activity that might provide a resolution that satisfies everyone and also engages the children in the mathematical principle of one-to-one correspondence. Taking advantage of the teachable moment, she provides an opportunity for learning number and social skills simultaneously.

To maximize children's input, the teacher designs her question using the phrase '*I wonder*' (line 90). This encourages children to offer their own ideas with less prescription over the course of the interaction (Houen, Danby, Farrell, & Thorpe, 2016a), a strategy that has shown to be more effective than 'wh-' questions in eliciting responses from children (Houen, Danby, Farrell, & Thorpe, 2016b). These intentional actions from the teacher prompt a proposal from Sara, that the marbles could be evenly distributed: '*two each*' (line 93). The teacher then offers this suggestion to the children for consideration, asking the children '*what do you think about that*?', nominating Rebecca as the respondent, given she suggested having *all* the marbles.

Extract 19.2c

95. Teacher: do you think? (0.2) what do you think about that
96. (.) Rebec:ca?
97. Rebecca: *((shakes her head))*
98. Teacher: well (.) what do you think, (.) Sara's say:ing:
99. you could have two: each: (.) which is really good
100. maths (.) Sa:ra? (0.3) Sara's say:ing (.) cos
101. there's ten? (0.4) marbles (.) and there's fi:ve
102. children (.) we could do thi:s (0.6) *((pushes two*
103. *marbles towards each child))* we could: di:vide
104. them up?(0.3)(x like that) and we could have two:
105. ea:ch?(0.2) O::R? (0.8) we ca:n (0.3) let one person
106. have ten mar:bles: first? (0.3) and then another
107. person has ten marbles? (0.2) and another (.) and
108. another (.) and another.*((holding all marbles and*
109 *gesturing to each child as she says 'another'))*
110. Teacher: what do you think is- (.) what do you want to
111. do:? =
112. Rose: =two (0.6) I want two: each.

The binary choice elicited from the children (i.e. Rebecca's suggestion for each child to have a turn with all the marbles, or Sara's idea to have two marbles each) is reformulated in the teacher's extended turn (lines 98–109). In presenting these two options for the group, the teacher embodies the distribution of the objects and the ownership or entitlement simultaneously. We see that 'body movement, including gaze, is a resource for displaying and projecting locally relevant kinds of participation … that this provides for the coparticipants to choose how to participate in the unfolding situation' (Rae, 2001, p. 272). The teacher creates this framework by dividing the marbles, pushing two marbles towards each child as she says '*we could: di:vide them up?, (.) and we could have two: each:?*' (lines 103–105). The teacher then uses gesture to reinforce what having all the marbles would entail; she collects all ten marbles in her cupped hands and proffers towards each child in turn while saying we can: '*(.) let one person have ten mar:bles: first: (.) and then another person has ten marbles (.) and another (.) and another (.) and another?*' (lines 105–108).

Not only does the teacher make salient what the distribution of marbles would look like, this embodiment once again underscores the mathematical knowledge embedded in the proposed solutions (see Goodwin 2007, pp. 55–56 and also Cohrssen, Chapter 11, in this volume). The teacher's praise of Sara for the '*good maths*' (lines 99–100) in response to Sara's prior proposal to have '*two each*' (Extract 19.2b, line 93) is notable. Although the teacher does not evaluate the children's suggestions to resolve the disputes, she positively assesses Sara's ability to use her math skills in proposing a solution.

Scaffolding Fair Dispute Resolution

To manage competing interests, the teacher scaffolds how the children can decide fairly – or at least democratically – on the two distinct propositions of how to allocate the marbles. As Rose responds quickly, '*I want two each*' (Extract 19.2c, line 112), the teacher moves to manage competing interests, explicit in Rebecca's subsequent, '*I want all of them*' (line 114, below), by explaining '*we will vote*' (line 115 below).

Extract 19.2d

113. Teacher: if you want to have two each (0.2) sit with A:va?
114. Rebecca: I want a:ll of them.
115. Teacher: if- listen (.) we will vote (0.2) if you want two
116. each? (0.2) sit with Sara? (0.8) *((children start*
117. *moving))* and if you want (.) all of them: (.) at
118. a ti:me? (.) sit with Rebecca.
119. (0.8)
120. Teacher: what about you Travis (.) do you want two- *((to*
121. *Travis))* Sara you've gotta stay- (.) you wan[t two:
122. *((to Sara))*
123. Travis: [I want. I want two. *((standing up))*
124. (0.5)
125. Teacher: °ok:ay?, (0.2) so let's count (.) how many
126. peo::ple? (0.4) want to have a:ll of them (0.3)
127. Sa:ra?=
128: Sara: =three.=
129. Teacher: =and how many want two.
130. (1.0)
131. Rebecca: two.
132. Teacher: so how does that vote wo:rk.
133. (1.2)
134. Sara: ten ea:ch.
135. (0.8)
136. Rebecca: ten each:.
137. Sara: ((to Rebecca))°(do you want) to do (.) eeny meney
138. miney mo?°
139. Teacher: ok:ay?, *((to all children))*

```
140. Rebecca: YEAH ((to Sara))
141. Rebecca  [eeny miney mo.=
```

The principle and practice of voting is one way of enacting fairness, in that the wants of the majority secure the outcome of the dispute (see Sigurdardottir, Williams, & Einarsdottir, 2019, on talking with preschool children about values). Children's acceptance of this as a fair solution is evident in their participating in and then accepting the outcome of the vote: two children want everyone to have two marbles each, and three of the children choose to have a turn with all the marbles. Importantly, the teacher facilitates the vote. Rather than instructing the children to vote, and then leaving them to it, she guides the process, advising children to sit next to either Sara or Rebecca to enact and make visible their choice, once again using this impromptu opportunity for mathematics in the everyday (see Garvis & Cohrssen, 2020).

Asking the children to engage in counting and to physically sit with Sara or Rebecca (lines 115–118) serve as scaffolding for those children who may not know what 'vote' means. Following the explanation of the process, the teacher checks for understanding when she asks the children a series of questions: '*do you want two-*' line 120), '*how many peo::ple? (.) want to have* all: *of them?,(.)*' (line 125–126) and '*how many want two?*'(line 129), '*so how does that vote wo:rk.*' (line 132). Asking the children questions helps the teacher evaluate their understanding of the concept of voting while allowing for the children's input. As the voting concludes and mutual understanding of the vote is reached, Rebecca, whose solution won the popular vote, is delighted and accepts Sara's invitation to arbitrarily select who goes first by doing the '*eeny meeny miney mo*' (lines 137 –141).

Extract 19.2 was one of *only two extended* sequences of teacher participation in scaffolding children's dispute resolution in 102 dispute interventions recorded in the data. Typically, teachers would make suggestions, direct children's next actions, or re-direct the children's attention elsewhere. When teachers did ask for children's input, the questions focused on eliciting the problem, rather than inviting solutions. The remarkable features of this particular intervention in the children's dispute in Extract 19.2, are that the teacher elicits possible solutions from the children themselves, then explains how the children might decide on the two solutions proposed. Supporting children to resolve the disputes themselves takes considerably more time, but invariably results in children being able to resume collaborative play (see Church, 2009a, 2009b).

In this extract we have seen the teacher explicitly establish a participation framework for the activity of resolving a dispute over resources, by instructing and overseeing the children to sit in a circle, with equitable access to both the teacher and the marbles she has sequestered. By establishing a public locus of attention (Goodwin, 2007), the teacher has involved all members of the group in the consensus of how the marbles will be shared. Inviting (and scaffolding understanding of) voting on proposed solutions is effective in securing compliance from the group, evident in the success of 'eeny meeny miney mo' selecting each child in turn to use all the marbles.

As the analysis of this example demonstrates, supporting agency in decision-making and scaffolding the children to resolve a dispute created a space where children were able to collaboratively engage with each other in a productive way. Structuring participation, eliciting children's ideas, and scaffolding choosing a fair solution allowed for the children to successfully engage in dispute resolution while remaining the decision-making parties. Additionally, collaborative participation allowed the teacher to take advantage of teachable moments in arithmetic (i.e. counting marbles) and vocabulary and concept development (i.e. 'vote'), all while restoring the peace and enacting the principle of fairness with the children.

Recommendations for Practice

The empirical evidence in this chapter – and the depth of EMCA research in young children's disputes – shows us that eliciting possible solutions from children proves more effective in resolving disputes than imposing a solution. Even more importantly, it provides children with a model of how resolution can be achieved, equitably, with a sense of fairness. Inviting children to suggest ideas for compromise, and then moderating these suggestions, enables the teacher to promote children's agency while encouraging next actions most likely to facilitate ongoing collaborative play. This scaffolding provides children with the opportunity to navigate dispute resolution with the support of a teacher as an experienced mediator. The key implications for teachers in talking with young children about resolving conflict are:

- Focus children's attention on a discussion and the task of resolving the conflict rather than the object of the dispute (i.e. rather than orienting to the accusations of wrongdoing, or establishing blame, move to a focus on a possible solution).

- Create opportunities for children to propose solutions themselves. Invite children to suggest possible next actions in resolving the dispute.
- Encourage children to contribute their ideas. Do not evaluate these ideas, but instead repeat or summarize the most equitable or productive suggestions for the group's consideration. Use gesture and props to support understanding.
- Invite or prompt children to respond to each other's contributions or suggestions.
- Ask children what they think. Open up multiple possibilities for all children to participate in the discussion.
- Recognize that children are not only learning about managing conflict in these interactions; extended sequences of interaction provide spontaneous opportunities for concept development (e.g. the integration of mathematics, literacy, or scientific concepts).
- Enable all children to influence the final outcome (e.g. the vote).
- Where possible, remain with children to provide encouragement and support as they implement the dispute resolution.

References

Ahn, J. (2020). Honorifics and peer conflict in Korean children's language socialization. *Linguistics & Education*, 59, 100736. https://doi.org/10.1016/j.linged.2019.05.002

Bateman, A. (2012). When verbal disputes get physical. In S. Danby and M. Theobald (eds.), *Disputes in Everyday Life: Social and Moral Orders of Children and Young People* (pp. 267–296). Bingley: Emerald.

Bateman, A. (2015). *Conversation Analysis and Early Childhood Education: The Co-Production of Knowledge and Relationships*. London: Routledge.

Björk-Willén, P. (2012). Being doggy: disputes embedded in preschoolers' family role-play. In S. Danby and M. Theobald (eds.), *Disputes in Everyday Life: Social and Moral Orders of Children and Young People* (pp. 119–140). Bingley: Emerald.

Boggs, S. T. (1978). The development of verbal disputing in part-Hawaiian children. *Language in Society*, 7, 325–344.

Brenneis, D., and Lein, L. (1977). 'You fruithead': a sociolinguistic approach to children's dispute settlement. In S. Ervin-Tripp and C. Mitchell-Kernan (eds.), *Child Discourse*. New York, NY: Academic Press.

Burdelski, M. (2020). 'Say can I borrow it': teachers and children managing peer conflict in a Japanese preschool. *Linguistics and Education*, 59, 100728. www.sciencedirect.com/science/article/pii/S0898589818303826

Cekaite, A. (2020). Triadic conflict mediation as socialization into perspective taking in Swedish preschools. *Linguistics and Education*, 59, 100753. www.sciencedirect.com/science/article/pii/S0898589818303978

Chen, D. W., Fein, G. G., Killen, M., and Tam, H.-P. (2001). Peer conflicts of preschool children: issues, resolution, and age-related patterns. *Early Education and Development*, 12(4), 523–544.

Church, A. (2009a). *Preference Organization and Peer Disputes: How Young Children Resolve Conflict*. Surrey/Burlington, VT: Ashgate.

Church, A. (2009b) Closings in children's disputes. In N. Thomas (ed.), *Children, Politics and Communication: Participation at the Margins*. Bristol: Policy Press.

Church, A., and Hester, S. (2012). Conditional threats in young children's peer interaction. In S. Danby and M. Theobald (eds.), *Disputes in Everyday Life: Social and Moral Orders of Children and Young People* (pp. 243–265). Bingley: Emerald.

Church, A., Mashford-Scott, A., and Cohrssen, C. (2018). Supporting children to resolve disputes. *Journal of Early Childhood Research*, 16(1), 92–103.

Cobb-Moore, C. (2012). 'Pretend I was mummy': children's production of authority and subordinance in their pretend play interaction during disputes. In S. Danby, and M. Theobald (eds.), *Disputes in Everyday Life: Social and Moral Orders of Children and Young People* (pp. 85–118). Bingley: Emerald.

Cobb-Moore, C., Danby, S., and Farrell, A. (2008). 'I told you so': justification used in disputes in young children's interactions in an early childhood classroom. *Discourse Studies*, 10(5), 595–614.

Cohen, R. (2009). Language and conflict resolution: the limits of English. *International Studies Review*, 3(1), 25–51.

Corsaro, W. A. (1988). Routines in the peer culture of American and Italian nursery school children. *Sociology of Education*, 61, 1–14.

Corsaro, W. A., and Rizzo, T. A. (1988). *Discussione* and friendship: socialization processes in the peer culture of Italian nursery school children. *American Sociological Review*, 53, 879–894.

Danby, S., and Baker, C. D. (1998). How to be masculine in the block area. *Childhood*, 5, 151–175.

Danby, S., and Baker, C. D. (2010). Escalating terror: communicative strategies in a preschool classroom dispute. *Early Education and Development*, 12(3), 343–358.

Danby, S., and Theobald, M. (eds.). (2012). *Disputes in Everyday Life: Social and Moral Orders of Children and Young People*. Bingley: Emerald.

Eisenberg, A. R., and Garvey, C. (1981). Children's use of verbal strategies in resolving conflicts. *Discourse Processes*, 4(2), 149–170.

Erickson, F. (1982). Classroom discourse as improvisation: relationships between academic task and structure and social participation structure in lessons. In L. C. Wilkinson (ed.), *Communicating in the Classroom*. New York, NY: Academic Press.

Evaldsson, A.-C., and Svahn, J. (2017). Staging social aggression: affective stances and moral character work in girls' gossip telling. *Research on Children and Social Interaction*, 1(1), 77–104.

Garvis, S., and Cohrssen, C. (eds.). (2020). Embedding STEAM in early childhood education and care. London: Routledge.

Genishi, C., and Di Paolo, M. (1982). Learning through argument in the preschool. In L. C. Wilkinson (ed.), *Communicating in the Classroom*. New York, NY: Academic Press.

Gilligan, C. (1988). Two moral orientations: gender differences and similarities. *Merrill-Palmer Quarterly*, 34(3), 223–237.

Goodwin, C. (2007). Participation, stance and affect in the organization of activities. *Discourse & Society*, 18(1), 53–73.

Goodwin, M. H. (1990). *He-Said-She-Said: Talk as Social Organization among Black Children*. Bloomington, IN: Indiana University Press.

Goodwin, M. H. (2001). Organizing participation in cross-sex jump rope: situating gender differences within longitudinal studies of activities. *Research on Language and Social Interaction*, 34, 75–106.

Goodwin, M. H. (2006) *The Hidden Life of Girls: Games of Stance, Status and Exclusion*. Oxford: Blackwell.

Goodwin, M. H., and Goodwin, C. (1987). Children's arguing. In S. Philips, S. Steele, and C. Tanz (eds.), *Language, Gender, and Sex in Comparative Perspective*. New York, NY: Cambridge University Press.

Goodwin, M. H., Goodwin, C., and Yaeger-Dror, M. (2002). Multi-modality in girls' game disputes. *Journal of Pragmatics*, 34, 1621–1649.

Haslett, B. (1983). Preschoolers' communicative strategies in gaining compliance from peers. *Quarterly Journal of Speech*, 69, 84–99.

Holm Kvist, M., and Cekaite, A. (2020). Emotion socialization – compassion or non-engagement – in young children's responses to peer distress. *Learning Culture and Social Interaction*, 28, 1–9.

Houen, S. Danby, S., Farrell, A., and Thorpe, K. (2016a). 'I wonder …' formulations in teacher-child interactions. *International Journal of Early Childhood*, 48(3), 259–276.

Houen, S., Danby, S., Farrell, A., and Thorpe, K. (2016b). 'I wonder what you know …' teachers designing requests for factual information. *Teaching and Teacher Education*, 59, 68–78.

Kendon, A. (2004). *Gesture: Visible Action as Utterance*. Cambridge: Cambridge University Press.

Kyratzis, A., and Guo, J. (2001). Preschool girls' and boys' verbal conflict strategies in the US and China: cross-cultural and contextual considerations. *Research on Language and Social Interaction*, 34, 45–74.

Mashford-Scott, A., and Church, A. (2011). Promoting children's agency in early childhood education. *Novitas – ROYAL: Special Issue: Conversation Analysis in Educational and Applied Linguistics*, 5(1), 15–38.

Maynard, D. W. (1985). How children start arguments. *Language in Society*, 14, 1–30.

Moore, E. (2020). 'Be friends with all the children': friendship, group membership, and conflict management in a Russian preschool. *Linguistics and Education*, 59, 100744. www.sciencedirect.com/science/article/pii/S0898589818303838

Moore, E., and Burdelski, M. (2020). Peer conflict and language socialization in preschool: introduction to special issue. *Linguistics and Education*, 59, 100758. https://doi.org/10.1016/j.linged.2019.100758

Newman, R. S., Murray, B., and Lussier, C. (2001). Confrontation with aggressive peers at school: students' reluctance to seek help from the teacher. *Journal of Educational Psychology*, 93(2), 398–410.

Rae, J. (2001). Organizing participation in interaction: doing participation framework. *Research on Language and Social Interaction*, 34, 253–278.

Roseth, C., Pellegrini, A., Dupuis, D., Bohn, C., Hickey, M., Hilk, C., and A. Peshkam. (2008). Teacher intervention and U.S. preschoolers' natural conflict resolution after aggressive competition. *Behaviour*, 145(11), 1601–1626.

Sacks, H., Schegloff, E., and Jefferson, G. (1974). A simplest systematics for the organization of turn-taking for conversation. *Language*, 50(4), 696–735.

Shantz, C. U. (1987). Conflicts between children. *Child Development*, 58, 283–305.

Sheldon, A. (1990). Pickle fights: gendered talk in preschool disputes. *Discourse Processes*, 13, 5–31.

Sigurdardottir, I., Williams, P., and Einarsdottir, J. (2019). Preschool teachers communicating values to children. *International Journal of Early Years Education*, 27(2), 170–183,

Theobald, M., and Danby, S. (2012). 'A problem of versions': laying down the law in the school playground. In S. Danby and M. Theobald (eds.) *Disputes in Everyday Life: Social and Moral Orders of Children and Young People* (pp. 221–242). Bingley: Emerald.

Theobald, M., and Danby, S. (2017). Co-producing cultural knowledge: children telling tales in the school playground. In A. Bateman and A. Church (eds.), *Children's Knowledge-in-Interaction: Studies in Conversation Analysis* (pp. 111–126). Singapore: Springer.

Vuchinich, S. (1990). The sequential organization of closing in verbal family conflict. In A. D. Grimshaw (ed.), *Conflict Talk: Sociolinguistic Investigations of Arguments in Conversations*. Cambridge: Cambridge University Press.

20 | Morality

ANN-CARITA EVALDSSON AND MAGNUS KARLSSON

Introduction

In this chapter we approach the moral work that is done in and through adult-child interaction within everyday preschool practices from an ethnomethodological conversation analytic perspective (EMCA) (Bergmann, 1998; Cekaite & Evaldsson, 2020; Theobald & Danby, 2012). In so doing, we focus on morality as an intrinsic quality of social interaction that is usually invisible but becomes relevant as participants deal with and manage problematic conduct (Garfinkel, 1967). Traditionally a cognitive developmental approach has dominated the research on children and morality, viewing morality as an underlying element of children's interior world and as an abstract entity that governs the individual's moral behaviour. For instance, cognitive research has focused on children's moral development and knowledge of rules and how children are able, at certain stages to distinguish between appropriate and inappropriate behaviour. In this chapter, we extend the research on morality by using an EMCA approach to explore the important, but often delicate, interactional work that childhood educators accomplish when they socialize children to manage problematic conduct and to take responsibility for their actions and feelings.

The selected data draws from a video recording of a regular circle time activity in a Swedish preschool with children 4–5 years old (Karlsson, 2018). We examine the remedial practices that teachers use to make children accountable for a problematic peer group conduct of excluding a child from play. We show how children in this process are renegotiating their responsibility for avoiding being blamed for faulty actions. Simultaneously the children are socialized to act in morally responsible and compassionate ways. The ideological and moral implications of the teachers' remedial practices are explored in respect to educational goals in preschool. Finally, we discuss how an EMCA approach to morality-in-interaction provides insights into how childhood educators can manage the interactional challenges of socializing children into moral accountability while recognizing children's agency and maintaining a democratic ethos.

Children Telling Problems to Adults

Previous research has shown how teachers assisting children in remedying problematic actions constitute a delicate situation that brings fore asymmetrical social relations between adults and children (Theobald & Danby, 2016). Teachers possess knowledge and moral entitlements to intervene in and critically evaluate children's behaviours, including their social relationships, expressions of feelings, and moral character (Cekaite 2012, 2020; Evaldsson & Melander Bowden, 2020). Although teachers support children's telling of problems in a seemingly neutral way, it is often the teachers' version of events, including what counts as appropriate moral and emotional conduct, that is asserted in the end (Cekaite, 2013; Evaldsson 2016; Theobald & Danby, 2012). While adults control and regulate children's actions and emotions, a child who does not comply with the teacher's moral order may be treated as disrespecting teachers' authority (Cekaite 2013; Evaldsson and Melander Bowden, 2020).

Adults regulate and control children's expression of emotions (such as anger, distress, and crying) in a moral manner and use affect as resources for enforcing children to act in accordance with moral expectations (Cekaite & Evaldsson, 2020). For example, Cekaite & Ekström (2019) demonstrate how teachers in a Swedish preschool in their responses to children's emotional expressions, instructed children to modify their social conduct (rather than treating these events as a place for discussions about emotions). In another study, Kyratzis & Köymen (2020) found that preschool teachers in the United States evaluated, corrected, and modified children's emotional and social conduct in conflict episodes. By doing this, the teachers gained insight into the children's peer group conduct, as well as socialized the children into the educational, moral, and emotional order at hand (Cekaite, 2013). As teachers invoke social and emotional rules of conduct in interaction for control purposes, such rules are tested and probed by children, who continually challenge and even subvert moral orders and rules for feelings. For example, Evaldsson and Melander Bowden (2020) demonstrate how a child, who claimed moral entitlement as 'victim' of peer harassment, used heightened affect (including crying) to undermine the teacher's version and strengthen her stance claims of being badly treated. In analysing children's subversive compliance of teachers' remedial actions in a first-grade classroom, Cekaite (2013, 2020) found that children were doing several things simultaneously. In displaying remorse, the children both complied with the teacher's orders, while simultaneously subverting responsibility for faulty actions.

Taken together, these studies demonstrate how children exercise moral agency in accounting for problematic conduct, while adults at the same time sanction children's actions and feelings in ways that simultaneously enforce and limit children's autonomy and responsibility for their actions.

Situating Norms of Conduct in Accounting Practices

Particular attention is given in this chapter to the ways in which norms of conduct and feelings, and moral accountabilities are mobilized and negotiated within the sequential and cultural contexts of accounting practices (Buttny, 1993; Cekaite & Evaldsson, 2020). The analysis addresses 'the lived morality' of everyday life (Bergmann, 1998, p. 281) in terms of how moral meanings and accountabilities for actions are negotiated and transformed in accounting practices (Buttny, 1993; Goffman, 1971). 'In ordinary language accounts can be identified as excuses, apologies, justifications, defenses, explanations, narratives and the like' (Buttny, 1993, p. 1). Accounting practices constitute a central part of what Goffman (1971, p. 108) define as remedial work, in which social actors strive to change the meaning of, mitigate, and modify a problematic incident while maintaining good (moral) character. The transformative and remedial features of accounts are captured in Buttny's definition of accounts (1993, p. 1), as 'talk designed to recast the pejorative significance of action and an individual's responsibility for it, and thereby transform other's negative evaluations'. In adult-child interaction, remedial work is initiated in situations of norm transgressions and in the participants' efforts to transform a problematic behaviour into 'what can be seen as acceptable' (Cekaite & Evaldsson, 2020). Requests for accounts provide, for example, adults with resources for morally evaluating children's actions and feelings, and for negotiating children's versions of events (Evaldsson & Melander Bowden, 2020; Sterponi, 2003; Theobald & Danby, 2016). Accounts are crucial resources for finding fault, justifying own actions, and blaming others to manage the social accountability of action (Pomerantz, 1978; see also Evaldsson, 2016, Sterponi, 2009).

In this chapter we consider how remedial moral work is done though accounting practices to make children socially accountable for a problematic peer group conduct (e.g. in response to a girl crying for being excluded in peer play). Marking an event as problematic creates a necessary condition for the launching of an accounting practice where the participants' moral accountabilities for an event can be negotiated and remedied in some way. As will be demonstrated, a child's expressions of strong emotions, in the form of sadness, distress, and tension are central for eliciting accounts, and consequential for constructing moral accountability (Evaldsson & Melander Bowden, 2020; Holm Kvist, 2018). We will show how children in this process are treated as moral agents who are being held accountable for their actions and feelings. At the same time, the socialization into moral accountability exerts a regulatory function that limits children's autonomy and their responsibilities in regard to their status and cultural norms of the community (Sterponi, 2009, p. 445).

Data, Ethnographic Setting, and Participants

The selected data are drawn from a video-ethnographic study in a Swedish preschool during a period of six months conducted by the second author (Karlsson, 2018). The preschool group consisted of twenty-five children (fourteen girls and eleven boys, 4 to 5 years old) with three female preschool teachers. As part of the data collection, the children were informed that they could at any time decline to be video-recorded. Written consent was secured from all participants, including the children's parents. In the analysis, all names are pseudonyms, to protect the participants' identities. The video-ethnographic study provided access to document the children's participation in routine activities such as play, games, mealtimes, circle time, and other pedagogical activities in preschool. In these activities, moral issues were recurrently brought up and made a topic of concern, often in relation to children's conflicts in peer play (Karlsson, Hjörne, and Evaldsson, 2017).

Educational policies in Sweden provide guidelines that preschools should provide space for children's active learning so that children evolve into responsible, compassionate, and caring persons (The Swedish National Curriculum for the Preschool, Lpfö 98, Revised 2018). Such democratic principles take different shapes in preschool practices in the meaning 'living together', where one shares perspectives and ideas together (Moss, 2007, p. 6). Exploration of the potentials of a particular educational policy therefore needs to be grounded in a detailed analysis of everyday preschool practices. Here, we demonstrate that by examining how preschool teachers talk with children about rules of conduct and feelings in peer play, we can gain knowledge about the processes through which children learn to act and feel in morally responsible ways. It will be shown how cultural norms of feelings in the Swedish preschool of strengthening children's ability to express empathy and compassion for other people (see also Cekaite & Ekström, 2019; Holm Kvist, 2018) are talked into being and negotiated through various accounting practices, emotional displays, and local interpretations. As we will show, the children's peer group is a powerful socializing agent in this process.

Moral Work in Accounting for Problematic Conduct

We use an ethnomethodological conversation analytic (EMCA) approach to talk-in-interaction (Sacks, 1992; Sidnell, 2010; see also Church, Bateman, & Danby, Chapter 1, this volume) to explore what the participants (here teachers and children) are interpreting as problematic and how they engage with and remedy undesirable moral conduct in social interaction (Sterponi, 2009). For the analysis, we have selected an extended account episode from a circle time event where a group of girls are requested to account for and take responsibility for a problematic peer group conduct of excluding one girl. The account episode is constituted of five chronologically ordered excerpts (Extracts 20.1–20.5) that involve a sequential pattern of distinctive actions (Buttny, 1993, p. 24; Sidnell, 2010, p. 78–79). To begin, the teacher identifies problematic peer group conduct (Extract 20.1) and asks some children to account for their actions (Extract 20.2). The fact that the children fail to provide a sufficient and reasonable explanation of their harmful peer play conduct results in an extended account episode (Extracts 20.3–20.5). In this remedial process the teachers initiate both general rules of conduct in preschool (Extract 20.3), and make use of hypothetical scenarios from the children's play (Extract 20.4a,b) and establish mutual agreements to make the children act in morally responsible and compassionate ways (Extract 20.5).

Identifying Problematic Peer Play Conduct

The first extract will show how the peer play incident that happened among a group of girls on the playground is transformed by the teachers into a problematic event and made a public concern for the whole group during a circle time event. At this point Mia, the excluded girl, is seated with her back towards the others covering her face, in ways that demonstrates her emotional distress and sadness.

Figure 20.1 Mia demonstrates her emotional distress.

When all the children are gathered, the teacher (TE1) announces the 'unhappy incident' 'do you see that someone is sad' (line 1). The teachers now engage in a form of indirect moralizing (Luckman, 2002) in which the children (and not the adult) become responsible for (1) finding out the nature of the problematic event (lines 3–5) and for (2) formulating an actor-agent responsible for the event (lines 11–13).

Extract 20.1

01 TE1: DE ÄR SÅHÄR att se::r n↑i:: att de e nån som e
IT'S LIKE THIS do y↑ou: see:: that someone is
02 lessen här N↑U:
sad here right N↑O:W ((looks at Mia)) *#fig 1*
03 CHI: ja:::
yea::: ((looks at Mia and points at her))
04 ELL: **MI:[A:::**
05 CHI: **[A:::**
06 (1.7)
07 TE1: **°mm:°**
08 (1.0)
09 TE1: för Mia- va va: de Mia du alltid får hö:r↑a
cause Mia- what i:s it Mia that they always te:ll yo↑u
10 (4.0)
11 MIA: att Li:n:da å ehm (.) Ne:lly (1.5) å ehm (1.5)
that Li:n:da e uhm (.) Ne:lly (1.5) e uhm (1.5)

12		ehm Emelie och Ellen allti säger att "dom vill
		ehm Emelie and Ellen always say "they want
13		va ifred å ~ja↓ ↑inte få va me~"
		to be alone and ~I↓ ↑can´t join~"
14		(2.0)
15	TE2:	↑o:ps då
		↑o:h my ((looks at the children))
16	TE3:	de var ju ↑inte bra
		that´s n↑o good

When the teacher, in lines 1–2, announces that someone is sad '`do you see that someone is sad`' she simultaneously looks at Mia, whose bodily position highlights her emotional distress and sadness (see Figure 20.1). The negative emotional ascription '`someone is sad`' transforms the excluded girl into someone whom the other children might feel sorry for (Holm Kvist, 2018). At the same time, it provides information about the occurrence of some problematic or blameworthy condition (Buttny, 1993, p. 87). The issue of moral responsibility is further developed as the teacher turns to Mia and asks her what happened (line 9). The teacher's request is designed as a 'possible description' (Sacks, 1992) that indicates an occurrence of a trouble for the particular girl (Mia). The use of an extreme case formulation, '`what is it that they always tell you`' (line 9), describes 'the behaviours as frequently occurring or commonly done' (Pomerantz, 1986, p. 220).

In what follows, Mia directs an accusation toward the four girls in the group (lines 11–13), which gives the selected girls the status of blamed parties. The attribution of blame is upgraded through an extreme case formulation (reusing the teacher's words), '`they always say`' together with reported speech (reusing the girls' prior words) '`~they want to be alone and I↓ ↑can´t join~`'. Mia further legitimizes her moral claims of being badly treated in a tremulous crying voice (~line 13), which justifies her version of the event and her feelings of sadness as reasonable (Evaldsson & Melander Bowden, 2020).

The four girls stand now accused of excluding Mia from their play. At the same time, Mia's emotionally charged narrated descriptions make available a contrastive category for her as a 'victim' and as 'socially excluded'. The teachers' uptakes in the form of negative assessments (lines 15–16), strengthen the 'factual basis and seriousness' (Edwards, 2005, p. 5) of the girls' actions towards Mia. The teachers simultaneously display strong alignment with the excluded girl, Mia, as in need of adult protection.

Requesting Children to Account for Their Actions

In what follows, requests for an account are used as resources to reveal the children's stances and alignments towards one another and the problematic peer group event. Requests for accounts are found to be common practices among adults across settings to position a child as (morally) responsible for his/her actions (Evaldsson, 2016; Sterponi, 2009; Theobald & Danby, 2012). As Sterponi (2009, p. 445) notes a request for an account 'grants autonomy to the individual as agent', as it offers an opportunity to mitigate the ascription of fault, i.e. to distance oneself from blame. At the same time, it limits the autonomy of action as it indicates a piece of trouble for the child who is cast as accountable for the misconduct (Sterponi 2003, p. 84).

In the beginning of Extract 20.2 the teacher uses a 'why-question' to elicit an account from the girls, 'why- why can´t Lin- Mia joi:n", is there anyone who can answer that'. As will be shown, the teacher's request for an account offers an opportunity for the girls both to mitigate their responsibility for excluding Mia and to defend their own actions.

Extract 20.2

01	TE1:	å då så sa ja såhär "vi får ju FRÅ:GA dom
		an then I said like this "we have to AS:K them
02		varf↑ör (1.0) varför får inte Mo-Mia va m↑e:"=
		wh:↑y (1.0) why can´t Lin- Mia jo↑i:n"=
03		=e de nån som kan svara på de↑
		=is there anyone who can answer that↑
		((leans forward))
04		(1.0)
05	GOR:	**fö- för** att (.) dom=
		ca-cause (.) they=
06	TE2:	=Tsch flickorna
		=Tsch the girls ((puts her hand on Goran´s mouth))
07		(2.0)
08	TE1:	de e dom här flickorna, Linda
		it is the girls, Linda ((points to the group))
09	LIN:	jag vill för att jag vill va .h själv ↑ofta
		I want because I want to be .h by myself ↑often
10	TE1:	du vill va själv ibland=så du har
		you want to be by yourself sometimes=so you have
11		aldri känt att int- att du har fått vart

never felt that you don- that you have been
12 utanför å du har frågat om du får va me:↑
left outside and asked others if you can joi:n↑
13 LIN: nä men ja- för ja för att jag har ofta velat
no but I- cause I have often wanted to be
14 vara själv
by myself
15 TE1: du vill leka själv H↑A:
you want to play by yourself R↑I:GHT
16 å Nelly ↑då har du sagt nåt?
and what about ↑Nelly have you said anything?
17 (2.0)
18 NEL: **((shakes on her head, leaning backwards))**
19 (1.0)
20 TE1: Ellen då?
Ellen then?
21 TE2/3: **((moves gaze towards Ellen))**
22 ELL: **((shakes on her head, looks down))**
23 TE3: har du sagt att Mia inte får va me?
have you said that Mia can´t join?
24 (1.0)
25 ELL: nä:e:
***noe:* ((rubbing her palms against each other))**
26 TE2: å så va det Emelie va?
and then it was Emelie? ((moves gaze towards Emelie))
27 EME: **((shakes her head))**
28 MIA: men innan sa ni att ni "ville va
but earlier you said that you "wanted to be left
29 ifred å att inte ~ja fick va me:~"
alone and that ~I couldn´t joi:n~"
30 TE1: vem va de som sa de då?
who said that?
31 MIA: Emelie Ellen å eh (1.0) Linda
Emelie Ellen and eh (1.0) Linda

The teacher's request for an account is first addressed to the whole group of children (lines 1–3) and then redirected to the four girls who now stand accused for the accountable action of not letting Mia join (lines 6–8). The four girls are singled out and addressed by their names, Linda (line 8), Nelly (line 16), Ellen (line 20), and Emelie (line 26), to take responsibility for and individually account for their faulty actions (lines 9–27). However, as shown, none of the girls comply with the teacher's request.

To start with, Linda reluctantly responds in a lowered tone of voice while she justifies her own play actions with '`I want to be by myself often`' (line 9). The use of a justification demonstrates Linda's recognition of the peer play event (rejecting Mia) as problematic. Through the justification Linda manages 'the negotiation of responsibility and the re-categorization of the problematic event/conduct' (Sterponi, 2003, p. 81). In that way she presents herself as having less responsibility to include Mia and in so making the rejection less problematic. However, the teachers do not accept the response but continue to question Linda to get a proper account from her (lines 10–12).

In what follows, the teachers treat the girls' unwillingness to take responsibility for their actions as a place for moral discussions about emotions. The references made to Linda's own feelings '`so you have never felt that you don- that you have been left outside`' (lines 10–12), works retroactively to evoke the girls' own experiences of being excluded and therefore as accountable. The use of a hypothetical scenario works to project moral and emotional insight to the girls about the hurt feeling experienced by the 'transgressed-upon child' (Kyratzis & Köymen, 2020, p. 624). In this way, the children are provided with interactional resources both to mitigate their offensive actions, and to become aware of their own and other children's (Mia's) hurt feelings and to refrain from similar actions in the future. However, none of the girls fully comply with the teachers' version. For example Linda only partly ties to the excluded girl's original version (i.e. '`they want to be alone`') (Extract 20.1, line 10). By altering the format in a preferred way (i.e. '`I want to be by myself`') Linda manages to justify her own play actions without openly rejecting the teachers' version (Buttny, 1993, p. 147). In response, the teachers (TE1 and TE3), one after the other, try to solicit an acceptable account from the rest of the girls (lines 16 and 23). Now proposing that the girls have prevented Mia to join their play, '`have you said that Mia can´t join`' (line 23). However, the teacher's efforts do not result in the girls taking responsibility for the faulty actions (lines 18, 22, 27). In her response Mia almost breaks out crying while she recycles her own version (line 29).

In this remedial process, two conflicting versions or sides of the problematic peer play event are co-constructed with the four girls' denying their responsibilities (for excluding Mia from play). In so doing, the girls invoke institutional rules of conduct '*to play on one's own*' without contravening the overarching rules in preschool '*everyone can play*' (Evaldsson & Tellgren, 2009). As shown, the teachers do not accept the girls' version.

Instead, they continue to request information about who is responsible for the untoward actions, 'Who said that' (lines, 16, 23, 26, and 30). A reason might be that Mia is still crying, which in turn amplifies her claims of being badly treated (Evaldsson & Melander Bowden, 2020). In what follows, we will look more closely into the role of negative emotions such as crying in shaping the teachers' efforts to engage in remedial moral work, to prevent children from hurting others' feelings, and from being left outside.

Invoking General Rules of Conduct

In the second part of the account episode, the teachers change their remedial moral work, in finding fault and questioning the children's actions, in an effort both to solve the girls' problematic conduct of excluding Mia and to socialize the children to act in compassionate ways towards one another (Extracts 20.3–20.5). In contrast to the first part of the account episode (Extract 20.1–20.2), where the teachers invited specific children (the four girls) to account for and explain their untoward actions, the teachers now transform the girls' problematic peer play into a public concern for the whole group of children. By using the collective address term 'you', the teachers request the whole group to take part in a shared moral discussion (Extract 20.3, line 1). The rhetorical question 'do you remember what we have talked about', invokes general rules of conduct, reminding the children of democratic principles of how to act towards one another in preschool. Interestingly, the teachers orienting the whole group of children to institutional rules of conduct linked to 'cooperation' and 'friendship' is formulated directly in response to the argument made by the four girls of their rights to play on their own.

Extract 20.3

01	TE1:	kommer ni ihåg va- kommer ni ihåg va vi
		do you remember wha- do you remember what we
02		pra:tade↑ om att vi skulle .hh hur hur-
		ta:lked↑ about that we should .hh how how-
03		va de va=
		what it was=
04	ISA:	=samarbeta
		=cooperate ((leans forward))
05	TE1:	å ja va bety:[der
		and yeah that mea:[ns
06	VER:	[å va vänner

[and be friends
07 TE1: å va vänner och samarbeta ja
and be friends and cooperate yeah
08 MIA: **((places her back turned**
towards the group))
09 **-------**
10 TE1: å så och så vänder du dig om Mia?
and then you turn around Mia?
11 .hh annars vet vi inte Ellen vad vi ska säga
.hh otherwise we do not know Mia what to say
12 **and then ((puts her hands on Mia´s shoulders))**

The teacher's reference in lines 1–3 to the children's collective remembering, 'do you remember', signals that the children together with the teachers often are involved in moral discussions about how to act towards one another. In the dialogue that follows, it is apparent that the teacher's rhetorical question is understood as a reason for further discussions and reflections about the general rules for conduct in preschool. One of the children (Isabel) immediately responds by leaning forward and continuing the teacher's question – that we should: 'cooperate' (line 4). The teacher (TE1) then invites the children to elaborate on the general rule, by asking: 'and yeah that mea:ns' (line 5). In overlap, another child, Vera, responds with her interpretation 'and be friends' (line 6). The discussion of more general rules (to cooperate and to be friends) (lines 1–7) works to provide the previous moral discussion with a general interest.

In the end the teacher shifts back to the particular play incident involving the four girls and Mia. The teacher now turns to Mia and gently asks her to turn her body towards the others: 'otherwise we don´t know what to say' (line 11–12). The teacher's action of placing her hands on Mia and turning her towards her peers works to position Mia as the main focus of attention for the current moral discussion about cooperation and friendship.

Modelling Children's Play Actions and Feelings

So far, the accounts offered by the accused girls have failed to provide proper and sufficient explanations of the problematic peer play event of excluding Mia. As Buttny (1993, p. 25) notes, for a problematic event to be remedied, the accounts offered need to be evaluated as acceptable by the recipient (here the teachers) and normalized in relation to cultural norms of the group. We will now show how the girls' lack of acceptable accounts results in the teachers continuing to treat the girls as morally accountable for the improper actions of excluding Mia. As Sterponi (2009, p. 446) shows in her work on morality in Italian dinner conversations, the socialization into accountability 'often consists of modeling the moves' that children seem not yet able to produce. The teachers' use hypothetical scenarios to perform this modelling, demonstrating for the children (1) how they should act and feel towards others (in compassionate ways), as well as (2) how they should remediate their conduct (compare with Sterponi, 2009, p. 454) (Extract 20.4a, lines 1–3, 5; Extract 20.4b, lines 8–12).

Extract 20.4a

01 TE1: Ellen (1.0) Ellen och Emelie å ni (2.0)
Ellen (1.0) Ellen and Emelie and you (2.0)
02 hur känn- hur skulle ni känna er
how does it fe- how would you feel
03 om nån säg- att ni får inte va me:↑
if someone say- that you must go and can't joi:n↑
04 ELL: då () vi leker (själva) o (gå) ↑igen
then () we play (on our own) and (leave) ↑again
05 TE1: vi men om du (1.0) °inte får va med nån°
we but if you (1.0)°can´t join anyone°
((points to Ellen))
06 (3.0)
07 TE3: **((looks at Ellen with wrinkled eye-brows))**

To start with, the teacher addresses the four girls, who now are cast as responsible for excluding Mia (line 1). The teacher (TE1) then uses a hypothetical scenario to model the children's actions and feelings, to make them (1) become aware of their own actions as harmful, and (2) to stop them from excluding others, 'how would you feel if someone says- that you must go and can't join' (lines 2–3). The teacher's use of a hypothetical scenario creates an imaginary situation that literally puts the accused girls in the shoes of the victim (i.e. Mia). In this remedial process, the teacher casts the girls' as accountable for causing distress, to elicit the girls' own feelings of remorse and make them feel and act as if they were the other person (Mia). The hypothetical scenario is performed with close retrospective attention to the format of Mia's prior account ('I↓ ↑can´t join') (see Extracts 20.1 and 20.2). However, none of the selected girls are willing to take responsibility for the actions of excluding Mia from play. Instead, one girl, Ellen, presents a solution to the problem, based on the girls' own experiences of wanting to play on their own (line 4). The format of Ellen's justification 'we play (on our own)' builds on and/reuses the format in Linda's previous response to the teacher ('I want to be by myself', Extract 20.2, lines 9, 13–14). The alternative account is defensive insofar as it deflects the blame away from the problematic peer play actions and 'implies that no offence or transgression has been committed' (Drew, 1998, p. 302).

The lack of an acceptable account from the four girls warrants in turn the teachers (TE1, TE2, and TE3) to collaborate in making the children accountable for their harmful actions (Extract 20.4b, lines 8–19). We will show how the teachers use hypothetical scenarios in the form of embodied enactments (voice, talk, gestures), to transform a problematic play event of excluding a peer into a place for discussions about the emotional consequences of harmful play actions.

Extract 20.4b

08 TE2: hon menar[såhär
she means [like this
09 TE1: [om du får gå ensam
[if you have to walk away alone ((points at Ellen))
10 TE2: hon menar såhär Ellen att om Emilie å Signe
she means like this Ellen that if Emelie and Signe
11 å al- å >alla< flickorna leker (.) tillsammans
and al- an >all< the girls play (.) together
12 å så kom- ↑"NÄE du få inte va me Ellen"
and then ↑"NO you can´t join Ellen"
13 hur känns de här inne ↑då
how would that feel here inside ↑then ((looks at the girls, puts her hands on the chest))
14 (0.5) **((looks at Ellen, frowning))**
15 ELL: då ( ) leka själv
then ( ) play myself
16 TE3: näe det känns nog inge bra
no it probably doesn´t feel that good
17 TE2: ja tror inte de känns sådär[jättebra] härinne
I don´t think that it feels [really good] inside ((looks at the children))

18 TE3: [näe]
[no]
((shaking her head))
19 TE1: de vet ja att du har sagt Emelie förut (.) att
I know that you've said before Emelie (.) that
((leaning forward))
20 du har tyckt de va jobbit .h å va ensam
you thought it was hard .h to be alone
21 EME: **mm ((looks down))**
22 TE2: **°Mm°**
23 TE3: å Rebecca också?
e Rebecca to? ((lifts her arm))
24 TE1: .hh ja:
.hh yea:
25 TE3: att du har sagt också Mia att du vill va ifred
that you also said Mia that you want to be alone

The hypothetical scenarios are designed to show the children what it means to be alone but also to become sensitive to other children's hurt feelings and to stop their own offensive actions (compare with Kyratzis & Köymen, 2020, p. 623). In this process the teacher (TE2) uses extreme case formulation together with hypothetical reported speech to deal with the children's rule violations in play, 'if Emelie and Signe and al- and all the girls play together and then comes-"NO you can´t join Ellen"' (lines 10–13). Simultaneously, as the words are spoken, the teacher puts her hand on her own heart while she looks at the girls one by one. The use of dramatic gestures intensifies the hurt feelings and localizes the negative feelings within the child's body, 'how would that feel here inside then?' (line 13). She then looks at Ellen, who instead of complying with the teacher, continues to justify her own play conduct (line 15). The other teachers (first TE3 and then TE2) now step in and ascribe emotions of being hurt also to Ellen (lines 16–18). In that way the teachers disqualify the girls' justifications of their play actions as playing on their own. In what follows, the three teachers collaborate in ascribing similar emotions of feeling lonely to the other girls (lines 19–25). Including Emelie: 'I know that you've said Emelie (.) that you thought it was hard to be alone' (lines 19–20), and then Rebecca (lines 23–24) and the excluded girl Mia (line 25).

The use of emotional ascriptions presumes that the teachers have access to and intimate knowledge of the children's inner feelings (Buttny, 1993, p. 96). By making claims of having knowledge not only of children's play actions but also of their inner feelings (of feeling alone), the teachers open up for further negotiations not only of children's responsibilities, but also children's agency and their control of emotions.

Establishing a Shared Agreement and An Activity Contract

In the end, the teachers, together with the children, establish a forward-looking 'activity contract' (Aronsson & Cekaite, 2011), to project morally appropriate play actions and feelings, and distinctive remedial moves. According to Aronsson & Cekaite (2011, p. 137), activity contracts constitute 'agreements that form a type of inter-generational account work around target activities'. We will show how the teachers once again use embodied enactments (voice, talk, gestures) and hypothetical reported speech to demonstrate the practical, moral, and emotional implications of rules for appropriate peer play.

Extract 20.5

01 TE3: men då är vi ju över↑ens (0.3) [bra:↑
but then we have an agr↑eement(0.3) [goo:d↑
((moves head around the circle))
02 TE2: [ja:]
[yea:]
03 CHI: men så får man ju inte säga
but you cannot say that
04 TE1: SÅ BRA:↑ (0.5) då får vi kanske tänka på
SO GOO:D↑ (0.5) then we might have to
05 tänka på de nu igen >lite<
think a bit about that again >a bit<
06 CHI: JA::
YEA:
07 TE1: KAN VI TUMMA PÅ DE att vi ska tänka på
CAN WE SHAKE HANDS ON that we should think
08 detta↑ i:gen
about this↑ a:gain
09 CHI: JA::
YEA::

10 ANN: **((talks with Emelie sitting next to her))**
11 TE1: annars får vi pra:ta om de igen EMELIE↑
or else we have to ta:lk about it again EMELIE↑
((points at Emelie))
12 å ANNA
and ANNA ((leans down towards Anna))
13 TE2: **((makes thumbs up))**
14 BEN: tummen ner betyder nej
thumbs down means no
15 TE1: Anna har du också tänkt på de (1.0) >mm< att
Anna have you also thought about (1.0) >mm< that
((leans fwd))
16 vi får tänka på de allihop att vi får sä:ga
we all have to think about that we have to sa:y
17 .hh att "du får gärna va me men nu har vi
.hh that "you can join but now we have
18 bestämt en lek som vi ska leka de får du va me"
decided a play that we will play that you can join"
19 på då (1.0) om man kommer in som nummer tre: mm
if one joins as number three: mm ((shows three fingers))
20 (1.0)
21 TE1: mm eller hur Mia?
mm right Mia? ((points to Mia))
22 MIA: **((Nods))**
23 TE1: man kan inte bestämma allt själv utan man får
one can't decide everything by oneself but one
24 lyssna lite på va dom andra leker också
has to listen to what the others are playing too
25 (2.0)
26 TE3: de där kan ju vara lite sv↑årt
that could be somewhat tr↑icky
27 TE1: **Mm**

The teacher (TE3) now moves her gaze around the circle. She sums up the extended moral discussion while pointing to the children and the teachers who now are described as having an agreement (line 1). The whole group of children is then encouraged 'to think about' (lines 4–8) and reflect on the current agreement (Goodwin & Cekaite, 2018, p. 105). At the same time the teacher (TE1) directs the children to shake hands (lines

7–14). In that way the teachers establish a mutual agreement with the whole group of children in the form of an 'activity contract' (Aronsson & Cekaite, 2011). The contract specifies how the children should act in future peer play, and that they are morally accountable for their actions, along with the various conditions. The teacher uses hypothetical reported speech as a modelling function to dramatize the practical implications of the shared rules of conduct (15–19). More specifically, the teacher (TE1) verbally enacts what the children should say when another child approaches their play (lines 17–18). This advice-giving activity (Theobald & Danby, 2012, p. 231) can be described as socializing the children into moral accountability by projecting or prompting children's future play interactions (Kyratzis & Köymen, 2020).

In the end, TE1 shifts to discuss more general implications of the rules of conduct (lines 23–24), '`one can't decide everything by oneself but one one has to listen to what the others are playing`'. Interestingly, this last part of the rule discussion is addressed to Mia (see line 21), the girl whose report about the other girls' unwillingness to include her in peer play started the moral discussion (see Extract 20.1). The teachers' discussion brings up the multiple and shared dimensions of moral responsibility for all the children involved in rule violations of cooperative play. By tying the rule discussion to the actions performed by the child who tries to join others' play, (i.e. the excluded girl, Mia), one can argue that the teachers are indirectly commenting on the problematic play situation brought up in the beginning; thus, indicating that the excluded party might have played a part in the problematic peer play situation, of causing her own exclusion. The final part of the moral discussion further allows the teachers to make the children collectively responsible for not following the moral rules of conduct in preschool, while avoiding blaming particular children of behaving inappropriately (compare with Evaldsson, 2016).

Recommendations for Practice

This chapter has shown how an ethnomethodological conversation analytical approach adds to our understanding of (1) the complex and often delicate moral and interactional work that is accomplished by preschool teachers when they engage in remedying children's problematic peer group conduct, and (2) how educational goals of encouraging children to act in responsible and compassionate ways are foregrounded in this process. We conclude by providing some recommendations for how preschool teachers can manage the moral challenges in remedying problematic peer-group conduct, while acknowledging children's agency and maintaining a democratic ethos.

- Teachers can notice how children carefully orchestrate their accounts to avoid being held morally accountable and blamed for faulty conduct. Close attention to how children design their accounts to mitigate blame, justify actions, and defend their rights to play on their own terms highlight children's moral agency and interactional competence to co-produce and even subvert teachers' moral order.
- The ways in which children respond to and subvert teachers' remedial actions reveal how children have some sense of what counts as a reportable offence in dealing with adults. Children's responses expose the importance for preschool teachers of being sensitive to how teachers and children orient to different and sometimes overlapping moral orders, and how children (in contrast to adults) are engaged in local peer group relations and peer cultures.
- Democratic principles of acknowledging children's moral agency and providing space for active learning are grounded in everyday practice for teachers. To avoid imposing moralization, and instead of confronting and condemning children, teachers can involve children in ethical discussions about how we behave with others, making morality a joint activity.
- By listening to children's accounts, teachers can encourage children's participation in establishing, negotiating, and enacting moral rules of conduct.

References

Aronsson, K., and Cekaite, A. (2011). Activity contracts and directives in everyday family politics. *Discourse and Society*, 22(2), 1–18.

Bergmann, J. (1998). Introduction: morality in discourse. *Research on Language and Social Interaction*, 31, 279–294.

Buttny, R. (1993). *Social Accountability in Communication*. London: Sage Publications.

Cekaite, A. (2012). Tattling and dispute resolution: moral order, emotions and embodiment in the teacher-mediated disputes of young second language learners. In S. Danby and M. Theobald (eds.), *Disputes in Everyday Life – Social and Moral Orders of Children and Young People*. Bingley: Emerald Books.

Cekaite, A. (2013). Socializing emotionally and morally appropriate peer group conduct through classroom discourse. *Linguistics and Education*, 24, 511–522.

Cekaite, A. (2020). Subversive compliance and embodiment in remedial interchanges. *Text & Talk*, 40(5), 669-693. https://doi.org/10.1515/text-2020-2078

Cekaite, A., and Ekström, A. (2019). Emotion socialization in teacher-child interaction: teachers' responses to children´s negative emotions. *Frontiers Psychology*, 10(1546), 1–19.

Cekaite, A., and Evaldsson, A.-C. (2020). The moral character of emotion work in adult-child interaction. *Text & Talk*, 40(5), 563-572. https://doi.org/10.1515/text-2020-2082

Drew, P. (1998). Complaints about transgressions and misconduct. *Research on Language and Social Interaction*, 31(3 & 4), 295–325.

Edwards, D. (2005). Moaning, whinging and laughing: the subjective side of complaints. *Discourse Studies*, 7(1), 5–29.

Evaldsson, A.-C. (2016). Schoolyard suspect: blame negotiations, category-work and conflicting versions among children and teachers. In A. Bateman and A. Church (eds.), *Children's Knowledge-in-Interaction: Studies in Conversation Analysis*. Singapore: Springer.

Evaldsson, A.-C., and Melander Bowden, H. (2020). Co-constructing a child as disorderly: moral character work in narrative accounts of upsetting experiences. *Text & Talk*, 40(5), 599-622. https://doi.org/10.1515/text-2020-2079

Evaldsson, A.-C., and Tellgren, B. (2009). 'Don't enter it's dangerous'. Negotiations for power and exclusion in pre-school girls' play interactions. *Educational and Child Psychology*, 26(2), 9–18.

Garfinkel, H. (1967). *Studies in Ethnomethodology*. Cambridge: Polity press.

Goffman, E. (1971). *Relations in Public: Microstudies of the Public Order*. New York, NY: Basic Bookss.

Goodwin, M. H., and Cekaite. A. (2018). *Embodied Family Choreography: Practices of Control, Care, and Mundane Creativity* (1st ed). London: Routledge.

Holm Kvist, M. (2018). Children's crying in play conflicts: a locus for moral and emotional socialization. *Research on Children and Social interaction*, 2(2), 153–176.

Karlsson, M. (2018). *Moral work in preschool. Rules and moral order in child-child and adult-child interaction*. Ph.D. Dissertaion. Gothenburg Studies in Educational Sciences, no. 417. Gothenburg: University of Gothenburg.

Karlsson, M, Hjörne, E, and Evaldsson, A.-C. (2017). Preschool girls as rule breakers: negotiating moral orders of justice and fairness. *Childhood*, 24(3), 396–415.

Kyratzis, A., and Köymen, B. (2020). Morality-in-interaction: toddlers' recyclings of institutional discourses of feeling during peer disputes in daycare. *Text & Talk*, 40(5), 623–642. https://doi.org/10.1515/text-2020-2081

Moss, P. (2007). Bringing politics into the nursery: early childhood education as a democratic practice. *Working papers in early childhood development, No. 43*. Bernard Van Leer Foundation. Netherlands: The Hague.

Luckmann, T. (2002). Moral communication in modern societies. *Human Studies*, 25(1), 19–32.

Pomerantz, A. (1978). Attributions of responsibility: blamings. *Sociology*, 12(1), 115–121.

Pomerantz, A. (1986). Extreme case formulations: a way of legitimizing claims. *Human Studies*, 9, 219–229.

Sacks, H. (1992) *Lectures on Conversation*, (vol. I and II). Oxford: Blackwell.

Sidnell, J. (2010). *Conversation Analysis: An Introduction*. Chichester: Wiley-Blackwell.

Sterponi, L. (2003). Account episodes in family discourse: the making of morality in everyday interaction. *Discourse Studies*, 5, 79–100.

Sterponi, L. (2009). Accountability in family discourse. Socialization into norms and standards of responsibility in Italian dinner conversations. *Childhood*, 16(4), 441–59.

Theobald, M., and Danby, S. (2012). 'A problem of versions': laying down the law on the school playground. In S. Danby and M. Theobald (eds.), *Disputes in Everyday Life: Social and Moral Orders of Children and Young People* (pp. 221–241). Bingley: Emerald Books.

Theobald, M., and Danby, S. (2016). Co-producing cultural knowledge: children telling tales in the school playground. In A. Bateman and A. Church (eds.), *Children's Knowledge-in-Interaction* (pp. 111–126). Singapore: Springer.

The Swedish National Agency for Education. (2018). *The National Curriculum for the Swedish Preschool, Revised 2018*. Stockholm: Skolverket.

21 | Families

AKIRA TAKADA

Introduction

Ethnomethodology established by Harold Garfinkel argued that studying people's (= ethno) ways (= methods) would lead to clarifying the processes by which society emerges within and through interactions (Garfinkel, 1967). This claim struck a chord with a number of excellent researchers, and various research domains were created to analyse people's everyday interactions in detail. In particular, conversation analysis and language socialization research influenced each other while crossing over both research topics and the researchers (including the author) who explore them. Since the background of conversation analysis is described in other chapters (see Church, Bateman & Danby, Chapter 1, this volume), the background of language socialization research is outlined below.

Elinor Ochs, a renowned professor in the Department of Anthropology at UCLA, studied at the University of Pennsylvania's graduate school under Dell Hymes, the founder of 'ethnography of communication' (Hymes, 1964). Hymes was a close colleague of Erving Goffman, a pioneer in interaction theory. Reflecting the work of Hymes and Goffman, Ochs started exploring why a child produces an utterance in a particular way at a particular time during interactions in the society under study. Motivated by these interests, Ochs began to enthusiastically develop language socialization theory with her colleagues Bambi Schieffelin, Alessandro Duranti, and others. Studies of language socialization have paid special attention to the analysis of recursive interplays between 'socialization to use language' and 'socialization through the use of language' observed in interactions between the expert members of a social group (e.g. caregivers) and the novices (e.g. children). Thereafter, studies of language socialization examined how 'each community's habitus of communicative codes, practices, and strategies is to be judged in terms of its own socio-cultural logic rather than external sensibilities' (Ochs et al., 2005, p. 548).

As a theoretical tool for this purpose, Ochs et al. (2005, pp. 552–553) further proposed the model of child-directed communication. A notable feature of this model is that it extends the scope of analysis of language socialization to modes of communication other than verbal utterances. As many studies on child development suggest, in caregiver–child interactions, facial expressions, gaze directions, nods, pointing, etc. are effectively used much earlier than the onset of verbal speech (e.g. Bruner, 1983; Povinelli et al., 2003; Tomasello, 1999). These semiotic resources – i.e. the actions, materials, and artifacts we use for communicative purposes – (C. Goodwin, 2000) are embedded in situation. At the same time, each participant can work on the situation by indicating where to pay attention in the course of interaction. Based on these findings, Ochs and her colleagues offered a perspective that children gradually take appropriate actions, according to the situation, by using a variety of semiotic resources, including non-verbal ones (e.g. Duranti et al., 2012; Ochs, 1988; Schieffelin, 1990).

In order to pursue this perspective, my colleagues and I conducted research on language socialization in Japan/Japanese. We call this research the 'cultural formation of responsibility in caregiver–child interactions (CCI) project'. The objective of this project is to clarify the process by which children gradually expand their spatiotemporal range to behave appropriately, according to the culturally framed situation of interactions, as exemplified by the explanation of Responsibilities 1 to 3 below (Cultural formation of responsibility in caregiver–child interactions, 2020). Needless to say, 'responsibility', which is the key concept of the CCI project, is one of the most important concepts in the humanities and social sciences. For example, in criminal law, the intention of an actor determines responsibility for the consequences of his/her deeds (Mizuno, 2000). Probably because of this widespread importance, however, there are various theoretical difficulties in defining the concept of responsibility in relation to the intention of the actor (Ohba, 2005). To overcome such theoretical difficulties, our approach seeks to find the foundation of responsibility in 'the ability of responses' (the etymological root of the word 'responsibility'), which enables call and response in actual interactions. Primordial forms of such ability can be observed in children even before they understand others' intentions (for example, crying for attention). From this perspective, responsibility can be classified into the following three sub-categories (Takada et al., 2016).

(1) Responsibility 1: Response in an interaction that has not led to an exchange of clear social meaning. In other words, an act that is the precondition of (2) (e.g. child responses, such as coordination of his/her gaze, to the caregiver's utterance/gesture, such as 'here you are', without clearly understanding its social meaning and the caregiver's intention).

(2) Responsibility 2: Response to a call found in the exchange of utterances that form an 'adjacency pair' (Schegloff, 2007), consisting of first pair part and second pair part (e.g. a child's 'good morning' greeting, as the second pair part, in response to the caregiver's 'good morning' greeting, as the first pair part).
(3) Responsibility 3: Response found in utterances that accompanied or extended from the exchange of utterances that form an adjacency pair (e.g. when a child gives the dispreferred response 'No', as the second pair part, to the caregiver's request, 'lend it to your sister', as the first pair part; the child further gives an account about the dispreferred response 'No': 'because this is mine').

The concept of responsibility in our approach is linked to, but not synonymous with, the vernacular concept of 'responsibility'. In actual exchanges, Responsibilities 1 to 3 are intricately intertwined and embedded in various patterns of interaction. By carefully unravelling such patterns and considering their development, we can gain a deeper understanding of the concept of responsibility. This approach has also contributed to language socialization and conversation analysis research by way of clarifying the mechanism of formation and coordination of the relationships between children and caregivers in everyday life (e.g. Takada, 2012, forthcoming; Takada & Kawashima, 2016; Takada et al., 2016).

Method and Data

In the CCI project, we conducted a longitudinal observation of eighteen families living in the Kansai area of Japan from 2007 to 2016. All families include children aged 0–5 years and their siblings (in total, nineteen males and sixteen females) at the time of filming, born of middle-class Japanese parents. The data set also includes mothers who were pregnant during the data collection period. The target families were selected from those who showed interest in the activities of the infant development research group of Kyoto University (Babylab, 2020). The members of our research group recorded interaction of the focal child with anyone in a natural home setting for about 2 hours per month. The recorded video totals about 528 hours. All conversations recorded in the video were transcribed. In addition, while repeatedly watching the video, we identified a person who performed a (non-verbal) behaviour that affected the progress of the interaction, and we described the behaviour. Also, at the beginning of the transcription, the situation was described as accurately as possible, and any changes that affected the progress of the interaction were noted. The descriptions were combined with the transcripts of the conversations to form a data set. Studies using this dataset have already been published in various books and papers (e.g., Takada et al., 2016; Takada, forthcoming).

From these products, this chapter focuses on three main topics: (1) sharing attention by pointing; (2) communication regarding directive; and (3) organization of attention, affect, and morality through storytelling, to explore which types of interactions are distinctive in Japanese family life. The implications for professionals in nursery and educational institutions, such as day-care centres for young children and preschools, will also be considered. Particularly, I would like nursery and preschool teachers to be aware of the richness of family interactions as a resource for the care and teaching of children. Moreover, I will suggest how they can establish a link between family life and educational settings for children in their care.

Sharing Attention by Pointing

Children and caregivers use various semiotic resources to align their behaviours and share attention in their interactions. Gestures, especially pointing, are often used for this purpose. Liszkowski et al. (2012) claimed that pointing is a universal feature that humans acquire as they grow up in society, regardless of cultural differences. Babies usually start pointing shortly before they start speaking. Use of pointing is thus considered to be closely associated with the development of symbols, such as language. Accordingly, child development researchers have been paying special attention to pointing from early on (e.g. Bruner, 1983; Povinelli et al., 2003; Tomasello, 1999). Moreover, pointing connects the lifeworld(s) of multiple individuals with the environment. Therefore, studying the use of pointing provides us with the opportunity to overcome the methodological individualism that has been the mainstream of child development research and to open up a new research domain that discusses how children and caregivers achieve mutual understanding within the structure of the environment. This new research domain has been pioneered by the works on pointing from the perspective of interaction studies (e.g. C. Goodwin, 2007; Mondada, 2007). It will clarify the various aspects of Responsibility 1, mentioned above, and the mechanism by which Responsibility 2 emerges from them.

Endo and Takada (2019) examined caregivers' reactions to children's pointing and discussed how pointing works as a resource for interaction in home activities. According to them, in order for pointing to do something in communication, it must first be seen by the other party. This may sound obvious, but that is not always the case for the pointing of young children. During infancy, expressive pointing, by which an infant shows (just) their own interest in an object or event by pointing, appears earlier than more communicative pointing, such as imperative pointing, which can work as a request to the observer (Franco & Butterworth, 1996; Grünloh & Liszkowski, 2015). For this reason, infants often point when the caregivers are not looking at them.

A child gradually comes to recognize circumstances in which their caregiver can see the target of interest, as indicated by the child's pointing. In this regard, Kidwell (2005) reports that children sensitively modify their behaviour according to the type of gaze (e.g. 'a mere look', in which the caregiver continues with the current activity, or 'the look', in which a caregiver projects an intervention in children's activities) directed by the caregivers.

Endo and Takada (2019) indicate that a child's pointing is often reacted to by the caregiver as being initiated by the caregiver or as part of an activity that is already underway, thereby working as a resource for achieving joint attention in caregiver–child interactions. In the example below, a 15-month-old boy, B, and his 50-month-old sister, S, were sitting facing a table. Mother, M, sat diagonally between B and S. S drank a cup of tea and ate rice crackers. Then, the following interactions occurred.

It should be noted that in the excerpts, each line includes the original Japanese utterance, word glosses, and the English translation. The original Japanese utterances are transcribed according to a modified version of the conventions developed in conversation analysis research provided at the front of this volume [for details, see Schegloff (2007); Sidnell & Stivers (2013)]. These transcripts provide empirical evidence of the subsequent description and analysis. Readers unfamiliar with the format of transcripts should first read the description and analysis of it and then return to the transcripts.

Extract 21.1 (Endo & Takada, 2019, p. 171)[1]

B (aged 15 months), S (aged 50 months), M (mother)

```
11             *(1.0)           +(1.0)              %*+(1.0)
     S body   *puts the cup   +bites a rice        % bite makes
                               cracker              a loud sound
```

[1] To transcribe body movements and gaze direction, the following method is used in Extract 21.1 (cf. Mondada, 2007; for Extracts 21.2 and 21,3 these signs are not used because the focus of analysis is less relevant to the detailed body movements and gaze direction). The part that starts with a sign such as *, +, and % indicates the part where the body movement or gaze direction continues. If the body movement or gaze direction continues to the following line(s), it is represented by →.

	M gaze			*gazes at S->
	B body			+moves the body slightly forward
12		%(1.0)	*+Fig. 21.1(0.5)	
	B body	%..............	*ptg to S-> line 15	
	M gaze		+gazes at B->	
13	B:u.	%Fig. 21.2		
	B gaze	%gazes at M->		
14		*(1.0)		
	M body	*nods twice		
15	M:	+*tabe+te haru na:* **she is eating, isn't she**		
	B body	+,,, +		

Figure 21.1 B starts pointing.

S makes a loud noise while eating rice crackers. In response to that sound, M turns to S (line 11). Then, the younger child, B, points to S with his left hand (line 12). In response to this expressive pointing, M immediately gazes at S (line 12, Figure 21.1). Then, right after B gives an utterance,

Figure 21.2 Right after B gives an utterance, 'u', M looks at B.

'u', M turns to look at B (line 13, Figure 21.2) and then nods twice (line 14). The nodding was used to acknowledge B's preceding action (i.e. pointing). B then returns his fingers and arm to the original positions (line 15), reflecting B has achieved joint attention with M. Here, B's pointing serves as Responsibility 1, namely a response in interactions that have not yet reached an exchange of clear social meaning.

After nodding, almost at the same time as B returns his fingers and arm to the original positions, M describes what is going on at the target of the pointing, saying '+*tabe+te haru na:* (she is eating, isn't she)' (line 15). This utterance indicates that B's pointing (line 12) and utterance, *u*', (line 13) were interpreted as a reminder of what was happening in front of him. It tells B that M also shares the understanding that 'she is eating'. In addition, an interactional particle, '*na:*' (cf. Morita, 2005), empathetically asserts that the understanding of the situation is shared. Moreover, it classifies the participation framework (see Bateman, Chapter 3, this volume) of this activity into (1) S, who is eating, and (2) B and M, who are seeing S eating.

In this way, M interpreted B's expressive pointing as an action of inviting M's attention. She then gave a verbal response to it and thereby located B's pointing in the frame of Responsibility 2. As shown in this case, caregivers often give a slightly advanced interpretation of child behaviour and thereby scaffold the development of children (Bruner, 1983). These interactions also serve as the basis for the child to develop more communicative pointing, such as imperative pointing, which is a manifestation of Responsibility 2.

Communication Regarding Directive

Of course, caregivers not only give an interpretation to children's behaviour and action but also direct children to take particular action. 'An utterance intended to get the listener to do something' is called 'directive' (M. Goodwin, 2006, p. 107). In our framework, it is understood as a typical example of Responsibility 2. Caregivers often issue a directive as the first pair part of an adjacency pair in order to elicit a desired behaviour from the child. A directive can take behavioural actions as well as verbal utterances as its second pair part. It is relatively easy for children who are not yet proficient in language use to respond to a directive (e.g. a request to take food) with a behavioural action (e.g. taking the food). For this reason, directive sequences are frequently observed in caregiver–child interactions across various cultures.

It should be remembered that, to the addressee, a directive is an inherently 'face-threatening' action, namely an action that may harm the recipient's self-image (Brown & Levinson, 1987; Clancy, 1986; Goffman, 1967). Thus, directive has variations that weaken its face-threatening nature and enable the speaker to effectively elicit the desired behaviour from the recipient. When a child does not comply with the caregiver's directive, the caregiver often repeatedly issues modified directives while monitoring the child's behaviour. In most languages, the variations of directive can be ordered in terms of a scale, ranging from very direct (imperatives: 'Gimme a match') to very indirect (hints: 'The matches are gone') (Clancy, 1986; Ervin-Tripp, 1976; Falsgraf & Majors, 1995). In this regard, Clancy (1986) proposed a 'scale of directness' for Japanese caregiver–child interactions, based on her data obtained from Japanese mothers while they were issuing directives to their two-year-old children. The study indicated that a wide range of grammatical forms in the Japanese language is used to moderate the directness–indirectness of directives.

As a revised version of Clancy's (1986) scale of directness, Takada (2013) proposed a multidimensional scale of directness. The first dimension is the intensity of directive found in the utterance form. It is the axis in which the force or compulsiveness to make the recipient do something is arranged, from relatively high to low. The grammatical features of the Japanese language make it possible to modulate the intensity of action by using particular grammatical items, such as *nasai* (command), *tte* (request), *tte-age-tara* (suggestion) and *tte-goran* (prompting) at the end of sentences. The directness of directive is also considered to decline in this order. These items, considered modal markers (cf. Pizziconi & Kizu, 2009), can reflect the speaker's interactional concerns and allow the caregiver to coordinate her or his actions with a child's behaviours while progressively monitoring the latter. As the second dimension, the directness of directive is influenced by the 'footing' of utterances. Goffman (1981, p. 128) defined footing as the speaker's 'alignment, or set, or stance, or posture, or projected self' in relation to an utterance. Caregivers often manipulate the footing of utterances to elicit the desired behaviour from their children.

Directive is closely associated with the activity of teaching (Ochs, 1988; Schieffelin, 1990). Particularly, researchers have claimed that directive sequence in Japanese caregiver–child interactions is used for the purpose of teaching *omoiyari*, which is considered as the distinctive value of Japanese culture and is often translated into English as 'empathy' (Burdelski, 2006; Clancy, 1986). Below, I will use an example to support this. In Extract 21.2, 37-month-old K was playing with toy trains at home. His father, F, watched him while sitting on the floor. His mother, M, who was 9 months pregnant with her second child, was also sitting on the floor.

Extract 21.2 (Takada, 2013, p. 429)

K (aged 37 months), M (mother: 9 months pregnant), F (father)

```
1    F:   (ru)kondo, akachan (ga) umare-tara keihan age-
          yo-kka, akachan ni.
          (r) when the baby is born next month, will
          ((you)) give the Keihan train ((i.e. a toy
          train of a particular railway company)), to the
          baby?
2    K:   datte(.)keita no:
          But(.)((it is)) m:ine.
          ((ten lines are omitted))
12   K:   zenbu keita no:
          All ((toys)) are m:ine
13   M:   kawaiso, akachan nai-chau yo:
          Poor ((baby)), the baby will cr:y
14   F:   ya: hidoi yatsu ya:
          O:h, ((you are)) awful
```

15 F: [*san, sansai-kun yaro demo.*
[Three, ((you are)) Mr. Three-Year-Old, aren't ((you)) though.
16 M: [*en e::n*
["en e::n
17 M: ↑*oniichan, nanka chouda:[i tte.*
↑big brother, give ((me)) something", [saying.

At the beginning of this interaction, F points to a toy train (*Keihan*) and then, in line 1, gives a suggestion to K, saying, 'When the baby is born next month, will ((you)) give the *Keihan* train to the baby?' Here, in the original utterance in Japanese, F used *-tara*, which indicates the action of suggestion and constitutes one of the modality markers that modulate the intensity of action. However, K claims his ownership (i.e. legitimacy) in line 2, saying, 'But(.)((it is)) m:ine'. Although F and M attempted to negotiate with K to give a toy to the coming baby (omitted in the excerpt), K does not accept that suggestion and reinforces his rejection by noting, 'All ((toys)) are m:ine' in line 12. In line 13, M says, 'Poor ((baby)), the baby will cr:y', which serves as an evaluation of the baby's status, and then complains to K by discussing the situation in greater detail. She then adopts the baby's perspective and voices the baby's imagined response, 'en e::n big brother, give ((me)) something' in lines 16 and 17. Here, by introducing the unborn baby as a figure (Goffman, 1981), M changed the footing of her utterance and spoke for the baby (Schieffelin, 1990) using a type of reported speech. The reporting frame is marked by the high-pitched voice and the citation marker *tte* in line 17, both of which designate the performative aspect of the utterance. In the transcript, I marked this reported speech by double quotation marks (lines 16 and 17). The utterance incorporates the unborn baby into the current familial relationship. The use of 'big brother' also emphasizes the familial relationship between the participants and the baby.

This particular style of communication provides a context for performing actions that are in line with moral beliefs, such as *omoiyari*. In other words, by using the utterances of a figure, such as the unborn baby, the caregiver creates a playful situation and encourages the child's active participation in the framework of interaction. Utterances through such a figure constitute actions that match the value of *omoiyari*, which is distinctive in Japanese culture. In other words, *omoiyari* arises as its 'result' rather than as a 'reason' for practising the strategy.

While caregivers frequently use directives, children are not always passive recipients of directives. At times, a child also becomes an active agent who escapes from the force of the caregiver's directive. Takada (2013) classified the child's response to the caregiver's directive into six types: 'acceptance', 'initiating repair', 'changing frame', 'claiming legitimacy', 'challenging', and 'rejection'. Among them, the combination of directive and acceptance or rejection is a typical example of Responsibility 2 (i.e. response to a call found in the exchange of utterances that form an adjacency pair), described above. On the other hand, initiating repair, changing frame, claiming legitimacy, and challenging are related to Responsibility 3 (i.e. response found in utterances that accompanied or extended from the exchange of utterances that form an adjacency pair) identified earlier, where there is some elaboration of the prior response. Of these, Takada (2013) pays special attention to the strategy of changing frame. This is a strategy to change the framework of conversation. For this purpose, in response to caregivers' directives, children often cite their involvement in a normative or pro-moral activity (e.g. in response to a caregiver's suggestion to give a toy to her younger brother, a girl says, 'I'll go to clean up my hands'). When this strategy works successfully, the disjunctive utterance elicits the caregiver's reaction, which may further develop the conversation about the normative or pro-moral activity. In other words, the child can avoid the face-threatening situation, and the child and caregiver may jointly shift the topic of conversation. In this way, the strategies related to Responsibility 3, such as that of changing frame, also contribute to establishing a context in which culturally shared morality is introduced. In these strategies, children make use of the implicature (i.e. the act of implying one thing by saying something else; Grice, 1975, 1978) of their utterances in the service of not complying with caregivers' directives.

Organization of Attention, Affect, and Morality through Storytelling

Another cultural tool that enables the (re)production of culturally shared morality is storytelling. Storytelling constitutes a type of extended telling, one that suspends the normal turn-taking arrangement – the most basic and fundamental rule of conversation – between the speaker and the addressee(s), while the speaker produces a multi-unit turn (Schegloff, 2007; Stivers, 2013; see also Filipi, Chapter 9, this volume). Through this, storytelling encourages children to cultivate the above-mentioned Responsibility 3, extended from Responsibility 2, in the course of caregiver–child interactions. The caregiver engages in storytelling and also lets the child do it to create a cultural framework that extends from the adjacency pair.

In other words, storytelling allows the speaker to narrate events that are removed from the here-and-now situation and to introduce cultural knowledge associated with broader contexts (e.g. a past birthday party) (Ochs & Capps, 2001; Reese, 1995). Storytelling thus constitutes an important language genre that provides effective tools for bridging the 'context of situation' and 'context of culture' (Ochs & Schieffelin, 2012) in many societies (see also Filipi, Chapter 9, this volume).

For the very reasons outlined above, it is a challenging task for verbally inexperienced young children to successfully participate in storytelling practices. While storytelling demands extended turns-at-talk on the part of the teller (Mandelbaum, 2013, p. 492), the recipient must, for their part, correctly perceive the story's beginning and ending and react appropriately throughout. Previous studies have shown that children, both as speakers and listeners, need considerable support from their caregivers to properly participate in storytelling practice (e.g. Bruner, 1983; Filipi, 2017). In this sense, 'stories are interactive productions, co-constructed by teller and recipient and tailored to the occasions of their production' (Mandelbaum, 2013, p. 492). Therefore, it is especially important to clarify how caregivers and children are involved in storytelling practice, including the perception, introduction, and deployment of the context of culture in their daily family interactions. From this perspective, Takada and Kawashima (2019) examined the strategies that caregivers use to facilitate two- to three-year-old children to launch, sustain, and end storytelling in the activity of picture-book reading, which is often observed in the early stage of language socialization in storytelling.

At the point of story launching, caregivers often tried to let the child start storytelling by repeating modified directives. Caregivers also frequently intervened in the child's position and posture, taking care to ensure the children were properly involved in storytelling (e.g. placing a toddler comfortably on the caregiver's lap to facilitate the co-telling of a picture book).

While sustaining the sequence of turns in a story, caregivers engaged in several strategies. The first strategy involves the caregiver's taking over of the child's utterance. In this vein, Japanese conversation has developed various means of negotiating and achieving joint utterance constructions (Hayashi, 2003). These means are often used in caregiver–child interactions and facilitate children to collaboratively construct an utterance with the caregiver. The second strategy is the formulation of the caregiver's utterance, which includes echoing the word or phrase of the child's preceding utterance. This strategy enables the caregiver to demonstrate the cooperative stance toward the child. The third strategy employed by the caregiver to help the child to sustain a storytelling is association of the story with the here-and-now, or a real-life situation. In the following Extract 21.3, 32-month-old C and her mother, M, are reading a picture book titled *The Hole of the Navel* (Hasegawa, 2006), in which an unborn baby is looking at the world around him through the mother's navel.

Extract 21.3 (Takada & Kawashima, 2019, p. 211)

C (aged 32 months), M (mother: 9 months pregnant)

80 M: *oheso no naka kara- ana kara mieru mieru.*
((I)) can see it from the hole of the navel.
>*mi-te-hann-de.*<
((The baby)) is looking at you. ((mother points to her belly with her left-hand forefinger.))
81 M: °*mi-te-haru*°
((She)) is looking at you.
82 C: ((C looks at the mother's belly, and then pulls up her sweatshirt a little and looks at her own belly.))
83 M: *chika, huhaha hhh*
Chika, ((Sounds of laughing)).

Having just read a line from the picture book, the mother produces an utterance referring to the here-and-now, '*mi-te-hann-de* (((she)) is looking at you)', while pointing to her abdomen with the forefinger of her left hand (line 80). This part of the utterance at line 80 is pronounced in a compressed manner. Subsequently, both C and the mother gaze at the mother's abdomen. In these ways, the pregnant mother's body (e.g. the foetus, her abdomen) is often used as a resource for communication (Takada & Kawashima, 2016). Taking these features together, the function of this utterance is to mark a change in the speaker's footing (Goffman, 1981; Johnson, 2017). The mother associates the story with the here-and-now situation. Accordingly, the baby in her tummy is treated as a legitimate participant, who is observing the situation through the navel, in a similar manner to the figure described in the picture book. The mother immediately repeats the phrase '*mi-te-haru* (The baby is looking at you)' in a slightly lower voice (line 81), as though they are secretly talking about the baby in the mother's tummy. The child then begins to examine her own abdomen by raising her sweatshirt a little and looking at her own belly (line 82). At line 83, upon observing C's behaviour, the mother addresses the child by name and exhibits signs of laughter, thereby communicating her assessment of the child's reaction as positive and amusing. Through such an assessment, the caregiver can associate the playful story with the child's lived experience and embody her moral stances that indicate what is good or appropriate (cf. Ochs & Capps, 2001).

At the point of story ending, caregivers tended to allow the children to finish telling the story, when the children suggested story ending according to the formulaic word (e.g. *oshimai* (It's finished)), even in the cases expected to have continued telling the story in the script of a picture book. The use of the formulaic word to express the story ending reflects cultural norms, which caregivers have often used for the purpose of jointly achieving story ending with their children.

Caregivers often use these diverse and multi-modal strategies to maintain the attention and involvement of children while launching, sustaining, and ending storytelling. This bridges Responsibilities 2 and 3, and enables children to participate in storytelling, which cannot be managed by themselves, in collaboration with caregivers. By voicing and animating the picture book texts, children are encouraged to experience the embodiment and self-reflection associated with rich cultural knowledge. Hence, by using the picture book as a set of environmental clues, storytelling functions as a valuable device in orchestrating attention, affect, convention and morality, and accomplishing language socialization in caregiver–child interactions.

Cultural Formation of Responsibility

As we have seen in this chapter, caregivers and children use a variety of strategies to monitor each other and mutually coordinate their behaviours. In these interactions, caregivers use a variety of strategies to attract children's attention and elicit their active involvement. The child's agency appears as a construct within their relationship with the caregiver. The construct is composed of the relationship between the action and the context in which the action is embedded. Moreover, performing an action prepares the context for the next action.

In this regard, studies of language socialization theory have examined how children and other cultural novices perceive the context of a situation and how they relate it to the context of culture, in the course of interactions. Caregivers try to involve children in the framework of cultural activities even before children can understand these contexts. Children use their limited choices to broaden the scope of contexts in which they make responses. In this process, children gradually expand the range and deepen the quality of their intimate social relationships. This is also the process by which Responsibilities 1 to 3 are culturally formed.

The perspective of 'cultural formation of responsibility' is effective for empirically analysing the interactions in which caregivers and children try to bridge the imbalance in their understanding of the context of situation and the context of culture. Moreover, it enables us to clarify the multi-layered function of semiotic resources used by caregivers and children. Research from this perspective enables us to deepen our understanding about the process of production, maintenance, and transformation of the lifeworld that is built on the accumulation of moment-by-moment negotiations among participants in culturally framed interactions.

Recommendations for Practice

In this chapter, I introduced the topics of sharing attention by pointing, communication regarding directive, and organization of attention, affect, and morality through storytelling as part of our research on language socialization in Japan/Japanese families. This work was conducted from the perspective that Responsibilities 1, 2, and 3 are culturally formed on the basis of the child's developing ability to respond during interactions with others. This perspective makes it possible to analyse caregiver–child interactions, both in terms of qualitative transformation and functional continuity. Professionals engaging with daycare centres for young children and preschools can contribute greatly to expanding and deepening children's social relationships by collaborating with caregivers and utilizing the strategies summarized below.

- During infancy, it is important to consciously seek to notice, recognize, and respond to a child's awareness of their surroundings, as indicated by the child's behaviour, such as pointing, and to share attention with the child associating with the situation (Responsibility 1). It is recommended that caregivers communicate to nursery or preschool teachers about their child's recent accomplishments in Responsibility 1 (e.g. pointing) so that nursery and preschool teachers can be more aware of them in their practices.
- Gradually, children begin to use different behaviours, depending on the different gazes that caregivers cast on them. One of the typical tools for

involving such child behaviour in the structure of linguistic meanings is directive. Being combined with the response to it, directive forms a type of adjacency pair (Responsibility 2). It is desirable for caregivers and nursery or preschool teachers to share the list of directives that they have used as well as the child's responses to them so they can elicit more positive responses from the child.

- It should be remembered that children often do not accept directives immediately. In order to elicit the desired behaviour from the child, it is effective to repeat the modified directives (e.g. change the intensity or footing of utterances) while respecting the positive self-image of children.
- Children who become proficient in the structure of adjacency pairs – that is, being adept at providing relevant responses – enjoy responding to more complex conversational structures (Responsibility 3). Storytelling is kind of like a toy box that is filled with historically accumulated cultural resources. In order to properly involve children in storytelling, it is effective for caregivers and nursery or preschool teachers to let children take a comfortable posture and position (e.g. placing the child on the caregiver's lap).
- Through the practices of storytelling, children go beyond the context of here-and-now situations and become socialized into the context of culture that sustains the speech community in which children dwell. Caregivers and teachers should share anecdotes about the child's behaviour in order to broaden the context of culture referenced in their interactions with the child.

References

Babylab, Kyoto University. (2020). Available from: https://babylab.educ.kyoto-u.ac.jp [in Japanese; last accessed 10 February 2022].

Brown, P., and Levinson, S. C. (1987). *Politeness: Some Universals in Language Usage*. Cambridge: Cambridge University Press.

Bruner, J. (1983). *Child's Talk: Learning to Use Language*. Oxford: Oxford University Press.

Burdelski, M. J. (2006). *Language Socialization of Two-year Old Children in Kansai, Japan: The Family and Beyond*. Ph.D. Thesis. Los Angeles: University of California.

Clancy, P. (1986). The acquisition of communicative style in Japanese. In B. B. Schieffelin and E. Ochs (eds.), *Language Socialization across Cultures* (pp. 213–250). Cambridge: Cambridge University Press.

Cultural formation of responsibility in caregiver–child interactions. (2020). Available from: www.cci.jambo.africa.kyoto-u.ac.jp/cr/en/index.html [last accessed 10 February 2022].

Duranti, A., Ochs, E., and Schieffelin, B. B. (eds.). (2012). *The Handbook of Language Socialization*. Malden, MA: Wiley-Blackwell.

Endo, T., and Takada, A. (2019). Child pointing and caregiver's response in family collaborative activities. In E. Yasui, H. Sugiura, and K. Takanashi (eds.), *Pointing in Interaction* (pp. 161–189). Tokyo: Hitsujishobo (in Japanese).

Ervin-Tripp, S. (1976). Is sybil there? The structure of some American English directives. *Language in Society*, 5(1), 25–66.

Falsgraf, C., and Majors, D. (1995). Implicit culture in Japanese immersion discourse. *Journal of the Association of Teachers of Japanese*, 29(2), 1–21.

Filipi, A. (2017). The emergence of story-telling. In A. Bateman and A. Church (eds.), *Children's Knowledge-in-Interaction: Studies in Conversation Analysis* (pp. 279–295). Singapore: Springer.

Franco, F., and Butterworth, G. (1996). Pointing and social awareness: declaring and requesting in the second year. *Journal of Infant Language*, 23, 307–336.

Garfinkel, H. (1967). *Studies in Ethnomethodology*. Englewood Cliffs, NJ: Prentice-Hall.

Goffman, E. (1967). *Interaction Ritual: Essays on Face Behavior*. New York, NY: Pantheon Books.

Goffman, E. (1981). *Forms of Talk*. Philadelphia, PA: University of Pennsylvania Press.

Goodwin, C. (2000). Action and embodiment within situated human interaction. *Journal of Pragmatics*, 32, 1489–1522.

Goodwin, C. (2007). Environmentally coupled gestures. In S. D. Duncan, J. Cassel, and E. T. Levy (eds.), *Gesture and the Dynamic Dimension of Language* (pp. 195–212). Amsterdam/Philadelphia, PA: John Benjamins.

Goodwin, M. H. (2006). *The Hidden Life of Girls: Games of Stance, Status, and Exclusion*. Malden, MA: Blackwell.

Grice, H. P. (1975). Logic and conversation. In P. Cole and J. Morgan (eds.), *Syntax and Semantics* (vol. 3, pp. 41–58). New York, NY: Academic Press.

Grice, H. P. (1978). Further notes on logic and conversation. In P. Cole (ed.), *Syntax and Semantics* (vol. 9, pp. 113–127). New York, NY: Academic Press.

Grünloh, T., & Liszkowski, U. (2015). Prelinguistic vocalizations distinguish pointing acts. *Journal of Child Language*, 42(6), 1312–1336.

Hasegawa, Y. (2006). *The Hole of the Navel*. Kobe: BL Press.

Hayashi, M. (2003). *Joint Utterance Construction in Japanese Conversation*. Amsterdam: John Benjamins.

Hyme, D. (1964). Introduction: toward ethnographies of communication. *American Anthropologist*, 66(6), 1–34.

Johnson, S. J. (2017). Multimodality and footing in peer correction in reading picture books. *Linguistics and Education*, 41, 20–34.

Kidwell, M. (2005). Gaze as social control: how very young children differentiate 'the look' from a 'mere look' by their adult caregivers. *Research on Language and Social Interaction*, 38(4), 417–449.

Liszkowski, U., Brown, P., Callaghan, T., Takada, A., and de Vos, C. (2012). A prelinguistic gestural universal of human communication. *Cognitive Science*, 36, 698–713.

Mandelbaum, J. (2013). Storytelling in conversation. In J. Sidnell and T. Stivers (eds.), *The Handbook of Conversation Analysis* (pp. 492–510). Chichester: Blackwell.

Mizuno, K. (2000). *Significance and Limitations of the Concept of Causation: For the Reconstruction of Tort Retribution*. Tokyo: Yuhikaku Publishing (in Japanese).

Mondada, L. (2007). Multimodal resources for turn-taking: pointing and the emergence of possible next speakers. *Discourse Studies*, 9(2), 194–225.

Morita, E. (2005). *Negotiation of Contingent Talk: The Japanese Interactional Particles* Ne *and* Sa. Amsterdam: John Benjamins.

Ochs, E. (1988). *Culture and Language Development: Language Acquisition and Language Socialization in a Samoan Village*. Cambridge: Cambridge University Press.

Ochs, E., and Capps, L. (2001). *Living Narrative: Creating Lives in Everyday Storytelling*. Cambridge, MA: Harvard University Press.

Ochs, E., and Schieffelin, B. B. (2012). The theory of language socialization. In A. Duranti, E. Ochs, and B. B. Schieffelin (eds.), *The Handbook of Language Socialization* (pp. 1–21). Malden, MA: Wiley-Blackwell.

Ochs, E., Solomon, O., and Sterponi, L. (2005). Limitations and transformations of habitus in child-directed communication. *Discourse Studies*, 7(4–5), 547–583.

Ohba, T. (2005). *What Is Responsibility'?* Tokyo: Kodansha (in Japanese).

Pizziconi, B., and Kizu, M. (eds.). (2009). *Japanese Modality: Exploring its Scope and Interpretation*. Basingstoke: Palgrave Macmillan.

Povinelli, D. J., Bering, J. M., and Giambrone, S. (2003). Chimpanzees' 'pointing': another error of the argument by analogy? In S. Kita (ed.), *Pointing: Where Language, Culture, and Cognition Meet* (pp. 35–68). Mahwah, NJ: Lawrence Erlbaum Associates.

Reese, E. (1995). Predicting children's literacy from mother-child conversations. *Cognitive Development*, 10(3), 381–405.

Schegloff, E. A. (2007). *Sequence Organization in Interaction: A Primer in Conversation Analysis* (vol. 1). Cambridge: Cambridge University Press.

Schieffelin, B. B. (1990). *The Give and Take of Everyday Life: Language Socialization of Kaluli Children*. Cambridge: Cambridge University Press.

Sidnell, J., and Stivers, T. (eds.). (2013). *The Handbook of Conversation Analysis*. Chichester: Blackwell.

Stivers, T. (2013). Sequence organization. In J. Sidnell and T. Stivers (eds.), *The Handbook of Conversation Analysis* (pp. 191–209). Chichester: Blackwell.

Takada, A. (2012). Pre-verbal infant-caregiver interaction. In A. Duranti, E. Ochs, and B. B. Schieffelin (eds.), *The Handbook of Language Socialization* (pp. 56–80). Chichester: Blackwell.

Takada, A. (2013). Generating morality in directive sequences: distinctive strategies for developing communicative competence in Japanese caregiver-child interactions. *Language & Communication*, 33, 420–438.

Takada, A. (forthcoming). Language socialization and cultural formation of 'responsibility' in Japan. In H. Cook and A. Takada (eds.), *Language Socialization in Japanese*. Tokyo: Hitsuji Shobo.

Takada, A., and Kawashima, M. (2016). Relating with an unborn baby: expectant mothers socializing their toddlers in Japanese families. In A. Bateman and A. Church (eds.), *Children's Knowledge-in-Interaction: Studies in Conversation Analysis* (pp. 211–229). Singapore: Springer.

Takada, A., and Kawashima, M. (2019). Caregivers' strategies for eliciting storytelling from toddlers in Japanese caregiver-child picture-book reading activities. *Research on Children and Social Interaction*, 3(1–2), 196–223.

Takada, A., Shimada, Y., and Kawashima, M. (eds.). (2016). *Conversation Analysis on Child Rearing: How Does 'Responsibility' of Adults and Children Grow?* Kyoto: Showado (in Japanese).

Tomasello, M. (1999). *The Cultural Origins of Human Cognition*. Cambridge, MA: Harvard University Press.

Index

Printed in the USA
CPSIA information can be obtained
at www.ICGtesting.com
LVHW050525051023
760095LV00010B/716

9 781108 845472